STUDIA HISTORICA UPSALIENSIA

published by

The Historiska Institutionen at the University of Uppsala, Sweden, through
Sven A. Nilsson and Sten Carlsson.

SCANDINAVIAN UNIVERSITY BOOKS

DENMARK MUNKSGAARD *Copenhagen*
NORWAY UNIVERSITETSFORLAGET *Oslo, Bergen, Tromsø*
SWEDEN LÄROMEDELSFÖRLAGEN *Stockholm, Gothenburg, Lund*

This book falls within the framework of the research project, "Sweden and America after 1860."

Within the framework of this project and in Studia Historica Upsaliensia the following books have been published:

31. Nilsson, Fred, Emigrationen från Stockholm till Nordamerika 1880–1893. En studie i urban utvandring. Sthlm 1970.

35. Runblom, Harald, Svenska företag i Latinamerika. Etableringsmönster och förhandlingstaktik 1900–1940. Uppsala 1971.

STUDIA HISTORICA UPSALIENSIA
XXXVII

Sture Lindmark

Swedish America, 1914–1932

Studies in Ethnicity with Emphasis on Illinois and Minnesota

LÄROMEDELSFÖRLAGEN

Also published by The Swedish Pioneer Historical Society
Chicago, Illinois.

ISBN-91-24-68684-0

Printed in Sweden
WRETMANS BOKTRYCKERI AB
UPPSALA 1971

BIRGITTA

Foreword

This book falls within the framework of the research project, "Sweden and America after 1860," which is directed by Professor Sten Carlsson at Uppsala University. Over the years that I worked on this book, I have received valuable assistance from a number of people. I have had the privilege of conducting my research under the supervision of Professor Sten Carlsson. He has offered constructive suggestions and penetrating criticism and equally as important personal encouragement. Professor Sven A. Nilsson of Uppsala University has examined the dissertation in manuscript form and provided valuable insights.

Professor Franklin D. Scott of Pomona College, Claremont, California (formerly of Northwestern University), has also been of great assistance. He has not only read through the manuscript and scrutinized the translation but has also helped me in tracking down elusive source materials in the United States. I am also greatly indebted to Professor Nils Hasselmo of the University of Minnesota, Minneapolis, who kindly permitted me to use as yet unpublished research findings. Doctor E. Gustav Johnson of North Park College, Chicago, Doctor Wesley M. Westerberg, President of Kendall College, Evanston, and Kermit B. Westerberg, M.A., have also sacrificed their time doing the translation.

Several of my friends at the Historical Institution of Uppsala University have provided me with valuable criticism. I would especially like to thank Ann-Sofie Kälvemark, Hans Norman, Harald Runblom, Nils Runeby, Sune Åkerman, and others connected with the American History Department. I have further received helpful advice from Lars Kritz of The Industrial Institute for Economic and Social Research, Stockholm. Inga Rosell of *Svenska Dagbladet*, Stockholm, has assisted me with the preparation of the manuscript.

My thanks go finally to my wife, Birgitta, who has assisted me in every way. She has drawn all of the diagrams and graphs and attempted to convey to me some knowledge of elementary statistics. It is largely due to her understanding and self-sacrificing spirit that this book has come about.

My research work in the United States has been made possible by a scholarship from the American Council of Learned Societies, New York, and by grants from the Anna Maria Lundin Fellowship Foundation of Smålands Nation, Uppsala.

Throughout this book, for practical reasons quotation marks are set in the Swedish fashion.

Uppsala, November, 1971.

Sture Lindmark

Contents:

I. The Background, Purpose, and Design of the Study

1. *Introduction*

> I was born here. My children were born here. What the hell do I have to do to be called an American?
>
> *Joseph Kennedy*[1]

From the beginning of the 1840s to the economic Depression of the 1930s streams of people flowed from Sweden in search of new opportunities for a livelihood in the United States of America. During these decades approximately 1.3 million Swedes – equivalent to 80 percent of the total emigration from Sweden – have sought their fortune in America.[2] By 1930 the Swedish emigration to America was a closed chapter; the number of immigrants was exceeded by the number of emigrants. The last wave of emigration to the United States came during the 1920s, when approximately 92,000 persons left Sweden. During this period, the peak was reached in 1923 with close to 25,000 emigrants, or more than one-fourth of all emigrants during the whole decade. The net migration for the decade, however, was less, inasmuch as the number of those returning to Sweden was considerable. There is no direct connection between the declining emigration from Sweden to the United States and the quota laws of the Twenties, since the mass emigration at the time that the quota laws were coming into force was a closed chapter in Swedish history. Emigration during the Twenties, with the exception of 1923, never exceeded the assigned quota.

In 1910 there were over 1.4 million first- and second-generation Swedes in America, 665,000 of whom were born in Sweden.[3] After 1910 the number of Swedish-born declined and had diminished by

[1] ***New York Times,* January 28, 1957, p. 26.**

[2] Florence Janson, *The Background of Swedish Immigration, 1840—1930* (Chicago, 1931); *Historical Statistics for Sweden,* Part 1.

[3] ***Fifteenth Census of the United States, 1930, Population,* Vol. II, p. 269.**

1920 to 633,000 and by 1930 to 595,000. The Swedish stock (first- and second-generation Swedes) continued, on the other hand, to increase until 1930, after which it was absorbed beyond distinction.

2. *Earlier Research*

Earlier research dealing with the Swedish emigration to America was chiefly interested in reasons behind the decision to emigrate, in the significance of the emigration from Sweden to America, and in the disposition of the Swedish emigrants to adjust quickly to the new land. The struggle to preserve the Swedish cultural heritage and Swedish identity has remained almost completely outside the interests of research. Because the latter aspect has not been adequately considered, the traditional view of the history of the Swedish stock in America is unbalanced. Previous scholarly investigations stress the Swedes' capacity for rapid assimilation. The view that Swedes were Americanized quickly has been generally accepted without questioning its validity. Carl M. Rosenquist, to name one example, says in the introduction to his doctoral dissertation, "The Swedes of Texas," that the dissertation itself is the result of his interest in "so-called easily assimilated nationalities in America."[4] Everett Arden in *Augustana Heritage* (1963)

[4] Carl M. Rosenquist, "The Swedes of Texas" (Chicago, 1930), p. ii. In the bibliography, *A Report on World Population Migrations. As Related to the United States of America* (Washington, 1956), which has been compiled at George Washington University, it is said: "An examination of the materials published in the field of immigration reveals an area of social investigation in which a relatively small amount of objective, scientific research has been greatly overwhelmed by a mass of subjective emotional thinking. . . . Humanistic impulses become confused with scientific conclusions and a definite viewpoint, rarely based on adequate evidence, emerges" (p. 17).

In addition to Carl M. Rosenquist's dissertation on the Texas Swedes, two other studies should be mentioned: Gene Lund, "The Americanization of the Augustana Lutheran Church" (Princeton, New Jersey, 1954. Unpublished dissertation.); and E. Eklund, "Acculturation in the Swedish Lutheran Congregations of the Boston Area: 1867—1930" (Boston University, 1964. Unpublished dissertation.) and "Swedish Lutheran Congregations of the Boston Area: 1867—1930" in *The Swedish Pioneer Historical Quarterly,* April, 1965.

Oscar A. Benson, "Problems in the Accommodation of the Swede to American Culture" *(University of Pittsburgh Bulletin,* Vol. 30, No 2, 1933), p. 47, says without qualifying it: "Because of his willingness to accommodate himself to his environment, use English, Americanize his name and acquire citizenship, the Swedish immigrant is readily assimilated into his new plurel."

maintains that Swedes took quickly to American customs and practices. They mingled, he says, with neighbors and friends in "the American melting-pot" and adjusted so readily to their new environment that they often claimed to have forgotten their old mother tongue before they had learned to speak English.[5]

The information that exists on Swedish Americans stems to a great extent from *Emigrationsutredningens betänkande* (Report of the Commission on Emigration) and 20 supplements to it (1908–14). Despite its shortcomings, the Report is still the most comprehensive study that has been made of the Swedish emigration. It is the basis of much that has been written since 1914. Helge Nelson *(The Swedes and the Swedish Settlements in North America,* [1943]) more than any other has studied the demographic conditions among Swedes in America. The purpose of the study is stated by Nelson as follows: "It is above all the geographic distribution of the Swedish stock in the United States and its causes that the author wants to give an account of in his work, with the emphasis laid on the decade of 1920 and the distribution of the Swedish stock at the census of the United States in 1930. . . ."[6] In addition to the census material, Nelson has made good use of his own experiences traveling around the American continent and of oral information received from Swedish Americans.

The significance of the religious denominations for the Swedish community has been treated by George Stephenson in *The Religious Aspects of Swedish Immigration. A Study of Immigrant Churches* (1932). Stephenson himself had close ties with Swedes and had followed their development in America at close range. His books and observations about Swedish Americans are given a prominent place in bibliographies on immigration history. *The Religious Aspects of Swedish Immigration* treats not only the origin and development of the religious groups but covers a wide area of Swedish-American history, not the least of which is the struggle of the churches to preserve Swedish individuality. Stephenson's *A History of American Immigration 1820–1924* (1926) also provides much valuable information about the Swedish immigrants in America. Inasmuch as Stephenson was the son of Swedish immigrants, he appeared very eager to present

[5] Everett Arden, *Augustana Heritage. A History of the Augustana Lutheran Church* (Rock Island, 1963), p. 234.

[6] Helge Nelson, *The Swedes and the Swedish Settlements in North America* (Lund, 1943), p. 2.

the positive aspects of the Swedes. He stressed the fact that they were easily assimilated – "quickly and thoroughly."[7] He attributes this propensity by Swedish Americans toward rapid Americanization to, among other things, America's supernatural and mystical power – "the magic of America" – over the immigrants. At the same time he was often critical of the Swedes in America, a fact which Fritiof Ander has explained as Stephenson's exaggerated fear of being considered partisan.[8] Stephenson was especially critical of the Augustana Synod. The reason, says Ander, is that he wanted to be objective. "He wanted to arrive at historical truth by eliminating his own prejudice. In doing so he stripped himself of the Augustana Synod. It became impossible for him to differentiate between his personal impressions and the historical reality."

Adolph B. Benson has also dealt with the Americanization of the Swedes in "The Assimilation of Swedes in America" (1956).[9] According to Benson the reason that Swedes found it easy to assimilate was a historically inherited tendency – in part through necessity – to get along with other people, foreign or otherwise, and to be a good, helpful neighbor. For Benson, the Swedes' interest in learning strange languages and customs was of invaluable help to those who emigrated to the United States. "One quality which undoubtedly has accelerated the rapidity of assimilation in foreign lands, especially in the United States, is the inherited internationalism of the Swedes. Of all national groups known to the writer, with the possible exception of the Dane, he is the least nationalistic."

There are, however, a few recent studies, where the group consciousness among the Swedish Americans is emphasized. Charles H. Anderson points out in *White Protestant Americans. From National Origins to Religious Group* (1970) that "empirical investigations into Swedish communalism confirm the view that structural assimilation was far

[7] George Stephenson, "Rip Van Winkle in Sweden" *SPHQ* (April, 1956), pp. 54 ff.

[8] Fritiof Ander, "Immigrationshistoriens utveckling i Amerika" (The Development of Immigration History in America), *Historisk Tidskrift,* 1961, pp. 291 f.

[9] Adolph B. Benson, "The Assimilation of Swedes in America" *SPHQ* (October, 1956), pp. 136 ff.

from complete 25 years ago and is not complete even today."[10] Wayne Wheeler's conclusion in "An Analysis of Social Change in a Swedish-Immigrant Community" (1959) is that Swedish solidarity was high as recently as the 1950s, when outsiders found it difficult to be accepted. W.W. Schroeder and Victor Obenhaus have found *(Religion in American Culture* [1964]) that Swedish Lutherans were slightly more likely to choose members of their own church as close friends than were members of other denominations. The Augustana Lutherans reported that 41 percent of their closest friends belonged to their own congregations and the Mission Covenanters declared that 60 percent did.

With respect to the language question, Nils Hasselmo's two articles, "Language Displacement and Language Influence in Swedish America" and "Language in Exile," deserve primary attention.[11] Nils Hasselmo in part has dealt with various attitudes toward the language question and in part has attempted to study the transition from Swedish to English against the background of the periodicals published by the Augustana Synod and the books published by Augustana Book Concern: the Swedish and English titles respectively and the editions in both languages.

The Swedish language newspapers and their contents have been the subject of very little research. Albert F. Schersten is the only one who has studied their importance in relation to, and their influence upon, Swedish American assimilation, and that with only Rock Island and Moline, Illinois, as point of focus *(The Relation of the Swedish-American Newspaper to the Assimilation of Swedish Immigrants,* 1935). Schersten has tried to determine, with respect to assimilation, if there is any difference between Swedish immigrants who read a Swedish-American paper and those who do not.

A study by Finis Herbert Capps, *From Isolationism to Involvement. The Swedish Immigrant Press in America, 1914–1945* (1966), shows

[10] Charles H. Anderson, *White Protestant Americans. From National Origins to Religious Group* (Englewood Cliffs, New Jersey, 1970), p. 52. Wayne Wheeler, "An Analysis of Social Change in a Swedish-Immigrant Community" (Doctoral dissertation, University of Missouri, 1959). W. W. Schroeder and Victor Obenhaus, *Religion in American Culture* (New York, 1964), pp. 87—88.

[11] I have also had access to two as yet unpublished works by Nils Hasselmo, namely: "The Swedish Language in Chisago County, Minnesota" and "Den amerikanska svenskan" (The American Swedish).

that the newspapers contain interesting information on Swedish Americans and their attitudes. Capps' work, the only exhaustive study based on the content of the Swedish-American press, treats the position of the Swedish-American newspapers with respect to American foreign policy. The part that deals with World War I shows how difficult it was for the Swedes to take a position between the belligerents. When they did, it was often in consideration of what was best for Sweden, rather than for the United States.

There are several studies that deal with individual denominations. In *Augustana Heritage* (1963) Everett Arden gives an account of the Augustana Synod and its development. Karl Olsson's *By One Spirit* (1962) gives a well-rounded view of the Evangelical Mission Covenant of America.

After an examination of the historical and sociological literature on the Swedish immigrants in America one asks why research has paid so little attention to the conscious struggle of the immigrants to preserve their own cultural heritage. Swedish Americans, it should nevertheless be pointed out, do not constitute an exception to the rule. The same observation, namely that research has been more concerned to prove the immigrants' disposition to adapt than to preserve their heritage, is universally valid. Joshua Fishman is one of the few scholars who have observed that "the cultural and linguistic self-maintenance efforts of American minority groups are surrounded by towering mountains of ignorance and vast oceans of apathy."[12] Fishman deplores that scholars have been concerned only with what he calls "disappearance phenomena" and have not paid attention to "maintenance phenomena": the efforts of the various immigrant groups to preserve and to transmit their specific heritage and to keep the countrymen together in order to strengthen national ties. Even Rudolph Vecoli has maintained that "ethnicity," group consciousness based on a sense of common origin, has been disregarded by historians. "Ethnic studies thus have long suffered from the blight of the assimilationist ideology. Because of their expectations that assimilation was to be swift and irresistible, historians and social scientists have looked for change

[12] Joshua Fishman, *Language Loyalty in the United States* (The Hague, 1966), p. 21.

rather than continuity, acculturation rather than cultural maintenance."[13]

3. *The Purpose*

In 1943 Helge Nelson asked, with respect to Swedish Americans, "How long do they preserve their national character before becoming assimilated with the American milieu?"[14] The fundamental objective in this dissertation is to attempt to answer the question put by Helge Nelson and to determine to what extent Swedish immigrants sought to preserve the Swedish language, Swedish churches, Swedish organizations, and the Swedish language press. Since the character of the Swedish-American source material is generally such that it underscores the conserving tendencies – the pressures that work against Americanization – the focus of this investigation has been placed on "maintenance phenomena" and only indirectly on Americanization – "disappearance phenomena."

It is understandably difficult to talk only about maintenance efforts, inasmuch as they have their opposites in the efforts toward Americanization. In other words, there was always an interaction in which the one trend was a reflection of the other. Both processes have an obvious connection which must be observed.

In order to answer the question of how long the Swedish Americans were able to preserve their national characteristics, I have attempted to determine the various phases in the transition to the English language, within the religious groups, within the secular organizations, and in the Swedish language press. The transition from the Swedish language to English can be determined rather exactly within the reli-

[13] Rudolph Vecoli, "Ethnicity: A Neglected Dimension of American History," *American Studies in Scandinavia* (Uppsala, Summer 1970), p. 19. Victor Greene has studied the patriotism of Polish Americans and discovered: "The emergence of their ethnic self-consciousness and that of their fellow Slavs was indeed a dramatic transition. ... America made its immigrants ethnocentric. ... The process of identity-consciousness went on continually with every group" (Victor Greene, "For God and Country: The Origin of Slavic Catholic Self-Conscience in America," *Church History* [December, 1966], pp. 446 f.) The word "ethnicity" stems from the Greek word *ethnos*, which means people."

[14] Helge Nelson, *The Swedes and the Swedish Settlements in North America*, p. 5.

gious groups by comparing the number of Swedish to the number of English services held in the churches. The minutes of the various congregational meetings often contain information about language change. I have used these minutes in order to establish the time for the transition to English within the churches of the Augustana Synod and the Evangelical Mission Covenant in Illinois. Not only the denominations but also the conferences (equivalent to the Swedish *stift*) and the individual congregations took action at their annual meetings on whether or not to strike the word "Swedish" from the name, print the minutes in English, or translate the bylaws, etc., into English.

Inasmuch as the possibilities of preserving the Swedish language and the Swedish institutions were directly linked to Swedish group consciousness, I have attempted to illustrate the internal unity and solidarity with respect to themselves and to their Swedish nationality. In the three sections on World War I, the passage of the quota law, and the Depression, I have also wanted to test and to show how strong the national ties really were. The section on intermarriage and citizenship has been included in order to measure partly the strength of group cohesion as opposed to the disposition towards Americanization. Both aspects, intermarriage and naturalization, have customarily been regarded as a measure of the immigrants' propensity to adapt to the host society.[15] The issue of citizenship also demonstrates the immigrants' determination, or lack of it, to take the plunge and break completely with the old country.

4. *Parameters of the Study*

The choice of subject field has been directly influenced by the character of the source material, particularly by the difficulties in localizing it. Because the possibilities of following the careers and activities of specific individuals are slight, it has been necessary at the outset to limit the study to institutions and their development. Large numbers not belonging to a Swedish church and a Swedish organization or not identifying themselves with Swedish America are not represented. It is impossible to determine exactly how large are the numbers of

[15] For references, see the respective chapters.

[16] Helge Nelson, *op. cit.*, p. 368. (Helge Nelson's estimation is that only a fifth part of the Swedish stock belonged to congregations founded and supported in America by Swedes and their descendants.)

individuals in these non-groups. It is customary, on the whole, to figure that approximately 25 per cent of all Swedes belonged to one or another of the Swedish-American denominations.[16] This does not mean, however, that the remainder – 75 percent – did not have religious affiliations, since many Swedish immigrants, and especially their American-born children, belonged to American churches. Those who did not belong to a Swedish church could also maintain contact with Sweden and their fellow countrymen by subscribing to a Swedish language newspaper or by belonging to one of the many Swedish societies and organizations which existed all over the country. In 1915, for example, there were 72 Swedish language newspapers with a total circulation of over 650,000.[17]

A general inadequacy of this study is that large parts of it will be based on the statements and opinions of Swedish Americans themselves. An obvious difficulty has been to determine to what extent certain source materials accurately reflected Swedish-American opinion. This is primarily the case with expressions of opinion from individual Swedish Americans and those which appeared in the Swedish-American press. It has proved almost impossible to obtain any collection of viewpoints which represent Swedish Americans as a whole. For this reason, I have confined myself to presenting clearly articulated opinion – in other words, the viewpoints of individual Swedish Americans or of the institutionalized segment of the Swedish-American community – the churches, the press, and various organizations. This means that those expressions of opinion which have been available for this study cannot unreservedly be assumed to reflect the overall Swedish-American opinion in various issues but rather should only be seen as one expression of opinion among Swedish Americans. For example, when I speak about Swedish-American attitudes to World War I, I am chiefly relying upon those statements of opinion which appeared in the Swedish-American press.

All that can be said with certainty is that most of the persons referred to are well known Swedish Americans and opinion-makers. Whether they represented a smaller or greater part of the Swedish immigrants, they set their stamp on "Swedish America" and the whole Swedish-American debate. To a great extent they can be said to have turned the face of Swedish America outwards.

[17] N. W. Ayers, *Newspaper Annual and Directory*, 1915.

The only way of reaching those who stood outside the Swedish community is to select a specific number of persons and follow them for a given period of time. It would be interesting to know what happened to the Swedish immigrants who tried to make their own way without the help that might have come from their own countrymen. Does strong involvement in a Swedish language church or a Swedish society mean that assimilation proceeded more slowly than if one moved directly into relations with Americans? Or did contact with their own countrymen mean that the newly arrived immigrants were more easily merged into the new milieu? These are questions that demand further study. Another interesting topic, which also demands further study, is the social stratification of the members of Swedish churches and organizations and of the subscribers to Swedish language newspapers.

This study deals chiefly with the period from 1914 to 1932. For the sake of perspective it has been necessary in certain instances, especially in the tables and diagrams, to go back in time. The year 1914 has been set as the earliest limit for the study. Originally it was my intention to begin with 1917, the year that the United States entered the war. But my interest was aroused during the study in comparing the attitude of Swedish Americans to the war both before and after America's official declaration. With the declaration of war by the United States, however, came a turning point in American immigration history. Attitudes toward immigrants changed; a growing opinion demanded measures for accelerating the Americanization process. The increased mistrust and animosity of the war years finally caused the earlier demand for the restriction of immigration to receive a more favorable hearing in Congress.

After 1910 the second-generation Swedes comprised a larger proportion of Swedish Americans. Judging, for example, from the population figures on the number of first-generation and second-generation Swedish Americans one can surmise that the transition to English must have been concentrated in one of the later decades. My aim has therefore been not only to establish a more exact date for the transition but also to show how it happened, what the arguments were which attended the linguistic shift, etc. The year 1932 has been set as the terminal limit of this study. The year thereafter brought the New Deal and the great economic and social changes that followed it, and ushered in a new era for Swedish Americans, as for all Americans.

If the choice of the chronological limits has not created any major difficulties, this can not be said for the geographical boundaries. Some form of regional determination has been necessary in certain instances due to the wide distribution of Swedish Americans throughout the United States. Generally speaking, the study has been carried out on two levels: the national and the regional, the latter being limited chiefly to Illinois and Minnesota. The work of the Augustana Synod and of other denominations, however, has been treated *in toto,* inasmuch as the annual reports relate to the denominations as such. At the same time it has been important to test the more general trends in smaller units, for example the transition from Swedish to English within certain congregations. With respect to the national development, I am basing my conclusions chiefly on earlier studies, while my own contribution to research will relate primarily to the regional and local levels.

A survey of American research in the area of this study reveals that there is no generally accepted definition of the concept of *assimilation,* but that it is subject to shifts in meaning and magnitude. Because I have wanted to avoid a fruitless discussion on the meaning of assimilation, I have purposely not used the term. Instead I have used the expression *Americanization* which, in this study, means the immigrants' gradual accommodation to the American community, naturalization, intermarriage, and the linguistic transition from Swedish to English. It is also possible to say that Americanization implies a decreased dependence on the immigrants' own language and institutions and increased contacts with other groups, a disruption of clanishness. This concept of Americanization corresponds to Milton Gordon's definition of cultural assimilation.[18] Gordon distinguishes between cultural and group or structural assimilation: the former refers to the content of a person's speech and behavior and the latter to a person's network of social interaction.

[18] Milton Gordon has analyzed assimilation into its component parts in *Assimilation in American Life. The Role of Race, Religion, and National Origins* (New York, 1964), pp. 60—83; Charles H. Anderson, *op. cit.,* pp. 6 f. He pinpoints that "speech and behavior must usually change in the direction of that found in the host society before a person is socially accepted. However, acculturation does not guarantee structural assimilation. A person may speak the same language, place value on the same goods and services, and share similar norms with his neighbors, but at the same time be denied or not prefer acceptance into their families, close friendship groups, clubs, and organizations."

5. *Source Materials*

The fundamental sources for this study have been the printed census reports which exist for every tenth year, the annual reports and other publications of the religious denominations, and the Swedish-American press. The Swedish-American denominations which have been included are the Augustana Synod (Lutheran), the Evangelical Covenant Church of America, the Swedish Methodists, and the Swedish Baptists. In general, the sections on citizenship and intermarriage are based on a review of literature, while the other sections are, for the most part, the result of my own research.

The demographic section is based largely on the published census reports and more specifically on the population figures for 1910, 1920, 1930, and 1940. These give a good overview of the geographical distribution of Swedes between town and country, age distribution, literacy and ability to write, and citizenship. On the other hand, they provide no breakdown by occupations or information on the proportion of intermarriages. The most interesting information, that which relates to specific individuals, is unfortunately not yet available for research purposes. Only when this material, sometime in the future, can be employed will one be able to get to the Swedish Americans who made it on their own without benefit of membership in a Swedish community.

The development within the religious denominations is reflected primarily in the various denominational proceedings and annual reports. In certain cases the denomination printed minutes and annual reports even at the local congregational level. The annual reports of the denominations as well as of the various conferences provide valuable information and data on the development. Even the minutes and parish papers of the local churches contain interesting facts about the congregations and their members. Finally, there is a wealth of source material available from the many activities of the denomination: publishing, schools, hospitals, homes for the aged, etc., each of which contributes to the total picture.

Church materials are usually well preserved. The Augustana Synod and the Evangelical Mission Covenant have systematized and preserved their materials at the Lutheran School of Theology and at North Park College, respectively, both in Chicago. The Commission on Covenant History is currently gathering as much information as possible on Covenant congregations.

Both Augustana and Covenant archives contain valuable records, such as correspondence of the most outstanding leaders of the denominations. Collections of letters which have been used are chiefly those of G.A. Brandelle, president of Augustana Synod 1918–35, and David Nyvall, president of North Park College, 1891–1908 and 1912–1923.

Information on the transition to English in the Augustana and Covenant churches in Illinois is derived chiefly from congregational minutes, anniversary publications, and parish papers. Information was also gathered from a questionnaire sent to the pastors of these congregations.[19] With 113 Augustana churches in Illinois in 1925, a personal examination of the records of every church would have demanded an inordinate amount of time, and many congregations would be found to lack any information whatsoever. It has been possible, however, in the case of 49 Augustana churches, to establish the date of transition to the English language. Of the 43 Covenant churches in Illinois it was possible to trace the development in 28. In those cases where individual congregations have published some kind of anniversary album or history, I have been able to compare information regarding the transition.

The Swedish-American newspapers have been a valuable source. News and notices about Swedish Americans provide a lively picture of conditions and impressions in the new country. The discussion and debate appearing in the newspaper columns reflect also the Swedish Americans' views on various issues and events. With wide latitude given to reports of various activities among Swedish Americans, the papers provide detailed information on the development within both the individual congregations and the non-religious organizations. The newspapers which have had primary use in this study were all in the Middle West and especially in Illinois and Minnesota. Those published in Illinois and Minnesota and available for the years 1914–1932 have been subjected to a systematic investigation.

[19] In this questionnaire I asked, among other things: When did you remove the word "Swedish" in the church's name? When was the first English service introduced? Was it an evening service? When were all regular services conducted in English? When did you begin to use English as the official language? When were the bylaws translated into English? Etc.

In spite of the fact that the Swedish language newspapers played a salient role in the lives of Swedish Americans, there is little information about these newspapers, their distribution, editions, number of newspapers per household, etc. The data on newspaper editions to be found in N. W. Ayers, *Newspaper Annual and Directory,* is not always accurate. Where current data have not been reported, estimates have been substituted. Despite the fact that information for certain years is not accurate, Ayers' statistics on editions provide a valuable source, not least because the foreign language newspapers are listed according to nationality. From all appearances the list of Swedish-American newspapers is complete.

With respect to Swedish Americans and World War I, the records of the Committee on Public Information (CPI) in the National Archives in Washington, D.C., in addition to the Swedish language newspapers, provide information on the actions of the Swedish Americans and their attitudes toward the belligerents. CPI's own activities among the Swedes in America also reflect the more official position towards the Swedish immigrants during the war years. In addition, the State Council of Defense in Illinois has information from the various draft boards on the attitudes of the Swedes toward military service. This information is to be found in the Illinois State Historical Library in Springfield. As to the attitude of Swedish Americans toward World War I and the belligerents, Finis Herbert Capps' book, *From Isolationism to Involvement. The Swedish Immigrant Press in America* (1966), has been of great help, not least for my own investigation of the Swedish-American newspapers. Capps' detailed citations have also helped me discover those newspapers and articles which reflected the newspapers' own position on the war. Despite Capps' painstaking investigation of the Swedish-American newspapers, I have been compelled to do my own systematic reading, inasmuch as we were looking for different things. While Capps tried to describe the Swedish-American attitude towards the war, I have tried to interpret the reasons for this attitude, what resulted from their affinity with the Germans, whether or not they dared to say what they thought, what feelings they experienced in the new country – not least the rising hostility towards immigrants. Other questions to which, I have sought answers are: How did they react to the increased demand for more rapid Americanization, for example to the prohibition of use of Swedish? What role was played by the immigrants' ties with Sweden?

Did the immigrant waver between Swedish and American loyalties?

Materials of secular Swedish organizations have not been collected or catalogued and were therefore not available for study. None of the large fraternities – Vasa Order of America, The Independent Order of Vikings or The Independent Order of Svithiod – has archives. The minutes of the meetings of the Vasa Order and of the district lodges nevertheless provide a great deal of valuable data on growth, number of members, number of new and defunct lodges, etc.

The Scandinavian Socialist Society *(Skandinaviska Socialistförbundet),* in contrast to the Vasa Order, seems not to have a single document preserved for posterity. The reason for this is the animosity towards immigrants following World War I. For fear of encountering trouble those who were involved in the Society chose to burn and destroy every document which could be used against them. In spite of this we know a great deal about the Swedish Socialists in the United States, thanks to Henry Bengston and his book, *Skandinaver på vänsterflygeln i USA* (Left-wing Scandinavians in the USA) 1955.[20]

The proceedings of the Swedish-American Relief Committee have completely disappeared, and any treatment of its activities is based chiefly on the accounts of Herbert Hedman, chairman of the Committee, and the Swedish language newspapers. It was quite customary for the newspapers to reproduce the minutes of business sessions and accounts of activities, both of which contain detailed information on the Committee's functions.

The proceedings of the Swedish National Society exist for a part of the period in question and are housed in the archives of the Swedish Pioneer Historical Society at North Park College, Chicago. Because there are large gaps in both the Swedish National Society's records and their collection of correspondence, it has often been difficult to follow their relief work among Swedish Americans. As a rule it has been possible to close the gaps only with the help of the Swedish language newspapers.

In general, the main body of material that deals with Swedish Americans and has not been used earlier has been the object of a methodical study or search. This material has been found scattered

[20] Henry Bengston, who is still living, was active in the Scandinavian Socialist Society and for a long time editor of *Svenska Socialisten* (The Swedish Socialist).

among many individuals. The records of the secular organizations, for example, would in some cases be found in the hands of the president or secretary – if, in fact, their predecessors in office had bothered to pass them on.

6. *The Organization of the study*

The investigation consists of four parts or problem areas, each of which deals with various aspects of the same theme, namely: to study group consciousness among Swedish Americans. The third and fourth parts, which build almost exclusively on the results of my own research, comprise the focal points of the dissertation. The first part is devoted to a more demographic description and charting of the number of Swedes of the first and second generations, their ages, their geographic distribution and mobility. The second part sheds light on intermarriage and citizenship. The third part, which concerns the Swedes during World War I, their position on quota legislation, and conditions during the Depression, is intended to reflect the internal unity during three periods of crisis. Through all of these periods people drew together in order to help one another and to protect the Swedish name. Finally, the fourth and last part depicts the transition from the Swedish language to the English, in particular within the Swedish religious denominations and in the decline of the Swedish language press.

II. The Demographic Development – Swedes in America

Prior to 1900 the majority of Swedish immigrants had come from rural districts and were farmers or in any case familiar with agriculture. To a large extent they settled in the large woodland and prairie areas west of the Great Lakes, first and foremost in Minnesota and Illinois, and then in Iowa, Michigan, Wisconsin, Kansas, and Nebraska. After 1900 the concentration of Swedes shifted somewhat eastward toward the industrial localities of New England and the states along the Atlantic coast.[2]

In 1860 the total number of Swedish-born people in the United States was only 18,625, of whom 63 percent lived in Illinois, Minnesota, Wisconsin, and Iowa.[3] By 1880 the number had risen to 194,337, which was 2.9 percent of the total of foreign-born. In 1900 the number of Swedish-born was 581,986. That year the Swedes reached their highest percentage, 5.6 percent of the total foreign-born. During the decade 1900–1910 the absolute number of Swedish-born rose to 665,183, but at the same time they decreased to 5.0 percent of the total foreign-born. After 1910 the number of Swedish-born gradually declined. During the period 1910–1940 their numbers were reduced from 665,183 to 445,070. The main reason for this was, naturally, the declining immigration from Sweden. In the single decade between 1930 and 1940 the number of Swedish-born decreased by 25 percent.

The number of Swedish Americans[4] was considerably larger than the figures of Swedish-born indicate. Thus in 1930 there was a total of

[1] In this section the author has used, unless other sources are indicated, Helge Nelson, *The Swedes and the Swedish Settlements in North America,* and A. B. Benson and N. Hedin, *Americans from Sweden* (Philadelphia, 1950).

[2] These latter states are New York, New Jersey, and Pennsylvania.

[3] Helge Nelson, *op. cit.,* p. 43 ff; *Fourteenth, Fifteenth and Sixteenth Censuses of the United States : Population.*

[4] The total number of Swedes — "the foreign stock" — includes those born in Sweden and those born in the United States of Swedish parents, and those who had either a Swedish father or mother; thus the first and second generations.

Table 1. Total number of persons born in Sweden and total number of persons born in the United States of Swedish parents or parent.

Year	Number of persons born in Sweden	Percentage of the total of foreign-born in US	Born in US of Swedish parents or parent	Percentage of the total of US born foreign stock
1900	581,986	5.6 %	542,032	3.7 %
1910	665,183	5.0 %	752,695	3.7 %
1920	625,580	4.6 %	888,497	3.6 %
1930	595,250	4.5 %	967,453	3.8 %
1940	445,070	3.9 %	856,320	3.7 %

Source: *Fifteenth Census of the United States, 1930, Population.* Vol. II, p. 269. *Sixteenth Census of the United States, 1940, Population. Country of Birth of the Foreign- Born Population,* p. 225.

1,562,703 Swedes of the first and second generations. While the number of Swedish-born in the U.S. decreased after 1910 that of second-generation Swedes continued to increase up to 1930, after which it decreased. Between 1930 and 1940 the second generation was reduced by 11.5 percent. Since then the number of the first- and second-generation Swedes in America has steadily declined.

Ever since 1900 the geographic distribution of Swedish Americans has changed. The concentration in the Middle West weakened gradually.[5] In 1890, 70.3 percent of the Swedish-born were to be found in the Middle West, while in 1900 the figure was 65.1 percent and in 1910, 58.9 percent. Simultaneously, the New England states and the Middle Atlantic states because of industrialization had attracted more and more Swedes. In 1900 there were 10.2 percent of the Swedish-born in New England and 12.7 percent in the Middle Atlantic states. States on the Pacific coast had 5.5 percent. In 1930 the geographic distribution was 11.1 percent in New England and 15.3 percent in the Middle Atlantic states, which means that more than one-fourth had concentrated in the Northeastern industrial states. The Pacific coast states had likewise continued to exert attraction for the Swedes and had that year 14.6 percent. In the Middle West the number had decreased to 52.7 percent of the total Swedish-born. (The fluctuations between the various parts are indicated in Table 2).

[5] Middle West states: Ohio, Indiana, Illinois, Michigan, Wisconsin, Minnesota, Iowa, Missouri, North and South Dakota, Kansas, and Nebraska. New England states: Maine, New Hampshire, Vermont, Massachusetts, Rhode Island, and Connecticut. Middle Atlantic states: New York, New Jersey, and Pennsylvania.

Table 2. The geographic distribution of the Swedes in US in 1910, 1920, 1930, and 1940 (in percentages).

	Swedish-born				Born in US of Swedish parents or parent			
Area	1910	1920	1930	1940	1910	1920	1930	1940
New England states	10.6	10.7	11.1	11.4	8.0	8.5	8.5	8.3
Middle Atlantic states	13.2	13.4	15.3	15.7	10.3	10.4	11.1	11.0
Middle West states	58.9	56.3	52.7	50.7	66.6	67.2	60.0	58.5
Pacific Coast states	10.3	12.5	14.6	15.8	7.5	9.3	12.4	14.2
Other areas	7.0	7.1	6.3	6.4	7.6	4.6	8.0	8.0

Sources: *Fourteenth Census of the US, 1920, Population. Country of the Foreign White Stock*, pp. 912–925.
Fifteenth Census of the US, 1930, Population. Vol. II, pp. 288,312.
Sixteenth Census of the US, 1940, Population. Nationality and Parentage of the White Population, pp. 42–51.

The geographic redistribution of second-generation Swedes, like that of the Swedish-born, was less extensive between 1930 and 1940 than it had been during prior decades. In contrast to the Swedish-born the second-generation Swedes preferred to move westward to the states on the Pacific coast. Between 1930 and 1940 their number in that region increased by 1.1 percent, while at the same time their number in the states along the Atlantic coast and in New England decreased by 0.3 percent. The concentration in the Middle West weakened successively. In 1920 there were 67.2 percent of the second-generation Swedes in that area while in 1930 the figure was 60.0 percent and in 1940, 58.5 percent. According to the Census reports a greater percentage of the Swedish-born than of the second generation lived in urban areas. More than half of the former – 68.6 percent – lived in cities in 1930, and of the latter 62.2 percent.

A little more than half of the Swedes – 52.6 percent – who lived in rural areas in 1930 were engaged in agriculture, and if we include the second generation, the figure becomes somewhat higher – 56.8 percent. A reason for this may be that the second generation had become landowners to a larger degree than the Swedish-born, and had thus become more closely associated with agricultural pursuits. It is also possible that the higher nativity among the farming population played a certain role. The average size of families of all the Swedish-born was 3.08 (in 1930), while it was 3.45 among those engaged in agriculture.[6] Finally, the economic situation of agriculture at the end of World War I had become less attractive, and many of the newly arriving immigrants sought their livelihood outside of agricultural pursuits.

The urbanization of the 1900s influenced also the Swedish immigrants in America. The "Emigration Report" states that "the farmers complained that their sons and daughters, in America just as in Sweden, finding life dull and tedious out on the farm, moved to the cities and found city employment."[7] The concern among the Swedish farmers to which the "Report" refers was not without basis. Both first-and-second generation Swedes were attracted to the cities. The drawing power of the cities on the Swedes was particularly strong during the 1910s and 1920s. However during the 1930s the cities lost some of their power of attraction. This was partly due to the prevalence of unemployment which was as a rule worse in the cities than in rural districts. In 1910, 60.6 percent of the Swedish-born lived in cities, compared with 68.6 percent in 1930; of the second-generation Swedes, 52.2 percent lived in cities in 1910 while in 1930 the figure was 62.2 percent. Of the Swedish-born living in rural areas, the number engaged in agriculture was reduced from 52.6 percent in 1930 to 50.2 percent in 1940. In-

Table 3. Swedish-born persons and persons born in America of Swedish parents — or parent — living in urban or in rural areas.

Year	Born in Sweden		Born in US of Swedish parents or parent	
	urban	rural	urban	rural
1910	60.6 %	39.4 %	52.2 %	47.8 %
1920	63.1	36.9	58.7	41.3
1930	68.6	31.4	62.2	37.8
1940	68.8	31.2	62.9	37.1

Sources: *Fourteenth Census of the United States, 1920, Population. Country of Origin of the Foreign White Stock*, p. 958.
Fifteenth Census of the United States, 1930, Population. vol. II, p. 270.
Sixteenth Census of the United States, 1940, Population. Nativity, and Parentage of the White Population, pp. 13—17.

[6] *Fifteenth Census of the United States 1930 : Population, Special Report on Foreign- Born White Families by Country of Birth of Head* (Washington, 1933), p. 16 f.

[7] *Emigrationsutredningen, XX* (1911), p. 118.

Table 4. Number of Swedes — the Swedish stock — living in cities having 100,000 or more inhabitants, and the percentage of the total number of foreign stock in 1910, 1920, 1930 and 1940.

City	1910		1920		1930		1940[1]	
	number	%	number	%	number	%	number	%
Boston	11 256	2.3	12 027	2.2	10 555	1.9	7 899	1.6
Chicago	116 740	6.9	121 326	6.2	140 913	6.5	110 198	5.6
Denver	8 900	8.9	8 910	8.5	9 429	9.1	—	—
Detroit	1 110	0.3	6 379	1.0	11 603	1.3	9 945	1.2
Duluth	—	—	—	—	16 968	24.2	—	—
Hartford	—	—	4 390	4.7	4 511	4.0	—	—
Los Angeles	6 150	4.5	10 462	4.1	23 126	5.1	22 484	4.0
Minneapolis	52 755	26.1	61 514	25.3	70 463	26.6	60 584	26.6
New York	55 278	1.5	57 750	1.3	66 978	1.3	55 161	1.1
Omaha	8 355	12.5	9 282	9.8	8 886	9.5	—	—
Philadelphia	2 429	0.5	5 115	0.5	5 003	0.5	3 752	0.5
Portland	8 383	8.8	10 114	8.7	11 559	8.9	—	—
Providence	5 953	3.8	5 187	3.1	4 794	2.7	—	—
St Paul	24 640	16.4	24 227	15.8	25 430	16.4	—	—
San Francisco	10 599	3.7	11 407	3.5	14 416	4.0	12 638	4.0
Seattle	14 299	11.7	18 855	11.6	21 001	11.9	18 010	11.5
Spokane	5 849	12.1	5 395	11.7	5 802	12.4	—	—
Worcester	—	—	15 856	12.4	16 002	11.8	—	—

[1] The Census Reports only give statistics on foreign-stock in cities of 500,000 or more.

Sources: *Fourteenth Census of the United States, 1920, Population: Country of Origin of the Foreign White Stock*, pp. 930—49.
Fifteenth Census of the United States, 1930, Population. Vol. II, pp. 314—337.
Sixteenth Census of the United States, 1940, Population: Nativity and Parentage of the White Population, pp. 13—17.

cluding the second generation, the reduction becomes larger: 56.8 to 52.4 percent.

Chicago had incomparably the greatest attraction for the Swedes. For most Swedes Chicago was the crucial point from which they traveled farther but where also many remained because for various reasons they were not able to go any farther. The second such place was Minneapolis, the third and fourth were New York and St. Paul. Despite the large total number of Swedes in Chicago, they constituted in 1930 only 6.5 percent of the total number of persons of foreign extraction. The same situation prevailed in New York where the number of Swedes in proportion to the population was very small and in 1930 made up only 1.3 percent of the foreign stock. In Minneapolis, on the other hand, the Swedes constituted all of 26.6 percent of the foreign stock in 1930.

There were Swedes not only in the above-named big cities. If one would use the term "Swedish centers" it must first of all apply to such places as Rockford, Moline and Rock Island in Illinois, and Jamestown in the state of New York. The Swedes concentrated, however, not only in the cities but also in rural areas. In the United States no county can show a more compact Swedish population than the counties of Chisago and of Isanti, both in Minnesota.[8]

In Rockford in 1930 there were 10,086 Swedish-born persons, constituting 55 percent of the total of foreign-born. Altogether, the first- and second-generation Swedes made up 26.0 percent of Rockford's total population. The same year Moline had 2,888 Swedish-born persons or 48.4 percent of the total of foreign-born. Rock Island, which has primarily become known as the home of Augustana College and Theological Seminary and of Augustana Book Concern, in 1930 had 652 Swedish-born or 16.1 percent of the total foreign-born in the city. In Illinois, Evanston, a suburb of Chicago, had a large percentage of Swedish residents: in 1930 a total of 2,342 Swedish-born, making up 24.3 percent of the total of foreign-born.

Of all the cities in the United States, Jamestown, in the state of New York, shows percentage-wise the largest number of Swedes and and Swedish descendants. In 1930 Jamestown had 7,738 Swedish-born people, constituting 62.7 percent of the total number of foreign-

[8] Helge Nelson, *op. cit.*, p. 190 ff; *Fifteenth Census of the United States*, 1930, *Population.*

born. Together, first- and second-generation Swedes made up 37.2 percent of the total population of the city, which was 15,155.

In Chisago County, Minnesota, there were 2,319 Swedish-born residents in 1930 and in Isanti County 2,165; together they constituted 85 and 84 percent of the total of foreign-born. If both the first and second generations of Swedes were included, 54.7 percent of the total population of Chisago County and 54.2 percent of Isanti's were of Swedish extraction. Besides these counties with a large Swedish population may be mentioned the counties of Kanabec and of Mille Lacs, both in Minnesota, which each had 1,023 and 1,292 Swedish-born persons or each a total 64 percent and 51 percent of the foreign-born.

According to a special investigation in 1930 of the total number of families of foreign extraction, there were that year 267,496 Swedish families in the United States of which both parents or either the father or the mother were born in Sweden.[9] Of these families 175,014 lived in cities and 92,487 in rural areas. Of the latter, 50,367 were engaged in agricultural pursuits.[10] Farmer families concentrated most strongly in the Middle Western States where they constituted a total of 68.5 percent of the Swedish families.[11] Of the separate states, Minnesota had the largest number of farmers (13,888), next followed by Wisconsin (3,071) and Washington (3,463).

If the number of real estate holdings and farms owned by Swedes, according to the census of 1930, is taken as the measure of value, the economic standard was high among the Swedes compared to that of other nationalities. Of the Swedish families 64.9 percent owned their own homes.[12] Next to the Swedes were the Finns with 64.8 percent, then the Germans with 63.9 percent and the Norwegians with 63.8 percent. For comparison it may be noted that for the Italians the corresponding figure was 42.8 percent. Of the Swedish families in the cities 59.1 percent owned their homes, followed next by the Germans with 58.2 percent.[13] Of the non-farming families in rural areas, only the Germans had in percentage more real property than the Swedes (77.4 vs. 72.3 percent).

9 *Fifteenth Census of the United States, 1930, Population: Foreign- Born White Families by Country of Birth of Head*, p. 6.

10 *Ibid.*, p. 10.

11 *Ibid.*, p. 44 ff.

12 *Ibid.*, p. 7.

13 *Ibid.*, p. 11.

Of the Swedish families engaged in farming 78.7 owned their farms, but were surpassed by, among others, the Finns, the Poles, and the Czechs. The number of owner-farmers was largest among the well-to-do Swedes in Michigan, Wisconsin, and Washington where respectively 91.8, 91.5 and 90.2 percent of the Swedish farmers owned their own farms. For Illinois the corresponding figure was 49.6 percent.[14]

Finally, the report of the 1930 census contains a close study of the age divisions of the total foreign-born. The median age of "the older immigration" from North and West Europe increased on the whole during the 1900s according as "the newer immigration" from South and East Europe streamed in. In comparison with other immigrant groups, the median age among the Swedes was very high.

Table 5. The median age of foreign-born from certain selected countries, 1910—1940.

Country	1910	1920	1930	1940
Sweden	40.7	44.6	52.0	58.0
Norway	40.7	46.2	50.3	56.3
Germany	47.3	—	53.0	56.6
Italy	29.2	34.7	40.6	48.8
Poland	—	—	41.3	49.9

In 1910 Hutchinson gives the median age only for Scandinavian.

Source: Edward Hutchinson, *Immigrants and Their Children, 1850—1950* (New York, 1956), p. 17.

When the emigration from Sweden was reduced the median age among the Swedes rose. As indicated in Table 5 the Swedes had next to the highest median age in 1930 and the highest in 1940. The Italians had the lowest, which may primarily be seen as a direct result of their relatively late arrival in the United States. The median age of the Swedish-born immigrants, according to the 1930 census, as Table 5 shows, was 52.0 years while for the Italians it was 40.6 years.

As to the occupational divisions of the various nationalities in the United States, the census records give scanty information. After 1910 the census records divide the population only in groups of "native-born" and "foreign-born." Occupational divisions of these two groups are substantially different. In 1930, for instance, foreign-born were

[14] *Ibid.*, p. 44.

percentually more (44.1 percent) employed in industry than native-born (27.5 percent).[15] It has also been pointed out that the foreign-born were in the main concentrated in industries that demanded only low industrial experience, or none.[16] In farming pursuits the division was 9.1 percent for foreign-born and 21.4 percent for native-born.

It is impossible to say to what extent the Swedes in this regard differed from the whole group of foreign-born. Helge Nelson found that the Swedes felt a special attraction toward certain occupations and that their technical training and aptitude made them particularly welcome in the metal industry, in factory work, in furniture manufacturing, and in the building trades.[17] A comparison between the censuses of the last half of the 19th century shows a tendency indicating that more and more Swedes were drawn from agricultural work to industrial pursuits. An investigation in 1950 emphasized further that a definite shifting from agricultural to industrial work had taken place among the Swedish-born.[18] As previously stated it is impossible to ascertain definitely the occupational division among the Swedes. The only thing we know is that a small percentage – 16.6 in 1930 – had a direct connection with agriculture and consequently a relatively large percentage was engaged in city employment and industry.

According to information from Swedish churches and organizations in 1930 the largest number of Swedes were employed in the building trades, in factories, and in the furniture-making industries. Recorded data and narratives of Swedish Americans show a similar picture. Andrew Stomberg found, in 1928, that the contribution of Swedes to America's industrial life was so significant "that if one could imagine that these resources could suddenly be rendered inactive, the whole nation's productive ability would suffer a serious damage."[19] Stomberg estimated that Swedes had done about 80 percent of all building projects in Minneapolis and about 35 percent in Chicago. Even if they are to be considered highly speculative, Stomberg's figures indicate

[15] *Fifteenth Census of the United States, 1930. General Report on Occupations*, Vol. V, p. 74.

[16] Maurice Davis, *World Immigration*, p. 244.

[17] Helge Nelson, *op. cit.*, pp. 67 and 380.

[18] Edward Hutchinson, *Immigrants and Their Children, 1850—1950* (N Y. 1956), p. 242 f.

[19] Andrew Stomberg, *Den svenska folkstammen i Amerika* (Stockholm, 1928), p. 11 ff.

that a large percentage of the Swedes in the United States were employed in the building industry. Henry Bengston estimates that about 50 percent of the Swedes in Chicago in 1930 were employed in the building industry.[20]

The demographic development among the Swedes followed the general pattern. The most noticeable fact about the distribution of the foreign-born including the Swedes is their concentration in the New England, Middle Atlantic, and North Central States. A majority of the Swedes, however, settled in the North Central States, while the foreign-born at large were concentrated mainly in the Northeast. The sections which have shown marked increases in the number of foreign-born and also native-born of foreign or mixed parentage are New England, the Middle Atlantic, and the Pacific, while the number in the North Central decreased. Most Swedes, as most immigrants, settled principally in the cities. The percentage of the foreign-born living in cities steadily increased. In 1930, 80.3 percent of all foreign-born lived in cities and 68.6 of the Swedish-born.[21]

[20] Henry Bengston, for many years editor of the paper *Svenska Socialisten* and author of the book *Skandinaver på vänsterflygeln i USA* (Stockholm, 1955), operated for over 50 years his own printing shop in the Lake View district of Chicago.

[21] Maurice Davie, *World Immigration,* p. 234.

III. Development of a "Swedish America"

In a geographic sense there has never been a "Swedish America," because the Swedish immigrants did not concentrate within any certain geographic area but have been found all over the American continent. Their concentration was further prevented as the immigration changed in character. And yet one may, in a more abstract sense, speak of "Swedish America" as a collective description of the cultural and religious heritage which the Swedish immigrants brought with them and perpetuated in America – a concept in which the core is Swedish. They developed a sense of peoplehood with other newcomers from their homeland. The sharing of a sense of peoplehood and commonality served to bind men together into kinship networks, cliques and organizations. The resulting system of social relationship constituted the ethnic group. The idea of a "Swedish America" took institutional form in the churches using the Swedish language, in a Swedish press, and in idealistic and mutual benefit societies. These institutions were kept alive by a stream of new immigrants from Sweden. This "Swedish America" was partly a product of the nationalism arising among the Swedes, as it did among other immigrant groups, after their arrival in America – a nationalism that was quickened into life through the immigration process. Louis Gerson has explained nationalism among immigrants as follows:

> One must bear in mind that the wellspring of immigrant nationalism is to be found not only in affection for the native countries, which is often absent at the time of emigrating, but perhaps even more in the compressed ghettos where group consciousness was fostered by loneliness, poverty, prejudice and periodic attacks from nativists and other ethnic groups.[1]

Nationalism among the Swedish Americans found its expression in emphasis on their affinity with Sweden, Swedish culture and Swedish history. Rivalry between the many immigrant nationalities stimulated

[1] Louis Gerson, *The Hyphenate in Recent American Politics and Diplomacy* (Lawrence, 1964), p. 5.

the Swedes, as it did other groups, to accentuate the superiority of their own nationality. One compensated for unfamiliarity with American history by recalling the old country's history and historical exploits. Among the problems confronting the immigrants in the new country was the absence of antiquity and of traditions, countered by remembrance of friends left behind. The only guide by which they could adjust themselves was the use of the ways of the old country. Language and traditions were transported to the United States. Belonging to the group – togetherness – gave them security and psychological strength. It is not strange, therefore, that they organized themselves according to their original nationality.

One may also say that "Swedish America" is synonymous with "Swedishness." Since the very beginning of immigration there have been forces actively at work for "Swedish America," or for the preservation of "Swedishness." They have maintained that Swedish Americans ought to be able to leave traces of themselves in American culture so that their lives will be not merely a record of their laboring, eating and sleeping, "somewhat like that of draught-oxen."[2] When the Swedes were numerically weak, it was considered necessary that they pull together as much as possible in order to be able to preserve their cultural heritage. The various ethnic groups in America, it was said, had each been given a mandate to contribute to the development of the country. A somewhat pointed contest ensued to determine which nationality would contribute the most and the best.[3]

While the immigrants defended "Swedish America," the opinions were very much divided about how to preserve it, and about what ought to be preserved. John A. Enander defined, for example, in a speech in 1899 what he considered to be the task of the Swedes in America:

> The goal which I have desired but also for which I have striven all my life . . . is this: to awaken to life the feeling of Swedish nationality, slumbering as if dead, to kindle in hearts that are lukewarm or cold a warm love to a common language, common historical memories, common song, and a common spiritual nurture in general, and to mold this into a harmonious whole with all the beautiful, the noble, the true, which the culture of the new

[2] *Förbundets Veckotidning,* June 7, 1917.

[3] See for instance, S. G. Öhman, "Vårt svenska arv" in *Korsbaneret* (1924), p. 116 ff; C. A. Lönnquist, "Vårt svensk-lutherska arv," in *Korsbaneret* (1925), pp. 96—105.

> fatherland has so freely offered the immigrant. I have wanted our nationality to be not only a receiving people, but likewise a people able to give.[4]

Because opinions about the preservation of Swedish culture, its content and extent, were divided, the ”National Society for the Preservation of Swedish Culture in America” initiated the publication of a series of articles in which the matter was analyzed and discussed.[5] David Nyvall wrote, as an introduction, that

> ”preservation of 'Swedishness' ” was a cultural commitment we have inherited from our fatherland which we cannot conscientiously get away from because of our removal to this country. With 'Swedishness' we do not mean so much using the Swedish speech in ordinary contacts but, in a wider extension, something of a contribution to the great totality of American idealism. We mean the translation in word and deed of Swedish thought, Swedish will, Swedish dreams, which we have brought with us as our essential wealth. We mean the planting in American soil of the seed we have not only brought with us but which we *are*.[6]

As examples of what he meant, Nyvall referred to the establishment of churches and schools that were altogether Swedish.

A form letter issued by the Northwest division of the Swedish Cultural Society and sent to Swedish Americans explained in definite detail what was meant by ”preservation of Swedish culture”:

> By the term 'preservation of Swedish culture' we do not mean, nor do we promote, political obligations to our forefathers' and maybe our own childhood's country, for we live in another country of which we must be good citizens, but we *do* mean and we do promote interest in the beautiful language inherited from our fathers, wherever the need to promote it exists, as well as all other great and noble aspects of the culture we have inherited and brought with us and which can be and ought to be injected into the American society and life.[7]

[4] Conrad Bergendoff, ”The Role of Augustana in the Transplanting of a Culture Across the Atlantic,” *The Immigration of Ideas* (Rock Island, 1968), p. 72.

[5] ”Föreningen för svenskhetens bevarande i Amerika,” organized in 1910, was a daughter-organization of ”Riksföreningen för svenskhetens bevarande i utlandet”; in 1923 the name was changed to ”Svenska kulturförbundet i Amerika' (Swedish Cultural Society). (See further, special chapter pp. 313 ff).

[6] David Nyvall, 'Svenskhetens bevarande,” *Augustana,* December 22, 1921, p. 818 ff.

[7] Form letter issued by the Northwest division of the ”Society for the Preservation of Swedish Culture in America” dated Minneapolis in July, 1922 (for the purpose of securing new members).

"Swedishness" was not only love of and pride in whatever was Swedish. It was also appreciation of the Swedish Americans themselves, and of the contribution of the Swedish people to world history, to man's development, of their incomparable exploits and martial deeds as defenders of human rights and freedom.[8] Knowledge of the Swedish language was also considered an expression of "Swedishness."[9]

C.A. Lindvall asserted (1917) that it was the duty of the Swedish Americans to preserve as much as possible of the Swedish heritage, while at the same time they had to realize that their adopted country had a greater authority over them than Sweden – which only harbored their recollections.[10] The same writer also said he was convinced that the longer they could maintain their glorious Swedish tongue the better it would be even if they thereby were accorded the blasphemous title "hyphenated Americans." It would be deplorable if the descendants of magnanimous forefathers were to stand non-plussed and weak-willed ready to relinquish all of their rich heritage.[11]

After this brief analysis, I propose to describe how the Swedes tried to preserve a distinctively Swedish America and describe the debate within the community on what was worth preserving and what was the essence of "Swedishness." Did they succeed in their efforts to preserve the traditional character of the Swedish language, Swedish churches, Swedish cultural organizations, and a Swedish press? Was a distinctively Swedish national consciousness maintained in the American environment? Did intermarriage become a common and accepted turn of events or did group consciousness among Swedish Americans remain dominant? These are a few of the questions which I will discuss in the following chapters.

[8] A. G. Witting, "Svenskheten och den äkta amerikanismen" (Swedishness and the real Americanism), *Meddelanden från Svenska Kulturförbundet i Amerika* (1932?), p. 6.

[9] V. Berger, *Svensk-amerikanska meditationer* (Swedish American Meditations) p. 126; O. A. Linder, "Svenskhetens bevarande" in *Svenska Amerikanaren,* November 25, 1926, p. 5.

[10] C.A. Lindvall, "Vårt stora kulturarv" (Our great cultural heritage), *Year-Book of the Swedish Historical Society of America* (1916/17) p. 14 ff.

[11] — "Svenska språket i Amerika" (The Swedish language in America), *Year-Book of the Swedish Historical Society of America* (1915), p. 16.

IV. Citizenship

It would seem natural that immigrants who came to America to stay would seek American citizenship as soon as possible, that is within five years after their arrival.[1] In most cases this did not happen. Most of the immigrants were in no hurry to become naturalized. Before World War I it took on the average 6.8 years before the immigrants filled out their "first paper" – the declaration of intention to seek citizenship.[2] After that a delay of five years, on the average, ensued before they would apply for citizenship – the final petition for naturalization – while the law prescribed only two years. This means that for the average immigrant it took 11.8 years to become an American citizen even though the law stipulated only five years.

Whatever the reasons for the long interval of time, it is noteworthy that the immigrants paid so little attention to citizenship when this conferred so many privileges. American citizenship was required for the privilege of becoming a voter. Further, a person's chances for

[1] Required for citizenship: "Declaration of intention, filing of a petition for naturalization after a minimum of two years' residence, and final admission after an additional three years in the United States. A speaking knowledge of English is required, and most judges require some ability to read English. The applicant must be of good moral character, bring witness to attest this fact, and also pass a brief oral examination on the principles underlying the government of the United States." See also William Bernard, *American Immigration Policy — A Reappraisal* (New York, 1950), p. 143; and *Fifteenth Census of the U.S.: Population, 1930,* p. 401 ff.

[2] John Gavit, "Americans by Choice," *Immigration an American Dilemma. Problems in American Civilization* (Boston, 1953), p. 90; Gavit bases his conclusion on an investigation, July 1, 1913 — June 30, 1914, of 26,284 petitions for naturalization. He made a selection from 28 courts in Eastern, Middle West and Western parts of the country. — Sune Åkerman has tested some one hundred naturalized persons in Dane County, Wisconsin, 1903—1906 and found that about half of them waited more than 20 years to petition for citizenship. (See PM of Sune Åkerman, "Citizenship Records as Source for Study of Assimilation in USA" [Uppsala, 1970], p. 40).

gaining a livelihood were enhanced by his being an American citizen.[3] After the outbreak of the war in 1917 it became difficult for an alien to get work. Some employers would not consider an application for employment unless the applicant could show that he had at least filled out a "declaration of intention." This was true also for Swedes. A statement of the National (Swedish) Social Welfare Board (Socialstyrelsen) in 1941 declared, for instance: "From various sources it has been learned that certain categories of our countrymen in America to a large extent have neglected to obtain American citizenship and have thus placed themselves in an unfavorable situation . . . that the absence of American citizenship in America in critical times may even entail the risk of deportation, and that thousands of poor Swedish workers without American citizenship, because of fear of that eventuality, have moved about from place to place."[4]

Still more important was the significance of naturalization itself which was indicative of a person's deliberate decision to assimilate with the American commonwealth and relinquish all thought of returning to the old country. Naturalization was a part of Americanization and therefore it has been used as an index of a nationality's or individual's ability or willingness to be Americanized. Naturalization was the technical and formal procedure that eradicted the constitutional and legal differences between "citizens" and "aliens." "The familiarity that they gain with the English language by going through the naturalization process and also the changed status in the community and in the eyes of their children that they acquire by becoming naturalized are advantages that they discover they can hardly afford to miss."[5]

The United States Immigration Commission of 1907 set forth some far-reaching conclusions based on citizenship statistics. From that

[3] H.F. Gosnell, "Non-Naturalization: A Study in Political Assimilation," *The American Journal of Sociology* (May, 1928), p. 930. Jerome Davis writes in the article: "The Assimilation of Immigrants and Our Citizenship Process": "In a period of economic depression, our society has definitely accepted the theory that American citizens should have preference in securing positions in the economie life. ... At the present time every state in the Union has some laws on its statute books that deprive the alien of the right to engage in certain occupations." *(Social Forces,* Volume XII [May, 1934] p. 579).

[4] *Utlandssvenskarna.* Statens Offentliga Utredningar (Stockholm 1941 : 36), p. 27.

[5] Gosnell, *op. cit.,* p. 934.

investigation the incorrect conclusion has been drawn that the "old" immigrants were more eager to seek citizenship than the "new." John Gavit pointed out already in 1922, in his book *Americans by Choice*, the Immigration Commission's deficiency.[6] He stated that the statistics on naturalized and aliens were not pertinent as long as the time period of immigration was not entered as a component. He contended that it was a matter of course that the number of naturalized was greater among Swedes, Germans, and Irish, etc., since they came much earlier than Italians, Poles, Russians, and Finns. The number of naturalized, however, did not prove that the former became Americanized more rapidly than the latter. Instead John Gavit found "that the desire to become citizens is as evident among these immigrants of the new races as among those of the earlier,"[7] something which few scholars would challenge.

The value of naturalization records as a measure of the immigrants' desire for assimilation is not, of course, an exact instrument. One must bear in mind that naturalization is not synonymous with Americanization.[8] In itself it indicates nothing of the individual immigrant's attitude toward the receiving country. In individual cases, citizenship does not necessarily prove anything, but when it comes down to large numbers of people, then the whole question of citizenship gives rise to certain interesting tendencies. During certain periods, as previously mentioned, naturalization was necessary, as for instance during World War I and during the depression years. "Thus desire for citizenship may no longer be a matter of pride and loyalty to America so much as a matter of bread and butter necessity."[9] Furthermore, it was not certain that naturalization changed the immigrant's loyalty to the old country. Finally, there were those who never obtained American citizenship yet became Americanized.

Despite difficulties in establishing exact motives for seeking naturalization one cannot ignore the fact that those who were naturalized

[6] Gavit, *op. cit.*, p. 85 ff. (Here reference is made to an article under the same title since the book was not available in Sweden.)

[7] *Ibid.*, p. 89.

[8] Niles Carpenter, *Immigrants and Their Children, 1920* (Washington, D.C., 1927), p. 250; Carpenter points out that naturalization was not "tantamount to Americanization."

[9] Jerome Davis, "The Assimilation of Immigrants and Our Citizenship Process," p. 580.

showed a deliberate will to be Americanized and become Americans for good.[10] Even if naturalization did not include complete Americanization it was yet a step in that direction. That may be said also about declaring their intention to apply later for citizenship – filing their "declaration of intention to become a citizen."[11]

The time period of arrival must be considered if the naturalization records are to be used as a measure of the Americanization of the various nationalities. An individual who is naturalized after five years must be considered more easily Americanized than a person who is not naturalized until the passage of ten to fifteen years. The investigators who contend that immigrants from Northern and Western Europe became Americanized more rapidly than those from Southern and Eastern Europe have, as a rule, quite neglected consideration of the time of arrival and have only reckoned the number of naturalized. They have not taken into account that immigrants from Southern and Eastern Europe arrived much later and therefore had a shorter time to fit into the new conditions. As indicated in Table 6 there were percentally more naturalized among the "old" immigrant groups than among the "new." With exception of Danes and Welsh, the Swedes had in 1930 percentally the largest number of American citizens, thus more than the English. Of the persons who, according to the census of 1930, lived in the U.S. and were born *e.g.* in Germany, Sweden or Wales, 50 percent had arrived by 1900 or earlier, while of those who were born in Poland, Italy or Greece only 20 percent had come in 1900 or earlier.[12]

A comparison of 1910 and 1930 shows that the number of naturalized increased from 45.6 percent of foreign-born to 62.0 percent. The largest increase occurred between 1920 and 1930, and is partly explained by the campaign for Americanization initiated during and after the First World War. This is further indicated by the large number of foreign-born who filed their "first papers" between 1910 and 1920: in 1910, 8.6 percent had filed their "first papers," in 1920, 16.5

[10] Niles Carpenter, *op. cit.,* p. 250.

[11] *Ibid.,* p. 253. "Consequently, in so far as the citizenship status of the foreign-born is studied with reference to this tendency toward assimilation, both those fully naturalized and those having first papers should be counted since both have started — and only started — along the road toward effective Americanization."

[12] Maurice Davie, *World Immigration,* p. 543.

Table 6. Naturalized and alien men over 21 years of age 1910—1930 (percent).

Nationality	1910 Naturalized	First Paper	Aliens	Unknown	1920 Naturalized	First Paper	Aliens	Unknown	1930 Naturalized	First Paper	Aliens	Unknown
England	—	—	—	—	64.8	12.8	14.1	8.3	69.6	11.8	14.6	4.0
Norway	57.1	15.2	16.2	11.5	67.3	15.0	12.1	5.6	70.8	12.2	13.2	3.8
Sweden	62.8	11.5	14.9	10.8	69.5	14.2	11.1	5.2	72.1	12.1	12.8	3.0
Denmark	61.6	12.6	13.8	12.0	69.6	14.1	10.0	6.3	75.3	11.4	10.1	2.2
Germany	69.5	7.2	9.9	13.4	73.3	11.6	8.5	6.6	72.3	13.3	10.8	3.6
Finland	30.6	15.9	45.9	7.6	39.2	21.7	35.5	3.6	50.5	16.2	31.0	2.3
Italy	17.7	7.8	65.7	8.8	30.2	18.6	48.9	2.3	55.3	12.1	30.3	2.3
Poland	—	—	—	—	27.9	23.2	46.3	2.6	55.4	16.6	25.8	2.2
Russia	26.1	13.0	52.4	8.5	41.7	18.7	36.1	3.5	67.7	11.4	18.2	2.6
All Foreign Born	45.6	8.6	34.1	11.7	49.0	16.5	29.3	5.2	62.0	13.6	21.1	3.3

Census of 1910 contains information only about the number of naturalized men over 21 years of age.
Beginning with the census of 1920 there are informations about both sexes — "subsequent to the 19th amendment to the constitution of the United States."

Sources: *Fifteenth Census of the United States, 1930, Population.*
Fourteenth Census of the United States, 1920, Population.

Table 7. Naturalized and time of arrival, living in urban and rural areas, 1930 (percent).

	URBAN							RURAL – FARM							RURAL – NONFARM						
	natu-ral-ized	period of arrival						natu-ral-ized	period of arrival						natu-ral-ized	period of arrival					
		1925 – 1930	1920 – 1924	1915 – 1919	1911 – 1914	1901 – 1910	– 1900		1925 – 1930	1920 – 1924	1915 – 1919	1911 – 1914	1901 – 1910	– 1900		1925 – 1930	1920 – 1924	1915 – 1919	1911 – 1914	1901 – 1910	– 1900
Norway	65.3	9.5	10.2	4.0	6.7	27.5	37.3	80.0	2.5	2.2	1.7	4.8	25.1	61.0	75.3	3.9	4.2	2.1	4.8	22.7	57.3
Sweden	70.0	7.3	8.8	3.3	6.9	22.9	47.7	82.9	1.7	2.2	1.9	5.2	22.1	64.7	73.6	4.0	4.9	2.4	5.6	20.4	58.0
Denmark	71.9	7.5	9.9	4.7	8.6	21.5	43.6	79.9	3.6	4.6	2.8	9.0	23.9	53.4	78.9	3.5	5.1	3.1	7.3	19.1	57.6
Germany	67.5	15.5	9.3	0.9	4.6	11.9	54.1	81.3	3.5	4.0	0.4	3.8	11.4	73.5	76.1	6.4	5.6	0.7	4.0	11.3	66.4
Poland	51.3	3.2	9.6	3.0	25.0	38.7	18.2	50.9	1.1	2.6	2.0	19.9	41.1	30.6	41.9	1.4	3.5	2.5	25.1	42.8	20.0
Austria	64.4	2.9	11.4	2.4	15.5	37.9	26.3	64.8	1.1	4.0	1.7	13.4	38.8	37.3	51.5	1.5	6.1	2.2	16.5	39.6	24.5
Russia	62.5	2.2	11.4	3.8	19.1	40.7	20.0	64.1	0.9	2.9	2.0	18.9	40.5	31.8	55.4	1.4	4.8	3.1	20.3	33.1	28.5
Finland	46.9	3.7	10.2	6.4	16.3	39.2	20.6	61.8	0.5	2.8	3.5	11.1	45.1	35.5	49.0	2.0	5.6	4.9	13.7	41.7	27.8
Italy	50.2	4.7	15.2	6.3	17.0	36.1	17.7	43.9	1.9	9.3	4.3	17.3	41.1	23.3	49.2	4.0	13.5	5.2	18.6	37.6	17.1

Source: *Fifteenth Census of the U.S., 1930, Population*, p. 505 f.

Table 8. Citizenship and Period of Arrival, 1930 (percent).

	Natura-lized	First Paper	Aliens	Period of Arrival					
				1925–1930	1920–1924	1915–1919	1911–1914	1901–1910	1900–earlier
Norway	72.1	8.7	14.6	6.7	7.1	3.1	5.9	26.0	47.1
Sweden	73.7	8.6	15.7	5.9	7.1	2.9	6.4	22.4	52.0
Denmark	76.1	8.7	12.0	5.9	7.8	4.0	8.5	21.6	48.3
Germany	72.5	9.9	13.5	12.7	8.0	0.8	4.4	11.7	58.3
Poland	50.7	11.6	35.6	2.9	8.7	2.9	24.8	39.2	19.0
Russia	63.0	8.3	25.0	2.1	10.7	3.6	19.1	40.3	21.0
Finland	51.5	11.2	34.8	2.6	7.5	5.4	14.5	41.2	25.7
Italy	50.5	8.4	38.4	4.6	14.8	6.2	17.2	36.4	17.8

Source: *Fifteenth Census of the United States: Population*, Vol. II, pp. 403 and 503.

percent. The increase of naturalized foreign-born may be further explained by the fact that in 1910 many of the "new" immigrants had not been in the country sufficient time to be eligible for American citizenship.

Women became naturalized somewhat more rapidly than men. In 1920 49.0 percent of the men were citizens, against 52.9 percent of the women.[13] For the Swedes the corresponding figures were 69.5 and 70.5 percent. During the 1920s a shift occurred so that the number of naturalized men among the foreign-born was percentally more in the census of 1930 – 62.0 percent of the men, 58.4 percent of the women. Among the Swedish Americans, however, no shift occurred. In 1930 there were percentally more naturalized Swedish women (75.7 percent) than men (72.1 percent).

Also, more of those living in rural areas applied for citizenship than those living in cities.[14] This has been explained by the fact that those living in rural areas arrived earlier than those who settled, for instance, in metropolitan areas.[15] Among the rural settlers, the number of naturalized was higher among the farm-employed than among the non-farming. In 1930 70 percent of the city-dwelling Swedes were naturalized, 82.9 percent of the rural farm-employed and 73.6 percent of the rural non-farming. As to the "new" immigrants the situation was the opposite. Among the Italians as well as the Poles, the number of naturalized was higher in the cities than in rural areas. The reason for this contrast seems to be that the earlier immigrants, to a greater degree than the latter, preferred to settle in country areas.

As indicated in Figure 1, the number of naturalized and the time period of arrival were quite dependent on each other. The figure is based on the number of naturalized according to the 1930 census, and on the number of immigrants arrived before the year 1900. The correlation between the two values is very high, or more definitely +0.90.[16] Even though the Swedish Americans have been able to show a larger number of naturalized than most other immigrant groups, it does not mean that they were naturalized more rapidly than, for instance, the Italians and Poles. If proper consideration is given to the

[13] *Fifteenth Census, 1930 : Population,* Vol. II, p. 409.

[14] *Ibid.,* p. 411.

[15] Carpenter, *op. cit.,* p. 259.

[16] A perfect correlation is 1.00, which means a perfectly positive connection.

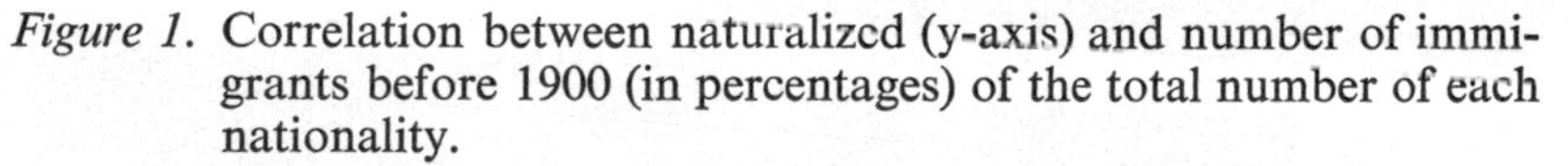

Figure 1. Correlation between naturalized (y-axis) and number of immigrants before 1900 (in percentages) of the total number of each nationality.

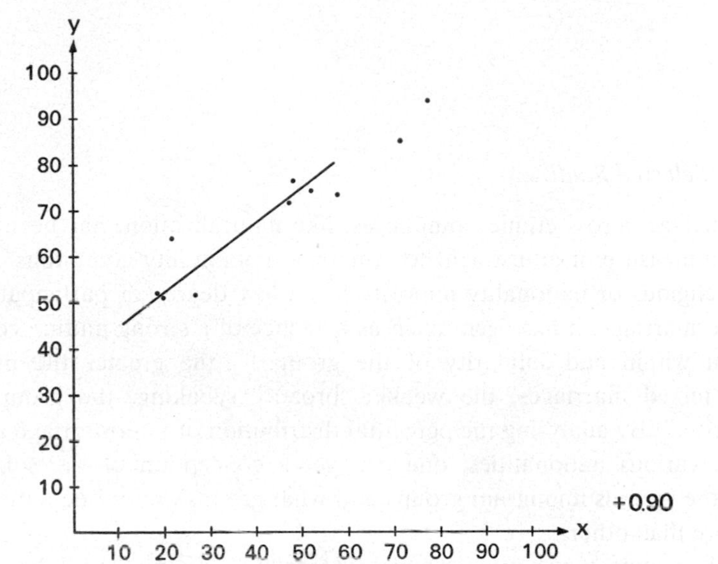

The correlation reckoned according to product-moment-correlation method. Y-axis — number of naturalized 1930 and X-axis = number of immigrants before the year 1900 (percent).
The coefficient of correlation is an arithmetical method of showing the connection between two variables. The coefficient range from + 1.00, wich means a perfectly positive connection, to −1.00, which means a perfectly negative connection. Thus, in this case, the correlation shows that a close connection exists between the number of naturalized and the period of arrival.

time period of arrival one cannot maintain that any one nationality is more easily naturalized than others. There is nothing, for example, to justify the idea that Swedes may, in this matter, be regarded as particularly outstanding. On the other hand, the conclusion must be that the differences noticed are so small that it is impossible to distinguish one group from another. Those who wish to prove that Swedish Americans became Americanized more quickly than other immigrants will find no evidence for this in the statistics of the number of naturalized.

V. Intermarriage

1. *Selected Studies*

Marriage across ethnic boundaries, like naturalization, has been taken as a measure of adjustment to American community conditions. When a religious or nationality minority has a low degree of participation in intermarriage, it has been taken as evidence of a strong mutual connection within and solidarity of the group – "the greater the number of mixed marriages, the weaker, broadly speaking, the group solidarity."[1] By analysing the percental distribution of intermarriage among the various nationalities, one can get a conception of the solidarity of the various immigrant groups and what groups prefer one nationality more than others.

The importance of intermarriage for the "melting pot" has never been clearly established. This, to a great extent, is because the official population statistics contain no information about intermarriage. The only statistical report that exists, by and large, is on the number of married couples listed as to race and nationality in New York State.[2] The census material has no information on the matter. One may, however, gain some conception of intermarriage by studying the statistics on children born of "mixed foreign parentage." Finally, there is a series of particular studies of marriage certifications in New York City, in New Haven, and in Wright County (Minnesota), to name a few examples. In Nebraska, New York, and Wisconsin, Edmund de

[1] Julius Drachsler, *Intermarriage in New York City* (New York, 1921), p. 18; James H.S. Bossard, "Nationality and Nativity as Factors in Marriage," *American Sociological Review* (December, 1939), p. 792. Bossard concludes that "intermarriage is a severely realistic index of the social distance between distinctive groups and peoples living within a given area." Ruby J.R. Kennedy, "Single and Triple Melting Pot," *The American Journal of Sociology* (January, 1944), p. 331. Kennedy agrees with those who contend that "intermarriage is the surest means of assimilation and the most infallible index of its occurrence."

[2] T.J. Woofter, *Races and Ethnic Groups in American Life* (New York, 1933), p. 204. Maurice Davie, *World Immigration*, p. 289.

S. Brunner has examined over 44,000 marriage certifications in 100 rural communities.[3] In the following a collation will be made, based partly on the above-named studies and partly on information in the census of the year 1920 on children born of mixed foreign parentage.

In general, it may be said that intermarriage has been more common among foreign-born men than among foreign-born women. The principal reason for this was the uneven distribution of the sexes. According to the 1930 census there were 117 foreign-born men over 21 years of age to every 100 foreign-born women over 21 years of age.[4] As

Table 9. Intermarriage with the Native-born White of Native-born White Parents, by Nationality, Nativity, and Sex, New York State, 1936.

Nationality	Percent Marrying Native-born Whites of Native-born White Parents					
	Foreign-born		Native-born of Foreign-born Parents		Native-born of Mixed Parentage	
	Male	Female	Male	Female	Male	Female
Group A						
Austria	25.1	13.4	29.6	29.4	43.1	42.5
Hungary	25.9	18.2	29.9	28.7	35.7	43.3
Italy	11.9	5.8	21.3	15.3	34.3	24.0
Poland	9.4	12.6	18.5	19.4	24.8	26.6
Russia	9.8	7.9	18.1	11.9	25.0	17.4
Group B						
Denmark, Norway, Sweden [1]	29.2	23.9	52.4	47.0	64.2	58.9
England, Scotland, Wales	41.4	37.9	55.8	56.7	62.1	60.6
Germany	27.1	20.9	51.1	43.9	57.6	56.4
Ireland	26.8	21.5	49.0	48.7	56.7	54.9

1) The Scandinavians are treated as one nationality, which means that a marriage, e.g., between a Swede and a Norwegian has not been counted as intermarriage. This is also true for the British Countries.

Source: James H. S. Bossard, "Nationality and Nativity as Factors in Intermarriage," p. 796.

[3] Edmund de S. Brunner, *Immigrant Farmers and Their Children* (New York, 1929).

[4] *Fifteenth Census of the United States, 1930 : Population,* Vol. II, p. 408.

Table 10. Percent Distribution of the Marriages of Foreign Born Brides and Grooms. New York State exclusive of New York City, 1929.

Nationality	To U.S. natives	To same foreign nationality	To other foreign nationality
Total foreign grooms	57.1	31.2	11.7
Denmark, Norway, Sweden	50.4	36.1	13.5
England, Scotland, Wales	59.6	29.0	11.4
Germany	37.1	55.5	7.4
Hungary	53.7	33.3	13.0
Ireland	43.4	46.3	10.3
Italy	64.6	31.8	3.6
Poland	54.2	37.6	8.2
Russia	52.6	29.8	17.6
Total foreign brides	42.3	42.1	15.6
Denmark, Norway, Sweden	32.2	59.7	8.1
England, Scotland, Wales	49.9	35.1	15.0
Germany	22.6	66.1	11.3
Hungary	34.7	37.9	27.4
Ireland	45.0	39.2	15.8
Italy	27.6	68.4	4.0
Poland	40.7	48.9	10.4
Russia	37.3	42.5	20.2

The Scandinavians are treated as one nationality.
Source: T. J. Woofter Jr, *Races and Ethnic Groups in American Life*, p. 207.

for the Swedes, the corresponding division was 128 men for every 100 women. Numerically speaking there was thus a greater possibility for a woman to find a man of the same nationality as herself. A man was obliged, to a certain extent, to choose between remaining unmarried or to marry an American woman. According to Niles Carpenter, most intermarriages took place between native-born women and foreign-born men.[5] This is corroborated by the marriage statistics of New York State.[6]

[5] Niles Carpenter, *Immigrants and Their Children,* p. 239.

[6] In New York State the immigrants preferred to marry within their own nationality. In 1936, 23.7 percent of the foreign-born men and 31.8 percent of the foreign-born women sought their mates within their own ethnic group. Including those who married second generation members, the ratio becomes still higher: 42.8 percent of the men and 40.8 percent of the women (See James Bossard, *op. cit.,* p. 796 ff.)

One of the more comprehensive studies of intermarriage between immigrants of various nationalities and native Americans was published in 1921.[7] It concerned New York City and was based on an examination of 100,000 marriage affidavits 1908–1912. For the period in question 14 of every 100 marriages were intermarriages. The study also showed that intermarriage was more common among the second generation than among the first.

The information from New York State indicates that the number of foreign-born men who married "native-born of native-born parents" was considerably smaller in group A – "new" immigrants – than in group B – "old" immigrants. This difference was not reduced, as one might expect, among the second-generation immigrants. The figures in Table 9, however, indicate that percentally considerably more of the second-generation immigrants in both groups married "native-born of native parents" than of the first-generation immigrants. If one further defines the second-generation immigrants as Americans born of foreign-born parents or Americans born in families where one parent – either the father or the mother – was foreign-born, he will find that the latter were more acceptable among the "pure" Americans.

An investigation of intermarriages in New York State, covering the years 1916–1918 and 1929 – by the latter year immigration had nearly ceased – indicates that intermarriage percentally increased toward the close of the immigration period.[8] Of all the foreign-born men in 1916, 38 percent married women born in America. In 1929 the figure had increased to 57 percent. The same was true of foreign-born women. The trend was alike for both urban and rural settlers.[9]

In New Haven, Connecticut, in-marriage was very common. In more than two-thirds of marriages during the period 1870–1940 both parties were of the same nationality.[10] The trend was the same in this as in other areas, namely that intermarriage increased, percentally, toward the end of the immigration period or as the immigrant became established: from 8.8 percent in 1870 to 36.4 percent in 1940. Of the

[7] Julius Drachsler, *op. cit.;* William Bernard, *American Immigration Policy,* p. 139; and Maurice Davie, *op. cit.,* p. 290.

[8] T.J. Woofter, *op. cit.,* p. 204.

[9] William Bernard, *American Immigration Policy,* p. 139 ff.

[10] Ruby J.R. Kennedy, "Single or Triple Melting-pot," p. 331 ff. Kennedy had investigated intermarriage in New Haven, 1870—1940; she based her conclusions on a total of 9,044 marriage affidavits.

investigated nationalities, in-marriage was least among the Scandinavian immigrants.

An interesting aspect of the New Haven investigation is that it shows that religious barriers were more difficult to overcome than the national. Contacts among immigrants, who consisted almost exclusively of Protestants, Catholics and Jews, were limited by the religious boundaries. It was unusual that a Protestant married a Catholic or vice versa. The rule was that Catholics married Catholics, Protestants married Protestants, and Jews married Jews. The conclusion regarding the situation in New Haven was that the idea of America as a "single melting-pot" would be changed to a "triple melting-pot."[11] "The future cleavages will be along religious lines rather than along nationality lines as in the past."[12]

The most interesting study, so far as it concerns the Swedish Americans, is one from Wright County, Minnesota (1942), where the Swedes comprised the largest group (4,073) next to the Germans (5,036) according to the 1930 census.[13] In two-thirds of the marriages among the foreign-born, both parties were of the same nationality. Among the men only the Norwegians, French and Irish married by more than 50 percent outside of their own nationality; among the women, only those who came from Norway or Ireland (see Table 11). The figures from Wright County indicate that in-marriage was particularly prevalent in areas where one and the same group was most strongly concentrated.[14]

[11] Ruby Kennedy, *op. cit.*, pp. 331, 339.

[12] Ruby Kennedy, *op. cit.*, p. 332. In 1870, 91.1 percent, in 1900, 90.9 percent, in 1930, 78.2 percent, and in 1940, 79.7 percent of Englishmen, Germans and Scandinavians intermarried among themselves, all three being of Protestant origin. August B. Hollingshead states in an article. "Cultural Factors in the Selection of Marriage Mates," in *American Sociological Review* (1950), p. 622: "Next to race, religion is the most decisive factor in the segregation of males and females into categories that are approved or disapproved with respect to nuptiality." He found that in 91 percent of marriages both parties came from the same religious background.

[13] Lowry Nelson, "Intermarriage among Nationality Groups in a Rural Area of Minnesota." The study is based on a sampling of 1,770 persons representing ten nationalities living in a farming district. (*The American Journal of Sociology*, March, 1943).

[14] *Ibid.*, p. 588 ff.

Table 11. Percentage of Husbands and Wives Marrying within the Same Nationality, Wright County, Minn.

Nationality	Per cent marrying same nationality Husbands	Wives	Foreign- stock in Wright County 1930	in sample
German	80.0	76.0	5 036	790
Swedish	61.8	69.4	4 073	368
Finnish	86.7	83.7	1 214	169
French	48.1	51.0	582	105
Irish	23.2	26.3	406	81
Polish	73.5	75.8	147	67
English	59.2	53.3	206	57
Dutch	58.3	82.4	323	41
Norwegian	18.2	11.4	667	57
Bohemian	50.0	52.9	324	35
All groups	68.2	68.2	12 978	1 770

Source: Lowry Nelson, "Intermarriage among Nationality Groups in a Rural Area of Minnesota," p. 588 ff.

The Germans made up the majority of the population in 14 of 20 communities, the Swedes in two, the Finns and the French in one each. Intramarriage was in direct relation to the numerical size of each nationality and was percentally very high among the three largest nationalities, namely the Germans, the Swedes, and the Finns.

Table 12. Percentage of in-Group Marriages for Three Nationality Groups in Communities Where They Were in the Majority or Minority.

Nationality	Majority	Minority
German	80.7	50.0
Swedish	72.5	49.7
Finnish	87.9	79.2

Source: Lowry Nelson, "Intermarriage among Nationality Groups in a Rural Area of Minnesota," p. 589.

In Wright County also the rule prevailed that intermarriage between different religious groups was less common than between different nationalities. The situation in Wright County was the same as in New Haven, namely that the theory of a melting-pot had not by far been substantiated. "As long as the in-group marriage rate is at least 50 percent, it is difficult to see how absorption or biological assimilation is going to take place."[15] The geographical concentration strengthened the cultural isolation considerably more than the melting-pot advocates could ever have imagined.

Table 13. Distribution of Women (by nationality groups) Having Swedish Husbands. Wright County, Minn. and New York City.

Women's Nationality	Wright County Number	Wright County Percent	New York City 1908–1912 Number	New York City 1908–1912 Percent
Sweden	120	61.5	681	79.8
Norway	15	7.7	36	4.2
Denmark	—	—	7	0.8
Germany	35	17.9	21	2.5
France	4	2.1	9	1.1
Holland	1	0.5	1	0.1
Finland	9	4.6	35	4.1
England	4	2.1	7	0.8
Ireland	6	3.1	30	3.6
Other Countries	1	0.5	27	3.3
Total	195	100.0	854	100.0

Sources: Julius Drachsler, *Intermarriage in New York City*, p. 129.
Lowry Nelson, "Intermarriage among Nationality Groups in a Rural Area of Minnesota," p. 589.

In Wright County 62 percent, and in New York City 80 percent of Swedish men married Swedish women. Otherwise they married Norwegian, German, French or Irish women. The nationalities mentioned thus belonged to the groups usually reckoned as "old" immigrant groups. Extremely few selected wives among non-Protestants. The religious barrier was difficult to overcome. C.M. Rosenquist made a similar observation among the Swedes in Texas. "Even marriages of Swedish girls to Irishmen or Frenchmen have been looked upon as undesirable because of the practical certainty that such marriages would fail."[16] According to Rosenquist the Swedes in Texas followed the same pattern in Travis County, Texas, as in Wright County and New York City. The first-generation settlers, to a large extent, married

[15] Lowry Nelson, *op. cit.*, p. 591 ff.

[16] C.H. Rosenquist, "The Swedes of Texas," p. 90.

Table 14. Swedish and Scandinavian In-marriage Rates in the United States, Selected Studies.

Location	Time	Percentage Expected In-Marriages [a]	Percentage Observed In-Marriages [b]	Percentage Difference
New York City [c]				
(Swedes only)	1908–1912	2	73	71
Minneapolis [d]				
(Swedes only)	1912	15	82	67
Nebraska [e]	1909–1913	21	77	56
	1921–1925	21	62	41
Wisconsin [e]	1908–1912	24	84	60
	1921–1925	24	64	40
New York State [e]	1908–1912	3	61	58
	1921–1925	4	44	40
Woonsocket, R.I. [f]				
(Swedes only)	1926	1	82	81
New York State [g]	1939	6	40	34
Wright County, Minn. [g]				
(Swedes only)	1942	20	62	42
Northeastern Minnesota [h]				
(Swedes only)	1956	17	30	13
New Haven, Conn. [i]	1900	2	83	81
	1930	2	33	31
	1940	2	18	16

[a] The expected in-marriage rates were computed and represent the percentage of Swedish or Scandinavians (females if given) in the sample or community population.
[b] The observed in-marriage rates represent the percentage of Swedish or Scandinavian males married to Swedish or Scandinavian females of all Swedish or Scandinavian males in a given sample except in Minneapolis, and Woonsocket, where the over-all male and female rate is given to maximize sample size.
[c] Julius Drachsler, *Intermarriage in New York City* (New York: Columbia University Press, 1921), first and second generations only.
[d] Albert E. Jenks, "Ethnic Census of Minneapolis," *American Journal of Sociology*, XVII (May, 1912), 280–81.
[e] Edmund deS. Brunner, *Immigrant Farmers and Their Children* (Garden City, N.Y.: Doubleday and Co., Inc., 1929), first and second generations only.
[f] Bessie Bloom Wessel, *An Ethnic Survey of Woonsocket, Rhode Island* (Chicago: University of Chicago Press, 1931).
[g] Lowry Nelson, "Intermarriage Among Nationality Groups in a Rural Area of Minnesota," XLVIII (March, 1943), 585–92, first and second generations only.
[h] Lowry Nelson, *The Minnesota Community* (Minneapolis: University of Minnesota Press, 1960).
[i] Ruby Jo Reeves Kennedy, "Single or Triple Melting-Pot? Intermarriage in New Haven 1870–1950," *American Journal of Sociology*, LVIII (July, 1952), 56–59.

Source: Charles H. Anderson, *White Protestant Americans*, p. 54.

within the Swedish colony. But the longer the Swedes lived in Texas the more common became marriages beyond the nationality boundaries.[17] The Swedes in Kansas followed the same pattern as the Swedes in the other mentioned areas. "Marriage with non-Swedes was looked on with some disfavor. The tradition existed that American girls were not good workers and were extravagant. Then, too, the other party was likely to be non-Lutheran."[18]

Table 14, in which Charles H. Anderson has summarized various studies of intermarriage, shows that rates of Swedish in-marriage have in the past been quite high. The rate of Swedish in-marriage was in the vicinity of 70 to 80 percent during the first few decades of this century, then manifested an over-all decline.

2. *The Census and Intermarriage*

The published census material, as previously mentioned, contains no information on intermarriage. But statistics on American-born children in families where either the father or the mother was foreign-born (native white of mixed parentage) is recorded, and thus a conception of the trend may be found. Since the number of children per family within the same nationality group undoubtedly remained quite constant (see Table 15) one may postulate that intermarriage increased among all foreign-born between 1900 and 1930.[19] Comparing the nationalities with each other – such comparison should surely be made with great caution – it seems that intermarriage had been more prevalent among Danes, Norwegians, and Germans than for example among the Swedes. That, in general, intermarriage was more common among the "old" settlers than among the "new" corresponds with the results of the studies in depth which have previously been noted. Also, it was more common among men than among women.

The census material of 1910 and 1920 is much more complete on

[17] *Ibid.*, p. 91 ff.

[18] Terence Pihlblad, "The Kansas Swedes," p. 39.

[19] It has not been possible to find any statistical information on the number of children per family.

Table 15. Native White of Foreign or Mixed Parentage, 1900, 1910, 1920 and 1930. Percent of the Total Number of Native White of Foreign or Mixed Parentage for selected groups.

Nationality	1900 Both parents foreign	Father foreign	Mother foreign	1910 Both parents foreign	Father foreign	Mother foreign	1920 Both parents foreign	Father foreign	Mother foreign	1930 Both parents foreign	Father foreign	Mother foreign
Sweden	84.2	10.2	5.6	79.7	13.0	7.3	74.6	16.3	9.1	70.0	19.7	10.3
Norway	78.5	14.1	7.4	73.1	17.5	9.4	65.2	24.4	11.4	63.3	23.9	12.8
Denmark	78.2	15.7	6.1	72.4	19.4	8.2	67.1	23.1	9.8	62.6	26.8	10.6
Germany	72.4	22.0	7.6	68.0	23.0	9.0	64.5	24.9	10.6	62.9	26.5	11.6
Poland	94.2	4.8	1.0	89.9	7.7	2.4	88.5	8.8	2.7	85,9	10.8	3.3
Russia	94.8	4.3	0.9	94.0	4.6	1.4	91.6	6.2	2.2	84.2	11.2	4.6
Finland	94.1	3.8	2.1	89.9	6.4	3.7	83.4	10.6	6.0	—	—	—
Italy	90.6	8.3	1.1	92.2	6.9	0.9	90.5	8.4	1.1	83.6	14.4	2.0
Total	67.8	21.5	10.7	68.3	20.8	10.9	69.2	20.0	10.8	67.1	21.5	11.4

Source: *Fifteenth Census of the United States, Population, 1930*, p. 269. Persons having a native mother and a foreign father were assigned to the country of birth of the father; persons having a native father and a foreign-born mother were assigned to the of birth of the mother (p. 264).

"mixed parentage" than 1930 and later.[20] Statistics in the former cases account for the nationality of both parents. As Figure 2 indicates, the Swedish Americans who married outside of their own nationality preferred to a large extent Norwegians and secondly Danes, Germans, and Finns. Somewhat surprising is that so many Swedes married Irish people, which may primarily be explained by the fact that the Irish, like the Swedes, belonged to the early settlers and were thus well established.

No significant change in dispersion occurred between 1910 and 1920. They married almost exclusively settlers from Protestant countries. The investigations mentioned in the foregoing give us a certain conception of marriage alignments among the immigrants even though they are in all cases geographically circumscribed. As the statistics are defective, however, one ought to be careful in drawing far-reaching conclusions. One deficiency is that statistics do not sufficiently delineate "natives." When, for example, the marriage of a Swedish-born man and an American woman born of Swedish parents is registered as "intermarriage," it may be difficult to decide whether it should be so designated since the nationality designation as a rule takes in both the second and third generations. It is also extremely difficult to establish to what extent such marriages accelerate Americanization. The ordinary conception is that this is true. "The natives of foreign parents have been reared in the American environment, have learned the American language, and have come in contact with American culture .... They are, by and large, American in speech and in manners . . . the marriage of these natives and foreigners are indicative of the beginnings of a real Americanization process."[1] Even though second-generation settlers as a rule were quite fully incorporated into the national community, one must, however, remember that an essential difference existed in the attitude of the first and second generations toward the old land of emigration. While the immigrants energetically defended their cultural heritage, the second generation

[20] In the *Fifteenth Census of the United States, 1930: Population,* Vol. II, p. 263, the following explanation why it no longer indicates the nationality of both parents in a "mixed parentage": "No such tabulation was made in 1930, nor could it be made, because the country of birth of only one parent was punched on the population card."

[1] Carpenter, *op. cit.,* p. 242.

Figure 2. Children of a Swedish-born Parent and Another Foreign-born Parent, 1910 and 1920

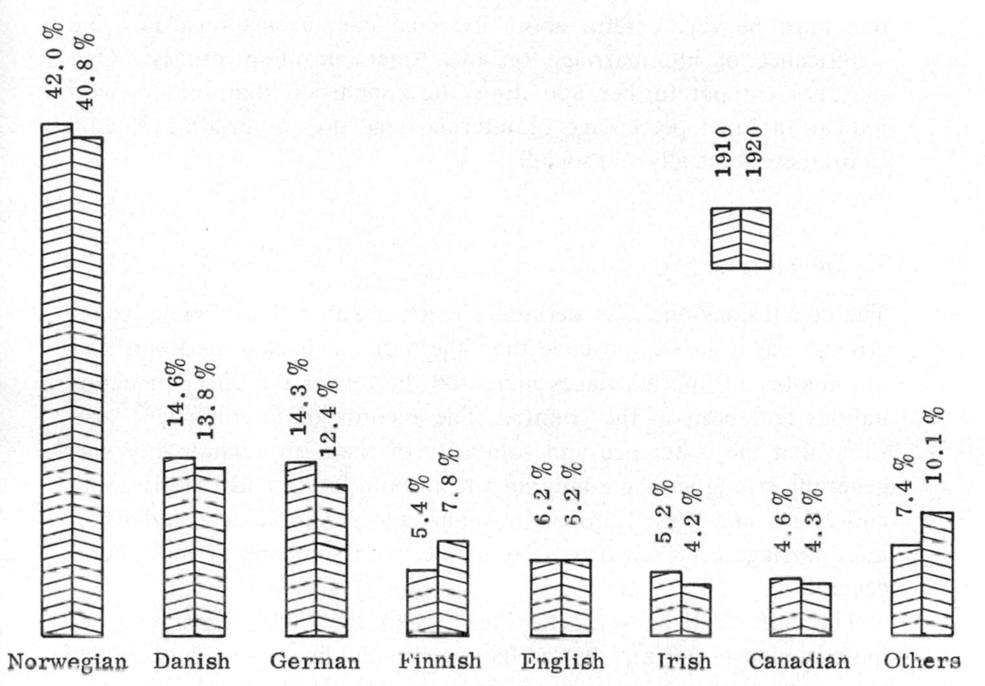

Sources: *Thirteenth Census of the United States, 1910, Population*, pp. 885–887. *Fourteenth Census of the United States, 1920, Population*, pp. 900–901.

were solicitous about revealing as little as possible of their origin. They were often ashamed of their origin and exerted efforts to eliminate traits that would identify them as "hyphenated" Americans.[2]

Aversion to marriage across ethnic boundaries and between members of different religions was undoubtedly due to other factors than demurral against Americanization. There have always been strong scruples against mixed marriages. The marriage of persons of different nationalities, race or religion has often been considered a direct provocation of conflict. When a marriage of persons of different back-

[2] Marcus L. Hansen, (*The problem of the Third Generation Immigrant* [Rock Island, 1938]) has perhaps most explicitly discussed the efforts of the second generation to break loose from both the emigrant country and the immigrant milieu.

grounds cracks up, the blame has been attributed to the mixed marriage even though other causes have undoubtedly been involved. Thus one must be very careful about eventual conclusions regarding the significance of intermarriage on the Americanization process. One may not without further ado draw the conclusion that settlers who indicate a small percentage of intermarriage do not become Americanized economically and socially.[3]

3. *Summary*

The conclusions one may definitely reach are that the religious background was a greater obstacle than the national background and that the number of intermarriages increased the longer the different nationalities had been in the country. The records of intermarriage also show that the coherence and solidarity of their own nationality was generally strong among immigrants from both South and East Europe, and North and West Europe. Intramarriage predominated, and when intermarriage occurred it was, as a rule, with someone of the second generation.

The difference between the "new" and the "old" immigrants is quite obviously not as great as has been maintained. The isolation of the "new" settlers in cities hampered their making contacts with other groups. The early settlers had built a solid footing on which to stand and were more acceptable to the "pure" Americans than, for instance, the Italians, Poles, and Greeks. Language, too, played an important role. Several of the nationalities comprising the early immigration spoke English or a language closely related to English, but immigrants from South and East Europe were linguistically handicapped. Intermarriage became significant because of the war. Great numbers of immigrants and children of immigrants were obliged to leave their immigrant milieu and go out in the war to fight for their new homeland. They were integrated with other categories of people and on the field of battle there was no difference between natives and foreign-born. The grim war-years and the struggle against the common enemy eradicated some of the nationality boundaries. The immigrants were

[3] Simon Marcson, "A Theory of Intermarriage and Assimilation," *Social Forces* (October, 1950), p. 78; Marcson is critical of those who use intermarriage records as a measure of assimilation.

imbued with the feeling of being a part of America. While the war forced the immigrants out of their own national commune and widened their sphere of contacts, the religious boundaries, however, were preserved.

In sum, the statistics show that intermarriage among Swedish Americans was no more customary than among other immigrant groups. In other words, the pattern is the same among the Swedish immigrants as among other ethnic groups in the United States. Swedish Americans who married outside of their own nationality preferred to a large extent Norwegians.

VI. World War I

1. *Growing suspicion of immigrants*

> Americanization is vital. The immigrant is anxious to become an integral part of America, and it is our privilege to assist him. But we must educate him, not suppress him; we must lead him, not drive him.[1]

The war created hardships for all immigrants in America but especially for the German Americans, who were constantly suspected of sabotage. German Americans were blamed for the smallest flurry of suspicious activity, but the Irish and Scandinavians were also being watched for any display of pro-German sympathies. Several statements by Theodore Roosevelt provide ample testimony to the type of public sentiment unleashed by the war. On one occasion he recommended that all unpatriotic German Americans be shot or hanged.[2] On another he demanded the deportation of all persons who could claim that 10 percent of their affections still belonged to their native countries: in his opinion, such people were not worthy of residing in the United States.[3]

After the declaration of war, the American government adopted drastic measures to stop political activities engaged in by the "foreign-born." The State Department and the Department of Justice together

[1] Oscar A. Benson, "Studies in Americanization," *The Lutheran Companion* (November 11, 1922), p. 718.

[2] John Higham, *op. cit.*, p. 209.

[3] Marguerite E. Jenison, *War Documents and Addresses* (Springfield, 1923), p. 405; In a speech in Illinois, August 26, 1918, Roosevelt said : "Nobody is obliged to come to this country, but if he comes, he is to take our constitution and our flag and our language. If he does not want to do that, he can go straight back to the land from which he came." (pp. 406—7).

with the FBI saw to it that criticism of American foreign policy was effectively stopped. The semi-official American Protective League, organized in March, 1917, became a powerful instrument in the war machinery and together with the National Council of Defense pursued an eager hunt of "aliens." Certain counties distributed special Loyalty Record forms calling for answers to personal questions such as conditions of bank accounts, opinions on the war, attitudes toward the different sides of the conflict, and so forth.

Personal liberty was curtailed by the enactment of restrictive martial laws. The Espionage Act of June 15 stipulated strict penalties for acts and utterances considered damaging to the country's foreign policy.[4] Later, the Trading with the Enemy Act was passed, which forbade the international exchange of seditious goods. Letters from and to foreign countries were subjected to strict censorship. Finally, on October 6, 1917, far-reaching regulations were adopted for control of anti-war newspapers. This also included controls over the publishing of articles on the war in a foreign language unless a translation had been delivered beforehand to the local postmaster. If he found the article contrary to American foreign policy, the paper or journal was impounded. No direct censorship was applied, although the Trading with the Enemy Act practically functioned as such. Articles critical of America's part in the war ceased almost completely, since no periodical dared risk its existence. The Sedition Act of May 16, 1918, extended the prison penalty for unpatriotic activities to a maximum of 20 years.

In addition to the previously mentioned organizations there was also the Committee on Public Information (CPI), which organized so-called "Loyalty Days" when immigrants had the opportunity to show their loyalty and patriotism. A pamphlet in several languages explaining why the USA was at war was distributed in five and a half million copies, including 76,500 in Swedish.[5]

Certain immigrants who persisted in showing affection for their native countries aroused an emphatic reaction among the American people – "the most pervasive nativism that the United States has ever

[4] Oscar Handlin, *America: A History* (N.Y., 1968), p. 798.

[5] *Complete Report of the Chairman of the Committee on Public Information, 1917, 1918, and 1919*, p. 15. For the activity of the CPI, see separate chapter.

known."[6] "Hyphenated Americans" were feared by the "genuine Americans" more than the enemy. It was a shock to discover that large groups of immigrants seemed to show as great an interest for their native countries as for the United States. Those who advocated Americanization found in that atmosphere ready listeners to their demands, and the watchword became uniformity and loyalty – "100 percent Americanism."[7] An increasingly large part of the general public clung to the belief that only a complete adjustment – what was meant by that was not explained – could unite the country during a national crisis.

In this atmosphere of hysteria Americanization became something of a popular movement. Federal organizations – the Bureau of Education, Bureau of Naturalization, and Committee on Public Information – state governments, and local and private organizations united in a common effort to persuade immigrants to learn English, become American citizens, buy war bonds, forget their native country, and stand up for their adopted country. This coercive Americanization included a contempt for everything foreign, "implicit disregard of the immigrants' own native culture."[8] Hundred percent Americans received valuable support from President Woodrow Wilson who, in an address in May 1915, expressly warned against hyphenated American's "dual loyalty."[9] Wilson said: "A man who thinks of himself as belonging to a particular national group in America has not yet become an Ameri-

[6] John Higham, *Strangers in the Land,* p. 195; Higham defines nativism as an intensive opposition to a minority because of its "foreign (un-American) connections" (p. 4). Discovering that a large segment of immigrants showed great loyalty to their native land disturbed many and is considered to have been the primary factor in heightening the hysteria aroused by the war. "The change in policy . . . was due partly to the realization that the immigrant whether naturalized or unnaturalized tended to maintain his loyalty to the land of his origin, even when it seemed to conflict with loyalty to the country of his sojourn or adoption." See E. Franklin Frazier, "Ethnic and Minority Groups in Wartime, With Special Reference to the Negro," *The American Journal of Sociology* (December, 1942), p. 369.

[7] Oscar Handlin, *Race and Nationality* (Boston, 1957), p. 74 ff.

[8] Milton Gordon, *Assimilation in American Life. The Role of Race, Religion, and National Origins* (New York, 1966), p. 100.

[9] William Bernard, *American Immigration Policy,* p. 18.

can."[10] The National Americanization Committee, formed in 1915, soon became the "brain trust" in the Americanization work.[11] The Committee considered its foremost task that of stimulating naturalization and forcing the immigrants to learn English. In the Congress and in state legislatures bills were introduced to provide increased resources for the work among immigrants; simultaneously came proposals for curtailing the foreign language press. Several states proclaimed prohibition of foreign languages in schools. The Governor of Iowa forbade public use of foreign languages. The ban went so far as to prohibit anyone from speaking on the telephone in any other language than English.

During the war and the immediate post-war period some 20 states prohibited the use of languages other than English in both public and private school instruction.[12] In industrial work only full-fledged American citizens or such immigrants who had declared their intention of seeking citizenship were offered employment.

The demands for a more rapid pace of Americanization were not novel. Even before the war there were those who thought it went too slowly and ought to be accelerated. Milton Gordon, in *Assimilation in American Life,* had found that attempts at what he called "pressure-cooking assimilation" already flourished during the 1890s.[13] "Other private groups, notably the 'lineage' patriotic societies, such as the Daughters of the American Revolution, the Society of Colonial Dames, and the Sons of the American Revolution, began to draw up and disseminate, in the decade or so before the war, educational programs designed to teach the foreign-born to understand American political institutions, to become naturalized, and to embrace patriotic sentiments." The Sons of the American Revolution used half of its income

[10] Oscar Handlin, *The American People in the Twentieth Century* (Boston, 1963), p. 121.

[11] Frances Kellor was chief for the National Americanization Committee. Since the beginning of the century she had been the foremost leader for Americanization of immigrants. She represented both sides: the humanitarian as well as the more nationalistic. In 1908, K. became secretary of the New York Commission on Immigration. In 1914 she organized the Committee for Immigrants in America whose main task was to assist immigrants and advise them about opportunities open to them (John Higham's *Strangers in the Land,* pp. 239—242).

[12] George Stephenson, *A History of American Immigration,* p. 227.

[13] Milton Gordon, *op. cit.*, p. 99.

in 1907 for making "aliens into good citizens."[14] Courses in English were arranged over the whole country in the belief that the immigrants' language skills were the real key to thorough Americanization. In spite of these occasional demands for a more active Americanization process, it was generally felt that the adjustment ought to be as compatible and uncoerced as possible for all immigrant groups and that social and humanitarian factors should be allowed to play deciding roles in the transition.

In the various states committees were appointed with dictatorial powers in all matters which might be related to the war. When war was declared, the Minnesota state legislature passed a series of laws which reflected its fear of the foreign-born.[15] The most important of these set up the Minnesota Commission of Public Safety and endowed it with the most sweeping powers probably ever accorded any state agency up to that time. Among the original members of the Commission were Governor J.A.A. Burnquist and John Lind, former governor and special emissary of President Wilson to Mexico in 1913. Pressure tactics were widely practiced by the Safety Commission. People were almost constantly alarmed by fears of unpatriotic elements in American society and by the general suspicions of everything alien. When it appeared that thousands of children were not offered an opportunity to learn English, the Commission instituted corrective measures. On November 20, 1917, it adopted a resolution to the effect "that school boards, principals and teachers be urged, as a patriotic duty, to require the use of the English language as the exclusive medium of instruction in all schools in the state of Minnesota, and to discontinue and prohibit the use of all foreign languages in such schools, except as a medium for the study of those languages themselves or as a medium for religious instruction."[16]

[14] John Higham, *op. cit.*, pp. 237 and 242. Higham writes: "Americanization pushed dramatically into the public eye in the spring and summer of 1915." Edward Hartmann, in *The Movement to Americanize the Immigrant* (N.Y., 1948) (p. 105) says that a change occurred in 1915. "From an attitude of indifference to the immigrant, the public changed to one of active interest."

[15] *Report of Minnesota Commission of Public Safety* (St. Paul, 1919); O.A. Hilton, "The Minnesota Commission of Public Safety in World War I, 1917—1919," *Bulletin of the Oklahoma Agricultural and Mechanical College* (Stillwater, Oklahoma, May 15, 1951).

[16] *Report of Minnesota Commission of Public Safety*, p. 23.

In January, 1918, the Commission directed the county commissioners to take a census of alien ownership of real estate, and provide the State Auditor with a list of its findings.[17] On February 25, 1918, it ordered the registration of all aliens. In the spring of 1918, aliens were prohibited from teaching in public or parochial schools or in any normal school which trained teachers for these schools.[18] Pressure tactics were widely practiced in boosting the sale of Liberty Bonds. The names of those who refused to subscribe were filed on blue cards.

As early as May 1917 steps were taken by the Commission to investigate German and Scandinavian language newspapers.[19]

The interest in Americanization work did not cease with the end of the war but continued for some years. Tactics and methods changed, however. Most important of all was that immigrants could now let their voices be heard: the fear of being accused of unpatriotic activities no longer had any magic force over them. At the beginning of 1921 "the Americanization crusade" was over, although many of the more attractive projects, such as the voluntary instruction in English, continued.[20] In the wake of coercive assimilation followed a demand for a restriction of immigration. Part of the reasoning behind this was that certain nationalities from Southern and Eastern Europe were less capable of responding to the assimilation process.

2. *The Swedish Americans and the War, 1914 – April, 1917*

At the beginning of the World War I, there was no doubt as to where the real sympathies of the Swedish Americans lay. Several of the Swedish language papers openly declared their support of the Central Powers. One paper described the Swedish Americans as the most pro-German-minded of all nationalities in the United States. Another paper said they were more friendly toward Germany than the Germans themselves.[1] Yet it must be stated that the Swedish-American press did

[17] O.A. Hilton, *op. cit.*, p. 11 f.

[18] *Report of Minnesota Commission of Public Safety*, p. 115.

[19] O.A. Hilton, *op. cit.*, p. 15.

[20] Milton Gordon, *op. cit.*, p. 101.

[1] *Svenska Amerikanaren*, December 31, 1914; *Missionsvännen*, May 2, 1916; Gustav E. Johnson, "The Swedes of Chicago," p. 55.

not give unequivocal support to Germany.[2] Simply in terms of numbers, few Swedish language papers declared themselves wholeheartedly in favor of Germany. However, since these were the more influential papers, they gave a pro-German stamp to Swedish Americans as a whole. Most of the papers in Illinois and Minnesota assumed a more cautious and impartial attitude which on the whole agreed with official American foreign policy. Without in any way being able fully to assess the Swedish-American opinion, one can still say with a good deal of certainty that Swedes were regarded as being pro-German.

When it comes to forming an idea of the attitude of Swedish Americans toward the war, the best source materials are to be found in the Swedish language newspapers. The reason for using Swedish-American newspapers in this study is that they are almost the only source materials which give a sample of Swedish-American attitudes to World War I over a period of time. This does not mean to say that they accurately or unconditionally represent the viewpoints of the entire Swedish-American community. As it seemed impossible to determine to what extent the newspapers did reflect the opinion of the entire Swedish-American community, I have not made any attempt to do so. Two scholarly investigations of the subject have been published, namely George Stephenson's "The Attitude of Swedish Americans toward the World War" (1919) and Herbert Capps' *From Isolationism to Involvement* (1966).[3] Both of these authors reached the conclusion that before the American declaration of war the Swedish Americans harbored pro-German sympathies. Capps observed further that the Swedes in Minneapolis were on more friendly terms with the Germans than in other parts of the country.[4] They considered Germany's cause was a legitimate one and criticized the American press for supporting England. *Veckobladet,* the chief newspaper of the Swedish Evangelical Covenant in Minneapolis, attacked those who regarded the war as a struggle between, on one side, free, democratic, and constitu-

[2] George Stephenson, "The Attitude of Swedish Americans toward the World War, "*Proceedings of Mississippi Valley Historical Association* (1918/1919), p. 84.

[3] I have systematically gone through the papers cited but have at the same time compared them with George Stephenson's and Herbert Capps' conclusions and source references. Since neither of these two authors provides a list of all articles on the war, it has been necessary to scrutinize the papers themselves.

[4] Herbert Capps, *op. cit.,* p. 37.

tional reform, and, on the other side, monarchical self-indulgence and militarism, and accused them of having an overly "warped shallow view of the war."[5] To what extent Herbert Capps' observations are correct is impossible to determine on the evidence of only two Swedish language papers. His conclusions should be accepted with some reservation, because they are based only on *Minnesota Stats Tidning* and *Veckobladet.*

Many factors determined the feelings of sympathy for Germany among the Swedish Americans. For the Swedish Lutherans in America Germany was Martin Luther's homeland and the stronghold against the barbarians' – in this case, the Russians – ambitions westward. Professor J.S. Carlson, one of the most energetic spokesmen for the preservation of the Swedish language in America, explained the pro-German attitude among Swedish Americans by saying that the Swedes received their form of religion and always took their literary impulses from Germany.[6] "Deutschland über alles" was also a tenet of faith in Sweden. It was therefore quite natural that some Swedish-American clergymen, particularly the older and less educated ones who had spent most of their lives in Sweden, adhered to their Swedish-German attachment as long as it was a matter of choosing between Germany and any other warring country. That some Swedish Americans at the beginning of the war sided with Germany was not considered treasonable as long as the United States was not in the war.

In popular discussion of the war the fate of Sweden was a recurring anxiety. It was generally held that Sweden ought to remain neutral. But opinions were divided as to which side Sweden ought to support if it were forced to abandon its neutrality. There were those who hoped Sweden would join its fate with Germany's if it ever abandoned its policy of neutrality *Gamla och Nya Hemlandet* expressed the hope in 1914 that a "higher power" would assist Germany and its Kaiser, "for in this war they battle for everything that a civilized people holds sacred."[7]

The Augustana Synod has been generally described as pro-German, with the exception of those groups influenced by *The Lutheran Com-*

[5] *Veckobladet,* August 25, 1914.

[6] J.S. Carlson, *Hvarför böra vi behålla och bevara, vörda och bruka svenska språket i Amerika?* pp. 6 ff.

[7] *Gamla och Nya Hemlandet,* August 6, 1914.

panion, which thought that while an English victory would be the best guarantee for a lasting peace, a German victory would only promote Catholicism.[8] The non-Lutheran denominations were more critical of Germany. Their newspapers urged their countrymen to rally behind President Wilson and his advice to the American people to be impartial – "especially since not only the United States, our adopted country, but Sweden also is neutral."[9] George Stephenson says it would be a mistake to believe that only Lutherans opposed the American entry into the war.[10]

The widespread hate of Russia was one of the reasons why Germany received the support of the Swedes. If Sweden abandoned its neutrality, Swedes argued, it ought to join with Germany in a last attempt to crush Russia,[11] the arch-enemy and Nemesis of all civilized nations.[12] It was said that this fear of Russia among Swedish immigrants was a direct consequence of the climate of opinion in Sweden during their childhood and the type of education in history they received in Swedish schools.[13]

The opposite, pro-British line of opinion accused Germany of having started the war, which was simply the work of the "devil of militarism" that had for so long held sway in Germany and throughout Europe.[14] If Sweden were forced to take a stand, they argued, it would win most by joining the Triple Entente. A third group, which was less outspoken in its views, sharply critized those who chose sides in either direction, since it would hurt Swedish Americans if the impression ever gained currency that they were not neutral. For this reason they advised

[8] *The Lutheran Companion,* November 21, 1914. At the outbreak of the war, the prospects of success for Sweden's policy of neutrality were considered rather gloomy. *Svea* and *Nordstjernan* were ready to receive monetary contributions to a special fund for aiding Swedish defense. In spite of appeals in both papers the results were disappointing. (Source: George Stephenson, "The Attitude of Swedish Americans toward the World War," p. 82n.)

[9] *Missionsvännen,* August 25, 1914; Herbert Capps, *op. cit.,* p. 36 ff.

[10] George Stephenson, *op. cit.,* p. 84n.

[11] *Gamla och Nya Hemlandet,* August 6, 1914; *Augustana,* August 13, 1914, p. 650.

[12] *Minnesota Stats Tidning,* August 12, 1914. The Irish-American papers agreed that German culture was threatened by Russian barbarism. Carl Wittke, *The Irish in America* (Baton Rouge, 1956), p. 277.

[13] *Svenska Amerikanaren,* December 31, 1914.

[14] *Svenska Kuriren,* August 6, 1914; *Svenska Amerikanaren,* August 13, 1914.

Swedish Americans to restrain their feelings and not set themselves up as judges of others.[15]

Despite their various stands toward the belligerent parties the Swedish-American papers were quite agreed that the United States ought to be neutral. As the tension between Germany and the United States increased President Wilson was warned against endangering American neutrality. There was even a tendency to brand neutrality as mere camouflage, because the government allowed export of arms to the Allies – something described as morally questionable. *Förbundets Veckotidning* criticized the American government for its reluctance to stop the export of weapons and ammunition to the belligerents. President Wilson's stand was described as "pitiful."[16] It deplored the fact that the United States' economy was flourishing on the "wretchedness of a bleeding Europe." Sweden was presented as a model. If President Wilson did not have such a "panicky dread" of offending England, it said, the war would have ended long ago.

The Swedish Americans attempted to help in setting a halt to arms exports to the belligerents. The Augustana Synod adopted a resolution sent to the President in which it asked him to issue an embargo on exports of weapons and ammunition.[17] The Chicago ministers of the Mission Covenant Church, in a resolution dated March 27, 1916, and addressed to the chairmen of the Senate and the House of Representatives Committees on Foreign Affairs, demanded an embargo on all exports of arms to the belligerents.[18] Several outstanding Chicago Swedes worked for a ban on exporting of arms. Carl Hjalmar Lundquist, a lawyer in Chicago and secretary of the American Embargo Conference, points out in a pamphlet entitled "Embargo on Ammunition and Weapons" that the word "neutrality" means "not participat-

[15] *Missionsvännen,* August 25, 1914.

[16] *Förbundets Veckotidning,* October 10, 1916.

[17] *Minutes of the Augustana Synod for 1915,* p. 167. The Iowa Conference — representing about 25,000 citizens in the State of Iowa — adopted a resolution on February 12, 1916, deploring the fact that arms exports had not been stopped (Source: *Iowa-konferensens referat för 1916*).

[18] The resolution was distributed to the Swedish language press (Source: Brochure published by the American Embargo Conference, 1916).

ing in, nor assisting either party."[19] One purpose of the pamphlet was to persuade Congress to speed the Embargo proposal through the Foreign Relations Committee. It was distributed together with a printed form which recipients were asked to fill in and send to their congressmen.

In 1916 the American Embargo Conference published a booklet in Swedish containing articles by Carl Hjalmar Lundquist, David Nyvall, Jacob Bonggren and Gustav Hallbom.[20] The preface criticized "those persons in Washington" who considered the war trade a healthy industry, beneficial to the country's economy. It demanded an end to the "traffic in murder weapons that provides pecuniary profits for a few by bringing suffering and death to many thousands . . ."

The authors of all the articles are sharply critical of the United States and its President, accusing him of fanning the flames of war by allowing the sale of war material. "The man who prays to God the war may soon end and at the same time sells murder weapons to the belligerents must surely have an easily comforted conscience."[1] There is no doubt that this was directly addressed to President Wilson. Poli-

[19] Carl Hjalmar Lundquist, *Embargo on Ammunition and Weapons.* The pamphlet, dated February 24, 1916, was published by the American Embargo Conference. The Conference was organized for the purpose of mobilizing that part of public opinion that believed in an embargo on war material. The headquarters was in Chicago, and the organization was very active among the Swedish Americans. Certain details about the Conference were supplied directly by Carl Hjalmar Lundquist in an interview, September 25, 1967.

[20] They were all born in Sweden. Jacob Bonggren became a member of the editorial staff of *Svenska Amerikanaren* in 1881 and was its editor in chief between 1908 and 1936. Gustav Hallbom was one of the leading Swedish bankers in Chicago. In 1922 he organized the Builders & Merchants State Bank where he served as president up to his death in 1928. Carl Hjalmar Lundquist worked as a newspaperman for *Svenska Tribunen Nyheter, Chicago-Bladet,* and *Hemlandet.* Later he became editor of *Svenska Posten* in Rockford. In 1916 he was secretary of the American Embargo Conference. He received the J.D. degree from the Chicago Law School in 1921 and thereafter worked as Assistant Corporation Counsel for the City of Chicago for more than 20 years. David Nyvall was one of the most prominent Swedish Americans in the United States in the decades before and after the turn of the century. In 1888 he was professor in the Swedish Department of Chicago Theological Seminary and served as president of North Park College, first from 1891 to 1905 and then again from 1912 to 1923 (Source: *The Swedish Element in America* [Chicago, 1931], Vol. III).

[1] Carl Hjalmar Lundquist, *Är vårt land fullt neutralt? En svenskamerikans åsikter ur freds- humanitets- och neutralitetssynpunkt* (1916), p. 5 ff.

ticians were called hypocrites and accused of being bootlickers for the money barons. Even if this particular article was a defense of neutrality, it could not disguise its sympathy for the German cause. England was charged with being the source of most of the trouble. There did not seem to be any reason to help England, which had always cunningly tried to defraud and even rob the United States. It was feared that ”shrewd English diplomacy” would seep into America like a poison and finally absorb the nation.

With the worsening of relations between Germany and the United States, Swedish Americans became increasingly fearful that the United States would eventually abandon its neutrality. After the sinking of the *Lusitania* the editors began to doubt that the United States could keep out of the war for any length of time. Germany's response to the English blockade was described as ”inhuman.” ”One steals and robs ... the other commits murder.”[2] Even those newspapers which had previously given their whole-hearted support to Germany expressed criticism of the U-boat war. The sinking of the *Lusitania* was considered ruthless. In spite of this change of attitude, it was too early to speak of a change of course.[3] The sinking of the *Lusitania* was blamed not only on Germany but on England as well.

During 1916 a noticeable change of attitude took place in the Swedish-American papers. In the first years of the war they discussed which party was most responsible for the war and criticized the American policy of neutrality for its camouflage tactics. However, during 1916 and the months before America's entrance into the war they devoted much space to commentary stressing the importance of American neutrality. As time went on the various papers worked more closely together on the basis of a common agreement and understanding that the war in Europe did not concern the United States. They condemned every step or statement that might threaten American neutrality. The Swedish-American newspapers regarded neutrality as an absolute, binding doctrine. They constantly urged the American government to follow the example of Sweden – to negotiate instead of ridiculously insisting on law and order. When the Germans increased their U-boat activity in the beginning of 1916, President Wilson was warned against insisting on ”law and order to a degree

[2] *Svenska Kuriren,* February 18, 1915; *Missionsvännen,* May 18, 1915.

[3] *Veckobladet,* May 18, 1915.

that may be unwise."[4] Instead of issuing an ultimatum, the American government should exhort its citizens to avoid traveling on armed merchant vessels belonging to the Allies. If this procedure were followed, difficult conflicts would be avoided. The President's ultimatum after the sinking of the *Sussex* was also considered unnecessarily provocative, especially since he did not have a united nation backing him.[5] He was warned against leading the country into war on England's side.

As war between America and Germany was drawing closer and Swedish Americans began to see the course being taken by the United States, they sharpened their criticism of the government. There was an almost paradoxical change in attitude in the Swedish-American press. Newspapers that earlier had been very critical of the German war policy now almost preferred American capitulation to participation in the war. Those newspapers which at the beginning of the war expressed pro- German sympathies now became more restrained and cautious in expressing their views. In an editorial under the rubric "In the Name of Humanity" *Svenska Kuriren* ironically spoke of the President's "marvelous" theory that the United States ought to emerge as a kind of superpower. In bold face type the paper declared it did not believe the American people felt prepared to go to war with Germany "in the name of humanity."[6]

The unrestricted U-boat war in the beginning of February, 1917, forced most newspapers to realize that war was unavoidable. But this

[4] *Svenska Amerikanaren,* March 2, 1916, p. 7. In an editorial on January 26, 1916, entitled "The Neutrality We Like," *Svea* advised the President to follow Sweden's example: "The Swedish people of America are good Americans. But, knowing what their old fatherland does, it is only natural that they think our own American government ought to be able to show the same strictness and independence as Sweden. The neutrality of Sweden has been set up as an example for the rest of the world. It is the neutrality we like. We Swedish Americans have followed it from the beginning of the war. . . . We want the government of this country to guard the independence and neutrality of this country with the same carefulness and the same manliness as shown by the Swedish government." See further George Stephenson, "The Attitude of Swedish Americans toward the World War," p. 87.

[5] *Svenska Tribunen Nyheter,* April 25, 1916. The paper indicated the Allegheny Mountains as the boundary: "While the East in general has taken his (the President's) side, the mood in the states west of the Allegheny Mountains is obviously against any break with Germany."

[6] *Svenska Kuriren,* April 20, 1916.

did not mean that they resigned their protests. On the contrary, they condemned to the very last those forces which tried to mislead the President into declaring war on Germany. In a signed editorial, Otto Högfeldt, editor of *Missionsvännen,* vigorously attacked the wealthy moneybarons and munitionsmakers who desired war:

> Shall we who have proudly exhibited the beautiful Monroe Doctrine get ourselves involved in the European controversies and shall the President who was elected with the motto 'He kept us out of war' now assist in getting us into it? . . . Why should our boys who have been singing under the protection of the free flying star-spangled banner be sent out to battlefields for the sake of European intrigues and for the protection of greedy militarists' interests? Why cannot the United States on this side of the globe maintain its neutrality when little Sweden can do it even when fires of war surround it close to its borders?[7]

It was a rather widespread belief that the capitalists and munitionsmakers wanted war in order to increase their wealth "through our own sons' blood and American mothers' and widows' tears."[8] The American people ought to protest every step that might lead the country into war. Everyone attempting to prevent such steps was within his rights to do so, since the majority of the people was against America's participation in the war.[9] *Sändebudet* was ill at ease about the President's being forced to declare war: "But if war is to be declared, even though our national existence is not threatened, only because some American adventurers have lost their lives in the war zone and our delivery of contraband material has been impeded, then we insist the question be submitted to a general plebiscite."[10]

When war seemed unavoidable, the Swedish Americans affirmed their loyalty to the United States. Several of the more influential papers requested their more critical colleagues to repress their utterances, since President Wilson had done the only thing he could do.[11]

The Swedish-American reaction to the European war was very much the same as that of German Americans and Irish Americans. Many Irish Americans accused President Wilson of "impartial neu-

[7] *Missionsvännen,* March 20, 1917.

[8] *Augustana,* March 15, 1917.

[9] *Svenska Tribunen Nyheter,* March 13, 1917.

[10] *Sändebudet,* February 6 and 13, 1917.

[11] *Svenska Kuriren,* February 8, 1917; *Svenska Amerikanaren,* February 8, 1917; and *Missionsvännen,* February 6, 1917.

trality."[12] Overshadowing all of Wilson's sins was the shipment of war material to the Allies by private American manufacturers. Many Germans and Irish like Swedish Americans demanded an embargo on the munitions traffic. A lot of German Americans and Irish Americans opposed the American declaration of war to the last possible moment.[13] After the American declaration of war they, like the Swedes, closed ranks to support a common cause.

3. *The Swedish Americans after America's entry into the War*

With America's entry into the war in April, 1917, Swedish-American newspapers' criticism of American foreign policy grew silent. The reaction to the declaration of war was restrained, although throughout the pre-war period the Swedes had clearly expressed their belief that the country ought to remain neutral.[1] The subdued reaction was undoubtedly due to fear and insecurity. War hysteria was strong, and utterances that might be interpreted as disloyal and unpatriotic could have serious consequences. Thus, when war was declared, the Swedish-American papers supported the American cause.[2] Swedes were asked to refrain from showing any sympathies for the enemy, whether in words or actions.[3] Those who had previously sympathized with the Germans – outwardly at least – made a complete reversal and, in some cases, became more intolerant of those who opposed the declaration of war than those who had supported the Allies from the very beginning.[4]

[12] Carl Wittke, *The Irish in America,* p. 278.

[13] *Ibid.,* p. 283.

[1] *Svenska Kuriren,* May 31, 1917; *Svenska Tribunen Nyheter,* April 10, 1917.

[2] George Stephenson, "The Attitude of the Swedish Americans toward the World War," p. 92.

[3] *Svenska Amerikanaren,* April 12, 1917.

[4] Gustav E. Johnson, "The Swedes of Chicago," p. 56. As for the German Americans, it is difficult to determine to what extent their change of attitude toward Germany reflected a self-imposed decision and to what extent both the change and the decision were forced upon them. Carl Wittke, *The German-language Press in America,* p. 263, says: "How much of the strategic retreat of the German-language press was dictated by expediency, and how much was due to the simple conclusion that loyalty to the United States was the first obligation of all naturalized citizens, can never be precisely determined."

Despite the fact they were always ready and willing to show their patriotism, the Swedes could not entirely hide their displeasure with the declaration of war. They were not convinced that it was justified. They questioned whether "a few" could determine such an important decision in a democratically governed country. They even called into question American motives in the war. *Förbundets Veckotidning* doubted that the government had acted "unselfishly" or that America's vital interests were threatened by Germany.[5] The Scandinavian Socialist Union completely opposed the war, and at its convention in Chicago, March 25–27, 1917, it adopted a resolution in which it called for a peaceful solution of the war.[6] After America's entrance into the war *Svenska Socialisten* continued to maintain that the country had nothing to gain through its participation.

The attitude of Swedish Americans to the war followed the same pattern as that of German Americans. Before the American intervention they, too, advocated full neutrality. After war was declared they were confronted with a choice between Germany and America. According to Carl Wittke, it was not a difficult choice – "the period of emotional readjustment was relatively brief."[7] In considering the attitude of Swedish Americans and other immigrants to the war, one ought not forget that even "genuine" Americans were opposed to American involvement. One ought not to forget that President Wilson was re-elected because he had promised to keep the country out of the war: he had campaigned on the slogan: "He kept us out of war!"[8] It was therefore natural that a large segment of the American people received the news of American intervention with dismay.

The Swedish Americans soon had other matters to think about than analyzing the reasons for declaring war. In the spores of the war nationalism was germinating. Among Swedish Americans, it was primarily members of the Augustana Synod who were said to sympathize with Germany. In an article in *The Lutheran Companion*, George Stephenson wrote that the pro-German sympathies expressed by Lutheran clergymen had damaged the whole Lutheran church.[9]

5 *Förbundets Veckotidning,* April 10, 1917.

6 Henry Bengston, *Skandinaver på vänsterflygeln i USA,* p. 107 ff.

7 Carl Wittke, "Fissures in the Melting Pot," *The Immigration of Ideas. Studies in the North Atlantic Community* (Rock Island, 1968), p. 151.

8 Oscar Handlin, *America : A History,* p. 784.

9 *The Lutheran Companion,* May 12, 1917.

"It has been a source of grief and humiliation, however, that a small – very small, fortunately – group of men calling themselves Lutherans have opposed the participation of America in the war . . . because of sympathy with the illegal and barbarous submarine warfare of Germany. For this reason the whole Lutheran church has been condemned by the enlightened opinion of the world."

Editor Ernst W. Olson wrote that public opinion had been given this impression by "politico-religious" agents – by which he meant the Catholics – who, in his opinion, tried to find ways of suspecting and discrediting the Lutheran church.[10] *Augustana* admitted that members of the Synod had divided sympathies when it came to choosing sides in the European conflict.[11] But when America was forced to intervene, the Synod unanimously rallied to its cause. The newspaper believed that all of the slanderous rumors against the Synod's patriotism were the result of intrigue on the part of the Catholic Church. "It is well known how the representatives of that church systematically cast suspicions on Luther and the church named for him."

In the official records of the Augustana Synod, however, there is nothing that would seem to indicate defeatism or disloyalty among its members. When any of its members seemed to waver or made statements which were open to misinterpretation, there was always some spokesman who hurriedly came forward with a clarification. When, for instance, the Synod was informed that one of its pastors had lived in the United States nearly 40 years without ever having become an American citizen, it immediately registered its regrets. G.A. Andreen hoped the report was not true, "for anyone who so conducts himself hurts thereby our whole synod and our whole denomination."[12] P.A. Mattson wrote he was sorry to hear that there was such a person in the Synod. At the annual meeting in 1917 the president of the Synod said it was the civic duty of members to call a halt to all opposition to the government's policy.[13] The president of Augustana College and Seminary expressed his pleasure that most of the members of the

[10] Ernst W. Olson, "A Word to Patriots in All Camps," *Ungdomsvännen* (August, 1917, p. 190).

[11] *Augustana,* July 26, 1917.

[12] Letter from G.A. Andreen to P.A. Mattson, April 1, 1918, and from Mattson to Andreen, April 4, 1918 (Archives).

[13] *Minutes of the Augustana Synod,* 1917, pp. 20 and 54; and 1918, p. 16.

school's music band had enlisted as volunteers.[14] At the annual meeting in 1918 the president of the Synod admitted "regretfully" there had been isolated cases that threw a shadow over the entire denomination. *Augustana,* the official publication of the Synod, condemned those individuals within the church who had been guilty of unpatriotic acts and proposed they be appropriately dealt with.[15] However, the newspaper felt it would be a mistake to blame the entire synod for their actions. The Synod's spokesmen concluded that Swedish Lutherans were basically as loyal as any other Swedes or minority groups, "for our Swedish people have not been rebels."[16]

The Lutheran Companion and *Augustana* declared that the majority of Swedish Lutherans had only one flag and one country.[17] "America is our country," asserted *Augustana,* "for which we would not hesitate to offer our lives even if it came to a battle against our old fatherland."[18] When J.P. McGee, director of the Minnesota State Fuel Commission and member of its Security Board, asserted that a number of Swedes had been disloyal, *The Lutheran Companion* refuted the accusation. It said there ought to be an end to those types of irresponsible accusations which were based on pure hearsay.[19] If one carefully investigated such reports, it said, one would find very few Swedes among the so-called "peace-at-any-price" propagandists. "Again we say that this talk of the Swedes and the Lutherans being disloyal and unpatriotic should be stopped." If there were Swedes guilty of unpatriotic acts and happened to be members of the Augustana Synod, the Synod should not be blamed for their conduct.[20] Those who simply equated Lutheranism with Germanism were described as representatives of the "low-minded know-nothingism."

14 *Augustana Observer,* Vol. XV, April 1919, p. 110. He declared: "Augustana is proud of its band and the country appreciates its patriotic spirit."

15 *Augustana,* October 11, 1917.

16 See note 12.

17 *The Lutheran Companion,* July 21, 1917, p. 354; *Augustana,* October 11, 1917; *Svenska Tribunen Nyheter,* April 17, 1917. Gustav Andreen, President of Augustana College and Seminary, said in a speech given in Chicago on the occasion of the 400th anniversary celebration of the Reformation that the Swedes were prepared to defend the flag of the United States.

18 *Augustana,* October 11, 1917.

19 *The Lutheran Companion,* May 11, 1918, p. 234.

20 *Augustana,* October 11, 1917, p. 672.

Further to show their support of American war policy, the Augustana Synod, as well as other religious denominations and Swedish-American organizations, all adopted resolutions attesting their loyalty.[1] At their respective annual meetings in 1917 the Central Swedish Conference of the Methodist Episcopal Church and the Baptist General Conference both passed resolutions assuring their complete loyalty to America's cause and full support of its President.[2] Although neither the Augustana Synod nor the Swedish Mission Covenant adopted similar resolutions in 1917, they did do so the following year at their annual church conferences. Moreover, separate conferences and congregations sent telegrams to President Wilson as tokens of their faith in the American war effort.[3]

[1] At its annual meeting in 1917, The Order of Vasa of America, the largest non-religious Swedish-American organization, sent a telegram to Washington, D.C., promising that its members, all "patriotic citizens," would do everything that might be required of them (*Minutes of the Eleventh Grand Lodge Meeting of the Order of Vasa,* June 26—30, 1917, p. 66 f).

[2] *Yearbook of the Swedish Evangelical Mission Covenant of America,* 1917/1918, p. 133. The resolution was sent to President Wilson and was worded as follows: "The Swedish Evangelical Mission Covenant of America, representing a considerable proportion of American citizens of Swedish birth or descent, hereby gladly record their undivided loyalty to the United States of America and pledge themselves to continue in wholehearted support of our government in the present crisis of the nation and of the world." At its annual meeting, June 5—11, 1918, the Augustana Synod also cabled President Wilson to affirm its loyalty and patriotic allegiance (*Augustana Synod Minutes,* 1918, p. 31). At the annual meeting of the Central Swedish Conference in 1917, the Swedish Methodists adopted a resolution "assuring devotion and faithfulness to the nation's government." They also promised the President their "intercessory prayers and our moral and material support; we promise anew our devotion to the flag, even the sacrifice of our lives if such sacrifice should become necessary. . . ." (*Minutes of the Central Swedish Conference of the Methodist Episcopal Church,* 1917, pp. 60, 61.) The Swedish Baptists also expressed their loyalty in a resolution, 1917 (Martin Ericson, *Baptist General Conference,* p. 74).

[3] At its annual meeting, May 1—3, 1918, the Ministers' Conference of the Nebraska Mission Association praised "the government's policy." At its annual meeting, April 9—13, 1918, the Iowa Conference adopted a resolution in which it warned its pastors as well as members of individual congregations against slacking or wavering in their patriotic spirit. "We, Iowa Lutherans of the Augustana Synod . . . desire to express to you our abiding faith in those principles of free government so wisely instituted by our Revolutionary fathers. Appreciating the privileges without forgetting the obligations of our citizen-

In speeches and in articles the Swedish Americans confirmed their allegiance to "the star-spangled banner." At first these statements confined themselves to expressions of patriotism and loyalty and avoided making outright attacks and condemnations of the enemy. However, as the war dragged on, their anti-German flavor became more pronounced and bitter. When the sons of Swedish Americans fought on the European fronts their parents grew just as intolerant of disloyal patriots back home as did American citizens.[4] The German "militarism's mad thirst for power" frightened even the formerly pro-German Swedes – "it was necessary to cripple the blood-thirsty savage beast called Prussian military autocracy."[5] In the spring of 1918 Edwin Björkman, chief of the Scandinavian department in the Committee on Public Information, declared that a change of attitude among the Swedes was taking place as they began to understand the import of the war and the reasons for American involvement.[6] An article by David F. Swenson, entitled "America's War Spirit," pointed out that understanding of the war itself and the nature of the United States' contribution was not only gaining strength and momentum among the Swedes but was giving rise to a belief "based on the heart impulses of faith and obedience regarding the intent of the United States and less and less characterized as simply a mere duty."[7]

Loyalty demonstrations became routine among the Swedes in America. Organizations and associations arranged so-called mass meetings to show their loyalty and to adopt resolutions relating to the war. The Swedish-American Women's Club attested their loyalty in

ship ... when our country demands the supreme sacrifice, we stand ready to offer our resources and our lives if need be ...." A similar resolution was adopted by the Minnesota Conference. (Sources: *Iowa Conference Minutes*, 1918, pp. 84, 85; *Minnesota Conference Minutes*, 1918, pp. 104, 105; *Förbundets Veckotidning*, May 28, 1918; and *The Lutheran Companion*, April 27, 1918, p. 210).

4 George Stephenson, *The Religious Aspects* ... p. 451.

5 *Förbundets Veckotidning*, May 28, 1918.

6 *The Minneapolis Tribune*, March 14, 1918. In a letter to George Creel, chairman of the Committee on Public Information, Edwin Björkman wrote: "There has been a very marked change in sentiment among the Swedes of the Northwest in the last few weeks. Events in Russia and Finland seem to be chiefly responsible ..." The letter is dated March 14, 1918.

7 David Swenson, "America's War Spirit," distributed by The Committee on Public Information, June 17, 1918. — Swenson was a professor of philosophy in the University of Minnesota.

the following words: "Resolved, that we, no matter what happens, stand loyally united as Americans in all our efforts and actions for the welfare and success of this our land, the land of the free and the home of the brave."[8] In September, 1917, the Swedes in Chicago began planning a loyalty demonstration. The intention was to show "Anglo-Americans" through a giant demonstration that the Swedes were prepared "to march under the star-spangled banner in the fight against oppressors."[9] All of the Swedish churches and congregations, societies and associations in Chicago supported the project. Guests of honor were "the Swedish mothers, wives and sisters whose sons, husbands and brothers had been called to war service."[10] The Swedish-American press praised the plan. At the meeting a resolution was adopted in which the loyalty of Chicago's 150,000 Swedes was affirmed.[11] The socialistic newspaper, *Svenska Socialisten,* described the meeting of "the-dyed-in-the-wool patriots" as a fiasco.[12] The paper considered the meeting totally insignificant since the participants represented only the "elite" of Chicago's Swedes. The paper was correct in its judgment insofar as the arrangers of the demonstration were members of the upper social class of Chicago Swedes and well known in political and banking circles. However, it has been impossible to determine to what extent this also applied to the actual participants in the demonstration.

All conceivable methods for mobilizing the Swedish Americans were utilized. The Swedish Historical Society of America made an appeal through the Swedish language press for submitting the names of

[8] *Svenska Kuriren,* September 20, 1917.

[9] *Svenska Kuriren,* September 20 and 27, 1917. In announcing the demonstration the arrangers expressed the hope that it would inform Anglo-Americans that the United States had never had more devoted citizens, more trustworthy men and stronger defenders than the Swedes. *Svenska Tribunen Nyheter* expressed the same sentiment in an editorial September 25, 1917.

[10] At first the intention seems to have been to secure Theodore Roosevelt as the main speaker. In a letter to Charles S. Peterson, chairman of the Loyalty Meeting of Americans of Swedish Descent, he congratulated the Swedish Americans for having such good patriots among them as Governor Burnquist of Minnesota and Harry Olson in Chicago. This letter is published in *Minnesota at War,* the official bulletin of the Commission of Public Safety.

[11] *Svenska Kuriren,* October 4, 1917.

[12] *Svenska Socialisten,* October 4, 1917.

Swedish men serving in the armed forces of the U.S. The intention was to preserve for posterity the names of Swedes sacrificed on "the altar of the foster-land."[13] President Wilson proclaimed July 4, 1918, as the foreign-born citizens' day. The Swedes praised the idea and initiated careful preparations. Newspapers urged all Swedish Americans to participate.[14] The American Scandinavian Foundation published at the time a special "National Service Number" of the *American Scandinavian Review.* President Wilson was praised for having taken the initiative in proclaiming a day when all foreign-born, regardless of race or nationality, could gather to celebrate. A project of that kind was considered much more attractive than the Know-Nothingism directed against "a loyal press, loyal churches and denominations just because they do not use English."[15] Everywhere in the country the Swedes harkened to the President's call. In an address in Minnehaha Park in Minneapolis, David F. Swenson said that all Americans, regardless of native origin, are citizens and that citizenship in the final reckoning did not depend on how long a person had lived in America nor on what language he spoke.[16] He rejected all rumors being spread about disloyalty among Swedish Americans.

Irritated by gossip and slurs on their patriotism Swedish Americans vociferously counterattacked. The *American Scandinavian Review* dismissed as absurd the whole question of whether or not Scandinavians were loyal.[17] *Svenska Kuriren* considered it below its dignity to answer charges from irresponsible sources regarding the Swedish Americans. However, the newspaper found it hard to follow its own advice and instead continued to take the lead in challenging all

[13] *Svenska Kuriren,* April 25, 1917.

[14] *Ibid.,* June 27, and July 11, 1918; *The Lutheran Companion,* June 29, 1918. In Chicago, the John Ericsson League of Patriotic Service distributed a broadside, signed by Harry Olson, containing the following: "The United States government intends to send out photographers throughout the country to take pictures of the different nationalities for record. Are the Swedish people going to show themselves 'slackers'? No, their splendid support of the Third Liberty Loan, War Savings Stamps, Red Cross, Enlistment ... are proof enough that they will go 'over the top' July Fourth."

[15] *American Scandinavian Review,* September—October, 1918, p. 287.

[16] David F. Swenson, professor of philosophy in University of Minnesota. (The Covenant Archives in Chicago has a typescript copy of his speech.)

[17] *American Scandinavian Review,* July—August, 1918; *Svenska Kuriren,* August 30, 1917 and March 28, 1918.

rumors of alleged disloyalty among Swedish Americans. When Judge Kenesaw Mountain Landis said that certain political candidates sought unpatriotic votes among "the disloyal Swedes," *Svenska Kuriren* was infuriated and retorted sharply that Swedish Americans were just as loyal as native Americans.[18] *Förbundets Veckotidning* thought this talk about disloyalty was "an irresponsible outburst of a sickly imagination," if not otherwise motivated simply by ill will.[19] On the whole the Swedish-American newspapers thought it was unfair to charge all Swedish Americans with apathy toward the war merely on the basis of a few isolated cases.[20] The American press was criticized for having spread unfounded rumors about citizens who had shown "the most striking evidence of true Americanism."

There is no doubt that in many circles Swedes were disturbed and offended by suspicions on their loyalty.[1] On August 8, 1918, Alexander J. Johnson wrote a personal statement in *Svenska Kuriren,* entitled "On the Thirtieth Anniversary," commemorating thirty years' service as editor of the paper, to the effect that he never could have believed the day would come when Swedes would be looked on with suspicion by the so-called "native Americans." He was disappointed too, he said, that the Swedes were denied the right "even to remember the land of their birth." The article recounts in a striking way the disappointments and the dilemma Swedes and many other nationalities faced during the war.

This atmosphere of suspicion, rumor, and allegation, all pointing to pro-German sympathies among Swedish Americans, soon caused them to focus critical attention on each other. A poem in *Ungdomsvännen,* entitled "The Fifth of June," aroused a thunder of protest.[2] A letter to

[18] *Svenska Kuriren,* December 6, 1917.

[19] *Förbundets Veckotidning,* July 30, 1918, p. 4.

[20] *American Scandinavian Review,* May—June, 1918, p. 160; *Svenska Tribunen Nyheter,* September 25, 1917. Gustav E. Johnson, in "The Swedes of Chicago" (p. 59), says that the Swedes were insulted by suspicions cast on their loyalty: "Most Swedes believed the foreign-born or so-called 'hyphenated' citizens to be as fully loyal towards their adopted country as any of the descendents of the first pioneers."

[1] George Creel wrote in an article in *Everybody's Magazine,* 1919: "It stung them (the Swedes) unbearably to be adjudged unpatriotic in any degree and to have their native tongues put under the ban along with German." (George Creel, "Our Aliens — Were They Loyal or Disloyal?", p. 70.)

[2] *Ungdomsvännen,* July, 1917. The poem was written by C.A. Lönnquist.

the editor, Ernst W. Olson, called the poem so unpatriotic "that it stamps your paper as utterly unfit to exist or to be read by our American citizens."[3] The letters Olson received in response to the poem forced him, in an open editorial, to challenge those he called hysterical patriots. In his opinion the immigrants were being caught in a web of suspicions woven by "altogether too many who believed they had a patent on patriotism. ... Naturally these will not go to Europe to fight foreigners in a war waged under the supreme direction of foreigners – oh, no! They prefer to stay home and slay imaginary Philistines ...."

Although prior to America's declaration of war some Swedish language newspapers displayed pro-German sympathies, there were, with the exception of a few minor incidents, no obvious examples of Swedish Americans turning their backs on the American war effort.[4] What is most surprising, however, is the lack of concrete examples of pro-German sympathies and un-American activities among the Swedes. Such charges were few and far between in American newspapers. When the Swedes defended themselves it was seldom because of direct accusations. For this reason readers of the Swedish language papers were easily given the impression that the Swedes reacted too strongly and thus themselves contributed to heightening the feeling among the American public that they were more pro-German than they really were. The criticisms Swedish Americans levelled at each other in their own newspapers amounted to something more of an exaggerated sensitivity on their part than a series of direct *faux pas*. It should further be noted that the Swedish-American papers, as well as the entire immigrant press, did not reflect the immigrants' inner feelings about the war. Seen solely in terms of the pressures under which these newspapers managed to function, any accurate and thoroughgoing analysis of Swedish-American opinion during the war will pose monstrous problems to any researcher or historian. It is obvious that

[3] Ernst W. Olson, "A Word to Patriots of All Camps," *Ungdomsvännen,* August, 1917, p. 191.

[4] *The Chicago Herald,* on March 6, 1918, attacked the Swedish Americans without any real reason. It wrote, for instance, that "the defenders of the Kaiser" have directed their efforts toward Americans of Swedish origin because of the friendship between Swedish and German aristocrats. To what extent the American government suspected Swedish Americans of disloyal activities cannot at this time be determined, for papers of the Department of Justice as well as documents of the Military Intelligence are not yet available.

no newspaper could risk publishing articles or letters from readers which criticized the American war effort, since reprisals would be immediately hurled against them. For instance, Andrew Tofft, the editor of *Svenska Tribunen Nyheter,* refused to publish an article by David Nyvall on the grounds that it might endanger the newspaper's policy of printing only contributions which were free of possible misinterpretation.[5]

Even though freedom of the press was sharply curtailed Swedish-American newspapers defended their rights whenever possible. When it was proposed in connection with the Sedition Act of 1918 that all foreign language newspapers be prohibited, they sent up an indignant protest. They regarded the proposal as an outright failure but even more as an "enormous mistake," because it implied that Swedish-American papers were less patriotic than their English language colleagues – an implication they vociferously denied.[6]

The foreign language press was threatened from two directions: so as not to damage the reputation of Swedish Americans they were forced to scrutinize all statements and articles which might be interpreted as critical of the American war effort; and once they did not censure themselves in this way they were faced with the prospect of official curtailment or legislative ban affecting all non-English printed matter. The fullscale assault on everything "foreign" scared away many would-be subscribers to foreign language newspapers. Among Swedish-American newspapers the worst attacks were levelled against *Svenska Socialisten,* which on several occasions had its editions impounded by the Post Office.[7] According to Henry Bengston, its war-

[5] Letter from Andrew Tofft to David Nyvall, April 11, 1918. Tofft returned the article with the explanation: "Your article is excellent and we would have liked to use it, but since it criticizes certain views, we thought it safest for us not to publish it."

[6] *Förbundets Veckotidning,* April 9, 1918.

[7] Henry Bengston, *Skandinaver på vänsterflygeln i USA,* p. 110. The issue of March 28, 1918, of *Svenska Socialisten* was impounded. The following issue explained that police authorities had refused to permit the distribution by mail of the whole edition. The paper commented that "the impounding is a complete puzzle." On June 13, 1918, the paper said the readers had waited in vain for two weeks for *Svenska Socialisten.* The explanation it gave reflected a rather common dilemma faced by socialistic newspapers at that time. It said that the postal authorities had refused to permit its distribution until the official censors in Washington had given their approval.

time editor, the paper exercised the greatest caution whenever the war was mentioned.[8] Immediately after the passage of "Trading with the Enemy Act" the management board of *Svenska Socialisten* decided to avoid publishing statements which could jeopardize the paper's existence.[9] The announcement was published on the first page of the issue of February 11. Several other Swedish language papers declared in editorials they did not intend to violate the Trading with the Enemy Act. *Augustana* made it clear for its readers that the paper intended to obey the law: "This act has now been made law, and Augustana's editors will not permit any deviation from it; thus we ask our correspondents not to include anything in their contributions pertaining to the war or any actions of the governments involved."[10] When they did publish articles on the war, most Swedish language newspapers informed their readers in a special insert that translations had been made and submitted to the Post Office. It has not been possible to identify which papers requested to be released from the editorial burdens such translations imposed.[11] For most papers the law required that a third of their content be translated.[12]

[8] Interview with Henry Bengston, September 20, 1967.

[9] *Svenska Socialisten,* October 11, 1917. The committee adopted the following resolution: "That until such time as we shall have acquainted ourselves with the law and its interpretation, so as to avoid coming into conflict with it, no news or information about the war shall be printed in this paper."

[10] *Augustana,* October 25, 1917, p. 705; *Ungdomsvännen,* December, 1917, p. 263.

[11] From David Nyvall's correspondence it is evident that he had intervened in behalf of *Förbundets Veckotidning* and *Missionsvännen* for securing permission to omit translating articles about the war. He appealed to Edwin Björkman who gave his sanction. The reasoning was that both papers were "absolutely correct in their war attitude and their tone is thoroughly patriotic." It seems *Missionsvännen's* petition was not approved, since it continued to indicate that translations had been submitted to postal authorities. *Förbundets Veckotidning* seems to have had its petition granted, for after April 9, 1918, it ceased to indicate translations had been made. (Sources: Letter from D. Nyvall to Björkman May 8, 1918; Letter from Carl Byoir, assistant chairman, Committee on Public Information, to Judge William H. Lamar, Dept. of Justice, April 25, 1918).

[12] Henry Bengston, *op. cit.,* p. 111.

4. *Swedish-American Congressmen and the War*

Not only the Swedish-American papers had divided opinions about what stand the United States ought to take with regard to the belligerents in Europe, but also the national politicians of Swedish birth or descent. Several outstanding men of Swedish origin were members of Congress: Irvine Luther Lenroot, Republican from Wisconsin, first in the House of Representatives, 1909 to 1918, then in the Senate, 1918 to 1927;[1] Charles A. Lindbergh, Republican from Minnesota, member of the House of Representatives, 1907–1916;[2] and Ernest Lundeen, who like Lindbergh was a Republican from Minnesota. The latter was elected to the House in 1916 but was not re-elected in 1918; he was elected to the Senate in 1930 on the Farmer-Labor ticket and remained there to his death in 1940.[3] Sidney Anderson, Republican, was a representative from Minnesota in the House from 1911 to 1925,[4] and Charles Otto Lobeck, a Democrat from Nebraska, was a

[1] Irvine Luther Lenroot (Lönnrot) was born of Swedish parents in 1869. The parents had come to the USA in 1854. Lenroot was not re-elected to the Senate in 1926. In 1929 he was appointed by President Herbert Hoover a judge in the Federal Customs Court and Patent Appeals in Washington, D.C., from which he resigned in 1944. He died in 1949. In 1920 he was mentioned as a possible candidate for the vice presidency but bowed out in favour of Calvin Coolidge.

[2] Charles Augustus Lindbergh was born in Stockholm in 1859 and was brought to America with his parents the same year. He secured his law degree at the University of Michigan. In Washington on Capitol Hill he began his fight against the money barons — the "Money Trust." After serving in the House from 1907 to 1917 he was a Republican candidate in the senatorial primary in 1916, but was defeated by Frank B. Kellogg. In 1917 Lindbergh wrote a book, *Why Is Your Country at War and What Happens to You After the War Is Over and Related Subjects,* which received much attention throughout the country. In 1924 he was nominated for the governorship on the Farmer-Labor ticket, but he died in the middle of the election campaign.

[3] Ernest Lundeen was born in 1878 in South Dakota of Swedish parents. His father was a pioneer Covenant preacher. Ernest became a lawyer and began his political career as a member of the legislature of Minnesota. He was a delegate to the Republican national conventions in 1912 and 1916. Elected to the House in 1916, he was one of the few who voted against the U.S. entry in the World War. He was not re-elected in 1918. He died in an air crash in 1940.

[4] Sydney Anderson, born in 1881 in Minnesota, had a Swedish father and a Norwegian mother.

member of the House of Representatives from 1911 to 1919.[5].

Among the politicians of Swedish or partly Swedish descent thus referred to, Ernest Lundeen and Charles A. Lindbergh became nationally prominent. Both were bitter opponents to the entry of the United States into World War I. Lundeen was one of the 50 congressmen in the House of Representatives who voted against the American declaration of war. He maintained consistently that a declaration of war was the people's prerogative and therefore ought not to be made unless a plebiscite were taken. "Before war is declared let the American citizen express his opinion."[6] In order to set a good example he arranged for a plebiscite in his home district. He sent the question by mail to 54,000 persons, but since mail delivery was slow – "on account of the ox-team mail service" – he did not receive all the returns by the time the war-declaration was being debated in the Congress. They indicate, however, he said, an almost unanimous answer – "my returns are not complete at this hour, but they run about 10 to 1 against declaring war on Germany." Lundeen said he was convinced that "if all of the congressmen had placed the ballot in the hands of the voters we would never enter the World War." "In obedience to that mandate, I was one of the 50 in the House who voted against war. For that vote I offer neither apology nor excuse."[7]

[5] Charles Otto Lobeck was born in 1852 in Illinois. His mother was born in Sweden and the father in Germany. The father, however, came to Sweden and became a Swedish citizen before his emigration to the USA in 1848.

[6] *Congressional Record,* 65th Congress, First Session, p. 362. According to Lundeen it was the first time in the nation's history the people in "a congressional district were given an opportunity to vote for or against war." *(Congressional Record,* March 3, 1919, p. 400). In a comment some years later he said that 8 were against the war declaration and one in favor — for war, 2023; for conscription, 3198; against war 16, 882; against conscription, 15, 381 *(Congressional Record,* Appendix, March 3, 1919, p. 402). Senator Robert M. La Follette mentioned in the Senate the vote taken in Minneapolis by Lundeen. The return of the war ballot showed, said La Follette, that nearly 8,000 voters were against declaring war as opposed to 800 who favored it. "Do not these messages indicate on the part of the people," he asked, "a deep seated conviction that the United States should not enter the European war?" (Belle C. La Follette and Fola La Follette, *Robert M. La Follette* [New York, 1953], p. 659).

[7] *Congressional Record,* Appendix, March 3, 1919, p. 400; *Congressional Record,* 65th Congress, First Session, p. 363 ff. The Senate passed a declaration of war, 82 to 6, on April 4; the House concurred, 373 to 50, on April 6. Ray S. Baker writes in *Woodrow Wilson. Life and Letters. Facing War, 1915—1917* (New

In a statement in the House on April 5, 1917, the same day Congress voted "yes" to the war declaration, Lundeen explicitly detailed his decision. He maintained that both England and Germany had violated America's maritime rights. "Let us frankly admit that both sides have wronged us." He exhorted America and his colleagues to follow the example of the Scandinavian countries. They have had, he said, "the good sense to put an embargo on ammunitions at the beginning of the war. Let us frankly admit that these countries were right, too, in warning their citizens to keep out of the war zones. . . . To choose between these war-mad nations and ally ourselves with one or the other is a crime against our civilization and our own citizens."

Lundeen criticized President Wilson for having only a half year earlier allowed himself to be re-elected on the promise of keeping the country out of the European war. He had no regard for those who asserted that it was now mandatory for all to close ranks around the President of the country. Somewhat ironically he asked: "Which one – the one that kept us out of war or the one that plunged us in?" He closed his long speech with the following declaration, for which, according to the congressional minutes, he received applause:

> Here in this hour I stand strong for peace with honor – the same honor that Sweden and Norway, Denmark and Holland, Spain, Switzerland, and the South American Republics regard as an honorable peace. They have refused to follow our President into war. Mr. Speaker, I vote "no" upon this resolution. God helping me, I can not do otherwise.

Lundeen's "no" and his speech aroused national attention. Among all the patriots closing ranks in back of the President's call he stood out as a traitor. He could hardly have been ignorant of what his "no" would provoke. Afterward he was subjected to much criticism from the 100-percent Americans.

Judging by the letters received by Lundeen, which he appended to the congressional minutes, he had many supporters among the Swedish Americans.[8] In letters and telegrams from Swedish-American churches and organizations he was encouraged to do his utmost to keep the country out of the war. Lebanon Evangelical Lutheran Church sent the

York, 1940), p. 516, that "the vote probably reflected the opinion of the people: that is, not more than ten or twelve in a hundred, the country over, were definitely opposed to the war."

8 *Congressional Record,* 65th Congress, First Session, p. 365.

following appeal: "Please keep our country out of the European war. Let England and the ammunition leaders care for their own affairs." A group of Mission Covenant pastors in Minneapolis and St. Paul opposed the war declaration: "This view is held widely by those with whom we come into contact."

Except for the war declaration itself and the general military conscription, Lundeen supported the motions propounded for a conclusion of the war. However, he held fast to the belief that it was a self-evident right of every American to discuss the war and the way it was being fought. He defended those who were characterized as disloyal and unpatriotic because they criticized the American war declaration. When a member of the Public Safety Commission of Minnesota questioned the loyalty of the Swedish Americans, Lundeen found this outrageous and called to mind that "they (the Swedish Americans had) fought in every war – the Revolutionary War, the War of 1812, the Mexican War, the Civil War, the Spanish American, and the World War. They have never been found wanting. The Swedish people first of all the nations in the world recognized American independence. No punishment is too severe for this character assassin who so traduces and slanders our very best citizens."[9] Lundeen's clearly defined stand against the declaration of war was observed naturally enough by the American press. According to his own statement, the American press referred to him as a Hun. "It was stated that I should be sent back to the Kaiser. ... I received letters questioning my loyalty and abusing me." In 1919, after the war, Ernest Lundeen was involved in "one of the outstanding instances of mob action" which occurred all over the country, when he tried to make a speech against the League of Nations at Ortonville, Minnesota. Before he began his talk, the local sheriff told Lundeen that "you can't talk here." Just as Lundeen commenced to speak, he was seized by the sheriff, and others, and escorted to the railroad depot where a train was just leaving. He was locked in a refrigerator car.

Lundeen was not the only one from Minnesota who was considered disloyal. Of the twelve congressmen – two Senators and ten members of the House of Representatives – eleven were denounced according to Lundeen "as Kaiserites by that large part of the press which was more

[9] *Ibid.*, March 4, 1919, p. 5060; H.C. Peterson and Gilbert C. Fite, *Opponents of War, 1917—1918* (Madison, 1957), p. 289.

active in promoting the interests of certain foreign nations than they were in protecting the lives of American citizens."[10] Lundeen was not afraid to turn upon his adversaries in retort. When Theodore Roosevelt called him "a shadow Hun" whom he wished to give "as a free gift to the Kaiser " Lundeen sent a telegram to Roosevelt (October 2, 1917) in which he asked for an explanation.[11] Their correspondence and their subsequent meeting resulted in Roosevelt's retraction of the accusation against Lundeen. At that meeting Lundeen explained why he had voted against the American declaration of war. In a letter to Roosevelt dated November 1, 1917, he further developed the reasons for his stand on the war question.[12] Roosevelt answered, November 7: "I understand now, as I did not before, the reasons that influenced you in your vote against the war, and while I can not agree with you, I appreciate your point of view, and I do not question your loyalty."[13] Roosevelt also admitted that Lundeen was fully within his rights in discussing the war. Finally, on December 18, 1917, the *Chicago Tribune* recorded, regarding this correspondence, that Roosevelt no longer thought of Lundeen as a "shadow Hun."

Charles A. Lindbergh was the second Swedish-American politician who figured in the headlines during the First World War. Though he no longer was in the Congress when the declaration of war was debated, he had at an early stage associated himself with those who felt the United States ought to stay out of the war. Already during the first war years he was very critical of those who would profit by the war. In March, 1916, he had made and officially included in the congressional minutes two statements, on the 10th and 20th, motivating his

[10] *Ibid.,* March 4, 1919, p. 5060. No attempt has been made to investigate the critique of Ernest Lundeen in the American press for in so doing this chapter would expand to an unproportionate length. The intention of this account has not been that of closely describing Ernest Lundeen and the reaction to his attitude, but only of demonstrating how one congressman of Swedish origin reacted to the war declaration.

[11] *Ibid.,* March 4, 1919, p. 5061.

[12] In the letter Lundeen reiterated that his electorate had clearly indicated they were against a declaration of war. "My enemies have stated to you (Roosevelt) that I conducted a referendum after war was declared. That I brand as an unqualified falsehood."

[13] *Congressional Record,* March 4, 1919, p. 5062.

attitude toward the war.[14] In both speeches he made forceful attacks on what he called "professional speculators." Characteristic for Lindbergh, he believed the USA ought to pursue a prudent policy so the country would not be drawn into the war and that the money magnates – "American dollar plutocracy" – ought not be allowed to profit by the war in Europe.[15] He deplored that the war "immediately developed into a case of 'dollar Americanism' against patriotic America, with the principal part of the press working overtime desperately attempting to deceive the public."[16]

In Congress Lindbergh proceeded resolutely against what he called "the lords of special privilege" who "in their selfish glee [were] coining billions of profit from the rage of war."[17] He analyzed the designation "preparedness" which he considered "the war-munitions lords" used as a substitute for "armaments." He maintained that the USA ought to avoid measures that could result in the country's being drawn into the war. He said *e.g.* that American citizens ought not to travel in merchant vessels, armed or unarmed, carrying war material. "A proclamation should be issued that Americans on such ships travel at their own risk." This would deter a patriotic citizen from traveling on such vessels.[18] He pointed out further that it was criminal to manufacture

[14] *Congressional Record,* 64th Congress, First Session, p. 497 f. Since Richard Lucas at the Historical Institution in Uppsala is working on a dissertation on Charles A. Lindbergh, "A Study on the Political Activities of Charles A. Lindbergh, Sr., Congressman 1907—1917," I will only mention his attitude to the First World War and how he motivated it. I have further limited myself to his role in Congress and to the book he wrote concerning the war.

[15] Lindbergh became known primarily for his attacks on the money aristocracy. Richard Lucas, "A Study on the Political Activities of Charles A. Lindbergh, Sr." A short paper presented at the Historical Institution, Uppsala, November 23, 1970, p. 5.

[16] *Congressional Record,* 64th Congress, First Session, p. 665.

[17] *Ibid.,* 64th Congress, First Session, p. 497 ff.

[18] In an article Lindbergh published in September, 1915, he wrote that "the tenacity with which the subsidized press demands Government guarantee of safety to foolhardy or inconsiderate American citizens who travel on armed belligerent merchant ships is for the purpose of involving us in war to protect speculators" *(Congressional Record,* 64th Congress, First Session, p. 498). According to his own statement he could not get the article into "the city press" but was forced to rely on the small-town press, because the former supported the war loans. In the article he hit hard at "professional speculators."

war material for export since that material might be used against the USA.

Lindbergh's term in Congress ended at the close of the year 1916. In his attempt to be elected to the Senate the same year he was defeated. Not silenced, however, he continued his critique of the money barons and war-agitators. In July, 1917, he published his book, *Why Is Your Country at War and What Happens to You after the War Is Over and Related Subjects,* in which he attacked the system and those who led the country into the war. In the main the book does not contain much that is new beyond what is in the minutes of Congress. He blames "big business" a great deal for getting America into the war because it created the conditions which made the belligerents violate the country's international rights.[19] Criticism was also leveled against the press that contributed to the heightening of the war fever, and against Congress for having "tied us to foreign nations by authorizing the credit of this country to exploit foreign peoples as well as our own."[20]

In 1918 Lindbergh tried to get nominated as candidate for the Minnesota governorship by the Republican party. The campaign proceeded completely in a time of war hysteria. Lindbergh, although supported by the Nonpartisan League, lost to another Swedish descendant, J.A.A. Burnquist. The voters gave Burnquist 199,325 votes to 150,626 for Lindbergh. Lindbergh had, however, polled a surprisingly large vote in light of the type of campaign which had been waged against him.[21] Burnquist and his supporters tried to accuse Lindbergh and the Nonpartisan League of disloyalty. Enemies of the League did everything possible to avoid economic issues and focus public attention on the loyalty question. When the League seemed to be gaining strength, more positive action was taken. League meetings were stopped. Of 250 meetings scheduled in the winter and spring 1917–1918, some 40 had to be cancelled. On one occasion a meeting had just begun when the county sheriff appeared and announced that no League meeting could be held in that county. Lindbergh could not speak, he said. Lindbergh then suggested that the meeting should adjourn a few miles south into the State of Iowa, and in 90 minutes the thousands

19 Lindbergh's *Why Is Your Country at War,* p. 80.

20 *Ibid.,* p. 126.

21 H.C. Peterson and Gilbert C. Fite, *op. cit.,* p. 189 f.

of automobiles and occupants had been transported to the neighboring state.

During the campaign Lindbergh's book, *Why Is Your Country at War,* was used as a cudgel against him. Clarence B. Miller, a Representative from Minnesota, declared in the House that he felt impelled to call the attention of Congress to the fact that the socialistic Nonpartisan League supported Lindbergh.[22] His book was considered to be of "deadly harm to this nation." The bitter feeling toward Lindbergh became so strong that he found it best to resign from the War Industries Board; certain persons said they would not be members of any Liberty Loan Committees while he was allowed to serve the government.

Of the Swedish-American congressmen only Irvine Lenroot of Wisconsin strongly defended the actions of the American government. According to him Germany had forced America into the war by having without warning killed American citizens.[1] Lenroot voted for the declaration of war. "A vote of 'yea' for this resolution means – and to my mind it means only – that we, the American Congress, propose to meet by war the war that is made upon us by Germany by war." He did not chide those who voted against the war declaration, but he himself could not do it, since that would mean that he acquiesced in the German transgressions.

Although Irvine Lenroot was loyal and supported the American declaration of war, President Wilson questioned his position. He said that Lenroot's record had been one of "questionable support of the dignity and rights of the country on some test occasions."[2] In 1918 Wilson asked Vice President Thomas Marshall to go to Wisconsin and speak for Democrat Joseph Davies, one of the candidates seeking the Wisconsin senatorial seat. The Republican candidate was Congressman Irvine Lenroot. On March 27, Marshall told a Madison audience that, regardless of how loyal Lenroot might be, he was bidding for the votes of traitors, pro-Germans, seditionists, and pacifists. However, Lenroot defeated Davies by a small margin.

[22] *Congressional Record,* 65th Congress, 2nd Session, p. 7542; George Stephenson, *John Lind of Minnesota* (Minneapolis, 1935), p. 338 f.

[1] *Congressional Record,* 65th Congress, First Session, p. 353.

[2] H.C. Peterson and Gilbert C. Fite, *Opponents of War, 1917—1918,* p. 164.

Sydney Anderson and Charles O. Lobeck also voted for the declaration. It may further be noted that another Scandinavian from Minnesota, the Norwegian-born Harold Knutson, like Lundeen, voted against the declaration.[3] In a statement on April 5, 1917, Knutson declared his intention of voting against the resolution because this attitude was in the interest of the people who had elected him. Further, he assailed the American press for having created hate against the Central powers.

Asle Jorgenson Gronna, a United States Senator of Norwegian descent (1911–1921) and a Progressive Republican from North Dakota, also opposed the declaration of war. He said:

> We criticize European monarchies for forcing their subjects into war against their will, but we refuse to ascertain by a referendum vote of the American people whether they desire peace or war. . . . I shall vote against the war because I believed it would have been possible to maintain an honorable peace.[4]

Gronna's conviction was assumed to have grown out of the democratic tradition of his Norwegian ancestors.

A third Congressman of Norwegian descent, Henry T. Helgesen, Republican from North Dakota (1911–1917), who was sick in a Washington hospital, sent a telegram to Robert M. La Follette, one of the most eager opponents to the war, with the request that La Follette read to the Senate a plea from a "North Dakota Farm Woman," typical of the thousands of messages which brought to him "one uniform protest against war."[5]

At the same time as Ernest Lundeen and Charles Lindbergh expressed their opposition to the war, two other Swedish-American politicians from Minnesota, Governor J.A.A. Burnquist and former Governor John Lind, whole heartedly supported President Wilson.[6]

[3] *Ibid.*, p. 22. Knutson was born in Norway in 1880; he came to the USA in 1886, and was a Republican Congressman 1917—1949.

[4] Belle C. La Follette & Fola La Follette, *Robert M. La Follette,* p. 655.

[5] *Ibid.*, p. 657.

[6] J.A.A. Burnquist, a Republican, became Governor in 1915, re-elected in 1916 and 1918. He was born in Iowa of Swedish parents, his father being a prominent pioneer lay leader among the Mission Friends, John Lind, born in Småland, Sweden in 1854, was elected to Congress 1886, re-elected 1888 and 1890 on the Republican ticket. In 1898 he ran as a candidate for the Democratic-Populist Party and was elected Governor. In 1902 he was returned to the House of Representatives, representing the Democratic party. In 1913 President Wilson sent him to Mexico as his personal emissary. Lind died in 1930.

Lind praised the President's efforts to keep the country out of the war. In an address under the rubric, "Peace and War," delivered by Lind in 1916 in the Swedish Mission Covenant Church in Duluth, he stated that the American people should thank Providence that Wilson was in the White House and not Theodore Roosevelt.[7] "Had Roosevelt been elected we would be at war with Germany now."

Lind did not place the blame for the war on any of the involved countries but sought it rather in "the struggle in Wall Street." In a letter dated February 16, 1916, he wrote:[8]

> I naturally took a great deal of interest in the European war at the outset. But it is waning. My feelings have become callous. I read the reports of the daily murders in the same spirit and I fear with no greater sympathy than I bestow upon the heroes and the vanquished who struggle in Wall Street. [In fact?] the conviction is forcing itself more and more upon me that the European strife in spirit is not unlike the struggle in Wall Street. The instrumentalities employed for the accomplishment of results differ, but the end sought is very much the same.

Lind's conception of the reasons for the war was much like that of Charles Lindbergh. Both blamed the money hunger – "the masters of finance consider little else besides their own profits."[9]

After the USA had declared war on the Central Powers John Lind offered his services to the country. He stressed, however, that he could not sympathize with the war spirit as such, but called to mind that he had always opposed imperialism – economic as well as military. "In the present situation, however, I find myself in absolute accord with President Wilson and I feel that there can be no world fit to live in until the Prussian military machine is destroyed."[10] The German Kaiser had not given America any choice. "We were face to face with the alternative whether we should surrender our sovereignty and submit to Hohenzollern rule, or whether we should meet force with force."[11]

John Lind, in spite of his loyal backing of the war policy of the country, was by no means an uncontroversial person. John F. McGee,

[7] George Stephenson, *John Lind,* p. 531 ff; Lecture, October 9, 1916, in *John Lind Papers.*

[8] Letter to Dr. Wm. Bayard Hale, in *John Lind Papers.*

[9] Lecture, October 9, 1916, in *John Lind Papers.*

[10] Letter to Albert Steinhauser, February 18, 1918 *(John Lind Papers).*

[11] Speech, September 5—7, 1917 *(John Lind Papers).*

a Minneapolis lawyer and a member of the Minnesota Commission of Public Safety, believed that Lind was a Socialist, and that "slipperyness" was one of his characteristics.[12] The immediate reason for the confrontations, primarily with McGee, was that Lind disapproved of the Safety Commission's undue interference with individual persons and united groups. Lind resigned in March, 1918, because he disagreed with the activities of the Safety Commission. Before he resigned he had accepted a position with the Department of Labor.

Both Ernest Lundeen and Charles Lindbergh used the same argument against the American declaration of war as, for example, Senator Robert M. La Follette and Senator George Norris. Lundeen and Lindbergh insisted, like the other anti war spokesmen in Congress and in the pacifist movement, that the chief beneficiaries of American participation were the munitions – makers, and in general, the bankers and industrialists.[13] They challenged the President to submit the war bill to a vote of the people before the declaration of war went into effect.[14] They also criticized President Wilson's policies as unneutral and declared that the vast majority of Americans did not want to go to war. They saw a great democratic nation gradually forced into war, in spite of the manifest indifference or reluctance of the majority of its population. Characteristic for both Lundeen and Lindbergh and also for the congressmen of Norwegian descent mentioned here was that they represented states in the Middle West, which was the main centre for the opposition to the American participation in the war. It should, however, be emphasized that most Swedish Americans holding political office appeared to be loyal to the President and blamed the American intervention entirely on Germany.

5. *Swedish Foreign Policy – A Swedish-American Dilemma*

Judged by the reaction in the Swedish-American press, the American annoyance with Sweden also affected the Swedish Americans. Swedish

[12] O.A. Hilton, *The Minnesota Commission of Public Safety in World War I, 1917—1919,* p. 5.

[13] Senator George Norris from Nebraska argued that munitions-makers and bankers were instrumental in taking the country toward war. H.C. Peterson and Gilbert C. Fite, *op. cit.,* p. 5.

[14] *Ibid.,* p. 7.

Americans were particularly embarrassed by Sweden's part in the Luxburg incident, which American newspapers soon capitalized on by depicting Sweden as Germany's secret confederate.[1]

In September, 1917, the American Secretary of State, Robert Lansing, disclosed that the Swedish legation in Buenos Aires had forwarded a coded telegram to Berlin, via the Foreign Department in Stockholm, from the German ambassador to Argentina, Count K.L. von Luxburg. For several weeks the "Luxburg Affair," as the incident was soon called, made front page headlines in newspapers throughout the world. The Swedish government was accused of having broken its neutrality. Both the British and the American press made violent attacks against Sweden and its government.[2]

Since Swedish Americans had respected Sweden's policy of neutrality more than America's, they were now faced with finding an acceptable explanation for what had happened. While they deplored Sweden's involvement in such a "precarious misunderstanding"[3] they expressed their satisfaction with the explanation given by the Swedish government. In their opinion, the United States ought not to have complained over the telegram in the first place, since it enjoyed the same diplomatic privileges as Germany. Despite the vindication of the Swedish government, *Svenska Tribunen Nyheter* thought it had been too credulous in delivering the telegram without having the faintest notion of what it contained.[4] Nevertheless, *Augustana* still claimed that Sweden had honorably maintained its neutrality: "If an official in the diplomatic corps acts unwisely, the whole country should not be held responsible."[5]

John Lind expressed his concern for the future of Sweden in light of the Luxburg Affair. Speaking at a patriotic meeting in September, 1917, Lind said: "I was astonished to see that the Government of Sweden had permitted itself to become the lackey of the Kaiser."[6] He reminded his Swedish audience that even though they were born in Sweden

[1] V.Berger, "De svenskes villighet att ge efter" in *Allsvensk Samling,* November 15, 1919, p. 4.

[2] For further information about the Luxburg Affair I refer to an article in *The Journal of Modern History* (March, 1969), "Wartime Diplomacy and the Democratization of Sweden in September—October 1917," by Steven Koblik.

[3] *Svenska Kuriren,* September 20, 1917.

[4] *Svenska Tribunen Nyheter,* September 18, 1917.

[5] *Augustana,* October 11, 1917.

[6] *The Princeton Union,* September 13, 1917.

they were no longer Swedes. "As to us Americans of Swedish blood or descent, they are our friends in peace, aye, more than friends, for they are kindred. But in war, if such should come . . . they are enemies."

The Luxburg Affair received a more critical reception in New York than in Chicago. According to an article in *The New York Times,* some New York Swedes, "in a position to voice Swedish-American sentiment," declared that the Swedish government could not expect any sympathy from Americans of Swedish birth or ancestry who live in this city unless an explanation was submitted to the telegraph dispatch officials.[7] At a loyalty meeting on October 13, 1917, the New York Swedes condemned the Swedish government's tendency to allow itself to be used by the Germans.[8]

An editorial in *The New York Times* praised their strong condemnation of the Swedish government's handling of German telegrams: "These Swedes, in other words, have taken care to make evident and indubitable that when they swear allegiance to a Government other than the one under whose flag they were born they meant what they said to the full significance of the words used, and that their Americanism though new, is real, unqualified, and capable of standing the test of disagreement with official action in the old home."[9] This was one of the finest recognitions the Swedish Americans received during the entire First World War. *The New York Times'* editorial concluded by saying that if these Swedes had stayed at home and never emigrated to America they would most likely be among those who were now fighting pro-German forces in their country. The sharp condemnation of the Swedish government made by the New York Swedes deviated considerably from the reaction among other Swedish Americans. It is also doubtful whether the New York Swedes mentioned in *The New York Times* even spoke for their fellow countrymen in the same city. Aside from this particular article in the *Times* there are no other indications that Swedish Americans in New York reacted more strongly than those in other parts of America.

Swedish Americans asked themselves: What would happen if Sweden were dragged into the war on the side of Germany? Gustav A. Brandelle declared that in such a case Sweden would have to face the

[7] *The New York Times,* September 11, 1917, p. 2.

[8] *Ibid.,* October 14, 1917, p. 3.

[9] *Ibid.,* September 17, 1917, p. 12.

same opposition from its former countrymen as Germany had from the German Americans. He admitted it would be horrible if American soldiers of Swedish origin had to go to war with Sweden, but, he said, "not a single one would hesitate."[10] Ernst F. Pihlblad, president of Bethany College, likewise affirmed that Swedish Americans would not hesitate to bear arms "against any of their own blood who went over to the Central powers."[11] Such statements were undoubtedly intended to serve two purposes: first, to indicate that Swedish Americans were not the victims of divided loyalties; and second, to discourage Sweden from concluding an alliance with the Central Powers. In a confidential statement directed to "Our Leading Citizens of Swedish blood" Edwin Björkman, chairman of the Scandinavian section of the Committee on Public Information, requested articles to be published in Sweden. These were intended to help convince Sweden that Swedish Americans would not hesitate to bear arms against Sweden if it joined the war on the side of Germany.[12] Björkman asked the "leading citizens of Swedish blood" to do their share by giving him one or more articles. Arrangements were made to give all articles received the "greatest possible circulation in Sweden."

> ... the moment has come for a united effort by our citizens of Swedish blood to make the position of the United States understood in Sweden .... The moment has come at last, when all classes in Sweden should be willing to listen to us. Let us speak up – for their sake as well as for our own.

In order to reach a wider section of the Swedish-American public and better educate it on the deeper implications of the war, leading spokesmen made frequent appeals on behalf of Sweden's national

[10] *Förbundets Veckotidning,* May 7, 1918. Since Brandelle's speech was reproduced without comments on the editorial page of the paper, it is likely that the paper shared his views. The article was distributed to Swedish language papers by the Committee on Public Information. The Jamestown District annual report to the Central Swedish Conference of the Methodist Episcopal Church, 1917, expressed the hope "that our fatherland will not be involved in the world catastrophe. If that should unfortunately happen, I feel quite convinced the Swedish Americans will be faithful to their adopted country."

[11] Ernst Pihlblad, "Amerikas öde vårt eget öde." Article distributed by the Committee on Public Information, released August 5, 1918 (see special chapter on CPI, pp. 109 ff).

[12] The statement is not dated, but it is possible to conjecture that it was written before March 30, 1918.

interests. Senator Irvine L. Lenroot said that Swedes in the United States ought to be doubly committed to winning the war since Sweden, Norway, and Denmark were all threatened by Germany's tide of victory.[13] According to Lenroot these three countries had just as much to gain by an Allied victory as the United States itself, even if they maintained their neutrality throughout the war. In a statement published in *Svenska Tribunen Nyheter* on April 2, 1919, J.A.A. Burnquist, Governor of Minnesota, G.A. Andreen, president of Augustana College, and others, said that to a certain extent the war had been fought more for Sweden and its own independence than for any other country in the world.

6. *Language Restrictions During the War*

Although the Swedish Americans supported the American government during the war and refrained from criticism, they strongly resisted attempts to restrict the use of the Swedish language. They wondered how it was possible that "the sons of the far North," who had not only pioneered and settled America's frontiers but more than doubled its agricultural wealth, could now suddenly become objects of suspicion.[1] Before the war no serious objections had been raised to immigrants using and speaking their own languages. However, when Theodore Roosevelt called for a ban on all foreign language newspapers in 1918, immigrant spokesmen were shocked enough to describe the proposal as a "malicious insult." The immigrant communities in Iowa reacted with particular bitterness and resentment to a proclamation issued by their governor in the spring of 1918 which banned the public use of all foreign languages. *The Bohemian Review* called the governor's decision "Prussianism – not Americanism."[2] Never in his wildest moment of fantasy, said *Förbundets Veckotidning,* could any Swedish American have imagined that Austria's ultimatum to the Serbian government would eventually mean that he could not speak Swedish on the telephone in Iowa. The paper could not understand what all the high-handed sabre-rattling between Germany and America

[13] *Förbundets Veckotidning,* June 4, 1918. Lenroot's article was distributed by CPI.

[1] *Svenska Kuriren,* July 18, 1918.

[2] *The Bohemian Review,* June, 1918.

had to do with the Swedish language.[3] However, the paper was not consistent in its views. At the same time as it defended the right to use Swedish in the churches, it endorsed the rallying cry from Roosevelt: "Away with the German language! The English is good enough for the instruction in our schools and our public life. . . ." *Augustana* commented that it had always believed religious freedom in America entitled people to use the language "by which they may best worship God."[4] Edwin Björkman also deplored the Iowa governor's proclamation, and he feared it would make his work more difficult.[5] He advised George Creel to persuade President Wilson to intervene in the situation and call for the measure's withdrawal.

G.A. Brandelle regretfully pointed out that America was doing everything in its power to eliminate foreign languages from its midst.[6] In Nebraska the Synod could no longer conduct church schools in Swedish. All languages but English were forbidden in schools except on Saturdays and Sundays. In Brandelle's opinion all of these laws and regulations amounted to nothing more than a conscious intent to eradicate every language except English from the American scene.

Lauritz Larsen, the secretary of the National Lutheran Council, worked diligently to bring a halt to such anti-immigrant controls. Organized in September, 1918, the National Lutheran Council (NLC) brought together most of the Lutheran churches in America, including the Augustana Synod, for the purposes of defending mutual interests and co-ordinating the post-war activities of the various social and charitable agencies of the Church. Lauritz Larsen vigorously corresponded with the Council of National Defense in an attempt to persuade it to repudiate any and all moves to outlaw foreign languages

[3] *Förbundets Veckotidning,* June 11 and 25, 1918.

[4] *Augustana,* August 1, 1918, p. 496.

[5] Letter to George Creel, July 17, 1918. Björkman wrote, in part: "There can be no question of reaching all these people effectively, so as to make them integral parts of our national organism, by prohibiting them from using the only language with which they are familiar." Björkman's letter seems to have been written at the request of Harry Olson (letter to B. June 7, 1918) and E.G. Hjerpe, president of the Swedish Evangelical Mission Covenant of America, who had originally proposed such a letter.

[6] *Protokoll för Augustana synoden,* 1919, p. 26.

in America. He was convinced that such a ban would hinder the Americanization process.[7]

"In many of the western states, for instance, South Dakota, Nebraska, Texas, and others, the state and local Councils of Defense have been very unreasonable in their rules with reference to the use of the German language."[8] Larsen reminded public officials that it was unconstitutional to deprive certain people of the right to use the language they themselves preferred. When the Council of National Defense did not act on Larsen's suggestions he turned to the Commission of Education. "Our church is anxious to cooperate with any government departments in a sane program of Americanization, but it realizes that a great injustice has been done to many people . . . in the injudicious prohibition of the use of other than the English language in public worship."[9] Larsen considered the situation so serious that he requested a meeting with the Commission. The Commission replied that neither the Bureau of Education nor Department of the Interior could intervene in the matter, since it concerned questions over which the Federal government had no influence.[10]

The Iowa churches were particularly victimized by the governor's proclamation. Worried pastors appealed to the presidents of both the Augustana Synod and the Mission Covenant for advice. One pastor in the Covenant begged for help: "People weep because the Word of God has been taken from them and we are not able to communicate the gospel in English."[11] These hardships were somewhat alleviated by shifting or substituting pastors and by securing those from other states who could speak English. E.G. Hjerpe was confident that nothing would happen to congregations who continued to worship in Swedish.

[7] Letter to Council of National Defense, December 3, 1918.

[8] Letter to the head of the Council of National Defense, December 30, 1918.

[9] Letter dated January 18, 1919.

[10] Letter dated January 21, 1919.

[11] Details are gathered from the E.G. Hjerpe correspondence file in the Covenant Archives, in North Park College. A pastor in Iowa wrote to Hjerpe that he had tried to preach in English to the best of his ability, but, he wrote, "if there is no change, I and several of the older preachers will not be able to keep it up for any length of time . . .. It is a pity that the older people in the congregation are thus robbed of the most valuable thing they own." The minister who wrote the letter asked that he be transferred to some other congregation where he could preach in Swedish. (The letter is dated August 12, 1918.)

However, he advised against this in practice, because he feared that public opinion would drum up violent resentment.

The correspondence between Hjerpe and several pastors in Iowa reveals how risky it was to preach in Swedish.[12] One minister wrote that the governor presumably would not arrest anyone who disobeyed the injunction, "but the people round about us, yes, even some of our own members are ready to brand the minister as pro-German, and threaten to paint our churches yellow or to burn them, yes, even to gather a mob and force the pastor out of the community."[13]

Both the Augustana Synod and the Mission Covenant discussed the Iowa situation at their respective annual conferences. Each of them deplored the governor's decision but requested their pastors to obey it.[14] In its annual report for 1919, the Iowa Conference of the Augustana Synod declared it was hopeless to fight the edict, since it was a popular plan of the governor.[15] The Conference considered it clearly contrary to existing constitutional statutes, but, it declared, "in war time there seems to be a law stronger than all others, namely 'public opinion'." Nevertheless, it accepted the edict in the interests of patriotism and in compliance with the rule of law in America.

In a "resolution on the language question," the Mission Covenant hopefully predicted that the edict was only a temporary measure "which will undoubtedly be revoked."[16] However, it categorically opposed the edict and denied that any ban on the use of Swedish or other foreign languages in religious worship could ever be accepted as reasonable, sensible, or just. On the other hand, the Covenant took pains to dilute its criticism with a mixture of patriotism and good will: "Under all circumstances we must remember, even when we defend our personal and national rights to our mother tongue and other cultural heritage, that first and last we are Americans and good and loyal citizens, willing to sacrifice even such a precious possession as our language." The edict caused great damage to the work of the

[12] Letter from E.G. Hjerpe to one of the pastors in Iowa, August 14, 1918.

[13] Letter to David Nyvall, July 22, 1918, from the chairman of the Iowa Conference of the Covenant.

[14] *Mission Covenant Yearbook,* 1917—1918, p. 132.

[15] *Minutes of The Iowa Conference Annual Meeting,* 1919, p. 14 ff.

[16] *Mission Covenant Yearbook,* 1917—1918, pp. 22 and 23; *Förbundets Veckotidning,* June 25, 1918.

Covenant. "Our preaching and almost all of our literature is in Swedish," complained *Förbundets Veckotidning*. In effect, regular worship in Mission Covenant churches was paralyzed, for the majority of the congregation was unable to appreciate, let alone take active part in rituals and readings given in English.[17]

Förbundets Veckotidning attacked the efforts to eradicate all foreign languages from American society as a blunder which could only damage the nation's health and future development.[18] *Augustana* called it an "injustice" to deny certain citizens the right to hold their own worship services in the languages they themselves best understood. Moreover, it was especially unjust to deny them this right in the name of patriotism. It rejected the notion that an individual's patriotism could only be measured in terms of the language that he spoke.[19] *Augustana* also noted that the war had brought about a change of attitude in America toward immigrant languages. Before the war, it said, Americans ridiculed Swedes who forgot their own language before they had learned English. However, once war was declared, these same Americans grimly demanded in the name of religion and patriotism that the children of these immigrants learn English.[20] *Augustana* characterized the anti-immigrant crusade as the work of "petty souls and bigoted creatures."

The Swedish Methodists seemed to suffer particularly among the immigrant churches in the wake of the language restrictions. In fact, their own conferences faced the threat of either being dissolved or absorbed. *Sändebudet,* the leading newspaper of the Swedish Methodist Church, warned that the persecution of immigrant churches and their traditional forms of worship might force the American Methodist Church to take over the functions of the Swedish Methodist conferences and absorb their congregations.[1]

In Swedish-American circles S.G. Öhman was perhaps the strongest critic of the restrictions on foreign languages in public and religious

[17] *Ibid.,* July 9, 1918.

[18] *Ibid.,* July 30, 1918.

[19] *Augustana,* August 1, 1918, p. 496.

[20] *Augustana,* December 6, 1917, p. 800; February 20, 1919, p. 121 and April 3, 1919, p. 222; *The Lutheran Companion,* February 15, 1919, p. 76.

[1] *Sändebudet,* July 9, 1918. The newspaper was more fearful of the attitude of its own bishops to the fate of immigrant churches and conferences than it was of an outright government ban on all foreign languages.

life. "Some Americans have lost all sense," he wrote in 1918.[2] "They prattle and scribble a mess of nonsense in the name of patriotism and misuse their temporary authority." He further maintained that each American immigrant group had a right to its own existence, and he deplored the fact that the war had caused the "melting pot" to boil over. However, he did not believe that American immigrants were ultimately in danger of losing their heritage and traditions. "For whatever is worth being melted down can naturally not be rooted up." David Nyvall also voiced protest over the restrictions. He suspected that party politics and cloakroom intrigues were behind the Iowa governor's proclamation. He particularly accused the Republicans of trying to win votes in the election by relying on the fanatical oratory of Theodore Roosevelt for a highly flavored, patriotic campaign slogan which would be music to the ears of English speaking Americans.[3]

7. *The Swedish Americans and the Committee on Public Information*

While Swedish language newspapers were muffling their criticism of the American war effort and Swedish Americans were keeping an eye on one another, the entire Swedish-American community was exposed to an intensively organized program of indoctrination. Instead of wasting any more words on the German military aristocracy, leaflets and broadsides called attention to the reasons for American intervention and presented its war aims in terms of a crusade for moral diplomacy.[1] The Scandinavian section of the Committee on Public Information (CPI), under the leadership of its chairman, Edwin Björkman, was directly responsible for propaganda efforts among Swedish

[2] S.G. Öhman, *Augustanasynodens självständighetsförklaring*, p. 101 ff.

[3] Letter dated June 14, 1918, to Erik Dahlhielm, former editor of *Veckobladet*. Nyvall even toyed with the idea of organizing a new political party. "I would want to call the party The New Democracy, and draw a large part of its platform from the President's ideas and from the English Labor Party's program. If anything like that could come about, I believe I would yet become interested in politics and become, as it were, a native American."

[1] Gustav E. Johnson, "The Swedes of Chicago," p. 58.

Americans.[2] The CPI was organized immediately after the United States entered the war and was then directed by George Creel. Its main purpose was to create and distribute propaganda favorable to the American war effort. It commissioned artists and illustrators to mass produce patriotic posters and other material for public consumption. A special Foreign Language Division of the CPI took charge of the "indoctrination" of foreign-born citizens. Congress officially terminated the functions of the CPI on June 30, 1919.

[2] George Creel, *How We Advertised America. The First Telling of the Committee on Public Information That Carried the Gospel of Americanism to Every Corner of the Globe* (N.Y., 1920); James Mock and Cedric Larson,*Words That Won the War. The Story of the Committee on Public Information, 1917—1919* (Princeton, 1936). Edwin Björkman is listed on the CPI payroll of January 5, 1918. During the two previous years, B. had been in Sweden working directly under the British Foreign Office. In his letter to George Creel in which he applied for appointment as head of the Scandinavian division, B. said that after the American declaration of war he felt "obliged" to offer his services to that country. Returning to the United States, he decided that the "time has come for me to look for a definite connection with the great movement for a national awakening — a movement which, I am sorry to notice, has not yet gathered anything like the speed and strength required if we are to bring the war to a successful finish within reasonable time." Born in Sweden but raised in America, Björkman considered himself qualified to handle the Scandinavian Division. He particularly prized his own understanding of pro-German sympathies and propaganda carried on by Swedish Americans. Moreover, it is clear from his correspondence with Creel that he was anxious to be appointed to this post. Now and then one is given the impression that it was not only the noble motives sketched in his application which prompted him to seek the appointment. In a letter dated January 18, 1918, he wrote: "Rank, title, position, authority play a tremendous part with all people of the Swedish race." Against that background it was desirable for him to have a title so that people might realize that the American government was backing his "mission." His work among the Swedish Americans indicates that he took pleasure in speaking as the representative of the government.

One correspondent points out that the campaign against foreign languages was not led by the wisest and most intelligent of individuals but by a crowd of reckless hotheads and bureaucrats. One Swedish American — and here only Björkman can be the intended target — "has during the time of the language persecutions particularly, made himself painfully obnoxious. . . . It was said, of course, that what was done, was done in the interest of the service, but he certainly loved to do what he did. Several Swedish-American papers were threatened with strangulation if they dared publish anything derogatory of him; he went further in his zeal than even the chief of the bureau in which he was serving." *(Allsvensk Samling,* October 1, 1919, p. 4.)

Edwin Björkman's foremost contribution, however, was the organizing of the John Ericsson League of Patriotic Service on March 4, 1918, the purpose of which was to co-ordinate the patriotic work of the Swedish Americans. Its headquarters were established in Chicago. According to its program prospectus, the organization had four main purposes: to support the national war policy; to act as the connecting link for all patriotic activity among the Swedes in the United States; to work for national unity; and to improve relationships between the United States and Sweden.

The John Ericsson Leauge was almost identical with the Scandinavian Division of the CPI, as indicated by both organizations' programs and agendas. It can be assumed that Edwin Björkman intended to accomplish his task in the CPI through the John Ericsson League. He perhaps believed that Swedish Americans would respond more enthusiastically to the League than to the CPI. Björkman's correspondence shows that he tried to communicate with his countrymen through the John Ericsson League. His contacts with Swedish Americans were almost exclusively limited to members of the League.[3]

Björkman's major responsibilities in CPI were the following: a) to stimulate Swedish Americans' wholehearted support of the American war effort; b) to accelerate the full assimilation and Americanization of Swedish Americans; c) to convince Sweden of America's high-minded and altruistic motives in the war, in order to promote friendship between the two countries both during and after the war.[4] According to the principles enunciated by Björkman, the Scandinavian Division of CPI should avoid presenting Swedish Americans as disloyal or unpatriotic, since this would only make its work more difficult. The overall intention was to persuade Swedish Americans to abandon the Swedish language, although for the time being they might continue

[3] *Chicago Examiner* and *Chicago Herald,* March 5, 1918; *Svenska Kuriren,* March 7, 1918. When the League was organized, the following officials were elected: Harry Olson, chief justice of the Municipal Court of Chicago, Chairman; Harry A. Lund, collector of Customs in Minneapolis, vice chairman; Edwin Björkman, secretary; Henry B. Henschen, director of the State Bank of Chicago, treasurer. Several honorary members were also elected: Ex-Governors John Lind and A.O. Eberhart, and Governor J.A.A. Burnquist. Besides the central office in Chicago, there were branches in New York, Minneapolis, and San Francisco.

[4] Letter to George Creel from Björkman, January 3, 1918, in which B. restated what he considered to be his task. The part of B's work alluded to in point *c* is not included here as it is outside the limits of this study.

to use Swedish without "hesitation" if this would improve contacts and communications with CPI.

In order to convince Swedish Americans that the war was necessary, Björkman requested leading Swedes in the United States to write articles for the Swedish-language papers which would then be distributed by the CPI. Such articles all shared a common theme: Germany was wholly to blame for the war, while the United States was valiantly fighting "in the name of humanity"; Germany had a long history of ruthless violence and deceitful intrigue, while America's rise as a nation was based on the advancement of humanity and liberty.[5] In sum, the United States did not seek to gain any territorial conquests nor any economic advantages in this war. Articles constantly appeared in the Swedish language papers asking the question, "Why are we in the war?" – and the answer was always the same: "We are fighting in behalf of liberty."

In his attempts to win the confidence of the Swedish Americans and convince them to show their best patriotic colors, Björkman kept a careful eye on them and scrutinized every statement that showed the least bit of uncertainty about the war. He was not always satisfied with his countrymen, although he publicly commended their patriotism. In his correspondence with George Creel he expressed his displeasure with the Augustana Synod and its lack of enthusiasm for the ideals for

[5] P.M. Magnuson, *Our Civilization, Democracy and the War* (St. Cloud, Minn., 1918), p. 22 ff. Magnuson was a professor of sociology in the State Normal School, St. Cloud, Minn. M. stressed repeatedly that the U.S. fought for higher ideals: "We have more than a mere national interest in this war. It is not only to save America that we go to battle — it is to save civilization, to save humanity." The Swedish-American press took up the same refrain once it finally accepted the declaration of war as an unalterable fact. *Augustana,* which had long been one of the most faithful champions of Germany's cause, asserted on April 18, 1918 (p. 282), that "the United States went to war on behalf of humanity's freedom and rights which are the greatest values on earth." — *Augustana Observer,* May, 1917 (p. 151), commented: "For this nation it is not a territorial war, for territory we have enough. It centers itself around something greater than territory — the principles of equality, liberty and justice." It has not been possible to determine the number of editorial articles distributed by CPI, nor to what extent these were used by the papers. Although we know that the newspapers generally accepted a certain number of these articles, it is impossible to determine which principles were used in selecting them.

which America fought.[6] However, he did not always exercise the greatest discretion in his surveillance of the Swedish-American press. There were instances in which his interference was totally irrelevant and uncalled for and inevitably led to disagreements with the editors in question. For example, an article by A.M.L. Herenius in *Ungdomsvännen* for March, 1918, entitled "Svensk Reformation," provoked Björkman's displeasure and interference on the grounds that it contained a great deal of "objectionable" material. Although the article was completely unrelated to the war, Björkman justified his action by charging that it displayed pro-German sympathies. In a letter to Gustav Andreen, he wrote that the article was contrary to regulations. He said that he had first thought of immediately reporting *Ungdomsvännen* to authorities in Washington, but since the Swedish Lutheran Church was already under close surveillance and his main task was that of uniting "our weak and straying elements," he decided that such a report would only cause more harm than good.

In a letter to George Creel, Björkman gave an account of his intervention against *Ungdomsvännen* and declared that if the Lutheran church could not guarantee that such an incident would not happen again, he would immediately report the paper to Washington and recommend "that the action taken be as severe as possible."[7] The Augustana Synod felt compelled to take some action in order to satisfy Björkman. The April issue of *Ungdomsvännen* announced that Carl J. Bengston hade now replaced Ernst W. Olson as editor.

Some months later the editor of *Svea* fell out of grace with Björkman. *Svea* had printed the contents of a speech given by Björkman on April 8, 1918, at an open-air meeting of Swedish Americans in Worcester, Massachusetts. Not only was Björkman furious at the way his speech was reported, but *Svea* itself expressed strong disapproval of Björkman's oratory, particularly the following: "and since the treachery no longer goes on in open daylight, it sneaks around at least at night whispering falsehoods into ears which are open. Sometimes it speaks with a German tongue; sometimes, I am sorry to say, it speaks Swedish."[8] In *Svea's* opinion, Björkman's comments were highly

[6] Letters from Björkman to Creel, March 28 and April 25, 1918; Letter from Björkman to Gustav Andreen, March, 1918; The article appeared in *Ungdomsvännen,* March, 1918.

[7] Letter to George Creel from E. Björkman, March 28, 1918.

[8] *Svea,* April 10, 1918.

improper and implicitly suggested that Swedish Americans were traitors. It said the accusation was totally false and commented that "Swedish Americans are neither blackguards nor traitors." Enraged by this commentary, Björkman asked George Creel to take retaliatory measures against the newspaper on his behalf. He specifically asked that *Svea's* permit to publish untranslated articles – Permit 273 – be immediately revoked. Björkman justified his indignation by saying that the editor of *Svea,* Karl G. Fredin, had purposely intended to disrupt his work in the CPI and discredit him personally.[9]

Björkman's attacks on *Svea* and *Ungdomsvännen* were two examples of the arbitrary manner in which the foreign language press was constantly harassed during the war. There was nothing in the articles of either newspaper which could possibly have been interpreted as un-American or unpatriotic.[10] *The Chicago Herald* praised those who had taken the initiative in forming the John Ericsson League at a time when Germany was encroaching upon their native country.[11] Through the League, said the *Herald,* "patriotic" Swedes assisted both the United States and their former fatherland.

8. *Liberty Bonds – a Measure of Patriotism*

The sale of Liberty Bonds was an important part of the war policy. The war was financed through loans obtained from the public.[1] Four Liberty Loan drives and one Victory Loan Compaign were conducted.

[9] Letter from Björkman to Creel, April 17, 1918.

[10] In his letter to Creel (note 9) Björkman makes several erroneous statements. For example, he mistakenly writes Fredin's first name as Edward instead of Karl; he asserts that Fredin's pro-German sympathies led to his dismissal as editor and his replacement by Reuben Heidenblad — which is incorrect, since Heidenblad was *Svea's* editor from the beginning of the war until April, 1918, when Fredin took over.

[11] *Chicago Herald,* March 6, 1918, p. 8.

[1] Theodore Calvin Pease, *The Story of Illinois,* pp. 226—240; Marguerite E. Jenison, *The War-Time Organization of Illinois,* pp. 187—223. The sale of war bonds was handled by the War Loan Organization of the Treasury Department formed in April, 1917. It administered its work through separate committees in the various federal reserve districts, which in turn established local committees. Each local district was allotted a definite quota in relation to its population, the economic conditions of the locality, and several other factors. The War Loan

The first sale of Liberty Bonds began on March 14, 1917.[2] For those on the home front, the number of Liberty Bonds they bought became a measuring gauge of their patriotism and resulted in competition between different national minorities. In order to reach those who did not understand English, special foreign language committees were organized, which in turn were divided into separate branches according to nationality. In the city of Chicago, which was a member of the Federal Reserve District Seven, the Swedes had a well organized branch in the Foreign Language Division. Its chairman was Henry S. Henschen, the prominent banker, founder of the State Bank of Chicago and Swedish vice consul. Circulars and pamphlets urged the Swedes to buy Liberty Bonds. "Prominent" Chicago Swedes appealed to their countrymen to respond in such a way as to kill any rumors of disloyalty. In full-page newspaper advertisements the Swedish branch committee exhorted Swedes to participate:

> Do your duty; show your true Americanism by buying United States government Liberty Bonds. Do your part in assisting this the greatest nation on earth to reach the goal it has set – to liberate the world from autocracy.[3]

Such advertisements were often re-enforced by editorial comments; readers were requested to accept the sacrifices the war demanded of them.

The Swedish-American papers seem to have completely accepted the Liberty Loans as a legitimate way of financing the war. All of them provided space for promotional advertisements and urged their readers to show their patriotism as actively as possible. *Svenska Tribunen Nyheter* summed up its own contribution during the war as follows: "Week after week the columns of our paper have been open for

Organization became an effective propaganda machine by printing posters, arranging competitions, sending out speakers, and so forth. Its methods were not always democratic. In certain places, the local committees decided on specific individual quotas and if the persons in question were unwilling to pay they were coerced into doing so.

[2] The second Liberty Loan was dated November, 1917; the third May, 1918; and the fourth September, 1918.

[3] *Svenska Tribunen Nyheter,* October 16, 1917.

articles and announcements of war loans and collections of contributions, and for communications, requests and appeals to the people from the government."[4] *Svenska Socialisten* was actually the only paper reluctant to provide space for the Liberty Loans. When the Swedish Liberty Loan Committee of Chicago wrote to the paper requesting it to insert a full-page advertisement for the Liberty Bonds, it was told that in so doing *Svenska Socialisten* would only be opening up its columns for war propaganda.[5] However, the paper's board of directors gradually gave way to the idea, mainly because they did not want to risk the paper's existence. The advertisement was printed without comment.

When the First Liberty Loan was announced, a group of leading Chicago Swedes made newspaper appeals asking Swedes to sign up immediately for the bonds.[6] Mass meetings were held where speaker after speaker praised the Liberty Loans. The advertisements warned that Abraham Lincoln's and John Ericsson's principles were being threatened by the war. Those unable to risk life and blood could show their patriotism by buying Liberty Bonds.[7]

According to *Svenska Kuriren* there were perhaps more patriotic rallies held in Chicago during the month of June, 1918, than at any

[4] *Svenska Tribunen Nyheter,* January 1, 1919.

[5] Henry Bengston, *Skandinaver på vänsterflygeln i USA,* p. 119. Interview with Bengston, September 25, 1967.

[6] *Svenska Kuriren,* May 31, 1917. The paper sought to impress its readers with the idea that buying bonds was not only a civic duty but also a good investment. *Svenska Tribunen Nyheter* endorsed the Second Liberty Loan in three separate editorials: November 6, 16, and 23, 1917.

[7] *Svenska Kuriren,* April 18, 1918. In an address given at Willmar, Minn., on April 5, 1918, Gustaf F. Johnson, pastor of the Swedish Tabernacle in Minneapolis, said that those who had not enlisted in the service of their country ought to buy bonds in order to insure the victory over Germany. For if Germany did win the war, it would only exact war damages from the United States, since neither England nor France would be in a position to make payments. Therefore, in his opinion, it was better to spend money on victory than to "give it away and receive a thrashing." (Gustaf F. Johnson, "A Glorious Duty" — a lecture. A summary of the lecture was published in Swedish by the Minnesota State Commission on Public Safety, 1918).

previous time in the history of Swedes in that city.[8] The Swedish section of the Illinois War Savings Committee took the initiative in arranging these rallies and were reportedly successful in their efforts. At one of the mass meetings held by Swedish-American women in Chicago $3,459 worth of bonds were purchased.

During the Third and Fourth Liberty Loan campaigns of May and September, 1918, sales competition among minority groups was more pronounced and better organized than in previous years. Special forms were issued which provided columns for registering purchasers' nationalities or native origins. When the Third Liberty Bonds were put on sale, the Swedish War Savings Committee sent out a circular in which it expressed the hope that Swedes would show their patriotic spirit and rally to the cause.[9] *Svenska Tribunen Nyheter* urged its readers to show that Swedish Americans really were "what prominent Americans have declared them to be: namely the best citizens in America."[10]

According to the figures published by the Treasury Department, immigrant groups purchased 17.4 percent of all bonds sold for the

[8] *Svenska Kuriren,* April 25 and June 27, 1918.

[9] The circular is dated April 15. Another circular, issued on April 22, made a similar appeal: "Time is short. The measure of our patriotism is now being taken in every part of this great state. . . . We must see to it that when this job is completed and anyone has the hardihood to use an interrogation point in discussing our loyalty, the record we now make will be a convincing and everlasting answer."

[10] *Svenska Tribunen Nyheter,* March 12 and 26, 1918.

Third Liberty Loan.[11] Since these groups made up only 13.2 percent of the total population of the United States, they more than filled their

[11] Information submitted by the Treasury Department. According to the Department's published statistics on the Third Liberty Loan, the various immigrant nationalities bought bonds in the following percentage amounts:

Sale of the Third Liberty Loan by nationality (millions of dollars)

Nationality	Millions of dollars	% of total number of bonds bought by foreign-born	% of all foreign-born
Germans	87.3	21.4	12.1
Italians	52.3	13.8	11.6
Poles	37.6	9.2	8.2
Czechs	31.8	7.7	2.6
Jews	16.7	4.1	—
Hungarians	8.3	2.0	2.9
Greeks	6.8	1.7	—
Swedes	6.0	1.5	4.5
Norwegians	6.0	1.5	2.6
Lithuanians	4.3	1.1	1.0
Yugoslavs	4.2	1.0	1.2
Russians	2.6	0.6	10.1
Danes	2.4	0.6	1.4
Frenchmen	2.1	0.5	1.1
Englishmen	0.3	0.1	5.8

The figures do not show the total sums subscribed by the foreign-born except in cases where it has been possible to identify the purchasers. According to the Treasury Department, more than seven million "foreigners" bought bonds to a total value of 741.4 million dollars. The Table records only about 270 million dollars, that is, about one third of the total value given by the Department. This means that the Table should be used with care. The Table is somewhat misleading in that it ignores any distinction between Jews of different nationalities. If it had made such a distinction, it is quite likely that the Russians would have received a much larger quota of the number of bonds bought. (Source: *New York Times,* September 5, 1918, p. 13.) *Svenska Kuriren* insisted in its issue of September 19, 1918, that the Swedish-American statistics were altogether too low; it believed they were really four times as large. *Svenska Tribunen Nyheter* declared on June 4, 1918, that through their participation in the Third Liberty Loan the Swedish Americans had conclusively demonstrated their patriotism and that all rumors which questioned their loyalty should now cease.

quota. Compared with other immigrant groups, the Swedes ranked fairly low on the list in total contributions. The Norwegians, Danes, Czechs, and Hungarians all purchased more bonds than the Swedes. The Czechs and Germans respectively bought the most bonds *per capita* of all immigrant groups.

The nation-wide statistics on bond sales largely correspond to those reported for the Chicago area. However, the Chicago Swedes appear to have made a better showing than their countrymen in other parts of the United States. This may have been due to the efficient propaganda machinery they had set up in Chicago.[12]

When it was revealed that one third of the bonds purchased by immigrant groups in the Third Liberty Loan campaign could not be traced back for identification, the Swedish Committee for the Fourth Liberty Loan energetically appealed to Swedes when buying bonds to register their purchases in the name of the "Swedish Division," in order that the real participation of Swedish Americans would be un-

[12] According to the Foreign Language Division for the Liberty Bond campaign, immigrant residents of the Seventh Federal Reserve District of Chicago bought the following percentage amounts of bonds in the Third Liberty Loan drive (sales in millions of dollars):

Nationality	Millions of dollars	% of total number of foreign-born in Chicago
Poles	5.6	17.0
Czechs	5.6	6.2
Germans	5.1	13.9
Italians	3.3	7.3
Swedes	3.0	7.2
Jews	2.4	—
Greeks	1.7	1.4
Yugoslavs	1.6	1.2
Lithuanians	1.4	2.3
Norwegians	1.3	2.5
Hungarians	1.0	3.2
Russians	0.4	12.6

Source: *Chicago Tribune,* May 2, 1918, p. 9.

failingly recorded.[13] In a letter to the *Chicago Tribune,* Oliver A. Linder, editor of *Svenska Amerikanaren,* complained that thousands of Swedes had bought bonds without properly registering their nationality.[14] When the Fourth Liberty Loan bonds were put on sale, the Swedish language press stepped up its propaganda campaign. Full-page advertisements and editorials alerted Swedes to their obligations as American citizens. This new campaign drive was clearly designed to be more competitive in spirit than ever before.[15]

The end of the Fourth Liberty Loan campaign marked the close of a hectic period of patriotic fervor which broke out after the American declaration of war. However, the Swedish-American press continued to urge its readers to purchase government bonds during the so-called Victory Loan drive. There was a new tone to these appeals in contrast to the war-time propaganda which had stressed an active display of patriotism by Swedes to their adopted homeland. When the Victory Loan was announced, there was a special appeal in *Svenska Tribunen Nyheter* to those who either were born in Sweden or were of Swedish descent saying that the war had been fought more "for Sweden – for its institutions, its independence and its political existence, than for any other country in the world."[16] It was said that by buying bonds Swedish Americans could explicitly show how much they loved Sweden.

If one accepts the notion that the sale of Liberty Bonds was an accurate measure of purchasers' patriotism, then it can be broadly

[13] *Svenska Kuriren,* October 3, 1918. The newspaper argued that if immigrant purchasers registered their national origins, sales totals would be comparatively higher than during the Third Liberty Loan campaign. Other nationalities besides the Swedes were equally as anxious to have their particular contributions registered. (Norman O. Jung, "Chicago's Foreign Language Press in World War I," p. 79.)

[14] *Chicago Tribune,* May 1, 1918, p. 9.

[15] *Svenska Kuriren,* October 3, 1918; *Augustana,* October 3, 1918, p. 640; *Svenska Tribunen Nyheter,* September 25 and October 19, 1918. The Swedish Liberty Loan Committee of Chicago ordered from the Committee on Public Information a total of 100,000 pamphlets in Swedish on the Fourth Liberty Loan. The CPI printed a total of 256,000 pamphlets for nation-wide distribution (War Loan Organization's records in the National Archives).

[16] *Svenska Tribunen Nyheter,* April 2, 1919. The public appeal was signed by J.A.A. Burnquist and G.A. Andreen among others.

stated that the foreign-born carried more than their share of the burdens of the war. Their contributions were praised by all official sources and spokesmen. Even the foreign language press was commended for its willingness to co-operate in the campaign.[17] The United States Treasury Department acknowledged that the foreign language press had performed an immense patriotic service during the war years.[18]

It is which should be stressed, however, obviously impossible to evaluate the patriotism of minority groups on the basis of the number of Liberty Bonds they purchased. In many cases they bought bonds only because they dared not do otherwise. Their actions were carefully watched by authorities, and those who refused to buy bonds were branded as unpatriotic Americans. Since all purchases were registered, it was easy to identify those who did not buy bonds. This particularly applied to residents of small towns and communities. Many bought bonds whether they wanted to or not merely because they feared reprisals. Thus, the sales statistics for Liberty Bonds cannot be relied upon to give any satisfactory or accurate evaluation of the immigrants' patriotism. It is not the number of bonds purchased by various minorities which is important but rather the enormous propaganda activity carried on by these minorities in order to persuade their own countrymen to buy bonds. Notably enough, the organizers and supporters of the various promotional appeals and advertising campaigns attached great importance to the registering of each minority's contribution. In the case of the Swedish Americans, for example, promoters were eager to have the total participation of the "Swedes" clearly indicated. On certain occasions this became such an over-riding concern that one almost suspects that Swedes were urged to buy bonds more for reasons of ethnic prestige than for the declared aim of assisting the war effort.

[17] Nathaniel Whitney, *The Sale of War Bonds in Iowa* (Iowa City, 1923), p. 2. Hans Rieg, head of the Foreign Language Division of the War Loan Organization, highly praised the foreign-born (*The New York Times,* April 13, 1918, part III, p. 6).

[18] *Svenska Tribunen Nyheter,* February 5, 1919 and January 7, 1920.

9. *Swedes in American Uniforms*

The best way for anyone to prove his patriotism was to enlist and fight on the European front. Those who were selected for military service could always point to their contribution whenever their loyalty was challenged. After the declaration of war in April, 1917, government officials were faced with the problem of deciding whether "aliens" should be required to perform military service even if they were not American citizens. Congress solved this problem by passing the Selective Service Act on May 18, 1917, which made military service mandatory for all men between the ages of 21 and 30.[1] However, it exempted all aliens who had not declared their intention of becoming American citizens. The Selective Service Act was so unpopular that Congress passed a new law in July, 1918, which excused from military service those aliens who had already received the first of their citizenship papers but stipulated that all of those who chose this option would be permanently barred from obtaining full citizenship status.

The Selective Service Act provided but few loopholes, and therefore it is impossible accurately to evaluate minority group patriotism on the basis of military service. Those who refused to enter the country's service were penalized and exposed to serious reprisals at the hands of militant groups of patriots and nationalists throughout the country. There were only a few examples of "slackers" among the Swedish Americans and, for that matter, among the American population as a whole. This probably had more to do with the enactment of compulsory military service than any private individual's attitudes toward the war.[2] It is unlikely that significant numbers of Swedish Americans had become so disenchanted with the United States that they would have gone so far as to refuse to perform military service. In this light it is obvious that a minority group's patriotism cannot be evaluated solely

[1] *Report of the Provost Marshal General to the Secretary of War on the First Draft under the Selective Service Act,* p. 5; *Second Report of the Provost Marshal General to the Secretary of War,* p. 88.

[2] *Augustana* (September 5, 1918, p. 576) advised those who questioned the patriotism of the Swedish Americans to take note of all the Swedish young men who had entered the service of the country: "they have shown the best aspects of true patriotism much better than all the spasmodic exhibits making much noise but accomplishing little."

in terms of the number of men it offered to the ranks of the American armed forces.

There were very few immigrants in America who leapt at the chance of avoiding military service by giving up the hope of securing citizenship. According to a Labor Department report, 1,692 persons turned in their "first papers." Most of these were Scandinavians – 738 Swedes, 479 Norwegians, and 68 Danes.[3] It should be added that these statistics applied only to citizens of neutral countries. In view of the fact that nearly one hundred thousand (99,995) Swedes were registered and a total of 48,173 had obtained their first citizenship papers, the percentage of those who took the advantage of avoiding military service was hardly a staggering one.

Even though only a few Swedes made use of the possibility to avoid military service, their numbers were sufficiently large to draw the attention of the newspapers. An article in *Svenska Amerikanaren* reported that a total of 1,745 persons, mostly Scandinavians, had turned in their "first papers." In its opinion, such statistics might signify a severe indictment of Swedish Americans if people were not informed that the majority of those involved were "newly arrived fanatical anti-militarists."[4] The article caused several readers to react against the

[3] *Hearings before the Committee on Immigration and Naturalization, Sixty-Sixth Congress, First Session:* "Proposed deportation of aliens who surrendered their first papers in order to escape military service," pp. 28, 29. The Army Appropriation Act of July 9, 1918, stipulated: "That a citizen or subject of a country neutral in the present war who has declared his intention to become a citizen of the United States shall be relieved from liability to military Service upon his making a declaration, in accordance with such regulations as the President may prescribe, withdrawing his intention to become a citizen of the United States, which shall operate and be held to cancel his declaration of intention to become an American citizen, and he shall forever be barred from becoming a citizen of the United States." V. Berger expressed his surprise over statistics which showed that Swedish Americans comprised a "considerable majority" among the total number of immigrants who returned their "first papers." An investigation revealed that these "slackers" were young socialists who had recently emigrated from Sweden. The crowning blow came when sixteen such Swedes in Jamestown, N.Y., who had returned their "first papers," were declared by the court as totally unworthy of American citizenship. In printing its news coverage of this episode, a New York newspaper placed it on the first page within a dark-ruled border and set above it in capital letters the headline "Swedes." *(Allsvensk Samling,* November 15, 1919, p. 4).

[4] *Svenska Amerikanaren,* October 23 and November 20, 1919.

paper's discussion of the question. *Svenska Amerikanaren* replied by saying that it could not see why it should hush up these reports, and it added that Swedish Americans had undeniably been given "a black eye." *Svenska Kuriren* considered the editorial in *Svenska Amerikanaren* to be in bad taste,[5] since the Swedes who returned their first papers had only made use of one of their legal rights.

The New York Times also took up the issue of military service among Swedish Americans and reported that by April, 1918, approximately 700 Swedes had requested the American government for exemption from military service. According to the paper "several thousands" had turned to the Swedish consulates in the same matter.[6]

The General Conscription Act of May, 1917, was received with mixed feelings. Those who had emigrated from Sweden in order to escape compulsory military service hardly appreciated the Selective Service Act. Those Swedes who had joined American socialist organizations were particularly bitter. In some circles there was talk about refusing to register, an idea that soon began to be discussed in the Scandinavian Socialist Union.[7] Some members of the Union considered adopting the idea but did not gain the support of the leadership. A preponderant majority of the Union members in Chicago concluded

[5] *Svenska Kuriren,* November 27, 1919.

[6] *The New York Times,* April 19, 1919, p. 11. Toward the end of January, 1918, most Swedish-American papers contained a communication under the heading "Information from the Swedish Consulates," in which it was stated that the Swedish Legation in Washington, with help from the various Swedish consulates throughout the country, would submit to the President petitions from Swedish citizens in the United States asking exemption from American military service. This reportedly concerned Swedish subjects who had not in any way applied for citizenship as well as Swedish subjects who had taken out their "first papers." The communication stated that Swedish subjects who had taken out their "first papers" were still required to do military service but that President Wilson considered granting exemption to Swedes who so desired. At the time this article was printed by *The New York Times,* the Army Appropriation Act had not yet been adopted, which is the reason why Swedes did not know that by returning their "first papers" they would forever lose any chance of obtaining American citizenship. If the statement in *The New York Times* is correct, it may be the reason why only 738 Swedes made use of the chance of being released from military service.

[7] Henry Bengston, *Skandinaver på vänsterflygeln i USA,* p. 113 ff. The statements were further substantiated in an interview with the author of this book.

that peace could not be won by illegal means. This opinion was shared by most of those liable to be drafted, except those who were members of the Socialist Club in Rockford. On the day of registration, June 7, 1917, 138 young men in Rockford were arrested for refusing to register, most of them Swedes. When brought to court a few days later, they were given the maximum penalty: one year in jail.

The Rockford incident aroused much attention, especially among the Swedes, and people were surprised that anything like that could happen in Rockford with its high percentage of Swedish residents. When it later became publicly known that 35 Swedes had been arrested in Belvidere (Ill.) the same day, many Swedes naturally became apprehensive over the consequences this might have for the Swedish-American community. The refusal to register was described as deplorable, regrettable, and, for the Swedish Americans, disastrous; there was no defense for such behavior. *The Lutheran Companion* found comfort in the fact that those who had refused to register were not American citizens, and thus would be deported as soon as they had served out their penalty.[8]

Information about the so-called slackers is very scanty both in newspapers and in official sources. Evidently the number of slackers was generally very low. Where they did appear it seems their own countrymen were more disturbed than the cases warranted. The Rockford incident, involving the arrest of a number of Swedes for refusing to register, does not seem to have attracted the attention of the American public to any significant extent. Undoubtedly, the fear of reprisals among the Chicago Swedes has been exaggerated. Several of the Swedish-American newspapers seemed to be working on the principle that it was better to anticipate such incidents than be caught flat-footed when they did occur, and thus they sharply condemned this incident in advance. On the other hand, the American papers had very little to say or report on slackers among Swedish Americans. *The New York Times* and *Chicago Tribune,* both of which have been carefully researched, devoted no more space to this matter beyond what has already been mentioned.[9]

[8] *The Lutheran Companion,* May 11, 1918, p. 234.

[9] The author has investigated the matter in *The New York Times* and *Chicago Tribune* for the years 1917 and 1918. To what extent smaller local papers were

The information from the various "draft boards" in Illinois is more illuminating than the statistical material. After the war the War Records Section sent out a questionnaire to all local draft boards in the state of Illinois.[10] This questionnaire took up the questions of military service and war sentiment among the foreign-born. Three questions in particular were asked about the foreign-born: Which nationalities resided within your registration area? What were their attitudes toward the war and military service? Did their attitudes change during the war?

The foreign-born were generally described as reluctant to perform military service. However, the Swedes appear to have been particularly reluctant to do so whether they were residents of cities or rural communities.[11]

more observant of the nationality of individual slackers has not been investigated. Judging by the Swedish-American papers, which usually took notice of and commented on attacks against their own countrymen, there was very little said in print about slackers — at least about Swedish slackers.

[10] The State Council of Defense, in the summer of 1918, appointed a special committee for the purpose of collecting and preserving all material relating to the war. This material was then to be preserved in the Illinois State Historical Library in Springfield. In July, 1919, the work of the special committee was taken over by the War Records Section of the Library where the material is now kept, although it is not yet organized and indexed.

[11] Only those local draft boards which indicated that Swedes or Scandinavians resided within their jurisdiction have been consulted in connection with this study. A few of the answers are reproduced here:

Local Board No. 77 answered: 1) Holland, Dutch, Greeks and Swedes; 2) All nationalities were strongly opposed to entering the service and made the most ridiculous claims to avoid service. Some of them actually surrendered their first citizenship papers; 3) Positively not.

Local Board No. 58: 1) The principal foreign elements were 65% Germans and 35% Swedish; 2) In my opinion there was a friendly feeling from all the foreign element with a few exceptions.

Local Board No. 50: 1) The principal foreign elements in our locality were Swedish and German. The Swedish element generally did not desire to go . . .

Local Board No. 17: The Swedes were decidedly lukewarm in their patriotism.

Local Board No. 8: The Scandinavians all through the war did what they could to evade service on the ground of their foreign citizenship . . .

Local Board, Belvidere: The Germans and the Swedes are about in equal number in our locality and both elements were right close to the line of being objectors . . .

Cook County: The Scandinavians . . . in the main seemed quite satisfied to

The negative attitude toward immigrants, which runs through all of these reports, undoubtedly reflects the general hostility of the American public toward the foreign-born. The exemption of aliens from military service aroused great indignation among draftees and their families. The main reason for this hostility was the feeling that aliens who stayed at home profited from the war by taking over the jobs of American workers in the service.[12] The officials responsible for the reports were undoubtedly influenced by this general attitude toward aliens. However, this does not explain why the Swedes were described as particularly reluctant to enter the country's service. Since there is no reason to suspect that Swedes were purposely defamed by those who drew up the local draft board reports, it may be assumed that they openly showed their preference to stay at home "and make honest peaceful money" rather than go to war.[13]

Volunteer companies were organized on the home front. In the fall of 1917 a Swedish home guard militia company was organized in

stay at home and make honest, peaceful money-making members of the community.

Cook County Board No. 5 : The attitude of our Mexican and Swedish aliens was as a whole somewhat less satisfactory than that of other neutral nationalities.

Rockford : The Swedes, being of a neutral country at first made one some trouble, especially the declarants, but the American born Swedes were as loyal and anxious as Americans. I noticed quite a change in the sentiments of our Swedish registrants after Finland declared her independence.

[12] A resolution adopted by the Citizens Committee of Board No. 82 may be cited as an example of the attitude toward aliens: "These same men by their manners and insolence caused more trouble to the Boards than any other registrants: they were cowardly, selfish, entirely lacking in any feeling of patriotism, not willing to do one thing for the country they have chosen to live in, their whole thought seemed to be to stay safely at home, make all the money they could, and gladly allow American boys to be sent away to the army. ... There is now a great surplus of unemployed labor in this country, and there never was room here for undesirable citizens. Be it resolved that we call upon all American citizens to use all honorable means to have Congress pass such laws as may be necessary, as well as put in force existing laws, to deport at once to the country of their birth all men who claimed exemption from military duty on the grounds of non-citizenship."

[13] See the answer from the Cook County draft board above.

Chicago, mainly comprised of members of the Swedish Club.[14] It was formed at the initiative of the Club's president, Charles S. Peterson, and became a part of the First Regiment of the Illinois Militia. The Swedish-American papers and the minutes from meetings of churches and organizations all contain reports which show that the Swedes willingly rallied around the American flag. "The young men in the Swedish community in Texas enlisted freely in the army and the navy."[15] Nearly 16 percent of the combined male membership of 221 congregations in the Minnesota Conference of the Augustana Synod enlisted in the American army. Out of this total of 3,730 men, 170 were killed in the war. Newspapers were rather consistent in making note of the Swedes who fought and died for the United States.[16] As Carl Rosenquist commented, "there is no question but that the Swedes in Texas were sincere in their patriotism."[17] Although there are examples of Swedish Americans who tried to get away from the military service, the majority were loyal to their new country. Very few took advantage of the chance to avoid military service by foreswearing the possibility of ever becoming an American citizen.

10. *The Treaty of Versailles*

The Treaty of Versailles was a shock to the Swedish Americans, for they had been lulled into believing the war was fought to create a better world. The Swedish Americans were avid followers of the peace negotiations from beginning to end. President Wilson was considered to be the only diplomat who could prevent the complete annihilation of Germany. The Swedish language papers emphatically declared that the peace negotiations were not to become a mere matter of revenge, where the victorious nations would try to grab off the largest possible gain. Instead, they insisted that the negotiations should aim at

[14] *Svenska Kuriren,* September 27, 1917, p. 11. In the same article, all Swedes 20 to 50 years of age were invited to join a second company that was being planned. The intention was that the militia was to replace the National Guard which had entered federal service. Its task was simply that of defending "house and home" in Chicago.

[15] Carl M. Rosenquist, "The Swedes of Texas," p. 250.

[16] Emil Lund, *Minnesota-konferensens och dess församlingars historia,* p. 229.

[17] See note 15.

insuring a permanent and lasting peace. This goal would not be benefited or achieved by the complete annihilation of Germany.[1]

There was a change of attitude in the Swedish-American papers after the Armistice pact. They muffled their criticism of Germany and gradually reflected an intense anxiety over what would happen in the peace negotiations. The Allies were warned against making Germany helpless. *Svenska Amerikanaren* believed – contrary to most of its Swedish colleagues – that these anxieties were exaggerated and that Germany deserved the reprisals after all its bloodshed. It criticized the Swedish language papers which now spoke of "violent peace" but in 1914 had not spoken of "violent war." The attitude of the Swedish Americans toward Germany after the Armistice largely corresponded with their views before the declaration of war. This may be explained primarily by the fact that control of and pressure on the foreign-born diminished when the war was over. One can notice that criticism of the peace terms sharpened as alien surveillance ceased.

Several papers wanted a revision of the peace treaty. With few exceptions the Swedish language papers were disappointed with the way things turned out.[2] *Missionsvännen* doubted "greatly" that the peace treaty would bring lasting peace.[3] *Svenska Kuriren* thought it unjust to Germany, considering that the German people had been led to believe that they served the welfare of the fatherland. The paper remembered how the Swedish Americans had been duped by the German propaganda.[4]

11. *Hundred Percent American Critized*

When the war was over and the harvests of victory were being reaped, the Swedish Americans saw to it that the foreign-born were not forgotten when plaudits were being issued. *Svenska Kuriren* declared that the Swedes could point with justifiable pride to their

[1] *Svenska Amerikanaren,* March 13, May 15, June 19, July 10 and August 21, 1919; *Svenska Kuriren,* March 27 and May 8, 1919; *Missionsvännen,* May 18 and July 1, 1919.

[2] Herbert Capps, *From Isolationism to Involvement,* pp. 65 ff.

[3] *Missionsvännen,* May 18 and July 1, 1919.

[4] *Svenska Kuriren,* April 10, 1919.

part in the "unselfish" heroic achievement, especially since they had unjustly been suspected of lacking loyalty toward the United States.[1] It also called the demand for Americanization an insult to the foreign-born who had devotedly fought for their new fatherland.

Carl J. Bengston, editor of *The Lutheran Companion,* thought the war had shown that the melting-pot had succeeded in uniting the various peoples of the United States.[2] However, he was disappointed in the Swedes, among other things, for neglecting to become American citizens. "Such people are not Americans. They are hardly Swedes, either, for then could just as well have stayed where they belong." He also thought it were about time the Swedes stopped that "stupid particularizing of the Swede in America, and that nauseating praising of his rich spiritual life."

The Swedish Americans gave a characteristic stamp to the immediate post-war period by regaining their self-assurance and openly criticizing the "100 percent Americans." *The Lutheran Companion* expressed its disappointment with the "Americanism"[3] that attempted to eradicate all traces of foreign languages and literatures. It admitted that certain immigrants were disloyal and unpatriotic, but it reiterated that there were just as many disloyal and unpatriotic persons among native-born Americans. *Förbundets Veckotidning* commented in 1919 that as the war hysteria died down, incident after incident took place which showed that the "presumptuous native Americans were no more patriotic than the foreign-born."[4]

Svenska Kuriren urged all patriots yelling about Americanization to look back upon things as they were before the war and compare them with the present situation.[5] It called attention to the fact that the United States had always been populated by immigrants, first as colonies and later as independent states. As long as the descendants of the English speaking settlers needed working people to do the rough labor which they themselves were too lazy or too dignified to perform, there was never any talk about Americanization. The paper blamed the

[1] *Svenska Kuriren,* December 26, 1918.

[2] Carl J. Bengston, "Varen Amerikanske," *Ungdomsvännen,* October, 1918, p. 238 f.

[3] *The Lutheran Companion,* February 1, 1919 and April 10, 1920.

[4] *Förbundets Veckotidning,* March 18, 1919.

[5] *Svenska Kuriren,* September 25 and November 6, 1919.

war for having awakened "all the slumbering passions of class hate, bigotry, and desire to suppress others."

In a subsequent article *Svenska Kuriren* compared "the hyphenate-worm" with the tape-worm, both of which were said to be destructive.[6] The essential difference was that the tape-worm attacked one individual at a time, while the "hyphenate-worm" threatened all of society at once. The Swedish language papers were generally critical of those who kept "hyphenism" alive. *Förbundets Veckotidning* feared that if Americanism were allowed to continue, it would become a new religion.[7] *Svenska Amerikanaren* maintained that it was impossible to force a true and genuine patriotism upon a person who had not himself learned to love America. It felt that the Americanization process was hindered by a general hostility toward "foreigners." It also wondered how anyone could believe that the Americanization program would actually appeal to immigrants, when those who happened to be born in America regarded the foreign-born as a disgrace to the nation. *Svenska Tribunen Nyheter* characterized the Americanization program carried on both during and after the war as so much hysteria. If Americanization were based on completely different principles and were extended to all persons regardless of their birth and nationality, the newspaper argued, then it might really become a significant means of educating the immigrants.[8] The Americanization program would never produce any "beneficial results" until it had assumed the character of study groups or lecture associations.

Even after the Armistice, immigrants continued to express their irritation with the official restrictions and public hostility directed against all foreign languages. When the governor of Minnesota, J.A.A. Burnquist, declared that only English ought to be taught in the schools and that all immigrants either ought to adopt English "or run the risk of deportation," one Swedish American "bluntly told the governor the facts in plain Swedish – a language which the governor, himself a native Swede, had now apparently forgotten in his patriotic

[6] *Svenska Kuriren,* January 22, 1920. On May 12, 1921, the paper said there was no reason why Swedish Americans should continue affirming their loyalty, since by now three generations of Swedes had in both word and deed shown their faithfulness to their adopted country.

[7] *Förbundets Veckotidning,* November 14, 1922; *Svenska Amerikanaren,* December 25, 1919, and January 27, 1921.

[8] *Svenska Tribunen Nyheter,* June 2, 1920; *Svenska Kuriren,* July 27, 1922.

zeal."[9] *Svenska Tribunen Nyheter* objected to the fact that some states had degenerated to such an extent "that they would deprive old people tottering on the brink of the grave of the right to hear sermons in the language of their fathers."[10] J.S. Carlson was perhaps the most outspoken critic of the intolerance of foreign languages during the war. In his book *Hvarför böra vi bibehålla och bevara, vårda och bruka svenska språket i Amerika,* published in 1923, (Why we ought to perpetuate and defend, cultivate and use the Swedish language in America) he attacked those who believed no one could be a true American as long as he retained his native language.[11] "They believe our brain is as small as theirs and not capable of containing more than one language." He said it was unpardonably naive and stupid to assert that anyone who spoke a language other than English was not a good American patriot. "Millions of those who broke the soil and built roads have not talked English to stumps and stones, but they have nevertheless cleared them away." There are a great many people, he said, who are Americans in spirit but do not know English. There are also many so-called Americans who speak an excellent English but nevertheless are "lazybones, tramps, thieves and swindlers" who in every way show themselves to be un-Americans and traitors to their own country. "The English language delivers no one from evil." He called the bans on foreign languages un-American: "As far as the Swedish language is concerned, that 'Prussianistic' measure was completely unnecessary and superfluous, for neither rebellion nor treason was to be feared from Americans of Swedish origin."

[9] *Allsvensk Samling,* June 16, 1919,p. 3. It must have been a great pleasure for the paper to publish this letter, for it had been irritated by the lack of criticism from Swedish-American newspapars. It said that its Swedish-American colleagues had protested against the language restrictions in words "the softness of which stands in striking contrast to the sharpness of style which usually characterizes them." *Allsvensk Samling* was of the opinion that the immigrants were forced to practice humility and submissiveness during the war. However, it hoped that the language restrictions of 1918 would at least awaken the Swedes and make them realize what a "priceless teasure the often neglected and despised mother tongue really is." (*Allsvensk Samling,* August 1, and September 2, 1918.)

[10] *Svenska Tribunen Nyheter,* May 7, 1919; *Augustana,* December 6, 1917, p. 800, February 20, 1919, p. 121, and April 3, 1919, p. 222; *The Lutheran Companion,* February 15, 1919, p. 76.

[11] J.S. Carlson, *op. cit.,* pp. 6—15.

12. *Summary*

World War I provided much food for thought for the theorists responsible for the idea of America as "the melting pot." When the war broke out in Europe it was discovered that the bonds with the old world were strong. The conglomerate of nationalities in America could not remain unconcerned about a conflict in which the fate of the old homelands was at stake. Meanwhile, America was revealing its deep-rooted intolerance of everything "alien" or "foreign": "nativism" and "100 percent Americanism" flourished side by side. The demand for compulsory Americanization was raised as soon as it was clear that the American melting pot had not succeeded in melting together all of the nationalities which had immigrated over the centuries.

The reactions of the Swedish Americans during the first years of the war, 1914–1915, indicate that ties with Sweden were strong. Their attitude toward the war and the belligerents was based to a great degree on what was best for Sweden. During their childhood they had learned that Russia was Sweden's most dangerous foe. They had also learned that Germany was the bulwark against the westward advance of barbarianism. It was therefore natural that many Swedes took Germany's side in the initial stages of the war. The Swedish Americans recommended that the United States remain neutral and not be lured into the war. However, this did not deter several of the Swedish language newspapers from taking a stand in the conflict. They openly declared their sympathies for Germany. Faced with the prospect that the United States might intervene on the side of the Allies, the newspapers intensified their demands that it remain neutral. On several occasions the Swedish language papers cautioned the American government against insisting on law and justice to such a degree that it frustrated its own neutrality. It is impossible to say how far the Swedes were prepared to allow the Germans to go before they thought the time was ripe enough for the United States to stop them. There is a lot which suggests that the Swedish foreign policy served as a model for their outlook. On several occasions they suggested that the American government follow the example of Sweden, namely by forbidding its citizens to travel on merchant vessels of the Allies. If Sweden succeeded in its maneuvering in spite of its proximity to the war, then the United States, with the whole

Atlantic ocean between it and the war, ought to be able to preserve its own neutrality.

The Swedish policy of neutrality was described as more honorable than that of the United States. When Sweden's neutrality was questioned, for example, after the Luxburg affair, the Swedish Americans replied that it was unreasonable to demand more of Swedish neutrality than of American neutrality. When America was neutral – that is, before the declaration of war – it exported arms and ammunition to the belligerents.

The Swedish Americans who, after the outbreak of the war, openly professed sympathy for Germany, ceased to do so after the American declaration of war. Newspapers, churches, associations and societies, and individual Swedish Americans supported every patriotic resolution as soon as it was adopted. There were probably many reasons why Swedish Americans muffled their criticism. For one thing, they did not dare to express any viewpoints which diverged from official American foreign policy. Such viewpoints were prohibited, and any violations were seriously dealt with. Every attempt to criticize the American war effort was silenced by a rigid control of the foreign language press. Consequently, it is impossible to determine from the Swedish-American newspapers how Swedish Americans really felt about the war. On the other hand, even if many Swedish Americans merely hushed up their true feelings because of their fear for American public opinion, there were undoubtedly many who changed their minds when they saw how the Germans were advancing in Europe. It would have been even more sensational if the American propaganda machine had not succeeded in influencing the Swedes more than it did. Finally, the war was seen in an entirely different light by all those who had sons, brothers or other relatives and friends fighting at the front. In such cases a change of attitude was quite natural. But in spite of energetic efforts, the Swedes never completely succeeded in clearing themselves of the charges that they were pro-German.

The Swedish Americans repeatedly asked themselves what would happen if Sweden were drawn into the war. Even though they realized the choice would be difficult, they declared they would not hesitate to go to war against Sweden if that should become necessary. A vital feature of the American war propaganda was the attempt to convince the Swedish Americans that Sweden had as much to gain by a victory of the Allies as any of the Allied nations themselves. Swedish Americans were encouraged to show their patriotism and loyalty by buying Liberty Bonds. The sales of Liberty Bonds led to fierce competition among different immigrant groups. Full-page newspaper advertisements and editorials called upon immigrants to show their active support of and undivided loyalty to their adopted country.

Since military service was obligatory for all men between 21 and 30 years of age, the statistics on those who served under the American flag provide no accurate means of evaluating immigrant's loyalty to their adopted country. Very few immigrants took advantage of the possibility to avoid military service by renouncing any hope of ever becoming American citizens. Those who did do so made front page news for themselves, especially in their own immigrant press. The Rockford incident in 1917, where 138 persons, most of them Swedes, refused to register for the draft, created a sensation in the Swedish-American papers, who expressed their disgust and called the incident an example of poor judgment. The information gathered by the various Illinois "draft boards" indicating that Swedes preferred to stay at home and make money rather than put on the American uniform may be said to support the idea that many young Swedes emigrated from Sweden to avoid compulsory military service. There may, of course, have been other reasons why they preferred to stay at home. For example, it is possible that they lacked a wholehearted feeling of affection for America. In light of the fact that many emigrated in order to improve their economic situation and status, it is easy to understand their reluctance to become involved in a war as soon as they reached America. However, the reports from the various Illinois "draft boards" seem to suggest that it was a rather generally accepted notion that the Swedes, more than any other immigrant group, preferred to stay at home and turn their backs on the war.

The war-time restriction on foreign languages infuriated the Swedes. They regarded the Iowa governor's decree as a malicious insult to the immigrants who bravely fought for the "Stars and Stripes." However, they obeyed the decree, in spite of the hardships it imposed, primarily because of their fear of American public opinion. The foreign language press was plagued by a host of troubles during the war and was severely threatened by two developments. Not only did it lose a great deal of its freedom of expression as a result of official curtailment, but it lost a good deal of its reading public as well, due to the fact that many people no longer dared to reveal publicly that they subscribed to a non-English newspaper. Foreign language newspapers were the objects of tight surveillance, and any indiscretion in the form of criticism of the American war effort was a step in the direction of official censure and ban. Of all the Swedish-American newspapers, *Svenska Socialisten* was hardest hit by the war-time regulations. On several occasions its editions were either confiscated or impounded. The war also meant extra expenditures for all foreign language newspapers, who were required to submit translations for all articles related to the war.

It should finally be noted that several Swedish-American newspapers openly re-declared their sympathies for Germany after the Armistice. There were some who, for example, expressed great dissatisfaction with the Treaty of Versailles and called it an insult to the German nation. Even ”100 percent Americanism” was critized after the war as both un-American and narrow-minded. There are, in other words, certain circumstances which suggest that while many Swedish Americans never fully approved of American intervention in the war on the side of the Allies, they refrained from criticism in fear of hurting themselves as well as their reputation as Swedes. The dominant impression of Swedish Americans during the First World War is one of strong inner resolve and unity – their conscious efforts to avoid discrediting their heritage and reputation and, on the other hand, to show that Swedes were equally as good patriots as other Americans.

VII. Restricted Immigration

1. *Increased Opposition*

The end of the nineteenth and the beginning of the twentieth century saw the growth of opposition to the rising tide of immigration. In 1897 Congress passed for the first time the Literacy Test, which stipulated that every immigrant was to be able to show that he or she could read and write his or her own language.[1] However, this bill was never put into effect, since President Grover Cleveland applied his right of veto. It did not become law until May, 1917, and then only over President Woodrow Wilson's veto. On two earlier occasions both Presidents William Taft, in 1913, and Woodrow Wilson, in 1915, had exercised their veto privileges in order to stop this legislation, on the grounds that "a literacy test could only test what opportunities had been open to the immigrant in his native land, and provided no proof of either his intellectual capacity or his moral worth."[2]

The Literacy Test was primarily a type of selective legislation intended to stop the immigration of those who could neither read nor write. The main motive with this measure and the chief expectation of its framers was a reduction of the immigration from Southern and Eastern Europe, "because the rate of illiteracy among the immigrants from the south and the east of Europe was much higher than among those from the north and west of Europe."[3] The strongest resistance to the legislation came from certain immigrant groups,

[1] Carl Wittke, "Immigration Policy Prior to World War I." *Immigration an American Dilemma. Problems in American Civilization* (Boston, 1953), p. 8 f; John Higham, *Strangers in the Land,* p. 101 ff; George Stephenson, *A History of American Immigration* (Boston, 1926), p. 156 ff. The literacy test included a long list of exemptions for, among others, the physically handicapped, persons under the age of 16, and the parents, grandparents, and wives of immigrants who met the literacy requirements of being able to read and write.

[2] Carl Wittke, "Immigration Policy Prior to World War I," p. 9.

[3] Maurice Davie, *World Immigration,* p. 374.

shipowners, and the railway companies, while, on the other hand, the American union movement expressed a positive attitude to a policy of restricted immigration. The American Federation of Labor feared that "Europe would do everything possible to retain the best men and to get rid of the disabled and inefficient."[4] The Literacy Test was further supported by the American Immigration Commission, which in 1911 published its 42 volume report. Aroused public sentiment during World War I was also made use of in passing the legislation over the President's veto. However, it should be remembered that the war provided only an extra push in the favored direction and hardly affected the matter *per se,* since the same legislation had been passed by the Congress two years earlier. Woodrow Wilson justified his veto on the grounds that he considered the legislation broke with traditional American policy toward immigration. Among other things, the law sought to "all but close entirely the gates of asylum which have always been open to those who could find nowhere else the right and opportunity of constitutional agitation for what they conceived to be the natural and inalienable rights of men."[5]

When it was seen that the Literacy Test did not reduce immigration in any significant degree, demands were then raised for a policy of restricted immigration. During the 1920s immigration legislation was finally subjected to a good many alterations which brought to a close more than a century of free immigration to the United States. In 1921 Congress passed into law the Quota Act which alloted a specific yearly quota of immigrants to each country of origin.[6] The Quota regulations drew upon a three percent figure of aliens of the same nationality who were residents of the United States at the time of the 1910 census.[7] By means of the Quota Act of 1924, which was based on the 1890 census, the earlier quota allotment was reduced to two percent.[8] This same legislation introduced further modifications of the quota allotment following the passage of the National Origins Law on July 1, 1927. These new regulations meant, in short, that the yearly quotas were projected and proportioned according to a definite

[4] George Stephenson, *A History of American Immigration,* p. 160.

[5] *Ibid.,* p. 167.

[6] The Department of State, *Visa Work* (Washington, D.C., 1957), p. 32.

[7] The Quota law was in force for the fiscal year July 1 to June 30.

[8] The Department of State, *Visa Work,* p. 33.

maximum number of immigrants – c. 150,000 – determined by the number of persons of the same nationality who were residents of the United States in 1920.

This later quota allotment met strong opposition and did not take effect until July 1, 1929, when President Herbert Hoover felt himself legally obliged to put it into effect after its passage by the Congress so many years earlier. However, he expressed his personal opposition to the legislation by saying that experience had taught him of the difficulties which could arise out of fixing quotas by individual countries.[9]

The quota laws of the 1920s must be seen against the social and historical backdrop. Certain groups of immigrants had been the targets of popular hatred and intolerance ever since they began to arrive in America. However, it was only in the twentieth century that a general xenophobia of this type began to draw serious attention. It showed itself most clearly after 1916 with the publication of Madison Grant's book *The Passing of the Great Race*. Grant's book was highly controversial, the object of much heated debate, and for many years ranked high on the "best seller" list. The book claimed to be a scholarly contribution and was said to be based upon research in biology and anthropology. Its theme was one of racial superiority.[10] If America desired to preserve the superiority of the Nordic race, Grant wrote, then it must close the doors on the inferior Central European and Jewish races as well as on the new arrivals from the Mediterranean countries. If these measures were not taken, the "great race," which alone possessed the qualities to make "soldiers, sailors, adventurers . . ., explorers . . ., rulers, organizers and aristocrats" would be replaced by "the weak, the broken and the mentally crippled of all races."

At the same time that xenophobia and a fear of everything non-American entered on the scene, a distinctively American nationalism was receiving fresh emphasis. New movements sprang up which saw it as their task to stand up for "the hundred percent American." These nationalistic tendencies were quickly acclaimed and accepted by students and intellectual circles. Books and magazines called upon

[9] William Myers, *Hoover Administration. A Document Narrative* (New York, 1936), p. 376.

[10] Carl Wittke, "Immigration Policy Prior to World War I," p. 10; Maldwyn Jones, *American Immigration,* p. 268; Madison Grant, *The Passing of the Great Race.*

people to stand up for their country and save it from the waves of immigrants who threatened the American culture "with unknown gods and rites" and constituted an alien menace "to our air."[11]

These nationalistic movements reached their fever pitch after World War I. Disappointment over the war itself and the unfortunate terms of peace increased the fear and suspicions of everything non-American. The aftermath of the Russian Revolution heightened these fears and anxieties and projected them against a vision of Communism and everything it might conceivably be associated with. Such feelings probably reached their peak immediately after the conviction in 1921 of the Italian immigrants Nicolo Sacco and Bartholomeo Vanzetti of the murder of a paymaster in South Braintree, Massachusetts.[12]

This xenophobia was intensified by the revival of the Ku Klux Klan in 1915.[13] Its membership rose sharply and in 1924 was estimated at around four million strong. The Klan pointed out the dangers of continued immigration and preached the doctrines of "pure Americanism," "white supremacy," and "Nordic superiority." On account of the size of its membership and the strength of its economic position, the Klan soon became a political force which could not be overlooked.[14]

Xenophobia was not limited to the Ku Klux Klan and similar extremist organizations but rather expanded in the post-war era to become a "study in the mood of America, displayed, among other things, in the frequent appearance of articles on this and related subjects in almost every new issue of leading American magazines and periodicals."[15] In one series of articles published by *The Saturday Evening Post* in 1922, Kenneth Roberts spoke out against a *laissez-faire* policy of immigration and the racial results of allowing different nationalities to mingle with one another: the "mixture of Nordic with Alpine and Mediterranean stocks would produce only a worthless race of hybrids."[16] Anthropologists and psychologists also objected to un-

[11] Carl Wittke, *op. cit.*, p. 10.

[12] *Interpreter Releases,* 1931, p. 29; Arthur Schlesinger, *Political and Social Growth of the American People, 1865—1940* (New York, 1947), p. 455.

[13] Oscar Handlin, *Race and Nationality in American Life* (Boston, 1957), p. 140.

[14] John Hichs, *Republican Ascendency, 1921—1933* (New York, 1963), p. 95.

[15] *Sociala Meddelanden,* 1924, p. 544.

[16] Maldwyn Jones, *op. cit.,* p. 275 f.

regulated immigration and expressed the opinion that altogether too many races and nationalities had already gained entrance to American society.[17] It was now said that one could prove the superiority of the Nordic race on the basis of the intelligence quotient tests carried out on American soldiers during the war. Published in 1922, the results of the tests showed that all soldiers from Southern and Eastern Europe had lower IQ's than those from Northern and Western Europe and the United States.[18]

It cannot be said that those groups and factions calling for strong legislative measures against immigration for reasons of racial or social sentiment exercised any direct influence on the formation of the Quota Law of 1921. The question of racial assimilation and the consequences of biological intermixing of nationalities does not appear at this time to have penetrated into the general public consciousness but rather seems to have been confined to intellectual circles and certain organizations and movements. Instead, one ought to see the first quota law legislation in terms of the American economic environment. Great numbers of American workers despised the immigrants because they increased competition for jobs. The workers were afraid that continued immigration would lead to a lowering of wages and a depreciation of living standards. Organized labor, which at that time was made up mostly of skilled and professional workers, was especially concerned by the great waves of immigrants who streamed into America from war-torn Europe and offered a ready market of cheap labor.[19]

However, the Quota Law of 1921 did not bring about the changes it was intended to produce. The immigrants continued to pour into America, and the debate they aroused went on as before. Restriction lists did not stop now at the three percent level but called for stronger regulations. The Ku Klux Klan continued in its nationalistic campaign, and its membership steadily rose. The daily press and the army of magazines and periodicals were instrumental in bringing the debate on the problem of immigration to the attention of the general public, and the resulting discussion of racial and national differences heightened the nationalistic atmosphere. An increasing number of Americans were won over to the idea that restrictive legislative was imperative, and by

17 Oscar Handlin, *op. cit.*, p. 140 f.

18 Maldwyn Jones, *op. cit.*, p. 276.

19 Carl Wittke, *op. cit.*, p. 10; Arthur Schlesinger, *op. cit.*, p. 494 f.

the time the 1924 Quota Law was drawn up it was obvious that purely racial motives and biological arguments weighed more heavily in people's minds than did economic considerations.[20]

As mentioned earlier, the Quota Law of 1924 was based upon the census of 1890. At the time of this census the mass immigration from Southern and Eastern Europe had not yet been unleashed. When voices were raised in Congress in opposition to setting the 1890 census as a framework for the Quota Law, it was decided that quota allotments would subsequently be made on a provisional basis until superseded by the National Origins Law of July 1, 1927.[1] The National Origin Law implied that quotas would no longer be accounted for on the basis of the number of aliens from respective nationalities who resided in the United States in 1890 but rather on the total amount of residents of "foreign stock" in the United States in 1920, scaled in proportion to the figure of 150,000.[2]

The House of Representatives' Committee on Immigration and Naturalization Questions issued a report in which it warned that continued immigration from Southern and Eastern Europe would lower living standards in America.[3]

With the stabilization of the economy after the post-war depression, economic motives for anti-immigrant legislation lost their formerly persuasive appeal. Even the pronounced intolerance previously prevalent among American employers against a strengthening of immigration legislation gradually diminished. It now appeared that they were more interested in legislation which would make possible the immigration of just that type of manpower which they felt was needed – in

[20] Maldwyn Jones, *op. cit.*, p. 276 f.

[1] Marion Bennet, *American Immigration Policies* (Washington, 1963), p. 47.

[2] The term "foreign stock" also designated persons born in Sweden and America whose father or mother was Swedish.

[3] Marion Bennet, *American Immigration Policies,* p. 50. The Committee went on to say in its report: "If immigration from Southern and Eastern Europe may enter the United States on a basis of substantial equality with that admitted from the older sources of supply, it is clear that if any appreciable number of immigrants are to be allowed to land upon our shores the balance of racial preponderance must in time pass to those elements of the population who reproduce more rapidly on a lower standard of living than those possessing other ideals."

other words, an immigration of quality, not quantity.[4] This change of attitude was apparently due primarily to the fact that the earlier forecasts of unfavorable economic repercussions as a result of the immigration regulations of 1921 failed to materialize.

The economic prosperity enjoyed by the United States after 1924 gradually allowed the furor of debate on immigration to subside until the Depression era. The Depression, however, revived and heightened the debate, and voices were once again heard calling for a more restrictive policy toward immigration.

2. *American Jobs for Americans*

During the Depression purely economic considerations again entered into the foreground of debate on immigration. Even if racial prejudice was not entirely absent from the scene, it was at least overshadowed or camouflaged now by the economic picture. "References to the homogeneity and racial character of the American people were conspicuous by their absence in discussion of immigration matters. ... The old cry of 'Keep America American' was replaced by the slogan 'American jobs for Americans'."[1] Immigrants were now accused of competing for jobs with American labor and increasing unemployment as well as lowering wages.

As the economic repercussions of the Depression grew progressively worse, the debate on proposed immigration legislation was intensified. There now seemed to be agreement among all parties concerned that a restriction of immigration was absolutely essential. Immigration was widely considered to be the primary reason for the severe unemployment which followed on the heels of the Depression. The Works

[4] *Sociala Meddelanden,* 1924, p. 288. Fritiof Ander wrote in an article in 1942 that "Republicans and Democrats alike supported restrictive immigration legislation in 1924, and the public was not displeased with it. The Congress had acted according to the will of the people .... A resentment toward Germans, retained from the war, undoubtedly influenced this reasoning, as did also a resentment toward the Swedes for having supposedly harbored German sympathies." (Fritiof Ander, "The Effects of the Immigration Law of 1924 upon a Minority Immigrant Group," *Annual Report of the American Historical Association,* Vol. III [1942], p. 345.)

[1] Robert Divine, *American Immigration Policy, 1924—1952* (New Haven, 1957), p. 108.

Projects Administration commented in its publication, *The Alien in Public Employment:* "When ever two or three are gathered together in friendly conversation nowadays, the talk first or last turns to the Depression, to the unemployment situation and what to do about it. And first or last some one is sure to suggest that the foreigner is in some way to blame .... That at least, under present conditions, the alien ... should stand aside from opportunities of employment in favor of citizens."[2] Articles constantly reappeared in the daily press and periodicals demanding or recommending a total ban on every type of immigration. In certain cases, such drastic measures were proposed as the deportation of immigrants already settled in the United States. Labor organizations demanded that all immigration cease. The chairman of the American Federation of Labor, William Green, called it "idiotic to let in 100,000 to 150,000 immigrants who only suffer themselves and further increase the already swelling ranks of unemployed."[3]

An editorial in *The Saturday Evening Post* in April, 1930, claimed there was a causal connection between immigration and the current unemployment.[4] The magazine was doubtful about the possibilities of relieving unemployment by stepped-up production, unemployment benefits, and the introduction of the five-day work week as long as new waves of immigrants were allowed to stream in. There were only two conceivable recourses in the fight against unemployment, it said: namely, to deport all immigrants who year after year gained illegal entry to the United States and, secondly, to successively reduce the quota levels. However, the magazine did not want to deny the fact that immigration had supplied the United States with vigorous, new blood. Yet at the same time it pointed out that the "best blood" had already arrived on American shores by 1890 – *i.e.,* during the period before the immigration from Southern and Eastern Europe took its start.[5] The magazine also argued that the United States would never have been faced with the current problem of assimilating its new citizens to the American environment had it restricted immigration forty years earlier and denied entrance to those "people we foolishly

[2] Work Projects Administration, *The Alien in Public Employment,* p. 4.

[3] *The New York Times,* September 10, 1930, p. 1.

[4] *The Saturday Evening Post,* April 19, 1930.

[5] *Ibid.,* March 4, 1933.

thought we could Americanize by dressing them in American clothes."

Even if the majority of people active in the immigration debate supported some sort of restrictive or prohibitive policy, there were those, if only a very few, who stated that the current unemployment level could not be reduced by merely continuing a policy of restrictive immigration. Samuel Dickstein, Representative from New York, pointed out that up to this point the restrictions on immigration had only proved to be a great "economic mistake."[6]

The Congress was also the forum for an intensive debate on the relation between immigration and unemployment. Senators and Representatives seemed to be rather firmly in agreement that a reform of existing legislation was crucial. However, they parted ways when it came to discussing where the lines would be drawn and which methods would be adopted. The leading question at the time was whether restrictions should be made on the administrative or the legislative level. Opponents of more restrictive legislation asserted that such a measure might all too easily be made into a permanent fixture of law, and they expressed the idea that administrative means of restriction were more readily adaptable to fluctuations in the economic situation.

During the spring session of the Congress in 1930, President Hoover, among other people, proposed to both Committees on Immigration that they work out the draft of a provisional bill which in the course of the following year would reduce the immigrant quota by 50 percent.[7]

However, no such draft was completed before the Congress adjourned. When the Congress did not come up with any new proposal for immigration legislation President Hoover announced on September 9, 1930, that he intended to put the brake on immigration to the United States in order to combat the rising unemployment.[8]

The immigration law stipulated, namely, that no one would be granted an entry permit if there were reasonable grounds for assuming that he would prove to be a "public burden." Since every worker who immigrated to the United States ran the risk of winding up on the list of unemployed, President Hoover requested consular authorities, on the basis of this new regulation, to help limit the actual number of immigrants by refusing visas to applicants who might possibly be

6 *The New York Times,* October 7, 1930, p. 11.

7 *Interpreter Releases,* September 11, 1930, p. 217.

8 *Press Releases,* September 13, 1930, pp. 176—7.

considered as future "public burdens." This administrative measure of restriction proved greatly effective in terms of dealing with the unemployment crisis. The instructions given to consular officials emphasized the importance of distinguishing between the so-called "new immigrants" and those who made the crossing in order to rejoin their relatives in the United States and who did not pose a burden on the American labor market.[9]

In his annual message to Congress on December 2, 1930, President Hoover underlined the fact that his action was only a temporary one, pending the passage of a new law.[10]

In spite of numerous and energetic attempts, supporters of a restrictive immigration policy never succeeded in winning the full support of Congress. When President Hoover left office American immigration legislation continued to rest on its traditional foundations. The Depression had not brought about any new legislation, even if the efforts at doing so were both numerous and vigorous. Public officials contented themselves with restricting the flow of immigrants through administrative channels. Moreover, President Hoover's measure had proved itself immensely effective. Secretary of State Stimson contributed the following comment to the debate on immigration before the House of Representatives' Committee on Immigration: "The restriction has resulted in the relief of unemployment in the United States by preventing the entry of aliens who would have entered into competition with American workingmen. This policy has received wide expression of approval of individual members of Congress and in the press throughout the United States."[11] In December, 1932, Stimson reported that the immigration policy introduced during the Depression had accomplished what it was intended to do and that over 500,000 new immigrants had been prevented from reaching American shores.[12]

[9] *Interpreter Releases,* March 31, 1935, p. 125.

[10] *Congressional Record,* December 2, 1930, p. 36; *Sociala Meddelanden,* 1931, p. 405, and 1930, p. 992.

[11] *Hearings No. 72 before the Committee on Immigration and Naturalization.* House of Represenatives, 72nd Congress, 1 Session (April, 1932).

[12] *The New York Times,* December 22, 1932, p. 22.

3. *Swedish Americans and the Quota Laws*

Throughout this period the immigrants themselves offered the strongest resistance to alterations and restrictions on legislation which affected them. As a rule, they opposed every measure which might conceivably have concerned the fate of their own countrymen. Their discontent spilled over in the foreign language press, which carried on an effective propaganda campaign for the immigrant cause. Every proposal for restrictive legislation was greeted with particularly bitter resistance from Southern and Eastern European immigrants, who felt they were the selected targets of discrimination. After World War I Scandinavians appeared to be one of the American minorities who were most inclined to accept a policy of restricted immigration.[1] Immigration legislation was a consistent issue of debate in the editorials of Swedish language newspapers between 1914 and 1932.[2]

The Swedish language newspapers passed over the Literacy Test without special comment. When they did comment on it, they did so in measured terms. Swedish Americans appear not to have opposed the law to any special degree. *Svenska Amerikanaren* believed that it ought to be adopted, since it was not directed against any particular group of people.[3] It was an obvious right everyone had to be master of his own house. "If restrictions are made on the immigration laws, they can only be of benefit to the whole country. The present restrictions are sparing us from the ignorant, superstitious hordes from Southern Europe who live under the sway of the Pope." The newspaper heaped praise on the immigrants from Northern Europe for their intelligent and firm resolve to work, their earnest and wholehearted desire to immigrate not only in order to improve their economic conditions, but "even for their zeal to live their lives as enlightened citizens under the honored banner of the 'stars and stripes.' They did not depreciate living standards nor did they lower the nation's cultural ramparts." The only ones who profited by immigration from Southern and Eastern Europe were the big industrial bosses and the Catholic Church. *Svenska Kuriren* shared the view of President Wilson that a person's character did not depend upon how much

[1] John Higham, *Strangers in the Land,* p. 304.

[2] Herbert Capps, *From Isolationism to Involvement,* p. 110 f.

[3] *Svenska Amerikanaren,* January 11 and February 8, 1917.

education he had received.[4] However, the newspaper criticized the Literacy Test with the observation that every sovereign state had the right to decide for itself how it would admit aliens to its shores. The leading newspaper of the Swedish Methodists, *Sändebudet,* agreed with *Svenska Kuriren* by saying that literacy alone "did not guarantee that immigrants would become acceptable additions to the national population."[5]

It is surprising that the Literacy Test provoked only a handful of protests. Immigrants were usually sensitive to such measures which restricted immigration in any way. In their eyes America was a free and open country to all who wished to come to its shores. It is possible that the general lack of criticism among all immigrant groups was partly due to the fact that all attention was drawn to the war and that the immigrants did not dare to criticize a law passed by Congress at a time when all immigrants were the objects of public suspicion.

Swedish-American congressmen held diverging opinions on the Literacy Test. Irvine Lenroot and Charles Lindbergh supported the proposal, while Charles Otto Lobeck opposed it. When the House of Representatives on February 4, 1915, tried to pass the Literacy Test over the veto of President Wilson, Lenroot attacked the President personally and accused him of caring more for "those abroad rather than (for) those now here."[6] Lenroot emphasized in his speech that it was the duty of Congress to pass the Literacy Test into law despite the President's veto.

Charles Lindbergh voted for the bill in 1914. However, he stated that he would not have done so if "the literacy provision had constituted the whole bill."[7] He explained that he did not believe "the literacy test provided by the bill is sufficient to insure the securing of good immigrants nor to exclude the bad ones." In spite of this he considered the bill contained so many good "provisions" that he promised to vote for it.

On the other hand, Charles Otto Lobeck was wholly opposed to the Literacy Test. In his opinion the job of weeding out desirable and undesirable aliens ought to be handled by the home authorities

[4] *Svenska Kuriren,* February 8, 1917.

[5] *Sändebudet,* February 6, 1917.

[6] *Congressional Record,* 63rd Congress, 3rd Session, p. 3037.

[7] *Ibid.,* 63rd Congress, 2nd Session, pp. 2610—11.

"before the intending immigrant embarks on the steamship."[8] The bill did not prevent undesirable aliens from emigrating, he said, "but it does prevent good, honest men who have not had the advantage of an education in their old homes, who wish to come and hope to make homes here for themselves and their families." Moreover, the bill did not amount to any effective barrier against immigrants, since increasing numbers were learning to read and write. When the Literacy Test was finally passed in 1917 it met with no resistance from Swedish-American congressmen.

The Quota Law of 1921 received a diversified and somewhat cool reception from the Swedish-American newspapers, who thought that it favored immigrants from Southern and Eastern Europe. As a result, they generally described the legislation as discriminatory to Scandinavian immigrants, whose importance for the destiny of the United States these newspapers constantly underscored.

When it was seen shortly after the war that the Literacy Test did not fulfill its expectations, Congress began to discuss other legislative means of restricting immigration. The reaction to this move was initially mixed in the Swedish-American press. Some newspapers were wholly negative in their attitude, others were more positive on the condition, of course, that the Swedish quota would not be affected.

Svenska Kuriren challenged the wisdom and the necessity of a restrictive immigration policy.[9] It believed that the high level of unemployment in 1919 was only temporary. Once employers had the chance to breathe more easily their demands for manpower would soon increase. It predicted that within the course of a year there would be a shortage of miners, and this could only be relieved, it asserted, by importing "raw manpower" from the Old World. The most effective means of combatting unemployment was a prompt return to the Republican party's principles of setting appropriate import duties on all goods which America itself could produce. *Svenska Kuriren* criticized legislators for laying themselves at the mercy and influence of the powerful labor unions.[10] It said that many congressmen were suffering from "that insanity unleashed by the war which has attacked such a great number of native Americans." The

8 *Ibid.*, pp. 2762—63.

9 *Svenska Kuriren,* February 6, 1919.

10 *Ibid.,* July 24, 1919.

newspaper did not go on in detail to describe what it meant by this "insanity." However, it is possible that it was referring to the high-flung oratory of "one hundred percent Americanism." It did not believe that this would be a prolonged epidemic, since all of the representatives and a third of the senators would be seeking re-election within the coming year. *Svenska Kuriren* was convinced that the election would then "usher in a quick therapy treatment which instantly cures these insanities." The newspaper defended a policy of unrestricted immigration by saying, in part, that there were still not enough miners available and willing to work in the coal mines and coal fields. In the immediate future America would need just as many additional workers in its labor force as it did during the pre-war decade.[11] Experience had shown that the immigration of European workers posed no threats to the balance of employment in America.[12] During the period of immigration before the war America's prosperity had soared extravagantly.

In May, 1921, a few months after the passage of the Quota Law, *Svenska Kuriren* came to terms with the idea of restricted legislation. It now said it saw no reason for its being a part of those movements which were working for unregulated and unlimited immigration "without taking into consideration the true welfare of the United States."[13] When Congress decided to extend the bill in force until July 1, 1923, the newspaper considered this was a wise decision.[14]

In contrast to *Svenska Kuriren, Svenska Amerikanaren* had from the very beginning accepted a certain restrictive policy on immigration.[15] In its opinion it was pure folly to allow America's doors to stand wide open at a time of national unemployment. An influx of a million immigrants, for example, would ruin the labor market. The newspaper saw that something had to be done to protect the American

11 *Ibid.*, September 18, 1919.

12 *Ibid.*, November 16, 1920.

13 *Ibid.*, May 12, 1921.

14 *Ibid.*, March 2, 1922.

15 *Svenska Amerikanaren,* February 6, 1919, and December 9, 1920; *Svenska Kuriren* predicted that when the war was finally over America would be inundated by the flow of immigrants from Scandinavia. It also believed that the Scandinavian countries would send over a higher number of immigrants in the immediate post-war era than at any time during the fifteen year period before the war.

worker "from a tidal wave of" immigrants which was expected to reach America after the reconstruction of post-war Europe. A year later, in June, 1920, *Svenska Amerikanaren* went one step further and demanded a restriction of the immigration from Southern Europe on the grounds that it contained grave risks for America.[16] It was no longer the quantity of immigrants the newspaper feared but rather the quality. Up to this point those who had come to America made up "the cream of the crop." "But," the newspaper commented, "it would not be long before the skim milk began to rise to the surface." It further sympathized with American workers and feared that uncontrolled immigration would only grant "certain interests the opportunity to exploit them."[17]

The Swedish-American religious denominations naturally took an interest in immigration legislation, inasmuch as their future existence was to a great degree directly dependent upon the course of immigration. When immigration declined they lost their importance as immigrant churches. Characteristically enough they did not object to more restrictive legislation as long as it only applied to immigrants from Southern and Eastern Europe. *Augustana,* the official newspaper of the Augustana Synod, considered that legislation of this type was unnecessary as long as there were guarantees that the immigrants who were allowed entry came chiefly from Northern Europe.[18] If this proved not to be the case *Augustana* preferred that restrictions be made to prevent the immigration of the Southern Europeans who were morally and physically weak. If this were not done America would have on its hands "millions of residents who, besides being ignorant and incapable of utilizing the rights of citizenship, had totally different conceptions of morality than those which gave the people of Northern Europe their pre-eminent position."

Förbundets Veckotidning, the official spokesman for the Swedish Evangelical Covenant Church, held principally the same viewpoint as *Augustana.* While the newspaper clearly perceived that America's development as a nation would be stunted if no new blood was furnished from abroad, it realized that "the current situation" could not continue.[19] Perhaps it was right, it said, to shut out immigrants

[16] *Svenska Amerikanaren,* June 3, and November 4, 1920.
[17] *Ibid.,* December 9, 1920.
[18] *Augustana,* September 15, 1921, p. 584, and March 16, 1922, p. 168.
[19] *Förbundets Veckotidning,* May 25, 1920.

who were menaces to society. However, any laws which, for example, excluded Scandinavians were out of the question. "Even we believe that a more congenial solution to the immigrant question can be found than an absolute ban."[20] A total restriction of immigration would be an unfortunate step in the wrong direction, as long as it was possible to enact laws which shut the doors on a great deal of the ignorant masses from Southeastern Europe. "It is from this area that we get the people who are menaces to society." Furthermore, as long as America boasted millions of acres of good arable land, it would not need to enforce a total ban on immigration. When the Quota Law of 1921 was enacted, the newspaper called it "nonsense" and contended that it judged neither the character nor the competence of immigrants for admittance or refusal.[1] It was a mistake to have a law where the almanac was the only deciding factor in the destiny of the would-be immigrant.

When Congress prepared to discuss ways of strengthening the quota regulations of 1921 the same arguments heard earlier in that connection were for the most part repeated. Senator Magnus Johnson was the only Swedish-American congressman who opposed the proposal of basing quota legislation on the census of 1890:[2] "I know that the bill is proposed to be passed for the purpose of discrimination." He stated in the Senate that reasons of principle forced him to oppose the measure, although he admitted that this would cost him votes in the next election. However, he refused to accept the notion that Swedes and Scandinavians at large were better than other Europeans: "I have met persons of all nationalities and I have met good and bad ones in all of them even in my own nationality." According to American opinion Magnus Johnson was radical in his views, which

[20] *Ibid.*, January 18, 1921.

[1] *Ibid.*, August 7, 1921.

[2] *Congressional Record*, 68th Congress, 1st Session, p. 6617. Magnus Johnson was one of the most colorful of Swedish-American politicians. Born in Eds parish in Värmland in 1871, he emigrated to America in 1891. In 1914 he was elected to the Minnesota State Legislature. He was nominated the Farmer-Labour Party's candidate for governor in the 1922 election but was defeated by a narrow margin. In 1923 he was elected to the United States Senate, though he lost his bid for re-election in 1924. However, in 1932 he gained a seat in the House of Represenatives and won re-election in 1934. He died during the election campaign of 1936. (Sten Carlsson, "Från Värmland till Minnesota," *Emigranten*, 2, 1970).

explains his scepticism toward the racial prejudice expressed by many Swedish Americans and native Americans.

The Swedish-American press adhered by and large to its stated principles. *Svenska Kuriren* now took the lead among the Swedish language papers in criticizing the move to strengthen existing regulations. In its opinion the action of Congress clearly showed that an overwhelming number of legislators and representatives of the American people were "unpractical" persons.[3] It called them "spineless gentlemen" who betrayed an alarming lack of moral fibre. The newspaper also ridiculed the talk about "the red scare" and the oratory which declared that America should only be populated by the "one hundred percent Americans." There were already more than enough such Americans, the newspaper assured its readers. What was needed now were more working class people to bridge the gap when the "one hundred percent American" gradually became more and more refined. "He (the hundred percent American) will no longer have anything to do with the miner. And this distaste for 'dirty' jobs is almost instinctively shared by the immigrants' children, who regretfully fancy that such an attitude is an integral part of the notion of being a one hundred percent American."

The outcome of the quota legislation of 1921 had made it clear that America could not shut its doors on the "undesirable" masses from Southern and Eastern Europe. For one thing, their quota allotments were filled much more rapidly than those of Northern and Western Europeans. However, this was no reason for further limiting the quotas, since America especially needed people who could work. What it did lack was people with good physical health and the willingness to take up whatever jobs were available.[4]

[3] *Svenska Kuriren*, February 22, and October 11, 1923. In the second of these two articles (October, 1923), the newspaper called this "red scare" talk "pure nonsense." In fact, it considered the "scare" so insignificant that it was prepared to let Bolshevik Moscow openly preach its doctrines in America. However, on this occasion the newspaper was not consistent in its views. During the war it had attacked communism as a threat to the security of America.

[4] The same arguments were used on more than one occasion. In its editorial of April 17, 1924, *Svenska Kuriren* accused the one hundred percent Americans of disregarding the country's pressing need for manpower in their blind fear that immigrants would cheapen the quality of the American race. "If further reductions are made on the number of immigrants from Northern and Western Europe, then it is rather certain that even the American employers who are fully

As time went on, even *Svenska Kuriren* seemed to accept the notion that the massive immigration from Southern and Eastern Europe was a disadvantage because these immigrant groups were not becoming Americanized.[5] The immigration regulations of 1924 would, in other words, be of advantage to those immigrants actually desired in America. *Svenska Kuriren* regarded the protests raised by Poles and Italians against the quota reductions as both unjustified and "considerably presumptuous." The Swedish-American press resorted to this line of reasoning whenever any non-Swedish minority raised protests.[6]

Förbundets Veckotidning and, at times, even *Svenska Amerikanaren* expressed the opinion that a reduction of immigrant quotas would harmfully affect America's economic development. *Förbundets Veckotidning* pointed out the need for immigrant workers and said that legislators would hardly have time to pass a law before American industry began to cry out for people who were willing to cast themselves into hard work.[7] For its part *Svenska Amerikanaren* feared that a total ban on immigration – a measure which was never seriously considered – would lead to severe setbacks in America's national development. Yet at the same time it was fully aware that America could not permit just anyone to be "dumped" on its doorstep:[8] in

hundred percent Americans will stand united to encourage new people to immigrate to America, without simultaneously turning up their noses at national origins and living habits or raising more of a fuss over deficiencies in the melting pot."

5 *Svenska Kuriren,* February 7, 1924. The newspaper referred to citizenship statistics which reported that these particular immigrant groups were slower than others in becoming Americanized. It maintained that, as a rule, those immigrants who were most enthusiastic about seeking citizenship made it known that they were getting along well in America and that they wanted to become citizens. *Svenska Kuriren* went on to argue that if quota legislation were based solely upon the immigrants' desire for citizenship, the lawful immigration from Northern and Western Europe would be three times as great as that from Southern and Eastern Europe. The chapter in this study which deals with this topic of immigrants and citizenship (pp. 41—49) has clearly shown that it is misleading to compare the "old" and the "new" immigrants, inasmuch as the statistics do not show the respective lengths of time the groups resided in America.

6 *Svenska Kuriren,* April 24, 1924.

7 *Förbundets Veckotidning,* April 24, 1923.

8 *Svenska Amerikanaren,* February 9, 1922.

other words, the newspaper was debating the issues in the same way that it handled the quota legislation of 1921.

The Swedish-American newspapers which were initially sceptical of the quota laws of 1921 and 1924 gradually accepted them. However, the National Origins Law was another matter: they considered it idiotic, unjust, and to a great extent discriminatory against Germans and Scandinavians. They indignantly regretted the fact that America no longer needed the contributions of the Swedish people who for so long had been praised as "the best of the immigrants."[9] None of the newspapers which have been mentioned here was convinced that the National Origins Law would produce a nation of one hundred percent Americans. For the most part, both the newspapers and Swedish Americans in general seemed to put their faith in President Herbert Hoover who, during the presidential campaign of 1928, pledged himself not to ratify the National Origins Law passed by Congress.[10]

In its opposition to the National Origins Law, as earlier in its opposition to the quota legislation of 1921 and 1924, *Svenska Kuriren* assumed the role of chief critic among the Swedish language newspapers. It regarded the law's provisions as a direct summons to eligible voters of Swedish descent to write their senators and congressmen and request them to vote for retaining the Quota Law of 1924.[11] The newspaper thought that Swedes ought to see to it that these provisions were revoked, "unless they seriously believed that the Swedes, whose family of settlers and nation-builders had worked side by side with Norwegian, Danish and German pioneers in setting star after star in the American flag, were less worthy and less desirable . . . than the Russians, Italians and English." It considered the primary obligation of all Swedes was to make legislators "understand what is in store for them if they fail to prevent a fanatic minority who shuns the broad light of day from achieving its goals by stealth and intrigue."[12] When it was clear that the law would become effective on July 1, 1929, *Svenska Kuriren* expressed its disappointment and regretfully pointed out that all of the talk about Swedes as the finest of American immi-

9 *Svenska Kuriren,* August 12, 1926.

10 *Ibid.,* March 21, 1929.

11 *Ibid.,* June 10, 1926.

12 *Ibid.,* February 21, 1929.

grant groups was evidently based upon a misunderstanding.[13] All of the fine words lavished on the Swedes were apparently only hollow phrases. The newspaper went on to comment that the reason for the quota reductions affecting both Swedish and Irish immigrants was probably connected with the fact that both groups were suspected of German sympathies during the war.

Svenska Tribunen Nyheter also opposed the National Origins Law on the grounds that it was impractical, unjust, and discriminatory. The law was only "a source of delight to white and colored persons who are subjects of the British Empire and to the great masses of Southern Europeans who live under the sway of the Catholic Church."[14]

Svenska Amerikanaren shared this view and further emphasized the discriminatory features of the law by claiming that it put the Swedes on equal footing with "those ignorant hordes of morally and physically inferior individuals who come to America from Mexico, Sicily, sections of the Balkan peninsula, and other places. One single Swede is worth more to the welfare of America than ten persons from such nationalities as these."[15] *Svenska Amerikanaren* had criticized the same legislation on a number of earlier occasions. It said, for example, that it could hardly imagine "a more absurd way, frankly speaking, of regulating immigration than the National Origins Law." In its eyes the law was directly aimed against the countries of Northern Europe "who had unquestionably given America and its people a more desirable type of immigrant stock than all the other nations put together, with the exception of England."

While the newspapers were debating the issues high and low, Swedish Americans were growing noticeably worried over the consequences the law might have for their own sphere of existence. Church-affiliated newspapers attacked the measure with particular bitterness. *Augustana* asked, among other things, that the law be changed in the name of justice.[16] It also requested its readers to write immediately to Congress and insist upon the following actions: the retention of current quotas based on the census of 1890; the repeal of regulations made in 1924; and the guarantee of legislators that they would not

[13] *Ibid.*, June 20, 1929.

[14] *Svenska Tribunen Nyheter,* July 17, 1929.

[15] *Svenska Amerikanaren,* August 21, 1930, and April 4, 1929.

[16] *Augustana,* December 8, 1927, and September 19, 1929.

propose any laws intended to reduce the quotas for Scandinavians. *Augustana* referred its readers to the resolution taken up with regard to the National Origins Law and adopted by the Synod in 1926 at its annual conference in Philadelphia. The newspaper's ecclesiastical views became the cutting edge of its protest: the new law would mean the curtailment of immigration by Protestants and the throwing open of the doors to the immigration of Catholics.[17] When the law was formally enacted the newspaper said that it was "necessary for all citizens who feel that the new regulations are unjust . . . to make their protests loud and clear to their respective Congressmen. Persons of Scandinavian descent especially ought to react to the new law as a slap in the face."[1] *The Lutheran Companion* charged that the legislation was a result of a "conspiracy" among certain groups of people, and it wondered how anyone could" figure out wherein the United States will be benefited by the immigration of more Italians, Poles and Irish . . . by reducing the quota of Germans and Scandinavians."[2] The various newspapers representing the Evangelical Covenant Church also voiced their opposition to the National Origins Law. *Förbundets Veckotidning* asserted that an infamous propaganda effort was responsible for the new regulations.[3] It, too, considered the law as an insult to Germany, Ireland, and the Scandinavian countries, all of which had given America the finest of citizens.[4] It was rather unusual for anyone reading a Swedish language newspaper at this time to hear the Irish being spoken of as some of "the finest of citizens." Swedes were more accustomed to seeing the Irish as their worst antagonists, especially when it came to political matters. In late 1930 *Missionsvännen* argued that the National Origins Law had not only been a bundle of problems from the very start but was directly responsible for unleashing a stream of lawlessness in America. The result of "our" policy of admitting destructive elements into "our" midst, "especially those from Russia and Southern Europe, has been an almost helpless struggle against crime and anarchy."[5]

[17] *Ibid.*, September 13, 1928, p. 584.

[1] *Ibid.*, April 11, 1929, p. 232.

[2] *The Lutheran Companion,* October 26, 1929, p. 1349.

[3] *Förbundets Veckotidning,* June 22, 1926.

[4] *Ibid.*, April 2, 1929.

[5] *Missionsvännen,* October 7, 1930.

The church-affiliated newspapers were joined in protest by other members of the Swedish-American press out of a common fear of the consequences the law would have for Swedish-American institutions. *Nordstjernan* thought that the Swedish heritage in America would die out.[6] *Svenska Amerikanska Posten* was so unnerved by the possible threat to Swedish-American organizations, churches, and schools that it predicted that everything the Swedish pioneers had built up under circumstances of great personal hardship would most likely vanish altogether.[7]

It is apparent from this analysis that the Swedish-American newspapers were fairly united in their reactions to the National Origins Law. They considered it particularly insulting to Scandinavians, whose quota allotments were lowered at the same time that immigrants from Southern and Eastern Europe were granted a relatively improved quota level. A persistent theme ran through all of the discussion brought forward by these newspapers: a concern for what was best for the Swedes. In an article published in 1926 George Stephenson pointed out the dangers of such feelings among Swedish Americans. Despite his opposition to the National Origins Law and his desire for having it repealed he warned against taking any steps which were rooted in racism or national discrimination. "Let the Scandinavians urge Congress to enact a law that will promote assimilation without deliberately offending certain nationalities."[8]

It appears as if the repeated requests from Swedish-American newspapers for an organized means of protest fell on deaf ears. The Augustana Synod, which was the largest and strongest religious body among Swedish Americans, was more interested in Prohibition than in the immigration question. The same seems to have been the case for all religious denominations. If there was any initiative taken for organized public protest, it came largely from private sources. Perhaps the largest protest meeting ever assembled during this period was that held in Chicago's Orchestra Hall in May, 1929, where 3,000 persons of Scandinavian, German, and Irish descent were on hand to participate.[9]

[6] *Nordstjernan,* May 28, 1926.

[7] *Svenska Amerikanska Posten,* January 30, 1929.

[8] "Immigration : A Symposium." *The American Scandinavian Review,* November 1926, p. 678.

[9] *Förbundets Veckotidning,* April 2, 1929.

However, various Swedish-American organizations adopted a series of resolutions. The Augustana Synod issued the following statement in one of the resolutions passed at its annual conference in 1926: "The synod disapproves of the Immigration Act of 1924 and, in particular, Section II of the Act, which, if put into operation would react inequitably against the immigrant to the United States, coming from Northern Europe."[10] In a resolution adopted by the John Ericsson Republican League of Illinois, the national origins provision was denounced as unjust, discriminatory, and impractical.[11]

Even Swedish-American congressmen showed strong opposition to the measure. Carl Chindblom, who called himself a restrictionist and had supported every attempt to curtail immigration, turned right around and fought the national origins provision.[12] Up to the very last minute he sought, in vain, to persuade Congress to delay its enactment as law. Congressmen of Scandinavian descent preferred that the quota legislation of 1924 – namely, the two percent quota based on the number of foreign-born residents of the United States in 1890 – be instituted on a permanent basis.[13]

4. *Comments on the Swedish Campaign against Emigration*

It has always been a predominant characteristic of Swedish Americans to react strongly against any negative comments made about America by Swedes back home. This was also the case when Swedes attempted to prevent the emigration to America. It is worth noting in this context the somewhat acrid remarks of *Svenska Kuriren* in reply to the proposal made by Adrian Molin that the Swedish-American Line carry only Swedes who were returning to Sweden and not those who

10 *Minutes of the Augustana Synod,* 1926, p. 163.

11 Reuel Gustav Hemdahl, "The Swedes in Illinois Politics," Ph. D. thesis (Northwestern University, Evanston, 1934), p. 230.

12 *Congressional Record,* 70th Congress, 2nd Session, p. 5194.

13 Fritiof Ander, "The Effects of the Immigration Law of 1924 upon a Minority Immigrant Group," p. 346.

were emigrating to America.[14] In an editorial on November 25, 1920, *Svenska Kuriren* expressed great irritation with "the notorius *Föreningen mot Emigrationen* (Anti-Emigration Association) and particularly its equally notorious director, Adrian Molin" and the alarms they were raising over increased emigration from Sweden. The newspaper declined to comment on all the scribbling in Sweden which talked about America as a wicked and odious nation. However, it did recommend one thing, namely that all Swedes who had thought about emigrating do so as quickly as possible. For it would only be a matter of time before "Adrian Molin and his compatriots in *Föreningen mot Emigrationen* no longer needed to campaign for a total halt to the emigration" to America. The newspaper believed that the reason why emigration from Sweden never got started after World War I was that Swedes were either frightened or discouraged from leaving the country.[15] It accused newspapers in Sweden of painting an altogether gloomy picture of the whole situation at the same time that Swedish Americans were advising their friends and relatives in Sweden not to emigrate. Under such circumstances *Svenska Kuriren* was reluctant to support the efforts being made to increase the immigration from Sweden. It was useless to do so when Swedes were being warned by relatives in America that it was difficult to find work. The newspaper also doubted whether Swedish workers were still suited for American society.

5. *Summary*

The Swedish-American newspapers usually lent their support to those who pressed for restrictions against the "new" immigrants – immigrants from Southern and Eastern Europe. However, as soon as the

[14] *Svenska Kuriren* also made a personal attack against Adrian Molin, "who more than any other living Swede has consistently made impossible that unity — which is known only by the slogan, 'the bridge over the waters' — through his methodical slandering of America and, in particular, the social relationships, organizations, and prominent individuals associated with Swedish Americans." This particular attack on Molin was characteristic of the prevailing attitude among the Swedish-American press. The newspapers replied just as harshly to every outburst of criticism from Sweden and every attempt by Swedish officials to restrict the flow of emigration.

[15] *Svenska Kuriren,* May 18, 1922.

talk turned to restricting immigration from Scandinavia, as was evident later on, they were less accommodating. They always took the stand which was most favorable for the Swedish Americans. Most editors seemed to be aware of the consequences restricted immigration might have for Swedish Americans and their particular community organization. The debate in the Swedish-American press on quota allotments soon became entagled in a web of suspicion and prejudice which sought out its targets among the Catholic minorities. Article after article emphasized the superiority of the Scandinavian and German peoples. This debate was often influenced by the overall public discussion on immigration.

It is surprising that the Swedish language newspapers took such a profound interest in the quota legislation, inasmuch as immigration from Sweden had almost entirely ceased by the time Congress enacted such measures. In fact, with the exception of one year – 1923 – immigration from Sweden never exceeded the authorized quota levels throughout the 1920s. However, there are signs which suggest that Swedish Americans believed that immigration would start up again. Several newspapers particularly clung to the idea that America had yet to see the last of the immigrants.

VIII. The Economic Depression and the Immigrants

1. *The General Situation*

The Depression came suddenly and few were ready for it. It was especially severe on the foreign-born, in particular, the aliens, who were not only deprived of their livelihood but found their dreams and illusions about the U.S. demolished. Many of the newly arrived immigrants had really not had opportunity to obtain a permanent job, much less set aside anything for the future. "Foreign-born families who had by years of ... effort raised themselves to a much better position were obliged to drop back to the level at which they started in America, or even lower."[1]

Immigrants were considered more or less as encroachers, and the indigenous workers thought that the native-born should have privileges on the job market, in which conditions for employment for the immigrants were often less desirable than for American workers.[2] Contrary to the situation in the 1920s, the attack was directed no longer chiefly against the Southern and Eastern Europeans, but against all immigrant

[1] Lillian Brandt, *An Impressionistic View of the Winter of 1930—31 in New York City* (New York, 1932), p. 14. It is often difficult to separate the designations, "foreign-born" (persons born outside the U.S.) and "aliens" (non-American citizens). This is explained partly by the fact that the boundaries between these two groups cannot always be identified. A clear difference is made in regulations and statutes, where according to American law all American citizens in principle are alike with one exception: one must be born in America to become president. Common opinion made no distinctions between the two groups, the reason being that even naturalized foreign-born, socially and economically, were identified with their nationality, even if legally and constitutionally they were equal with native Americans. The sense of identity with the respective national group was not necessarily lessened with citizenship, and the actual difference between citizens and non-citizens among the foreign-born became blurred, not least in the eyes of the people themselves.

[2] Ross Eckler, "Immigration and the Labor Force." *The Annals of the American Academy of Political and Social Science* (March, 1949), p. 96.

groups and strangers in general. People with strange languages and customs often were harassed for their deviations from the norm.[3]

Discrimination against non-citizens had severe consequences for large groups of immigrants. It assumed a serious nature when it asserted itself on the job market in that more and more jobs and employers demanded citizenship as a qualification. "In thousands of cases foreigners are being dismissed because of this 'all-American' policy."[4] There are many examples of workers being denied work because they lacked citizenship. There are likewise many examples of foreigners being dismissed in order to make place for American workers. "For instance, in December, 1932, fourteen hundred non-citizens were fired from New York hospitals. Only six hundred citizens were hired to replace those dismissed."[5] Harold Fields found in a study made in 1928 that a large number of immigrants lacked work because they were not American citizens.[6] In spite of the prevailing favorable working conditions, Fields found that three out of five jobs were reserved for American citizens and that four out of five trade unions demanded citizenship as a condition for membership. Only in the group of non-skilled workers was the demand for citizenship less pronounced. Fields also found that there were silent agreements regarding prohibitions against the employment of foreign workers.[7]

Discrimination was not limited to private undertakings or trade unions but was even encouraged by Federal authorities. In the year 1932 the Treasury Department was upheld in prohibiting the employment of non-citizens in public construction.[8] In the same year

[3] Jane Clark, *Deportation of Aliens from the U.S. to Europe* (New York, 1931), p. 31.

[4] Harold Fields, "Where Shall the Alien Work"? *Social Forces,* December, 1933, p. 213.

[5] Dwight Morgan, *The Foreign-Born in the U.S.* (New York, 1936), p. 45.

[6] Harold Fields, "The Unemployed Foreign-Born." *The Quarterly Journal of Economics* (May, 1935), p. 534 f.

[7] Dwight Morgan, *op. cit.,* p. 45; Foreign Language Information Service: "How Unemployment Afflicted the Non-Citizens," *Svenska Amerikanaren,* May 28, 1931, p. 4.

8 Harold Fields, *op. cit.,* p. 539.

Congress voted $132.5 million for the construction of public roads, employment for which was limited to American citizens.[9]

Harold Fields even gives evidence that discrimination was most common within the individual states.[10] In 1931 seven states adopted laws that prohibited the placement of non-American citizens in public jobs. Professionals who required more extensive education, like doctors, lawyers, teachers, *et. al.,* demanded citizenship.

The Ellis Island Committee, appointed under Franklin D. Roosevelt's administration, criticized the frequent discrimination and declared every kind of discrimination against newly-arrived immigrants as morally indefensible.[11] The Committee also criticized the tendency to dismiss foreign workers in order to create places for American workers. Discrimination on the job market was a vicious circle with respect to the living conditions of the immigrants. "In essence, they cannot work because they are not citizens and they cannot become citizens because they cannot work."[12] Between 1929 and 1934 the fee for attaining citizenship was so high that a person without work could not possibly afford it. The fee was increased in 1929 from $5 to $20. In addition there were other expenses for witnesses, travel, *et cetera,* increasing the total cost of the process to between $50 and $100.[13] By comparison, the average weekly wage for an industrial worker was $25.03 in 1929 and only $17.05 in 1932.[14]

Favoring American citizens was not confined to the job market. According to American law, in principle every person living in the U.S. was entitled to economic help – "relief" – as needed.[15] There are nevertheless many examples of American citizens receiving advantage in the distribution of aid. Resources were often inadequate and therefore it became the responsibility of the organizations to weed out in an equitable manner the less pressing cases. Considering the almost

[9] Read Lewis, "Immigration Issues," *The Survey* (May 15, 1932), pp. 189 f.

[10] Harold Fields, *op. cit.,* p. 536; Read Lewis, *op. cit.,* p. 189.

[11] *Report of the Ellis Island Committee,* 1934, pp. 7 f.

[12] *Report of the Ellis Island Committee,* 1934, p. 126.

[13] Harold Fields, "The Unemployed Foreign-Born," p. 540.

[14] *Hist. Stat. of the U.S.,* p. 92.

[15] Donald Young, *Research Memorandum on Minority People in the Depression* (New York, 1937), p. 64; C. White, *Administration of Public Welfare* (New York, 1940), p. 184.

hostile attitude not only to aliens but even to the foreign-born, it is easy to understand how they would become subject to a certain arbitrariness.[16] It was also commonly assumed that immigrants could manage on less and for that reason were not in as much need of help.[17]

There was no co-ordinated relief program for the entire nation. It varied from state to state and from place to place. The concepts of unemployment compensation and social welfare were still unknown, and public aid supported by public funds was strictly limited.[18] The basic principle was that aid should occur with private initiative and should be dispensed as "grudgingly and humiliatingly as possible in order to discourage spongers and to point up the disgrace of poverty."[19] In spite of the fact that the foreign-born comprised a high percentage of the total population (1930, 10.9 percent), there was no general organized relief program for this group or for aliens. The Department of Labor, in 1923, investigated possibilities for the immigrants to receive social welfare from the states. The conclusion reached was that any social welfare in behalf of immigrants in general was marked by an obvious inactivity.[20] There was hardly any improvement after 1923. *The Ellis Island Committee* concluded, on the contrary, that a decline had occurred.

With respect to relief work, by 1933 no less than 18 states had

[16] C. White, *Research Memorandum on Social Aspects of Relief Policies in the Depression* (New York, 1937), p. 72.

[17] Broadus Mitchell, *Depression Decade* (New York, 1947), pp. 103 f.

[18] Until 1932 relief activities in behalf of those suffering from the Depression were based almost exclusively on voluntary contributions. Committees on unemployment were formed and relief stations were established in most places for collecting and distributing contributions to the needy. In order to co-ordinate and to increase the effectiveness of the relief activities, several governors during 1930 and 1931 appointed relief committees within their respective states. In 1931 and 1932 the first state legislatures voted funds to assist the local relief committees. New York and Illinois each approved $20 million to meet the most pressing needs. (Clarence Enzler, *Some Social Aspects of the Depression 1930—1933* [Washington, D.C., 1939] pp. 94 ff.

[19] Dixon Wecter, *The Age of the Depression 1929—1941* (New York, 1948), p. 45.

[20] *Report of the Ellis Island Committee,* pp. 113 f.

laws which limited this program to American citizens.[1] In 1934 the senate in the state of New York proposed that all aliens should be excluded from relief work.[2] Even certain federal laws exercized a noticeable favoritism. The Secretary of Labor, in his report for 1935, pointed out that discrimination of non-citizens was quite common.[3]

From articles and pronouncements of that period one can easily draw the conclusion that foreign-born and especially aliens comprised a relatively large proportion of the nation's needy. The conclusion, meanwhile, has never really been supported with statistical data.[4] There is no breakdown by nationalities of the number seeking relief in the entire U.S.[5] Judging by the few local investigations the number of foreign-born who received help corresponds to their proportionate share of the population. A study of unemployed persons in Minneapolis who were registered between 1900 and 1936 with the Board of Public Welfare shows that the foreign-born during the Depression were not an especially oppressed group.[6] According to the 1930 census the foreign-born accounted for 17.6 percent of Minneapolis inhabitants. In 1935 and 1936, 19.2 percent and 18.4 percent respectively of the foreign-born received aid – in other words between 1 and 2 percent more than their proportion of the population. The same study reveals that the number of foreign-born who received aid between 1900 and 1936 showed a successive decline. Between 1920 and 1924, 34.9 percent of the aid went to the foreign-born. A comparison between citizens and aliens indicates that "contrary to public opinion" very few of the aliens received aid.[7]

[1] Donald Taft, *Problems Arising from Minorities. Our Racial and National Minorities, Their History, Contributions and Present Problems* (New York, 1937), pp. 26 f.

[2] Harold Fields, "The Unemployed Foreign-Born," p. 533.

[3] David Fellman, "The Alien's Right to Work," *Minnesota Law Review* (January, 1938), p. 138.

[4] *Interpreter Releases,* May 23, 1935.

[5] *Ibid.,* October 19, 1936.

[6] Paul Segner, *Minneapolis Unemployed. A Description and Analysis of the Resident Relief Population of the City of Minneapolis from 1900 to 1936.* WPA. (Minneapolis, 1937), pp. 21 f.

[7] *Ibid.,* pp. 23 and 114; *New York Times,* February 3, 1935; *Interpreter Releases,* October 19, 1936, p. 293.

> Percentage of foreign-born applying for relief has been somewhat higher than the percentage for the general population of Minneapolis calculated from the 1930 United States Census. However, the percentage of foreign-born applying in more recent years is only slightly higher than that for the general population. Only among those applying for relief prior to 1920 did the percentage of aliens in the relief population exceed the percentage shown by the general population of Minneapolis for the 1930 census.

However, it should be emphasized at the outset that, inasmuch as no consideration has been taken of demographic differences, discretion must be applied in comparing the statistics for the total number of foreign-born in America with the statistics for the number of immigrants who received aid. Compared with the rest of the American population the high average age prevelant among immigrant groups should, in theory at least, imply that a high percentage of immigrants requested financial or social assistance.

In several respects it was hazardous for non-citizens to demand aid. According to American law, as mentioned earlier, persons who were a burden to the public were subject to deportation.[8] During the Depression the number of deportations increased rapidly, while it seemed to be a common assumption that the U.S. in the long run would benefit from the deportation of non-desirable aliens.[9] The

[8] *Report of the Ellis Island Committee,* p. 74. The first law to be directed against a whole nation — the Chinese Exclusion Act of 1882 — stipulated that Chinese who had entered illegally should be deported. These decisions have since been supplemented. After 1921, when the first quota law became effective, the number of deportations increased rapidly, due primarily to the fact that the enforcement of relevant decisions was intensified. Deportations occured according to two main principles where the time of arrival was decisive. In the one instance, deportation must occur within five years after the latest arrival in the United States. In the other, there was no limitation as to time. In the first category mentioned were persons, who, among others, were found to be illiterate or had violated the Contract Labor Law. This category also included persons who could be shown, on arrival, to have carried a communicable disease or had arrived in such a state that they later became public charges. The largest and most important group, nevertheless, was the second: those who could be deported regardless of time of arrival. To this group belonged such persons who had arrived illegally after July 1, 1924: criminals, prostitutes, drug addicts, anarchists, and "dangerous" radicals.

[9] Jane Clark, *Deportation of Aliens,* p. 28.

"likely-to-become-public-charge" clause became especially meaningful.[10] According to this clause every person who was not an American citizen and who within five years after his latest arrival had become a burden to the community was subject to deportation. This clause had a devastating result for many aliens. The fear of being deported had a psychological effect in that many unemployed and distressed aliens, and even foreign-born, refrained from seeking aid, giving substance to the statement that "no other form of discriminating treatment has been so serious, or, until recently, has been so cruelly administered, as our deportation laws."[11]

Between 1930 and 1932 the number of deportations increased rapidly.[12] In 1929, 12,908 persons were deported. In 1930, the number increased to 16,631 and finally in 1932 to 19,426, which was the highest number of deportations that ever occurred. The chief of the Immigration Bureau wrote in his annual report for 1929–30 that a tough deportation policy should be conducted: "The task of house-cleaning has practically just begun."[13] While unemployment during 1930 grew worse and many of the immigrants were undeservedly left without income, the Department of Labor was forced to accommodate the regulations to the new situation. During the greater part of 1930 the Department did not approve deportations in those cases where unemployment was "the sole cause of the alien's dependency."[14] In January, 1931, the Immigration Bureau further declared that immigrants who depended on public aid only on the grounds of unemployment need not fear deportation. The fear that other conditions leading to deportation would be discovered, however, deterred many from seeking assistance.

2. *The Swedish Americans during the Depression*

If the development within the Swedish-American organizations and the religious denominations is to be taken as a standard, it would

[10] *Report of the Ellis Island Committee,* p. 74.

[11] Donald Taft, *op. cit.,* p. 27; Foreign Language Information Service, *Svenska Amerikanaren,* April 16, 1931.

[12] *Annual Report of the Commissioner General of Immigration,* 1929—1935.

[13] *Annual Report of the Commissioner General of Immigration,* 1930, p. 7.

[14] *Interpreter Releases,* March 3, 1931, p. 17.

appear that the privations were severe. Religious and non-religious organizations worked under severely pressing economic conditions, at the same time as the demands on them increased. The financial problems created a vicious circle: the need to help individual members became more demanding at the same time that members found it more difficult to fulfill their economic obligations. Minutes and accounts generally indicate that individual contributions were seriously reduced as the crisis intensified and as unemployment increased.

The records of the local relief organizations give a concrete picture of the economic conditions among Swedish Americans. A study of unemployed people at the family service bureaus in Minneapolis reveals that the number of unemployed within the various nationalities was almost in proportion to the population. The number of Swedish families who were registered at one of the family service agencies in Minneapolis between 1900 and 1936 (31.1 percent) corresponds almost exactly to their portion of the foreign-born (31.8 percent), which would indicate that Swedes fared neither better nor worse than other nationalities taken together. After Swedes came Norwegians and Poles, who had relatively more need than Swedes. It can also be pointed out that families from Eastern Europe and Germany were less dependent on, or less inclined to ask for, relief.

Among the many "Swedish centers," Chicago appears to have been the most vulnerable. Employment was a severe problem long before 1929. Between 1922 and 1929 the number of unemployed showed a steady increase, which meant that Chicago reacted quickly to the stock market crash.[1] The great unemployment therefore put Chicagoans through severe ordeals during the Depression years. Relief activities here, as elsewhere in the country, were based largely on private initiative, and due to lack of stable organization it was impossible to meet the need that now arose.[2] The difficulties during the winter of 1930–31 were especially marked since the possibilities for the unemployed to manage things on their own began to diminish, because their own savings had as a rule come to an end.

[1] Rom Gudrun, "The United Charities of Chicago. Its History, 1857—1957" (Manuscript, Chicago), p. 268; Illinois Emergency Relief Commission, *First Annual Report,* 1933, p. 3.

[2] Illinois Emergency Relief Commission, *op. cit.,* p. 3.

Table 16. The proportionate distribution of unemployed foreign-born families and males, according to nationality, in Minneapolis who received help from 1900 to 1936 and the total number of foreign-born families and males, 21 years and older, in Minneapolis in 1930.

Country	Number foreign-born families 1930 %	% families who received help	Foreign-born males 1930 %	% males who received help
Austria	1.6	3.6	1.6	4.6
Canada (French)	1.6	0.5	1.5	0.9
Canada (other)	5.6	4.6	5.3	2.7
Czechoslovakia	3.1	3.4	2.9	1.7
Denmark	3.2	3.6	3.5	3.3
England	3.1	2.4	3.0	1.6
Finland	1.3	1.2	1.3	3.0
France	0.3	0.1	—	0.2
Germany	7.7	6.6	7.2	5.2
Ireland	1.3	1.0	1.3	1.8
Italy	1.1	2.1	1.1	0.8
Jugoslavia	—	0.2	—	1.4
Netherlands	0.5	0.4	0.5	0.1
Northern Ireland	0.4	0.8	0.4	0.2
Norway	18.7	21.0	18.7	20.6
Poland	5.7	8.8	5.7	7.6
Rumania	2.0	0.8	1.9	0.4
Russia	5.9	2.9	5.8	4.1
Scotland	1.3	0.7	1.3	0.6
Sweden	31.8	31.1	32.1	33.2
Switzerland	0.4	0.3	—	0.3
Other Countries	3.5	3.9	4.9	5.7
Total	100.0	100.0	100.0	100.0

Sources: *Fifteenth Census of the United States, 1930, Population, Special Report on Foreign-born White Families by Country of Birth*, p. 132; Paul Segner, *Minneapolis Unemployed*, pp. 68, 69.

Responsibility for family relief in Chicago, up until the fall of 1931, rested chiefly on the five large private relief organizations – American Red Cross, Catholic Charities, Jewish Social Service Bureau, Salvation Army, and United Charities – together with a public agency for Cook County, Cook County Bureau of Public Welfare.[3] Because of the

[3] *Social Service Yearbook*, 1932, p. 9.

increase in the number of unemployed, Governor Louis Emmerson, in October, 1930, appointed a special committee – Governor's Commission on Unemployment and Relief – responsible for co-ordinating and making more effective the raising of funds to aid unemployed families in Cook County.[4]

By the end of 1931 the private relief committees demonstrated a greater ability than the public agencies to secure funds, and during 1931 the private sector accounted for two-thirds of all relief work in Chicago.[5] In 1932 the picture changed and over 90 percent of the same activity was carried on with public funds, due to a series of changes regarding the administration of relief for the unemployed in Chicago. "Public funds, first State and then Federal, were relied on after March 1 to furnish money for relief."[6] The reason for this change was that private funds were no longer adequate to the situation. During the winter of 1931–32 it became obvious to the Illinois State Legislature that something dramatic must be done. In February, 1932, the State of Illinois voted $20 million for unemployment relief for Cook County for the period March 1, 1932, to February 28, 1933.

According to the records of the local relief organizations, the foreign-born experienced their share of unemployment. The years 1931 and 1932 appear to have been especially severe since an unusually large number turned to the United Charities for help (see Table 17). The United Charities stated in its annual report for 1932: "Every day things happen in many Chicago families that are worse than lack of material goods – worse than illness. The effects of the Depression are as devastating as war."[7] There were considerably more foreign-born families turning to United Charities in 1931 and 1932 than at any previous time. One of the chief explanations is undoubtedly that many families, on their own or with the help of friends, managed to get through the year 1930, while their own resources played out in 1931 and 1932. The sharp decline in 1933 must be seen in the light of the entrance of Federal and State governments into relief activities, with the result that the private organizations lost much of their importance.

[4] Cook County corresponds roughly to the City of Chicago.

[5] *Social Service Yearbook,* 1932, p. 18.

[6] *Ibid.,* p. 15.

[7] United Charities of Chicago, *Annual Report,* 1932.

Table 17. Number of families of various nationalities which in some form or other received aid from United Charities in Chicago, 1929—1933, and percentage of all foreign-born families in their own nationalities in Chicago.

Land of birth	1929 Number	%	1930 Number	%	1931 Number	%	1932 Number	%	1933 Number	%
Austria	30	0.3	52	0.5	320	3.0	276	2.6	108	1.0
Czechoslovakia	36	0.2	69	0.3	345	1.5	362	1.6	94	0.4
Denmark	12	0.2	18	0.3	150	2.7	104	1.9	27	0.5
England	26	0.3	57	0.6	314	3.0	259	2.5	69	0.7
Finland	2	0.3	4	0.5	35	4.4	26	3.3	9	1.1
France	8	0.5	27	1.6	136	7.9	113	6.6	19	1.1
Germany	136	0.3	355	0.7	1737	3.6	1611	3.4	292	0.6
Greece	41	0.7	75	1.3	342	6.0	335	5.8	119	2.1
Ireland	48	0.2	121	0.6	545	2.6	457	2.1	87	0.4
Italy	228	0.7	620	1.8	2562	7.5	2089	6.1	435	1.3
Jugoslavia	20	0.3	59	0.8	108	1.5	162	2.3	93	1.3
Lithuania	17	0.1	59	0.4	223	1.6	260	1.9	77	0.6
Norway	14	0.2	43	0.5	304	3.5	225	2.6	46	0.5
Poland	375	0.5	553	0.9	2468	3.5	2622	3.7	778	1.1
Russia	32	0.1	59	0.2	288	0.9	265	0.8	16	0.1
Sweden	44	0.2	126	0.5	656	2.5	628	2.4	114	0.4

Comments on the table: The table is based entirely on the lists which were kept at the various relief stations of United Charities, where the nationality of those registered was indicated. The names of all persons — about 40,000 — registered during the period named have been examined.

While the author has no figure for the total number of foreign-born registered with United Charities, the number of relief recipients from the respective nationalities has been compared with the total number of families of the same nationality.

Again, the table includes only those families which received help over a continuous period. The figures, in other words, do not show the number who sought help. Aid was provided almost exclusively in the form of food, clothing, rent, fuel, and medical service.

In conclusion it can be said that United Charities was the largest private family relief bureau in Chicago which assisted families in need of economic aid without regard to religion, race, and nationality. In addition, United Charities took on a somewhat official character inasmuch as Cook County assigned a large portion of its family relief work to United Charities.

Sources: *Fifteenth Census of the United States, 1930, Population, Special Report on Foreign-born White Families by Country of Birth of Head*, p. 129. United Charities register of persons who received aid during 1929—1933 at the various relief stations in Chicago.

Table 18. Number of families of various nationalities who registered at the larger public and private family welfare bureaus in Chicago in June, 1934, and all foreign-born families in Chicago according to the 1930 census.

Land of birth	Percent of all foreign-born families	Foreign-born families at family relief bureaus, June, 1934	
		Number	Percentage of own nationality
Italy	9.5	8,448	24.7
Greece	1.6	1,334	23.2
Austria	2.9	1,663	15.9
Poland	19.6	10,493	14.9
France	0.4	254	14.7
Norway	2.4	1,017	11.8
Germany	13.3	5,466	11.4
Ireland	5.9	2,384	11.2
Russia	9.2	3,450	10.4
Lithuania	3.7	1,422	10.2
Czechoslovakia	6.3	1,933	8.6
Sweden	7.3	2,235	8.5
Denmark	1.5	466	8.4
Canada	2.9	693	6.8
Other Countries	13.5	7,218	14.8
Total	100.0	48,407	

Sources: *Fifteenth Census of the United States, 1930, Population, Special Report on Foreign-born White Families by Birth-place of Head,* p. 129; *Statistics,* Published by the Statistical Bureau, Council of Social Agencies of Chicago (Supplement), August, 1934, pp. 1–17.

It seems to have been especially difficult for the Southern European families during 1931 and 1932. Among Swedish families, on the other hand, there was less need of help from United Charities, and in 1931 only 2.5 percent of Swedish families received aid from this organization in contrast to 7.5 percent for example, of Italian. Swedish families seemed to manage better than most other nationalities.

Of the families who in June, 1934, were registered at the larger private and public family relief agencies in Chicago, 38 percent were foreign-born.[8] (According to the 1930 census foreign-born comprised 26 percent of Chicago's population.) The number who were registered was greatest among the Italian and Greek families, one-fourth of

[8] Council of Social Agencies of Chicago, *Statistics* (Supplement), August, 1934, p. 5.

whom received help from family relief agencies in Chicago (see Table 18). Only 8.5 percent of the Swedish families received aid from the agencies mentioned, which means that by comparison with other nationalities Swedes required less aid than other nationalities, with the exception of Danes and Canadians.

Table 19. The number of homeless males who in 1931 and 1932 were registered with the Chicago Clearing House and the percentage of foreign-born males, 21 years and older in Chicago, according to the 1930 census.

Land of birth	All foreign-born males 21 years and older in Chicago, 1930	Registered at Chicago Clearing House Number	%
United States	–	3,695	61.4
Poland	17.8	427	7.1
Ireland	5.9	248	4.1
Austria	2.8	205	3.4
Sweden	7.9	202	3.4
Germany	12.7	178	3.0
Lithuania	4.2	147	2.5
Russia	9.2	106	1.8
Norway	2.5	105	1.8
Mexico	0.1	103	1.7
Italy	9.5	88	1.5
Other Countries	27.4	496	8.3
Total	100.0	6,000	100.0

Sources: *Men in the Crucible*, Illinois Emergency Relief Commission, Chicago, 1931–1932, p. VI.
Fifteenth Census of the United States, 1930, Population, Vol. II, p. 470.

The Illinois Emergency Relief Commission discovered that 61.4 percent of the homeless males who registered at Chicago Clearing House in 1931–32 were Americans and 38.6 percent were foreign-born. With the foreign-born constituting 26 percent of the population of Chicago, it is evident that unemployment affects the foreign-born more extensively than the native-born.[9] Of all persons registered 7.1 percent were Polish, 4.1 percent Irish, and 3.4 percent Swedish. Germans comprised 3.0 percent and Italians 1.5 percent. If these

[9] Illinois Emergency Relief Commission, *Men in the Crucible,* Chicago, 1932. p. vi.

figures are compared with all foreign-born males 21 years and up, it is evident that Irish and Austrians especially were relatively overrepresented. Swedes corresponded almost to their portion of those registered, while Germans and Italians were notably underrepresented. These figures are surprising by comparison with foreign-born families, especially with respect to the low number of homeless Italian males who were registered at the Chicago Clearing House.

As is evident from the foregoing the differences were not only between native-born and foreign-born but between the various nationalities. Tables 18 and 19 show that Swedes comprised a lower number of families registered with United Charities in 1931–32 and with Chicago's family relief agencies in June, 1934, than most other nationalities. From this perspective at least the Chicago Swedes must be considered as having managed relatively well. This does not imply that the difference was necessarily as great as the statistics in the tables above indicate, while the internal relief activities among the different nationalities either decreased or increased the need of aid from external agencies. The number of Swedes with private and public family relief agencies would certainly have been considerably greater if the internal activities among the Swedes had not been as intensive as was the case.

The Swedish-American newspapers and the annual reports of the Swedish organizations provide a great deal of information regarding conditions among the Swedish Americans. Bitterness and disappointment with respect to America comes to light in a letter to *Svenska Amerikanaren* (1930):

> It is not a pleasant outlook to live in a city and not be able to find a day's work because there are thousands standing and waiting before you. . . . Certainly a country like this ought to be able to do something to relieve the need. But you have to fend for yourself or die. At home they arrange relief work so people can earn something, but what is being done here? . . . They had better stop boasting now about America, because I believe it is better in Sweden than here . . . one has to look again to Sweden, and many are doing just that these days . . . . But there are also many who do not have money enough for the trip home, and it's too bad about them.[10]
>
> An Östgöte

[10] *Svenska Amerikanaren,* August 28, 1930, p. 11.

The letter reflects a mood not infrequent among the Swedes. In letters to the editors of the Swedish newspapers there are frequent complaints about discrimination in the labor market. The following comment from "An Unemployed Swede" appeared in *Nordstjernan* (August 7, 1930):

> With respect to Swedes here in New York, their situation is anything but enviable. Many of them are construction workers. . . . In New York City there are obviously some large buildings under construction but it takes a "pull" to get work on these projects, and as a rule preference is given to Irish and Italians.[11]

A Chicago Swede found the same conditions in Chicago.[12] The newspapers carried a rich flora of events and tragedies that resulted from unemployment and economic misery. For many the future seemed hopeless. In *Svenska Amerikanaren* during the Depression years appeared a recurring headline: "Swedes tired of living." Under this heading were listed the names of persons who had committed suicide. Often the motivation for their action was attributed to the Depression. Only a few examples are given here:

> In desperation over being unemployed and even ejected from his apartment . . . attempted to commit suicide.[13]
> Financial difficulties produced disgust with life.[14]
> Unemployment is one cause of the great disenchantment with life.[15]

These examples reflect a bit of the tragedy that followed in the wake of the Depression. As a whole the frequency of suicide increased in the United States between 1928 and 1932 from 13.6 per 100,000 inhabitants to 17.4.[16] These statistics indicate, however, that there was little difference in the frequency of suicide between a period of economic boom and a depression. By 1935 the number had fallen to 14.8 per 100,000 and by 1939, at the outbreak of World War II, to 14.1

This picture of the situation among the Chicago Swedes can be complemented by the view which the Swedish papers in Chicago took

11 *Nordstjernan,* August 7, 1930, p. 15.

12 *Svenska Amerikanaren,* November 13, 1930, p. 9.

13 *Svenska Amerikanaren,* January 1, 1931, p. 1.

14 *Ibid.,* January 22, 1931, p. 1.

15 *Ibid.,* February 19, 1931, p. 1.

16 *Historical Statistics of the United States,* p. 26.

of the scene. According to one study made by *Svenska Tribunen Nyheter,* poverty among the Swedes was greater than appeared on the surface.[17] "It is undeniable," says the paper, "that Swedes in Chicago were hit especially hard – even harder than others – by the Depression and the resulting unemployment, because many thousands of Swedes were skilled workers in the building industry, which has been at a complete standstill for over a year here in Chicago." The paper also discovered that not only had construction workers been unemployed for a long period but "many, many others . . . walk the Chicago streets in search of work – starving, freezing, and without a roof over their heads." The more fortunate Swedes were urged, in the same issue of the newspaper, to be faithful to their unfortunate countrymen.

During the whole period from 1930 to 1932 the Chicago newspapers asked the Swedes to stay together and assist one another. *Missionsvännen,* like *Svenska Tribunen Nyheter,* found that the difficulties reached their worst in Chicago where Swedes, among others, lost their savings in bank failures.[18] The hardships encountered by Chicago Swedes were noted even by *Dagens Nyheter,* published in Stockholm, which stated as follows:

> The many bank failures which have occurred in Chicago this summer – 12 in one day! – just happened to strike those financial houses which had a significant Swedish-American clientele. As a matter of fact, there has not been a single bank crash in the city this year (1931) in which a large number of Swedes did not lose their money.[19]

The bank closings caused great anxiety not only for individuals but equally for Swedish organizations. The president of the Illinois Conference of the Augustana Synod declared at the annual meeting in 1931: "Not only have our people the unemployment condition to contend with, but the numerous bank and business failures as well."[20] Several of the better-known Swedish banks were forced to close. "Swedish bank" means that the majority of the stock was owned by Swedes or that the bank was located in a Swedish center. According to Charles Albers, manager and chief examiner, Chicago Clearing House Association "the Swedish banks were more ethnic than others.

17 *Svenska Tribunen Nyheter,* October 22, 1930, p. 1.

18 *Missionsvännen,* September 15, 1931, p. 4 (editorial).

19 *Dagens Nyheter,* September 20, 1931, p. 5 (Sten Hammarskjöld).

20 *Illinois Conference of the Augustana Synod, Minutes,* 1931, p. 19.

When a Swede heard that one of his countrymen had started a bank he very often patronized this bank."[1] Swedes were hit especially hard when the Lake View State Bank closed in August, 1930, and only 48 3/4 percent was paid out on deposits. Several thousand persons who had their savings in the Lake View bank and similar institutions suffered severe losses.[2]

Another Swedish bank that closed in April, 1931, paid out 52 percent. In 1930, the Chicago Bank of Commerce opened.

> The Chicago Bank of Commerce has come into existence especially to serve the Swedish element in the city and has in a short time become the Swedish bank. Of the stockholders, 80 are Swedish, and the chief officers are our countrymen.[3]

Unperturbed by the uncertain conditions, many Swedes transferred their savings to what was considered to be a safer institution. When it also closed in June, 1932, disappointment was great. The bank later paid out 71 1/4 percent of deposits.[4]

It was not only in Chicago that bank failures devastated the savings of the Swedish people. In Lindsborg, Kansas, two out of three banks closed. By contrast to Chicago, Lindsborg was a small town whose chief industry was agriculture. The low prices on farm products caused farmers to default on mortgage payments on farms which had been purchased when prices were high. Defaults on mortgage payments in turn increased the problems of the banks.

> The First National Bank closed its doors in October, 1930. . . . The Commercial State Bank followed with similar action in December, 1930. The Farmers State Bank was able to weather the violent financial storm which threatened Lindborg's only remaining bank.[5]

In Rockford, where first- and second-generation Swedes accounted for 26 percent of the city's population, unemployment was severe. Rockford was an industrial city dominated by furniture and machine

[1] Interview with Charles Albers, May 28, 1965.

[2] *Svenska Amerikanaren,* January 22, 1931, p. 13.

[3] *Sändebudet,* July 17, 1930, p. 15.

[4] Interview with Charles Albers, May 28, 1965. Information from Albers' own records on the closed banks in Chicago.

[5] Emory Lindquist, *Smoky Valley People. A History of Lindborg, Kansas.*(Lindsborg, 1953), pp. 160 f.

industries – "the second largest furniture center of the world."[6] Swedes owned the majority of the furniture factories. During the 1920s Rockford enjoyed great prosperity. "An economist of the day wrote that Rockford was the most prosperous city in the United States."[7] With the Depression, however, expansion ceased, and because of its production of materials sensitive to economic fluctuation Rockford felt the full impact. "With the speed of a dive bomber Rockford plunged to the depths of business stagnation in the early 1930s." The situation was especially critical in the summer of 1931, and in one day no less than three of the city's banks were closed. In December only two of eight former banks were still open.

The main body of Swedes seem to have worked in the tool and furniture industries. "Most of the factories had to close on account of the mortgages. Most of the Swedes were in these factories and that was mainly the cause of their unemployment."[8] Unemployment among the Swedes was considerable, which is evident in the fact that income for the Rockford churches which belonged to the Augustana Synod diminished by 41 percent from 1928 to 1932,[9] and in the fact that Baltic Lodge, Independent Order of Vikings, lost approximately 50 percent of its members.[10]

3. *Relief Work among Swedish Americans*

As mentioned earlier, the foreign-born were subject to discrimination in the relief programs. In addition, anxiety over the possibility of deportation was an indirect factor in deterring needy families and individuals from seeking help at public relief stations. In order to rush aid to their countrymen, the various nationalities formed their own relief committees.

The Swedish community developed new strength through the Depression. People closed ranks in order to assist unemployed and

[6] *Rockford,* compiled by the Workers of the Writers Program, 1941, p. 50.

[7] Wayne Whittaker, *The Rockford Story 1852—1952* (Rockford, 1956), p. 11.

[8] Letter to the author from The Reverend Albert Loreen, July 16, 1965.

[9] *Illinois Conference of the Augustana Synod, Minutes,* 1929—1933, statistical appendix.

[10] Interview with Adde Carlson, August 3, 1965. Information derived from records of the lodge.

needy members of their group and most of the Swedish organizations formed their own agencies. No help could be counted on from Sweden. In general, little attention was directed from that end toward Swedish Americans.

> It . . . is evident that Swedish immigrants in severe circumstances as a rule have no alternative but to depend on private generosity and relief efforts, whether from organizations or individuals. No help can be anticipated from the Swedish government except in unusual cases.[1]

The unwillingness of the Swedish state to help Swedish Americans stems from the pronouncement of the Bureau of Social Affairs *(Socialstyrelsen)* on June 24, 1930, in connection with a proposal for state aid for the unemployed Swedes in Canada.[2]

> It is further known that the present situation on the labor market in the United States is probably more troublesome than in Canada and that many Swedes there suffer from unemployment. If the present proposal is adopted, it would be difficult in the future to reject similar proposals from other quarters where Swedish immigrants are in distress.

As a rationale for rejecting the proposal in question, it was pointed out that decisions on obligations of this kind are based on "the internationally accepted opinion that it is the responsibility of the authorities in the country of residence to provide poverty-stricken foreign subjects the primary necessary assistance."

At the beginning of the Depression internal relief programs for needy Swedes were organized as a rule in the centers of Swedish population. Requests for help and voluntary contributions were made through the daily press and Swedish-American newspapers. In one paper after the other appeared announcements of benefit concerts and collections of clothes and funds. As a rule the initiative for relief activities was taken by an older immigrant or a second-generation Swede.

Since it is impossible to treat all of the places where Swedes were found, only a few of the larger centers will be selected, and since Chicago had the largest number of Swedes, it is appropriate to let this city, among others, serve as an example of Swedish activity.

[1] *SOU,* 1928 :8, p. 45.

[2] Statement from *Socialstyrelsen* (Bureau of Social Affairs) to Minister of Social Affairs. First Bureau, June 24, 1930, p. 481.

While help from the larger private relief organizations was far from adequate, Chicago Swedes made several attempts on their own to help their countrymen. In order to assist them effectively the churches in Chicago formed a special co-operative agency, the Swedish Church Federation.[3] One of its first actions was to bring into being a relief committee in each congregation with the responsibility for aiding its own members. The church members who were better situated were urged to help their countrymen who became victims of the economic crisis.[4] The next step was to organize a relief station where clothes and food coupons could be dispensed to those Swedes who were not members of a Swedish denomination.

When church effort proved to be inadequate, the Swedish-American Relief Committee was formed. It was a co-operative committee on which all of the larger Swedish organizations in Chicago were represented.[5] Its task was to "assist Swedish men and women who had encountered trouble through unemployment or bank failure."[6] At the organizational meeting it was declared that Swedes ought to take care of their own needy and that this could best be accomplished through a united effort by Swedish organizations. Through appeals in Swedish-American papers and in special communications, the Swedish-American Relief Committee set forth for the general public the situation of those in dire straights.

The Committee collected money and basic necessities. "We met frequently and developed a series of plans for raicing money through concerts, picnics and dances."[7] After the formation of the Committee the following plea appeared in the Swedish-American newspapers:

> Each and every one should participate in this worthy project: clothes and food items should be sent to a center set up for that purpose . . . or to one of the Swedish Churches, or to one of the nine Swedish Salvation Army Corps in the city. Hurry! The hungry need food immediately.[8]

[3] *Svenska Standaret,* December 16, 1930. (The Federation was formed in November, 1930).

[4] *Missionsvännen,* December 16, 1930.

[5] The Swedish-American Relief Committee was formed October 17, 1930, on the initiative of Herbert Hedman, who also became its chairman.

[6] *Svenska Tribunen Nyheter,* October 29, 1930, p. 18.

[7] Letter to the author from Herbert Hedman, October 21, 1964.

[8] *Svenska Amerikanaren,* October 20, 1930, p. 13.

The distribution of the necessities which had been assembled occurred through the Swedish Church Federation's relief station and the Swedish National Society *(Svenska Nationalförbundet)*, which was founded in Chicago October 10, 1913. The Society was an alliance of Swedish organizations and churches.[9]

The initiative taken by the Swedish-American Relief Committee provided a valuable benefit. Among other things a concert was arranged in Orchestra Hall September 21, 1930, netting a profit of $7,300. Meanwhile the need was great, and by January the money had been dispensed. In order to face the severe winter the need was placed on the consciences of the more prosperous Swedes with a plea for help.[10] *Svenska Tribunen Nyheter* praised the initiative in an editorial:

> Here in the city are thousands and thousands of Swedes who need not have the least anxiety for their existence, and every such person ought to contribute to relief funds.

To raise the funds the Committee decided that its members should each approach five of their closest friends and acquaintances and request of each a gift of five dollars.[11]

In order to be prepared for the worst in the face of the winter of 1931–32 the Chicago Swedes began to plan well ahead. On August 7 the representation of all of the larger organizations met and planned a Swedish National Day.[12] The total income from the festival would benefit the Swedish National Society. The decision was well received, and a total of 450 organizations were considered to have participated in the National Day on September 20. The advance preparations were extensive and the planning group was not ignorant of the value of publicity. Through the press, radio, public transportation, business houses, churches, and other organizations, all of Chicago was alerted to the Swedish National Day.[13] *Svenska Amerikanaren* found the proposal for the festival to be "genuine" and thought that

[9] "The objectives of the Association shall be to form, within Cook County (Chicago), a central organization for Swedish culture and to work for moral, intellectual, and economic development . . . to aid deserving persons of Swedish origin." *Bylaws of Swedish National Association in Chicago,* p. 1.

[10] *Svenska Tribunen Nyheter,* January 28, 1931, p. 4 (editorial).

[11] *Svenska Amerikanaren,* March 12, 1931, p. 13.

[12] Circular from Swedish National Association to Swedish organizations, dated August 13, 1931.

[13] John P. Miller, *Vart togo de vägen?* (Chicago, 1945), p. 142.

> here is where Chicago Swedes can be united on a common goal, here is where there should be no room for Swedish jealousy, here is where it is a matter only of going out and raising the largest possible fund which can become the means for helping our own people who are freezing and starving – milk in the pitcher and coal in the bin, food in the mouth and clothes on the body.[14]

The National Day gave evidence of great solidarity among the Swedes. The benefit netted $6,500.[15] The evaluation was so positive that the Society decided "that we, as Swedes, should plan a similar Swedish National Day annually in the future."[16]

The funds from the National Day were apportioned to the relief program of the Swedish National Society.[17] The need was great, and according to a report from the Society on December 18, 1931, over 900 requests for aid were received between October 1 and November 16.[18] The National Day fund did not reach very far during the severe winter that followed. By November the Society had to urge the organizations and lodges in Chicago to donate a dollar a week for a period of 26 weeks beginning December 1.[19] On December 11 the finance committee of the National Society sent out a communication pleading for further help: "We are making a desperate effort to assist the needy and unemployed among the Swedish Americans in Chicago. We need your help."[20] The purpose of the communication was to solicit a number of continuing contributors who would give 25 cents a week over a 20-week period. The difficulties of the National Society in stretching its resources to meet the need are evident from the correspondence between the Society and the authorities in Chicago. During the autumn months October–December, 1931, the Society

14 *Svenska Amerikanaren,* September 10, 1931, p. 4 (editorial).

15 Report of Treasurer, The Swedish National Day Relief Committee, January 18, 1932.

16 Circular to Swedish societies and lodges in Chicago, October 12, 1931.

17 Beginning September 30, 1931, the Swedish-American Relief Committee ceased to be and conveyed its responsibility to the Swedish National Society. The reason for its termination seems to be that the committee felt that it had been by-passed in the planning of the National Day. (*Svenska Tribunen Nyheter,* October 7, 1931, p. 16.)

18 Report on Swedish National Society's relief work in Chicago, December 18, 1931.

19 Undated circular from Swedish National Society of Chicago.

20 Circular from Swedish National Society, December 11, 1931.

received only one grant – $3,000 – from the Joint Emergency Relief Fund.[1] A letter to the Illinois Emergency Relief Commission on April 25, 1932, stresses the need of further help:

> We are in need of more funds this year, and we haven't a penny left in our treasury at the present time, so you see the matter is very urgent. Last year we distributed $18,000 in cash for food, etc. outside of donated clothing, furniture, etc. and employment assistance.[2]

It is evident from the same letter that the Society was threatened by legal procedures for non-payment of rent. The Illinois Emergency Relief Commission replied on May 5 that the National Society could not count on a grant since "this Fund cannot be distributed through private agencies."[3] The Society replied on May 6 that on that very day it had decided to close two of its three relief stations – "our South and West Side agencies" – for lack of funds.[4] Bitterness over the negative reply from the Illinois Commission is evident in the same letter:

> If we are to "close up," other charitable agencies, operating at a higher cost, will be called upon to take over our work, as there is no getting away from the fact that the NEED is there, and will have to be taken care of by someone – and immediately.

The Society reported in March, 1932, that during the winter it had distributed cash, food, coal, medicine, etc., at a value of $11,924. During March alone the Society assisted 461 Swedish families with food and fuel for an average of $3.48 per day.[5]

Preparations for the winter of 1932–33 included plans for a new National Day on September 11, 1932. It was expected that 50,000 persons would attend and that the 300th anniversary of Gustaf II Adolf's death would be observed in connection with the event. *Svenska Amerikanaren* was of the opinion that "every Swede and Swedish descendant should seize the opportunity to remind himself of our

[1] Receipt from Joint Emergency Relief Fund, February 15, 1932.

[2] Communication from the president of Swedish National Society to William Sexton, Corporation Counsel of the City of Chicago, April 25, 1932.

[3] Communication from Illinois Emergency Relief Commission to Carl Hjalmar Lundquist, President of the Swedish National Society, May 5, 1932.

[4] Communication to William Sexton, May 6, 1932.

[5] Statistical Bureau, Council of Social Agencies of Chicago, "Report for March, April 16, 1932."

fatherland's share in Protestantism's world victory."[6] The National Day aroused not only enthusiasm. Only one paper, namely the Scandinavian communist newspaper in Chicago, *Ny Tid,* expressed criticism:

> The imposing program is only one trend in the Gustaf II Adolf campaign of the Swedish middle class .... It is 300 years since this arsonist-king blessedly slept away on the battlefield at Lützen .... This is not the first time that these royalist hypocrites have set up similar campaigns. ... This exhibition is nevertheless the boldest of its kind in pushing monarchistic propaganda in the name of help for the unemployed. Damn! What humbug![7]

The Gustaf Adolf festival was a disappointment for the planners. The net benefit was only $1,577.[8] The president of the Society gave the following explanation after the festival: "This is not of course commensurate with the efforts we spent, but the Depression was against us."[9] The most acceptable explanation for the failure of the festival was that those who earlier had the means either had become poorer or, after three years of depression, had become more or less indifferent to charity. The Swedish relief work in its earlier phase can be said to have ended with the Gustaf Adolf festival, even if the need did not diminish but perhaps increased instead. When the public relief programs assumed the heaviest share of the burden after the change in the White House in 1933, the desire to contribute and the interest in private relief programs cooled. This did not mean that the need of private initiative disappeared. The Swedish National Society continued its relief work throughout the decade even if on a significantly smaller scale.

The work within the Swedish-American Relief Committee and the National Society was not restricted to material support but was also directed extensively to helping the unemployed find work. The Swedish Relief Committee opened an employment bureau in the beginning of January, 1931, under the name of Swedish-American Unemployment Agency.[10] Beginning in September the bureau became a part of the work of the National Society. Through the press and in churches and organizations employers were urged to give preference to

[6] *Svenska Amerikanaren,* August 4, 1932, p. 11.

[7] *Ny Tid,* September 8, 1932.

[8] *Svenska Tribunen Nyheter,* February 8, 1933.

[9] Letter from Swedish National Society, September 22, 1932.

[10] *Svenska Amerikanaren,* January 22, 1931.

the hiring of Swedes. *Förbundets Veckotidning* appealed with large headlines: "Work! That is the plea and the prayer of the masses of unemployed."[11] From January 1 to September 1, 1931, the agency received 1,280 inquiries about employment, and 419 of these were given assistance. The agency continued to work during 1932 but seems to have found it more and more difficult to help the unemployed. In August, 1932, it was reported:

> Now and then we were successful in finding a job for someone, but it is only a drop in the bucket among the thousands of our countrymen who wander the streets of Chicago without finding a single day's work. . . . We have hundreds of housewives who want "day work" in order to earn a little for maintaining their homes while the husband is without work for long stretches.[12]

In addition to the above mentioned areas of activity the National Society helped people who wanted to return to Sweden.

> Persons and families, unemployed, who desire to return to Sweden where they have better prospects and where relatives can help them are helped to obtain reduced rates on the railroads and steamships. Where necessary we pay their traveling expenses.[13]

Among the religious denominations the Swedish corps of the Salvation Army carried on the most far-reaching relief program. In contrast to the Swedish Relief Committee and the National Society, the Salvation Army concentrated all of its work on unemployed unmarried men. In the winter of 1930–31 the Scandinavian corps fed approximately 700 persons a day.[14] Between January 1 and March 7, 1931, 40,966 persons received help from the Swedish divisions in Chicago.[15]

In addition to Chicago, Swedish relief committees were organized in Minneapolis and New York, among other places. The situation

[11] *Förbundets Veckotidning,* January 27, 1931, p. 8.

[12] *Missionsvännen,* August 16, 1932, p. 8.

[13] Communication from Swedish National Society of the Joint Emergency Relief Fund of Cook County, April 29, 1932.

[14] *Stridsropet,* March 7, 1931. The Salvation Army carried on an intensive and inclusive activity and provided meals daily for unemployed Swedes. The reason that their contribution receives such scant treatment in this document is that no information or records are available on their relief activities.

[15] *Missionsvännen,* March 7, 1931, p. 8.

among Swedes in New York was so difficult that Consul General Olof Lamm on October 25, 1930, took the initiative for the Swedish Relief Fund for the purpose of alleviating the need among the Swedes.[16] The committee consisted of representatives of churches and societies in New York and served as a central organization with financial support from the Swedish organizations, which should "be able to plan and centralize help for the unfortunate compatriots who in these hard times have neither roof over their heads nor food for the table." The aid was intended primarily for the unemployed who were not family heads and who could not count on any help from city or state. It consisted further of material aid in the form of clothing, meals, lodging, and, in exceptional cases, rent and fuel. The relief work was administered through the Swedish Immigrant and Seaman's Home because it was already organized for and committed to this kind of work.

Nordstjernan found the Consul General's initiative commendable and on the editorial page expressed the hope that the more well-to-do Swedes would come to the aid of their needy compatriots. The paper thought that "nothing could be more sensible or necessary than to centralize and organize charitable measure within Swedish circles in this area."[17] The most important help was considered to be help in generating selfhelp. Swedish employers were therefore requested, wherever possible, "to increase their personnel even if it should mean a temporary sacrifice; and other Swedes to put into motion contemplated repairs, new construction, landscaping, gardening, or whatever one could think of . . . which would provide an opportunity for Swedes who are idle but willing to work." A bit later the newspaper declared that it was convinced "that no Swedish organizations or individuals who had a penny to spare would abandon their beautiful Swedish traditions in the defense of charity."[18] It maintained that wherever Swedes earlier had established their homes they had taken pride in caring for their less fortunate countrymen.

The Swedish Relief Fund was active during the entire winter of 1930–31, and when it ceased on May 17, 1931, it had, among other things, housed 428 Swedes who collectively spent 15,210 nights at

[16] *Nordstjernan,* October 30, 1930, p. 6.

[17] *Ibid.,* November 6, 1930, p. 6.

[18] *Nordstjernan,* November 20, 1930, p. 6

the Immigrant Home. The Fund had also served 33,570 meals to those in need.[19]

In the fall of 1931 Consul General Olof Lamm resurrected the Swedish Relief Fund. The reason was the dire outlook for the coming winter, which to a greater degree than the previous one threatened to harbor unemployment and the resulting privation and need among "our" compatriots.[20] A special committee was given the responsibility to see to it that Swedish families participated in both state and local relief. From the discussion at the organizational meeting it is evident that the resources were by now severely strained and that people could not hope to receive help to the same extent during the coming winter. The Consul General reported in a special communication on the serious conditions in New York:

> The prevailing Depression has dealt a severe blow to the Swedish-American population. If the information that has been received is correct – and it appears to be – the treasuries of many organizations this year have melted away and are severely strained. Many organizations during the year have seen their membership and the dues derived from it diminish while the difficulty of raising temporary funds through special events, collections, etc., has increased.[1]

In order to raise funds for its work the committee began a "mite box" collection in which approximately 3,000 persons participated. When the committee's work was done on March 28, 1932, a total income of $7,751 was reported. The Immigrant Home stated that during the winter it had provided work for about 40 percent of its guests.[2]

Difficulties during the winter of 1932–33 forced the committee to resume its work, and when it organized itself on October 11, it was agreed that the relief for fellow Swedes in distress was more necessary than ever.[3] While it proved to be very difficult to obtain money and other necessities the committee concentrated its activities chiefly on securing employment for the needy. The committee also felt obligated to broaden its activities to include families. A special committee –

19 *Ibid.,* May 21, 1931, p. 16.

20 *Ibid.,* October 29, 1931, p. 16.

1 Olof Lamm, an article on the relief question, *Nordstjernan,* November 12, 1931, p. 2.

2 *Nordstjernan,* March 31, 1932, p. 11.

3 *Ibid.,* October 20, 1932, p. 12.

Swedish Relief Fund for Families – was appointed for that purpose.[4] Every Swedish family in need of assistance and judged so by the committee was given the privilege to claim about 30 pounds of food – enough for one week – at the nearest relief station.

When currency proved hard to come by, Consul General Lamm made an appeal in *Nordstjernan:*

> The thought has occurred that we could utilize for this purpose the gold that is still to be found here and there and that has little value for the owner. In the strongboxes of most people are broken trinkets, necklaces, brooches, or rings, old spectacles, unused dental pieces, etc., which have no value in and of themselves but which if collected and melted down could still be converted into money.[5]

When the committee was dissolved in March, 1933, the income was reported as $5,370.[6]

In Minneapolis representatives of the Swedish churches and organizations formed a special relief committee on November 18, 1930.[7] By comparison with the committees in Chicago and New York, the Minneapolis group pursued a less inclusive course. The work was restricted to the collecting of food and clothing.

The locations mentioned above are examples of the way Swedish Americans rushed to help each other. Similar committees were organized even in places where Swedes constituted only a group.[8]

4. *Summary*

The privations which followed in the wake of the Depression affected the country's population in various ways, but the impact was especially serious on the foreign-born and, of these, the aliens most of all. The primary reason for this was discrimination, which was very obvious during the greater part of the Depression. Discrimination seems to have been applied rather consistently and, with respect to aliens, was often approved by high authorities. These injustices had profound consequences for both of these groups in terms of gaining a livelihood and

[4] *Ibid.,* December 15, 1932, p. 12.

[5] *Nordstjernan,* January 26, 1933, p. 12.

[6] *Ibid.,* March 30, 1933, p. 12.

[7] *Svenska Amerikanska Posten,* November 26, 1930, p. 30.

[8] The Swedish language newspapers provide information on relief activities among their own countrymen in places other than those cited here.

greatly diminished their possibilities of managing things for themselves. The relationship between foreign-born and native-born in America in the 1930s was not entirely unlike the situation in America today between blacks and whites.

A common characteristic of the various nationalities was to draw together and strengthen their sense of belonging. The external pressure from the so-called "100 percent American," who tried to make the immigrants scapegoats with respect to the widespread unemployment, strengthened their solidarity with their own groups and hastened their efforts in behalf of their distressed countrymen.

It was a predominant characteristic throughout of Swedish Americans to demonstrate great solidarity and a sense of belonging with their fellow Swedes and with the needy among them. Activities within the societies and the *ad hoc* relief committees show that the Americanization process of the 1920s did not weaken national affinities.

The Swedish-American newspapers make it clear that the need and the poverty were great among Swedish Americans. The constant appeals for help for their own countrymen show that there were many Swedes among the masses of unemployed.

It is obvious that the Depression had long-range consequences for Swedish Americans and their institutions. The progress and lofty plans of the 1920s suddenly came to an end. While their concern during the 1920s was for the future and what it would bring, after 1930 the Swedish Americans stood face to face with immediate problems. The period after 1930 was characterized by energetic attempts to conserve what had been built up over decades. The effect of the Depression in the process of Americanization is difficult to determine. It nevertheless appears most likely that the Depression, in spite of several indications to the opposite – among other things the intensified relief work within the Swedish national group – hastened Americanization. It can perhaps be said that the relief work during the Depression was a final desperate but vigorous attempt to hold together the Swedish population in America. The Depression enforced a series of economic and social reforms especially after the inauguration of President Franklin D. Roosevelt in 1933. This meant that private immigrant relief organizations lost their former importance and that, consequently, national solidarity was weakened. It can also be assumed that private relief organizations used up all of their resources during the first years of the Depression.

IX. The Language Question

1. *Swedish as the Mother Tongue*

The only official data on non-English mother tongues in the United States are those reported in the census. Data on mother tongues have been gathered in 1910, 1920, 1930 and 1940. As the population statistics cover only ten-year periods and the language of customary speech in the homes of the immigrants prior to immigration, it is not possible statistically to investigate the various immigration groups' transfer from their mother tongue to English. Although the census reports deal primarily with self-reported mother tongue claims rather than with indicators of current language use, the mere act of claiming a particular mother tongue is, according to Joshua Fishman, of substantial interest to students of language maintenance and language shift. "These two variables [claiming a mother tongue and current language use] are undoubtedly related to each other, although the exact nature or consistency of the relationship is still unknown."[1]

The American census reports on mother tongues for the years 1910, 1920, 1930 and 1940 show that 1930 is a demarcation year in American history in so far as it indicates that the number of persons who reported their mother tongue clearly declined. For the earlier immigrants – from Scandinavia and Germany – 1920 is the demarcation year. The reduction was a natural consequence of the diminishing immigration. The first generation of immigrants decreased rapidly. Because of the hostility occasioned by the war hysteria, many people of German origin did not dare to indicate German as their main language. This may even have been the case with immigrants of Swedish origin. The transfer from one language to another was undoubtedly more rapid in areas having few immigrants as well as

[1] Joshua Fishman, *op. cit.*, p. 34. In 1940 "mother tongue" was formally defined as the principal language spoken in the home of the person in his earliest childhood. This definition was frequently interpreted as referring to the language spoken by the person himself.

among nationalities small in number. "If the number of such individuals drops too low, then formal institutions of language maintenance (press, schools, organizations) cannot be maintained and creative potential must soon disappear."[2]

As for the Swedish Americans' part, the number of those who indicated Swedish as their mother tongue decreased from 683,218 in 1910 to 643,203 in 1920. In 1930 the number had decreased to 615,465, and in 1940 to 423,200. The American census of 1930 reported for the first time the immigrants' "inability to speak English." These accounts, in themselves quite interesting, lose much of their comparative value because no such tabulation had been recorded earlier in the published material. In other words, it is not possible to make a long range comparison of the various nationalities.[3]

The census of 1930 indicates that Swedish Americans learned English easily. In 1930 only 1.5 percent of all Swedish-born over 10 years of age could not speak English; only the Danes showed a lower percentage (0.9 percent). Among the Portuguese the same year 23.2 percent were non-English speaking, among the Italians 15.7 percent, among the Poles 12.8 percent and among the Germans 2.9 percent. That South and East Europeans were lesser inclined to speak English was chiefly due to the fact that they came to America later than the North and West Europeans. It may also be assumed that the high average age among the Swedes, other Scandinavians, and Germans played a significant role in this connection. There was, in other words, a greater proportion of people in the age bracket immediately over 10 years among the immigrants from South and East Europe than among those from North and West Europe.

Also of interest in this connection is the ability among immigrants to read and write. The census of 1930 shows that only 1.5 percent of all Swedish-born over 10 years of age were illiterate.[4] Distributed according to age, 2.1 percent in the age group 10 to 24 years were illiterate; 0.9 percent in the group 25 to 44 years; 0.9 percent in the group 45 to 65; and 3.6 percent in the group 65 years and over. By way of comparison it may be mentioned that among the Italians 25.3 percent were illiterate. Compared with other immigrants the

[2] Joshua Fishman, *op. cit.*, p. 47.

[3] Maurice Davie, *World Immigration*, p. 266 ff.

[4] *Fifteenth Census of the United States, 1930: Population*, Vol. II, p. 1315.

number of illiterate Swedes was percentage-wise among the lowest.

In a study of 1921, Riverda Jordan shows that the immigrants in Minneapolis and St. Paul clung to the language of their birth. The study was made during the school year 1917–1918.[5] The Germans led the list of those acquiring the English language as the medium of the home. Of 201 German-born parents listed, 123, or 61.2 percent spoke English habitually in the home. The next best record was made by the Danes, 26 out of 63 parents (or 41.3 percent) speaking English. The Swedes and Norwegians, "generally considered to be loyal Americans," did not show up as well as one would expect: only 33 percent Swedes and 32.3 percent Norwegians had acquired the new language as a part of their new heritage. When it is noted that 11 per-

Table 20. Comparative table of nationalities, showing number and percentage of foreign born parents who have adopted English as the language of the home.

Nationality	Total Parents	Number Speaking English	Percentage Speaking English
Bohemian	36	6	16.6
Slovak	77	5	6.5
Norway	396	128	32.3
Sweden	802	265	33.0
German	201	123	61.2
Austria	126	10	7.9
Danes	63	26	41.3
Finns	86	1	1.1
Roumanian Jews	234	35	15.0
Russian Jews	526	45	8.5
Italians	37	3	8.1
Average			21.0

Source: Riverda Harding Jordan, *Nationality and School Progress*, p. 28.

[5] Riverda Harding Jordan, *Nationality and School Progress* (Bloomington, 1921), made this conclusion in his doctoral dissertation. In order to get at the facts of nationality and progress of school children, Jordan gave a question blank to the children in Minneapolis and St. Paul. The blanks were to be taken home and filled out. The questionnaire was sent to the pupils of the three highest grades only, namely the 6th, 7th, and 8th. High school pupils were not included in the inquiry. From the thirteen schools investigated, 2653 questionnaires were collected (p. 26 f).

Table 21. Persistence of foreign language shown by number and percentages of foreign born parents, who retain the foreign tongue as the home language, although they have lived in America ten years or more.

Nationality	Total Parents	Years lived in the United States 10–19 inc. No.	%	20–29 No.	%	30–more No.	%	Total %
Germany	201	14	7.0	9	4.4	22	10.9	22.3
Denmark	63	5	7.9	7	11.1	5	7.9	26.9
Norway	396	69	17.4	48	12.1	76	19.2	48.7
Sweden	802	93	11.6	166	20.7	134	16.7	49.0
Austria	126	30	23.8	23	18.2	12	9.5	51.5
Roumanian Jew	234	123	52.6	18	7.7	5	2.1	62.4
Italians	37	5	13.5	16	43.2	3	8.1	64.8
Bohemians	36	6	16.6	10	27.7	10	27.7	72.0
Slovak	77	22	28.5	20	25.9	18	23.3	77.7
Russian Jews	526	237	45.0	145	27.5	32	6.1	78.6
Finnish	86	38	44.1	23	26.7	14	16.2	87.0
		Aver.	24.4	Aver.	20.4	Aver.	13.4	58.2

Two Swedes, one German, one Finn, and one Russian have lived in this country fifty years, and still speak the home language! Six Norwegians and five Swedes have been in this country forty-five years or more, and speak their native language in the home.

Source: Riverda Harding Jordan, *Nationality and School Progress*, p. 29.

cent of the Germans, 17 percent of the Swedes, and 19 percent of the Norwegians, have lived in the United States over thirty years and still use their native languages in the home, it must be admitted, Jordan writes, that among the several generally accepted tests of Americanization this particular test throws definite doubt on the real success of assimilation. The tables show that only a fifth of the immigrants in Minneapolis and St. Paul adopted English as the language of the home, and that more than one half did not speak English even after they had lived there for ten years or more.

2. *The Significance of the Swedish Language*

> There are many other valuable aspects of Swedish culture which we ought to maintain and preserve. However, if we keep and perpetuate the language it becomes comparatively easy to maintain and preserve the other values, but if we lose the language, all other worthy aspects will soon be lost.
>
> (J. S. Carlson, *Hvarför böra vi behålla och bevara, vörda och bruka svenska språket i Amerika?* [Minneapolis, 1923], p. 3)

The language question has occupied a central place in Swedish-American discussions. Few matters have been more emotionally accentuated than the transition from Swedish to English, and this has been explained by the observation that the language "touched the very heart of the immigrant's dilemma."[1] It has been said that the language is more than a means of communication. It symbolizes also the Swedish Americans' history and traditions, home, parents and childhood, religion, etc: that is to say, it holds the widely spread immigrants together.

Language was of great importance not only to the immigrants but also to the native Americans who believed that more than anything else the ability to speak English promoted the Americanization process. If the immigrants were trying to use the new language in their home life and home circle, if they were attending church services conducted in English, then it was assumed that they were really on the road to becoming Americans. If, on the other hand, they clung to the language of their birth and were not willing to adopt the language of the new home, they were not at heart ready for citizenship. In this study of

[1] Nils Hasselmo, "Language in Exile," p. 121 ff; Carl M. Rosenquist writes in "Linguistic Changes in the Acculturation of the Swedes of Texas," *Sociology and Social Research* (January/February, 1932) p. 221: "Every group feels that its language is peculiarly its own, and any attempt by other groups to impose a substitute calls forth stubborn resistance. ... Language serves more effectively than any other social trait to hold individuals together in social relationships."

1921, Riverda Jordan considered the encouragement of foreign language directly subversive and definitely antagonistic to the interests of the immigrants in their desire to compete with the native-born Americans in the struggle for survival.[2] Jordan concludes that it was clear that the language superiority of the American child placed him at an advantage during his entire elementary school education, and even into the high school.[3]

> When the situation continues to such an extent that the American born child himself continues the foreign language as the home language even when he is married and has a home of his own, as was shown to be the case in an appreciable number of instances, the fact of his language handicap is accentuated, and worse yet, the handicap is perpetuated as a national heritage to the third generation, at least. . . . The real position to be taken is that this handicap is a formidable obstacle to proper progress of the foreigner not only in school, but in all walks of life, and that it is the concern of every American to see that all possible steps are taken to remove the difficulty.

Gene Lund is of the opinion that the language was a key factor in the Americanization process:

> As long as Augustana congregations retained the Swedish language, the synod retained its predominantly old-world character and outlook. But as soon as the English language was adopted by the pastors and congregations, the process of Americanizing Augustana was completed almost over night.[4]

Since the Swedish language to a large extent composed the foundation of the Swedish-American religious denominations, it occupied a prominent place in the Americanization process. The principal reason why the Swedish immigrants established their own denominations and organizations for Swedes was that they did not understand English.

[2] Riverda Jordan, *op. cit.*, p. 102.

[3] Riverda Harding, Jordan, *op. cit.*, pp. 96 and 99.

[4] Gene Lund, "The Americanization of the Augustana Lutheran Church," p. 159; The Methodists believed that the more the Swedish language was removed from their midst the more insipid Swedish Methodism would become in the U.S. (*Svenska metodismens allmänna konvent 1914,* p. 28); A. Serenius, "Varför svenskan i Amerika?" in *Missionsförbundets Ungdomstidning,* May 21, 1912, p. 6. Serenius believed that the contribution which the Swedes owed to the USA could not be made if their language was lost, "because as a consequence of that loss would follow also the loss of essentially all that is characteristic for us Swedes in our sphere of thought and our spiritual life."

The extinction of Swedish, it was said, would mean the disintegration of the Swedish nationality, because "the language is the nationality's very source of life and the strongest bond holding us together." It was also said to be the key to the "national strong-box." "For Swedish America the entire Swedish culture will become only a fairy-tale if the language is lost."[5]

The transition from Swedish to English was a difficult and complicated process involving many factors. The so-called "pure" Americans took for granted that the immigrants would learn English rapidly. If they failed it was interpreted as a lack of loyalty – "disloyalty to the basic principles of American life."[6] The transition to English was largely a struggle between on the one hand, an automatic transfer to English and, on the other, a conscious effort to preserve the Swedish language as long as possible – "self-maintenance."[7]

It should be noted that Swedish Americans not only actively endeavored to preserve the Swedish tongue but also presented their own views of Americanization and the import of language for assimilation.

Thus, they did not accept a complete program of Americanization if this implied a total break with Sweden and Swedish culture. "The Swedish American best served America by contributing his spiritual treasures to the new world."[8] Americanization or the transition to English was not tantamount to rattling off the catechism answers or the multiplication table.[9] Americanization had to depend on its own power of attraction. If peremptory decrees were used the result would be the opposite. Swedes absolutely rejected the assertion which was sometimes made that it was un-American to speak any other tongue than English, since not even the best English was any guarantee that a person might become a good citizen. There were those, it was said,

[5] *Missionsförbundets ungdomstidning*, April 22, 1913, p. 12; Theodore W. Anderson in *Covenant Memories* (p. 101) wrote the following about the change-over to English: "The adoption of English as the language of worship opened the way to a much wider sphere of influence and a more hopeful outlook."

[6] Einar Haugen, *The Norwegian Language in America. A Study in Bilingual Behavior* (Philadelphia, 1953) p. 2.

[7] Joshua Fishman, *Language Loyalty in the US*, p. 15 ff.

[8] Conrad Bergendoff, "The Role of Augustana in the Transplanting of a Culture across the Atlantic," *The Immigration of Ideals. Studies in the North Atlantic Community* (Rock Island, 1968), p. 70.

[9] George Stephenson, *A History of American Immigration*, p. 237.

who speak English fluently and yet become traitors – "a good-for-nothing or an awkward bumpkin."[10]

There have been many arguments for the preservation of the Swedish language in America. The foremost, however, have been of a patriotic, cultural and religious nature – matters that are not always easy to keep separate. There were at the same time purely sentimental reasons and arguments which came into play. This can undoubtedly be said to have been the case even when the defenders of the Swedish language motivated their stand realistically. It was considered a self-evident right for anyone to speak whatever language he pleased for as much as he liked. Those who advocated transition to English maintained that the sooner this was accepted and the earlier preparations were made for a transition, the smoother the process would be. On the other hand, there were those who altogether questioned the retention of Swedish, since the attempt to implant a new language in a foreign country violated the fundamental principle of the immigration process. When a person decided to emigrate he ought immediately to lay aside the old and accept the new as rapidly as possible.

"Will the Swedish language in America live on forever?" This was a question Gustav Andreen asked in 1900.[11] It was a rhetorical question, and he was convinced it would not be the case. English would in the long run be the universally prevailing language. Although he knew at the same time that the Swedish language would sooner or later be lost, he stressed the importance of a certain power of resistance: it would be sad if the Swedish Americans too hastily abandoned their language.

One who perhaps most intensely discussed the preservation of the Swedish language in America was Professor J.S. Carlson in his brochure *Why We Should Maintain and Preserve, Cultivate and Use the Swedish Language in America.* His initial point was that the person who knows two languages is better equipped than the one who knows only one language, and the one who knows several languages is, in turn, better equipped than one who knows only two languages.[12] In other words, the more languages a person knows the better it is for

[10] S.G. Öhman, *Augustana-Synodens självständighetsförklaring,* p. 105.

[11] Gustav Andreen, *Det svenska språket i Amerika* (Stockholm, 1900), p. 17 ff.

[12] J.S. Carlson, *op. cit.,* p. 8.

him. It seemed preposterous to Carlson that schools taught Latin and other dead languages while at the same time despising Swedish. Swedish Americans should be exhorted not to abandon the Swedish language too soon. That sooner or later they will have to abandon it is, of course, natural, but they ought not do so until the time is ripe.[13]

In contrast to Latin, J.S. Carlson pointed out, Swedish was a living language – "living both as to body and soul – a beautiful and glorious language. . . . Sweden is the ancestral home of liberty, and America is liberty's great new home on earth, and Swedes carried liberty along from the ancestral home to its new habitation."[14] According to Carlson, the Swedish language should also be preserved for reasons of filial piety. "The person who at once and without a sense of loss forgets his parents and the parental home as soon as he leaves that home, is not a fully normal person – he has a screw loose somewhere."

J.S. Carlson's argument is reiterated continuously by those who defended the Swedish language. A.G. Witting maintained, as did Carlson, that the more languages one knows the better it is.[15] The cultural reasons for the preservation of Swedish seem to have dominated the debate. The Swedish language, it was said, was a cultural language of equal standing with other languages. Those who did not care about Swedish ought to be ashamed of themselves. On the other hand, no one ought to be ashamed of speaking "our sonorous, beautiful tongue."[16] M. Wahlström declared that Swedish Americans had to develop Swedishness side by side with Americanism and lend color and prestige to the Swedish language.[17] It was imperative, he said, to have people understand that it was just as elegant to study Swedish as French, Spanish or German. David Nyvall could not find that Swedish was better than other languages, but it was a glorious language, a

[13] *Ibid.*, p. 17 ff.

[14] *Ibid.*, pp. 10 and 20 ff.

[15] A.G. Witting, "Svenskheten och den äkta amerikanismen," pp. 18,19; David Nyvall wrote in *Svenskhet i Amerika* (1893), p. 20 ff that "one must study several languages to completely learn *one* language. There is an enormous advantage in knowing several languages — an advantage the children of emigrants have over natives who know only English."

[16] C.A. Lindvall, "Har det svenska språket någon framtid i Amerika"? *Ungdomsvännen,* No 7, July, 1916, p. 210.

[17] M. Wahlström, "Svenska språkets framtid i Amerika." p. 25.

virile language with a clear ringing sound.[18] American culture was enriched by the language. The "language of honor and heroes" was an inseparable part of the Swedish cultural heritage.[19] The language was the key to the rich Swedish cultural heritage.[20] It could not be emphasized enough how important it was to retain the Swedish language for the purpose of preserving the Swedish heritage.[21] The animosity toward foreign languages following in the wake of the war was considered menacing, since it left deep traces behind.

Another argument offered in defense of the Swedish language was based on the observation that the language was a bridge by means of which the best in Swedish culture could be further advanced. By allowing the language to die out, America would block the natural and surest means of acquiring the intellectual treasures to which the language gives access. "A multilingual people has the very best prospects of becoming an intellectually rich people."[1] Another reason for the preservation of the Swedish language was its importance for the Swedish national character.[2] Not only was it important for the private individual but collectively as well for the whole Swedish-American community and identity.[3]

Knowledge of the Swedish language did not, *per se,* constitute an indication of Swedishness. It meant, however, that one could learn to appreciate the rich treasures of Swedish literature which, according to Vilhelm Berger, for instance, was a prerequisite for the preservation of Swedishness.[4] It was also said that a literary culture could not be attained except by means of the language one had first

[18] David Nyvall, *Svenskhet i Amerika,* p. 13; Emeroy Johnson, "The Duty of the Augustana Synod in Regard to the Swedish Language," in *The Lutheran Companion,* February 9, 1924, p. 90. Emeroy Johnson could not understand why, for example, French and Spanish should have priority over the Swedish language.

[19] Erik Wahlgren, "Vårt svenska språk" in *Svenska kulturförbundets minnesskrift 1938,* p. 29 ff.

[20] S.G. Öhman, *Augustana-Synodens självständighetsförklaring,* p. 114.

[21] S.G. Öhman, "Vårt svenska arv," p. 119 ff.

[1] J.S. Carlson, *op. cit.,* p. 41.

[2] E.A. Zetterstrand, "Engelskans inflytande på det svenska språket," *Ungdomsvännen, 1904,* p. 244.

[3] Jacob Bonggren, *Sånger och sagor* (Rock Island, 1902),

[4] Vilhelm Berger, *Svensk-amerikanska meditationer,* p. 126.

learned. Examples were cited showing that practically all authors who wrote in Swedish had been born in Sweden.[5] Vilhelm Berger did not share the idea that the language was necessary for "Swedishness." He criticized those who believed that knowing Swedish was the Alpha and Omega of Swedishness. When the Swedish language has been hammered into English speaking young people, it has never been anything but a "veneer, sometimes thick, sometimes thin: but genuine Swedishness – the Swedish culture, the Swedish ideals, the Swedish thought-life – is never reached, it lies deeper." It is, he wrote, a "shameful ingratitude that Swedishness has been allowed to become only a kind of display of Swedish speech and Swedish provincial costumes." Berger did not think that Swedishness and the Swedish language were a pair of Siamese twins who had to keep together to avoid dying.[6] He thought that the effort to preserve Swedishness was unfortunate when it expressed itself by flattering Swedish ancestors with "pretty phrases, Swedish recitations, Swedish provincial costumes, Swedish 'evenings,' Lucia festivals, and so forth." The efforts for preserving Swedishness ought instead to concentrate on presenting Sweden as it really was. Efforts should be made to explain to Americans of Swedish ancestry the significance of being descendants of people with an ancient culture.

The importance of the Swedish language for religious activity was often stressed when the language question is discussed. Even if God could be approached in any language whatever, it seemed ridiculous to some that a person whose native tongue was Swedish would try to approach God in English.[7] It was thought that the Swedish language would be needed long into the future as a language of religious worship, since Swedish Americans in their worship would need a common language understood by all.[8] Sympathy was felt for the

[5] Martin Allwood, *Amerika-svensk lyrik genom 100 år,* p. IX.

[6] Vilhelm Berger, *Svensk-Amerika i målbrottet,* p. 12 ff. His book which was published in August 1933, consists of a number of essays which Berger published in *Nordstjernan,* of which he was the editor. In the introduction he relates that the articles in the paper were received with mixed feelings. There were both sharp rebuttals and approving expressions.

[7] J.S. Carlson, *op. cit.,* p. 27 ff.

[8] David Nyvall, *op. cit.,* p. 22 ff. See more about the importance of the Swedish language for the religious activity in the chapter devoted to the language debate within religious denominations.

elderly in particular, "who could just as well be ordered to travel to the moon as to learn a new language." There were also the younger ones who, to be sure, could speak English but not understand it readily enough so that it might be used in worship. The language of religious feeling cannot be translated with the help of lexicons, thought David Nyvall. Those who would rather preach in English instead of Swedish he characterized as follows: "For my part I regard their Americanization as a declaration of their emptiness and lack of real religiosity. And the American mission aimed at catching fish of that kind will not gain them enough even to pay for their nets and fishing gear."

The language question also served as a cudgel in the rivalry between the different nationalities in America. There are many examples of the use of the Swedish language in the competition with other immigrants. In M. Wahlström's opinion, if no other motive existed for the preservation of Swedish, the Swedish immigrants ought for their own sake to defend the language, something which other nationalities for themselves considered as a matter of course.[9] The Swedish Americans ought to emulate the Germans in their glowing love for their language. It would then be easy to maintain the Swedish.[10] Those who were infected with rickets (that is, the "English sickness") and abandoned the Swedish language were very much open to blame. The longer the language was preserved, the better the Swedes could keep together, "for the language is the tie that binds a people together better than anything else."

An argument that often reappeared in the language debate was the individual's right to speak the language of his own choice. Every immigrant, had the obvious right to preserve his native speech. It was pointed out that there is no paragraph in the American constitution forbidding the Swedish language. This country approves of and recommends Swedish schools, said David Nyvall. As long as there are parents who cannot learn to speak another language than Swedish, it is their duty as citizens to teach their children Swedish.[11] It was lamentable also that Swedes, through a false modesty, so easily forgot their own national characteristics. This fault was considered to be an

[9] M. Wahlström, *op. cit.*, p. 25.

[10] C.A. Lindvall, "Svenska språket i Amerika," p. 19; and "Har det svenska språket någon framtid i Amerika?" in *Ungdomsvännen*, July, 1916.

[11] David Nyvall, *op. cit.*, p. 18.

old hereditary weakness which in thoughtful people aroused ridicule and pity.[12] Of secondary import was whether Swedes spoke one or the other language. The essential thing was that Swedish strengthened the consciousness of their common origin.

Those Swedish Americans who battled for the preservation of the Swedish language were not pleased with countrymen who forgot their native speech. They condemned those who spoke contemptuously about Swedish or forgot it before they had learned English passably well. "They are Americans according to the newly hatched Americanism's 'patriotic' teachings, but such 'Americans' this land can well get along without – without any damage to its present or future."[13] True Americans are only those who for honor or advantage for themselves and their new homeland "maintain, preserve, cherish and use" the good, old Swedish language. He who forgets his native land may just as easily forget his new homeland. Memories of the childhood home cannot die even though they may grow faint. If the inner bonds are broken, the result is spiritual death. Language is the most important medium by which spiritual treasures are acquired. "The best Americans are those who maintain the old good they have, at least until they have been really able to grasp the new, and maintain the old good and make it fruitful even after they have grasped the new; for whatever is good one ought never to relinquish."[14]

Those who relentlessly drove for a solution of the language question were characterized as un-American. They deserve "our displeasure for their cruelty" if they "do not otherwise deserve our contempt for their folly."[15] This was directed against those who thought it next to rebellion that Swedish sons and daughters spoke the language their parents understood. Johan Person lamented that Swedish parents did not teach their children Swedish.[16] A significant reason why the children of Swedish parents were reluctant to speak Swedish, he explained, was that their schoolmates scoffed and jeered at them for their outlandish speech.

Adolph B. Benson thought it shameful and ignominious that

12 S.G. Öhman, "Vårt svenska arv," *Korsbaneret,* 1924, p. 117 ff.

13 J.S. Carlson, *op. cit.,* p. 18 f.

14 *Ibid.,* p. 25.

15 David Nyvall, *op. cit.,* p. 19.

16 Johan Person, *Svensk-amerikanska studier,* p. 134 f.

citizens of Swedish birth actually worked for abolishing the Swedish language.[17] It is not just as absurd as it is shocking, he commented, that while Americans with education and culture have the highest respect for Sweden, its people, and history, children and young people of Swedish origin disregard or show contempt for it? The person who befouls his own dwelling is really a wretched creature.[18] A.G. Witting interpreted the scant interest the Swedish Americans had for the Swedish language as a lack of self-confidence – "our timidity, our abject fear of doing something that might in the least be thought unacceptable by one of the screaming American big-mouths, who thinks he has a patent on what it is to be an American."[19]

Even those who, now and then, smuggled an English word into their Swedish were criticized. No other immigrants, it was said, were so completely linguistically Americanized as the Swedes. It was merely a shame that it was done at the expense of the Swedish language and that people did not become aware of "the Swedish beam in their own [eye]."[20] "Even those who had learned a good and beautiful Swedish in Sweden did not hesitate to follow the example of the crown and inoculate their fathers' tongue with the "most grotesque new forms." To give up the Swedish language was, according to Ernst Lindblom, a sign of moral weakness. In verses entitled "Contrasts" he wrote:

> The lisping Yankee speech she learned
> right quickly on the spot;
> her pay was raised, but also then
> her Swedish she forgot.
> . . .
> American expressions now
> she mimicked as she walked;
> at last that foolish brand of speech
> of half and half she talked![1]

Has the Swedish language managed to live on, now that immigration has ceased and the first generation is about to disappear? Have the

17 Adolph B. Benson, "Det svenska kulturproblemet i Amerika," *Årsbok utg. av Samfundet S:t Erik,* pp. 46—52.

18 S.G. Öhman, *Augustana-Synodens självständighetsförklaring,* p. 115.

19 A.G. Witting, *op. cit.,* p. 19.

20 C.P. Peterson, *Sverige i Amerika,* p. 203 ff.

1 Ernst Lindblom, *Stjärnbanerets land* (Stockholm, 1910), p. 51 ff.

second and third generations any interest in their origin and in Swedish speech? The questions can be answered with both yes and no. The interest for both Sweden and the Swedish language has surely been preserved longer than anyone had ventured to anticipate. However, the motives for preserving the language have changed during the course of the years. For the Swedish-born the language was not an end in itself, but a necessity. It was kept alive without effort as long as the need existed. For the second and third generations the need has been replaced by a desire for at least a passable knowledge of their ancestors' language, a longing for a feeling of affinity with the land of their origin. This desire can be said to be in part a product of two phenomena, one being the American social custom which considers it good fashion for one to be able to trace his origin, the other the actual structure of American society, which continues to be divided into ethnic groupings. This has nothing to do with the time periods for immigration, but with "American life generally."[2]

3. *Swedish and English Literature*

Even though a strong desire to preserve the Swedish language existed, the inevitable development continued. When immigration from Sweden ceased the interest for the Swedish language waned. Nils Hasselmo has made a quantitative estimate of Swedish-American literature in order to survey the retrogression of the language. The analysis comprises the authors and book titles contained in Fritiof Ander's Swedish-American bibliography, *The Cultural Heritage of the Swedish Immigrant*. Among the writings of the more than 150 authors included is found most of the literature produced in the last century.[1]

A compilation of titles by five-year periods from 1865 to 1950

[2] Nathan Glazer and Daniel P. Moynihan, *Beyond the Melting Pot* (1963), pp. 290, 291. Glazer and Moynihan give the following explanation: "It is not the temporary upsetting inflow of new and unassimilated immigrants that creates a pattern of ethnic groups within the nation, but rather some central tendency in the national ethos which structures people, whether those coming in afresh or the descendants of those who have been here for generations, into groups of different status and character."

[1] Nils Hasselmo, "Den amerikanska svenskan," p. 14 ff. Hasselmo has included the titles found in the chapter "The Religious and Secular Literature."

shows that prior to 1885 few books were published by Swedish-American publishers. Subsequently came an acceleration. The maximum number of publications was reached in the 1910–1915 period; after that the number declined substantially (see diagram 1).

Nils Hasselmo also has analyzed the Swedish-American press on the basis of Fritiof Ander's bibliography which contains references to a total of 832 periodical publications. Among these publications are found newspapers and journals issued during a period of years. To a large extent they are yearbooks, occasional sheets of advertising and news, newspapers and journals, which mostly met a speedy death. As indicated in Diagram 2, the peak year was 1910. In the following five-year period a strong decline began which has since continued unbroken. In 1950 only 13 periodicals remained, and at the close of 1969 it was said the number had been reduced to a total of six.[2]

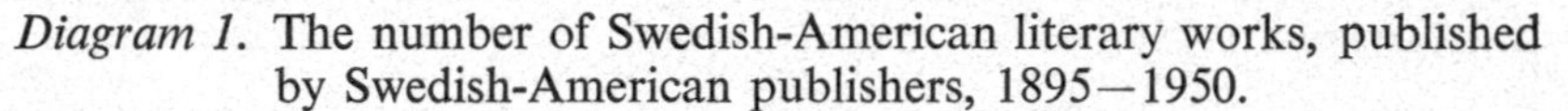

Diagram 1. The number of Swedish-American literary works, published by Swedish-American publishers, 1895—1950.

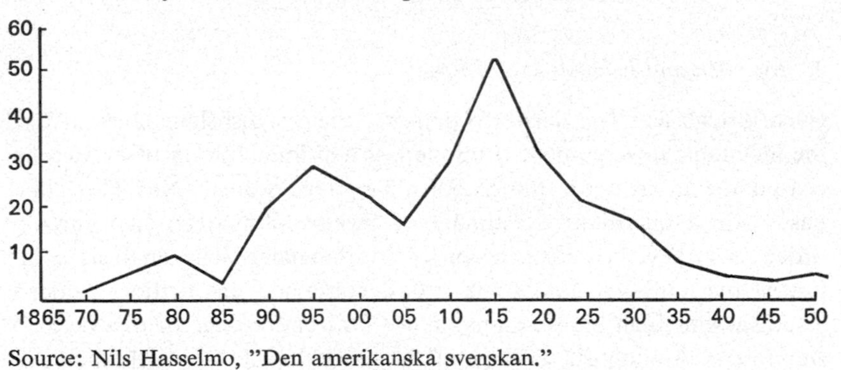

Source: Nils Hasselmo, "Den amerikanska svenskan."

The change over to English was directly reflected in the various denominations' publishing activity. Augustana Book Concern (ABC) reacted immediately to every change in the requests for literature in English. Before 1908 ABC published, with few exceptions, only Swedish books, but with the coming of the Association of English Churches (an association within the Augustana Synod of churches which had changed over to English) the publication of books

[2] *Riksdagstrycket, Utrikesutskottets utlåtande,* 1969 :22, p. 1.

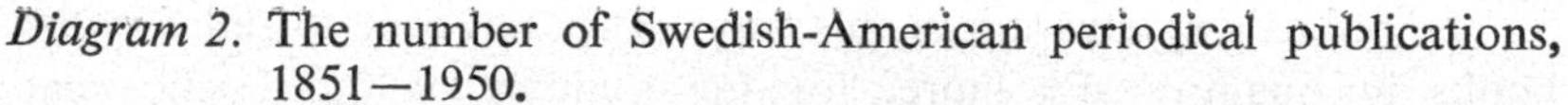

Diagram 2. The number of Swedish-American periodical publications, 1851—1950.

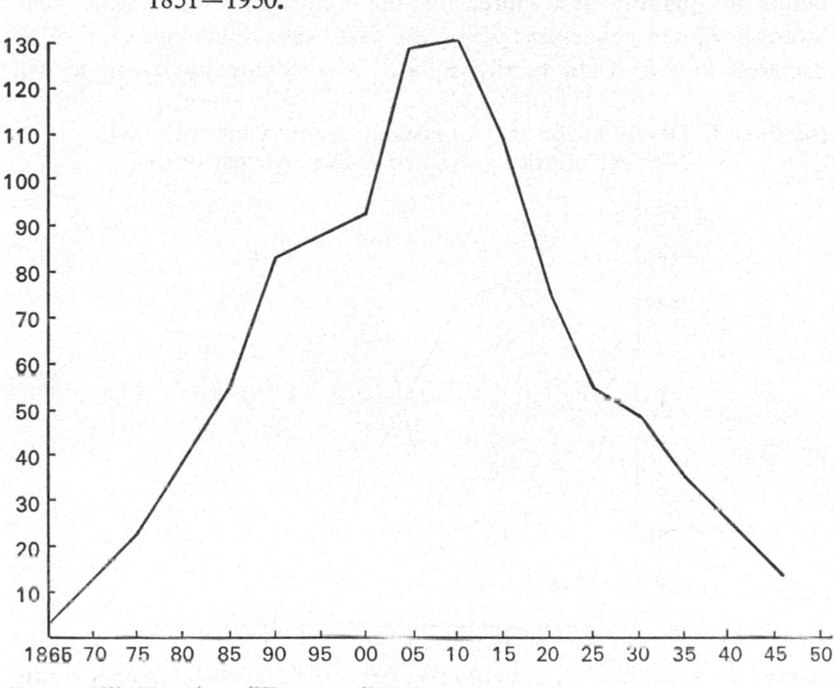

Source: Nils Hasselmo, "Den amerikanska svenskan."

in English increased rapidly after 1908.[3] The first necessity was an English hymnal and prayer-book, but there was an even more pressing need for textbooks for young people's activities. The increase in the production of English literature was quite slow up to 1910. After the close of World War I it became more and more difficult to sell Swedish books. The Synod's annual report for 1920 accounted

[3] Ernst W. Olson, *Augustana Book Concern. Fiftieth Anniversary, 1884—1934* (Rock Island, 1934), p. 60; Daniel Nystrom, *A Ministry of Printing,* (Rock Island, 1962), p. 70; Augustana Book Concern was one of the largest enterprises in Swedish America. Its activity goes back to 1889. The publishing firm belonged to the Augustana Synod, and each year it published a considerable number of books as well as pamphlets and tracts and several periodicals and journals. Hasselmo has not included works containing both Swedish and English text nor textbooks for teaching Swedish; Carl Sundbeck, in *Svenskamerikanerna* (p. 201) designated ABC as the best support for the Swedish language in America.

for the publishing situation in this way: "It is not easy to sell Swedish books in quantity any more, for the number of those who read Swedish diminishes every year.[4] In fact, the following year ABC declared that it could hardly square its accounts by trying to sell

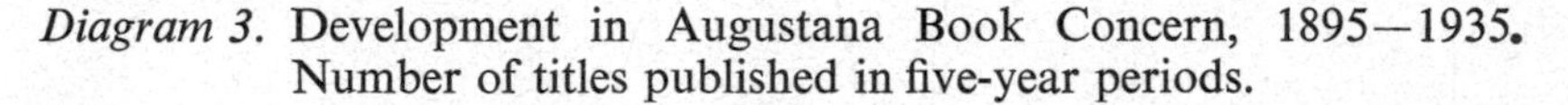
Diagram 3. Development in Augustana Book Concern, 1895—1935. Number of titles published in five-year periods.

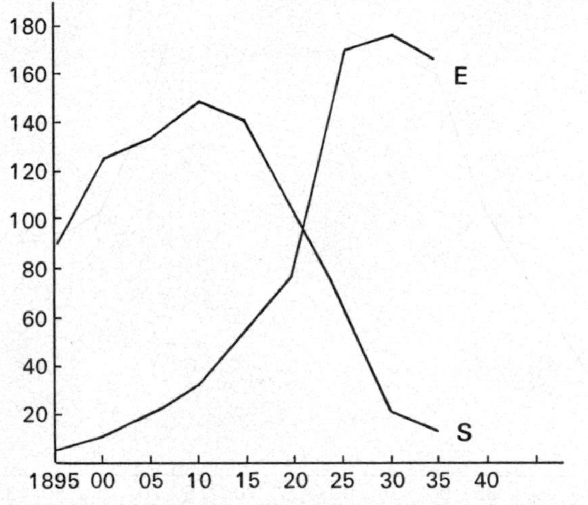

Source: Nils Hasselmo, "Den amerikanska svenskan," Hasselmo based his investigation on the annual reports of ABC, published each year in the *Minutes of the Augustana Synod.*

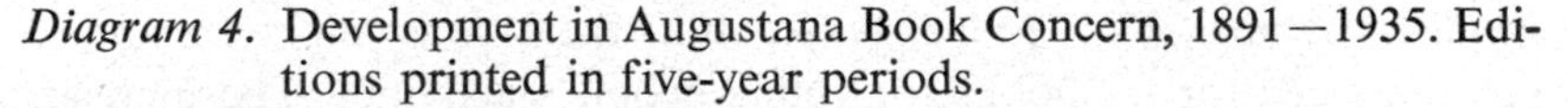
Diagram 4. Development in Augustana Book Concern, 1891—1935. Editions printed in five-year periods.

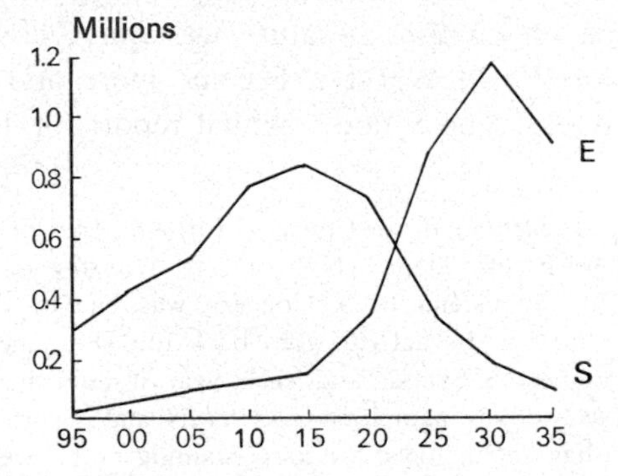

Source: Nils Hasselmo, "Den amerikanska svenskan."

[4] *Augustana-Synodens protokoll,* 1920, p. 23.

Swedish books to a public that either wanted no books at all or requested only English.[5]

Nils Hasselmo has investigated the development of ABC on the basis of the number of Swedish and English titles in its annual reports and the size of the editions in both languages.[6] He records the publications in five-year periods. The first period, 1891–1895, shows an overwhelming preponderance of Swedish language literature in the way of new titles and reprinted titles and editions. During these years a total edition of 310,000 Swedish and 3,000 English books were printed. In 1910 there was a total of 151 Swedish titles in a total edition of 750,000 copies and 31 English titles in a total of 82,000 copies. In the period 1921–1925 the English titles surpassed the Swedish. There were then 63 Swedish titles of 310,000 copies as against 165 English of 880,000 copies. After 1935 only the annual *Korsbaneret* and an almanac were published in Swedish, and in 1949 the production in Swedish ceased altogether. It should be noted that the diagrams of the number of titles and editions show great similarity. In both cases the intersection point occurs shortly after 1920.[7]

A comparison between the literary works and the two periodicals published by the Augustana Synod shows that the members of the Church were more conservative when it was a matter of shifting from the Swedish language *Augustana* to the English language *The Lutheran Companion*. Nils Hasselmo has investigated the published editions of both papers for the period 1896 to 1956.[8]

In 1896 *Augustana* was issued in average editions of 13,228 copies and the predecessor to *The Lutheran Companion* in 2,130 copies. Both papers increased markedly in the beginning of the 1900s and

[5] *Ibid.*, 1921, p. 21.

[6] Nils Hasselmo's investigation, "Den amerikanska svenskan," has not been published. However, I have been given the privilege of using the material in the unpublished manuscript.

[7] According to Ernst W. Olson, *Augustana Book Concern* (p. 64), the intersectional point had already been reached in 1919. He writes that the language transition proceeded slowly up to 1918. The hysterical enmity toward foreign languages during the war, however, immediately affected the production. In one year, between 1918 and 1919, the situation changed. Whereas ten Swedish books to five English were sold in 1918, the figures were nine English to three Swedish in 1919.

[8] Nils Hasselmo, "Den amerikanska svenskan," p. 15 ff.

Diagram 5. Number of subscribers for *Augustana* (Swedish language) and *The Lutheran Companion* (English), 1896–1956.

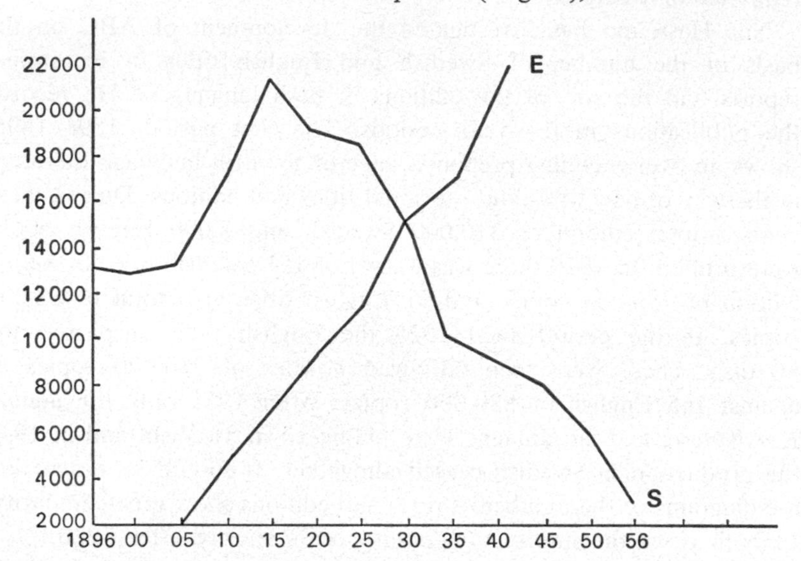

Source: Nils Hasselmo, "Den amerikanska svenskan." Hasselmo bases his figures on the annual reports of the ABC.

up to 1914, when *Augustana* was printed in editions of 21,594 copies and *The Lutheran Companion* in editions of 6,726 copies. By 1920 *Augustana* still had twice as many subscribers as *The Lutheran Companion.* The latter did not surpass *Augustana* until 1927. The editions that year were 18,965 for *The Lutheran Companion* and 18,358 for *Augustana.* During the Depression, the Swedish language readers seemed to be more loyal to their paper than the English language readers. *Augustana* reduced its editions to 14,873 copies in 1930 and to 10,535 in 1933, while *The Lutheran Companion* diminished to 15,316 copies in 1930 and to 11,501 in 1933. For a short time in 1931 *Augustana* surpassed *The Lutheran Companion,* but when its own period of decline set in *Augustana* never recovered. When the paper was discontinued in 1956 it had only 3,132 subscribers, while *The Lutheran Companion* had 88,345.

The trend with regard to the Synod's Sunday school papers was similar to that of *Augustana* and *The Lutheran Companion.* In 1921 the English language paper, *The Olive Leaf,* had more subscribers than the Swedish language *Barnens Tidning. Our Young People* was started in 1923. As indicated in Table 22, the size of the editions increased rapidly. *Barnens Tidning* was discontinued in 1932.[9] Prior to this, *Teologisk Tidskrift* ceased to be published in 1917 and likewise *Ungdomsvännen* in 1918.

Table 22. Number of subscribers for the Augustana Synod's Sunday school papers: *Barnens Tidning* (Swedish) and *The Olive Leaf* (English).

Year	Barnens Tidning	The Olive Leaf	Ungdoms-vännen	Our Young People
1916	37 583	20 500	5 035	—
1917	35 833	21 833	4 650	—
1918	33 375	24 625	4 049	—
1919	30 417	26 950	—	—
1920	24 237	23 122	—	—
1921	22 134	40 816	—	—
1922	18 933	44 480	—	—
1923	15 054	42 279	—	12 404
1924	10 643	32 432	—	17 727
1925	9 219	42 372	—	21 480
1926	7 174	39 774	—	22 850
1931	2 110	32 436	—	34 347
1932	—	28 368	—	34 952

Source: *Yearbooks of the Augustana Synod.*

Seen in the light of the general trend set by the younger generation of Swedish Americans with regard to the transition to English, it is quite natural that the English language Sunday school paper, *The Olive Leaf,* had a larger circulation than *Barnens Tidning* long before *The Lutheran Companion's* circulation surpassed that of its competitor, *Augustana.* It is also evident that the development regarding the papers of the Augustana Synod was very much the same as that of its Norwegian counterpart (see Diagram 6).

[9] Ernst W. Olson, *Augustana Book Concern,* pp. 64, 65 and 69. See the yearbooks of the Synod for the years concerned. *The Lutheran Companion* was called the *Young Lutherans' Companion* from January 1907 to 1911 and was then a young people's paper but developed into the synod's official English organ. In 1911 its name was *The Lutheran Companion.*

Diagram 6. The development of the circulation of the Norwegian Lutheran Church papers, *Lutheran Church Herald* (English) and *Lutheranen* (Norwegian language).

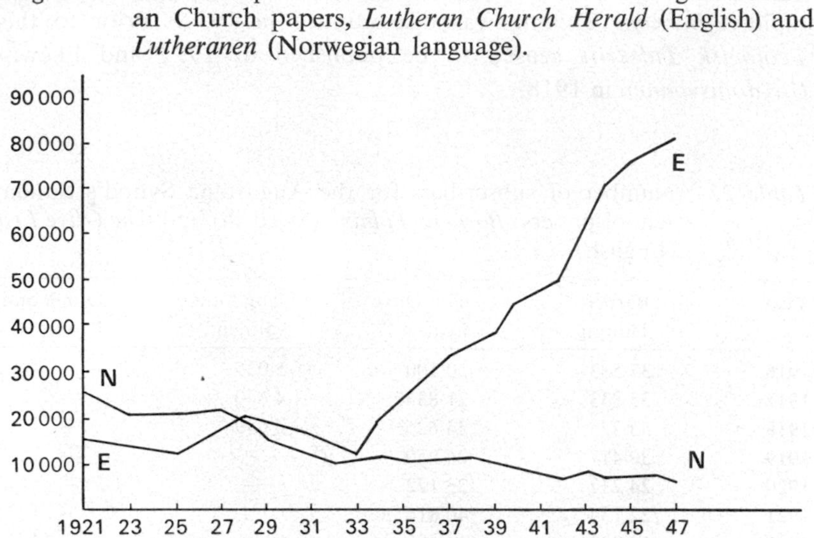

Source: Einar Haugen, *Norwegian Language*,p.276.

4. *The Importance of Schools for the Swedish Language*

Swedish schools have played an important role in maintaining the Swedish language in the U.S. The immigrants often sent their children to a Swedish school or to a school where they could learn Swedish. David Nyvall recommended more of good and elegant reading of Swedish for the young, and first and foremost, more conversation with them.[1] He called for more primary schools, as opposed to schools for higher instruction, with the aim of teaching "our" children the Swedish language. He went so far as to assert that it was their "duty and obligation under this country's constitution" to retain Swedish schools. He proposed that places which had a sizeable number of Swedish residents should demand that Swedish be added to the school curriculum. Where it was impossible to have it adopted in the public schools as an obligatory language, it was necessary to introduce

[1] David Nyvall, *op. cit.*, p. 16 ff; S.G. Öhman lamented that the historical connection with Sweden was neglected in both homes and schools. S.G. Öhman, "Vårt svenska arv" in *Korsbaneret,* 1924, p. 112; Johan Person was more sceptical than Nyvall and Öhman about the possibilities the schools might have in promoting the preservation of the Swedish language: see Person's *Svensk-amerikanska studier,* p. 137.

classes in Swedish "and within the regular school hours." Swedish week-day schools during the summer were an emergency measure, he said, and were not advisable, since they deprived the children of their summer vacations.

Colleges and theological seminaries were founded by Swedish-American religious denominations.[2] "It is significant that no enduring institutions of higher learning have been founded by the Scandinavian Americans apart from the church."[3]

Some of the Swedish-American colleges have had departments of secondary or college-preparatory education, usually referred to as academies. The four colleges of the Augustana Synod have discontinued their academies: Bethany College in 1927, Upsala College in 1928, Gustavus Adolphus in 1931, and Augustana College in 1932.[4]

In replying to a questionnaire circulated in 1941 as to why they gave instruction in Swedish, Norwegian or Danish, the Scandinavian colleges stated that it was mainly "to preserve the language and cultural heritage of the founders of these schools."[5] Esther Meixner points out that the founders of the Scandinavian-American schools, wanted instruction offered in their own language, and that later the schools continued to give this instruction in order to preserve the cultural heritage of the group. Though immigration had ceased by the 1920s, the interest in Swedish remained alive. Even after 1920, at Augustana College approximately 100 students, or a fifth of the total enrollment, participated in one of the Scandinavian courses offered in the curriculum.[6] At Gustavus Adolphus the interest in the Swedish language and Swedish literature was likewise maintained. In 1931 a total of 116 students enrolled in some course having a connection with Sweden. Between 1932 and 1939 the figures were as follows: in 1932, 116; 1933, 93; 1934, 116; 1935, 108; 1936, 148; 1937, 171;

[2] Peter Person, "*A History of Higher Education among the Swedish immigrants in America,*" p. 54. He writes (p.83): "These colleges originated as institutions stressing the Swedish language and culture but there is at present but little left of the Swedish except the name. Swedish is taught the same as any other foreign language." See also Esther Meixner, *The Teaching of the Scandinavian Languages and Literatures in the United States,* pp. 17 and 28.

[3] Esther Meixner, *op. cit.,* p. 18.

[4] Peter Person, *op. cit.,* p. 55.

[5] Esther Meixner, *op. cit.,* p. 29.

[6] *Ibid.,* p. 36 ff.

1938, 161; 1939, 143. At North Park College the interest was highest during the period 1891–1914. Then interest diminished from 1914 to 1920 but rose again from 1920 continuously to 1940.

Those who wished to study Swedish could also do so at non-Swedish-American colleges. From 1858 up to World War I, no less than 36 universities and non-affiliated colleges added some instruction in one of the Scandinavian languages to their curricula.[7] In Minnesota the State Legislature enacted a law in 1883 establishing a professorship of Scandinavian Language and Literature in the State University.

Parallel with the decline of interest in and need for the Swedish language came the abolishment of required courses in Swedish for students preparing for the ministry and for preaching. In the beginning Swedish was used as the main language of instruction, but was later placed on equal footing with English. For entrance to some of the Swedish colleges and academies knowledge of both English and Swedish was originally required. The demand for knowledge of Swedish, however, was gradually abolished. At Augustana College and Theological Seminary the requirement of an "ability to read and spell Swedish" is mentioned for the last time in 1899–1900.[8] Thereafter, a statement was made instead to the effect that "students of Swedish parentage are urged to devote as much time as possible to the study of the beautiful language of their forefathers. Sentimental considerations aside, the practical advantages of such study to the clergyman, the teacher, the physician, the lawyer, the businessman, the cultured man in any walk of life, are sufficiently obvious without being specially pointed out." This provision for the Swedish language prevailed up to 1931–32, when it was permanently given the same status as other foreign languages. The Theological Seminary had retained the requirement of Swedish until 1912–13. In 1932–33 the Swedish language in both the College and the Seminary was for the first time put on the same level as other foreign languages.

Certain American public secondary schools also began to offer courses in the Scandinavian languages. In 1900 the Norwegian language was introduced in a high school in Story City, Iowa, and in

[7] Gösta Franzén, "The Development of Scandinavian Studies in the United States," p. 43; *Minnesota University. A Compilation of State Laws Relating to the University of Minnesota* (Minneapolis, 1892).

[8] Nils Hasselmo, "Den amerikanska svenskan," p. 17 f; "Language Displacement and Language Influence in Swedish America," pp. 62—84.

1910 Swedish was offered in the curriculum of a high school in Minnesota.[9] The year 1910 is considered the year when Scandinavian languages gained their foothold in public schools.[10] In 1912 no less than 45 high schools were reported to have some Scandinavian language in their curricula. Among these schools, 26 were in- Minnesota, five in Wisconsin, six in Illinois, four in Iowa.

The interest for these languages increased in 1912, when the Society for the Advancement of Scandinavian Study appointed a special committee for the purpose of seeking to induce more public schools to introduce Swedish, Danish or Norwegian.[11] As a result of these efforts, Danish, Norwegian and Swedish studies flourished for a few years as never before or after. In 1917 no less than 63 'secondary schools' offered such instruction. In Swedish alone 1,822 students received instruction.[12] The teaching of Swedish, as in general the teaching of any foreign language, was dealt a hard blow by World War I. Many schools were forced to discontinue the teaching of Swedish. During the war, the Society for the Advancement of Scandinavian Study dissolved its Committee on Secondary Schools.[13]

During and after the war, 22 states enacted laws which more or less prohibited the offering of foreign language study in school curricula. Within a period of ten years after the war 65 percent of the public schools which had previously offered courses in the Scandinavian languages discontinued them. During this same period the number of students was reduced by 75 percent. A change was noted only after 1930, when the interest again began to increase.

How did it come about that public school systems began to take up Swedish or Norwegian into school curricula? There is no clear-cut

9 Gösta Franzén, "The Development of Scandinavian Studies in the United States," p. 43 ff.

10 Esther Meixner, *op. cit.*, pp. 73 and 75.

11 The Society for the Advancement of Scandinavian Study was organized in 1911 by persons interested in Scandinavian culture and preservation of the Scandinavian languages. Most of the founders were college professors engaged in teaching these languages. The organization was founded in order to "promote the study and teaching of the languages, literature and culture of the Scandinavian North." See Gösta Franzén, *op. cit.*, p. 51; and Esther Meixner, *op. cit.*, p. 75.

12 Esther Meixner, *op. cit.*, p. 80.

13 Esther Meixner, *The Teaching of the Scandinavian Languages*, p. 82.

Table 23. Public Secondary Schools with Courses in One of the Scandinavian Languages in Their Curriculum, 1900—1940.

Year	Approximate number of schools	Approximate number of students
1900	1	?
1905	2	?
1907	3	?
1910	5	?
1911	18	?
1912	45	1 190
1915	50	1 965
1917	63	4 526
1925	36	1 155
1927	22	1 080
1934	15	1 227
1940	17	1 544

Source: Esther Meixner, *The Teaching of the Scandinavian Languages*, p. 126.

answer to that question. In 1941 Esther Meixner asked a number of public secondary schools about this and, as indicated in Table 24 below, found that it was mainly because of requests from the public or from an interest group. The case of Chicago may be cited as an example of how a nationality tried to interest school authorities in instituting Swedish language instruction. In 1911 an intensive effort was made to persuade the Chicago Board of Education to introduce Swedish as an optional subject in Chicago's high schools. In December, 1911, a campaign was organized among the Swedes in Chicago, resulting in a mass petition, supported by Swedish churches, societies, newspapers and individuals.[14] "Through the distribution of this petition, which has already been signed by thousands of Swedish men and women, a public opinion has been created and an interest for the teaching of the Swedish language established, which can no longer be ignored by the city's Board of Education." The campaign resulted in the Board of Education's decision that instruction in any foreign language whatever would be initiated when a sufficient number of students applied.

[14] "Skall svenska språket införas vid Chicagos skolor?" (Should the study of the Swedish language be introduced in Chicago schools?) *Yearbook 1912*, published by Riksföreningen för svenskhetens bevarande i utlandet.

It is impossible to determine to what extent the instruction in Swedish in American schools affected the interest in the Swedish language. Undoubtedly the schools played a secondary role, because the future of the language depended on the will to preserve it.[15] It is also obvious that many parents preferred to send their children to American schools instead of their own schools and colleges. This of course, was not looked upon favorably by those who were zealously working for the preservation of the Swedish language. For example, *Augustana* wrote in 1921 that with many it was simply an idiotic pride which prompted them not to send their children to the Augustana Synod's colleges.[16] The paper had reached the conclusion that this applied especially to the economically well-situated who were deluded into thinking that it was more elegant to possess a diploma from a school not founded by Swedes.

Table 24. Reasons why Public Secondary Schools introduced classes in a Scandinavian language in the schools' educational program.

Reason	Number of schools
Demand by the public or by a Scandinavian organization	13
Population consisted mainly of Scandinavians	8
A wish to preserve the Scandinavian language and literature	4
For individual use	1
Other reasons	2

Source: Esther Meixner, *op. cit.*, p. 93.

5. *Summary*

The language question occupied a central place in the Swedish-American debate. The most common conception was that Swedishness could not be preserved without knowledge of the Swedish language.

15 C.A. Lindvall, "Har det svenska språket någon framtid i Amerika," *Ungdomsvännen*, July 1916, No. 7, p. 210.

16 Editorial in *Augustana*, July 28, 1921, p. 472.

As long as immigration continued on a wide scale, there was definitely a need for Swedish in churches and in social and fraternal meetings. Parallel with the cessation of immigration came increasing demands for a change over to English, especially among the younger generation who found it difficult to understand why they should be forced to learn a language for which they felt hardly any affinity. The older generation, however, zealously guarded the life of the Swedish language. The death of the language, they said, would result in the disintegration of their Swedish identity. Those who advocated the preservation of Swedish asserted that the more languages a person knows, the better off he is: The language was the best way to disseminate knowledge of Swedish culture and Swedish history: Those who forgot their mother tongue or depreciated it were not looked favorably upon. Those who easily forgot their fatherland were assumed to be just as likely to forget their new homeland.

Despite all efforts to preserve the Swedish language, time took its toll. Interest for Swedish diminished as quickly as the first generation of immigrants learned English or died out. The publishing of Swedish literature reached its zenith in the 1910–1915 period and then tapered off continuously. Not even the Swedish schools and colleges, despite courses both in the Swedish language and Swedish literature, could stem the tide.

X. The Swedish-American Press

1. *The Foreign Language Press – an Educational Agency*

Robert E. Park has emphasized the importance of the foreign language newspapers for the Americanization process.[1] Louis Gerson says that the non-English newspapers had two functions: to promote Americanization and to preserve ethnic identity.[2] He pinpoints that these newspapers welded the nationalities together and kept up the contact with the native country. "The foreign language press has . . . in isolated ethnic communities, kept alive old-country disputes, evoked pride and nationalism for the lands of origin." American historical scholars are quite unanimous in considering the immigrant press as important for the immigrants because the press made it easier for them to adapt to American conditions and strengthened their national identity. The foreign language press has often been charged with consciously working against Americanization. This was especially the case both during and after World War I. It should be noted, however, that American historical research indicates just the opposite. The newspapers' detailed accounts of American social conditions, printed in the language the immigrants understood, made adjustment easier for them – especially for those who did not know English. The Swedish-American newspapers also served to promote both Americanization and nationalism among the immigrants by spreading news from both

[1] Robert E. Park, *The Immigrant Press and Its Control* (New York, 1922), p.358 f; Maurice Davie, *World Immigration,* p. 484. Davie maintains that the immigrants need their newspapers because there is no other possibility for them to get acquainted with the ideals of the American community.

[2] Louis Gerson, *The Hyphenate in Recent American Politics and Diplomacy,* p. 22; William Carlson Smith, *American in the Making* (New York 1939), p. 191 ff; Smith points out, as does Gerson, the importance of the newspapers. "They [the immigrants] could not wait until they mastered the English language before learning anything about America. . . . The foreign language press, then, in spite of many shortcomings, has been an educational agency."

the new and the old homeland. Those who have studied the Swedish language papers have – perhaps to counteract criticism – stressed their significance for the conscious efforts to promote Americanization. "Instead of hampering, the Swedish-American papers at all times help and encourage in every way the Americanizing of their readers."[3] According to Conrad Bergendoff, the papers have meant just as much as the religious denominations in terms of immigrant identity and Americanization.[4] It has been said that those who do not take any notice of a Swedish-American newspaper are not interested in either Swedish America or Sweden.[5] The papers have continually encouraged their readers to defend the Swedish cultural heritage, and they have sought to keep the widespread groups together by informing them about events, activities and personal experiences among their countrymen, not only in their area of circulation but also in other parts of the country. They covered contemporary news from Sweden, not the least of which was the generous space devoted to the various provinces. Throughout the years such reporting strengthened the ties with Sweden and the old home districts. The papers have been considered the natural link between Sweden and the Swedish people in America. Their news items have been described as the oil that keeps the lamp of Swedish culture burning.[6] Naturally enough the Swedish newspapers in America addressed themselves to the Swedish immigrants in their own language. "Wherever these papers reached

[3] Oliver A. Linder, "The Swedish-American Press," *The Swedish Element in America,* Vol. II (Chicago, 1931), p. 341; A.B. Benson and Naboth Hedin, *Americans from Sweden,* p. 319. They also maintain that "the newspapers in his native tongue acted as a comforting stabilizer until his feet were more firmly planted in the new, foreign soil."

[4] Conrad Bergendoff, "The Role of Augustana," p. 68; Robert E. Park, *The Immigrant Press and Its Control,* p. 50; G.H. von Koch, *Emigranternas land,* (Stockholm, 1910), p. 385. Koch writes that "beside the church, it [the press] plays the greatest role in preserving the Swedish language and Swedish culture." Bergendoff comments: "Foremost of the instruments in the creation of Swedish-America was the press."

[5] Vilhelm Berger, *Svensk-amerikanska meditationer,* p. 79.

[6] K.A. Kilander, "Svenskhetens bevarande," *Augustana* (January 3, 1924), p. 3; Albert Schersten, *The Relation of the Swedish-American Newspaper to the Assimilation of Swedish Immigrants,* p. 97 ff. Schersten maintains that the Swedish papers intensified the existent interest for Sweden and kept alive the feelings the immigrants associated with Sweden and the past.

they proclaimed a solidarity for the Swedish population."[7] The papers stimulated both directly and indirectly the preservation of the Swedish language. While the churches and secular organizations successively transferred to English, the Swedish newspapers have stubbornly held fast to the language of the old country. "Don't forget the Swedish language!" has throughout the years been a common motto for the newspapers and their publishers.[8] The clear and understandable reason for this is that their very existence was directly dependent on the Swedish language. There was no possibility for the newspapers who represented non-confessional churches to change over to English: it was a foregone conclusion that they would fail in competition with the large American news media.

2. *A Continuous Struggle for Existence*

The foreign language press has from the very beginning fought a hard battle for existence. It has been said that the high mortality rate has been "the most important single characteristic of the foreign language press."[9] Between 1884 and 1920, 3,444 papers were started, while 3,186 ceased publication.[10] According to Maurice Davie the mortality among the foreign language papers has been so high and the records at various periods so variable that it is difficult to get an idea of the extent of the foreign language press[11] A specialist on the German language press calls attention to the fact that it has been quite easy to start a foreign language newspaper, but it has been a great deal more difficult to keep it alive.[12] The competition for gaining a reading public was particularly keen for new immigrant papers because of two factors: they had to compete with the papers already established among their countrymen as well as with the American press.

[7] Conrad Bergendoff, *op. cit.*, p. 69.

[8] *Ibid.*, p. 70.

[9] Jerzy Zubrzycki, "The Rôle of the Foreign-Language Press in Migrant Integration," *Population Studies*, 12 (1958), p. 76.

[10] D.N. Taft and R. Robbins, *International Migrations: the Immigrant in the Modern World*, N,Y., 1955, p. 533.

[11] Maurice Davie, *World Immigration*, p. 486.

[12] Carl Wittke, *The German-Language Press in America*, (1957) p. 2.

Table 25. Number of Mother Tongue Weeklies, 1910—1960.

Languages	1910	1920	1930	1940	1950	1960	Percent increase or decrease	
							1910—1930	1930—1960
French	18	17	18	14	13	8	0 %	−55 %
Spanish	30	39	39	18	18	10	+30	−74
German	433	172	106	68	35	29	−76	−73
Yiddish	8	16	7	3	8	2	−12	−71
Hungarian	7	16	28	25	26	19	+300	−32
Ukrainian	1	5	3	2	3	2	+200	−33
Italian	48	66	73	29	28	12	+52	−84
Polish	37	54	64	43	35	18	+73	−72
Greek	5	8	6	7	6	3	+20	−50
Czech	34	29	27	28	12	9	−21	−67
Other Slavic	11	31	28	22	26	20	+155	−29
Scandinavian	94	73	51	32	26	14	−46	−73
Other Germanic	16	13	11	8	3	1	−31	−91
Other Romance	8	12	12	10	6	4	+50	−75
Near Eastern	5	6	2	1	6	8	−60	+300
Far Eastern	4	5	8	3	5	3	+100	−62
All Other	17	32	28	24	29	26	+65	−7
Total	776	594	511	337	285	188	−34	−63

Source: Joshua Fishman, *Language Loyalty*, s. 55.

The history of the foreign language press has been rather dismal since 1910. The downward trend has been felt most of all by the German and the Scandinavian language newspapers.[13] Between 1910 and 1930 the number of Scandinavian papers in America decreased by 46 percent and between 1930 and 1960 by 73 percent. A study of the circulation figures among the foreign language papers (weeklies) reveals that with the exception of the German and Scandinavian the peak figures were reached in 1930. Between 1910 and 1930 circulation figures for the German papers decreased by 60 percent and the Scandinavian by 33 percent.[14]

It has been estimated that approximately 1,500 Swedish-American periodicals of various kinds – weeklies, monthly journals and annuals – had been published between 1851 and 1910.[15] Of these only a dozen or so had a national circulation. Most of the Swedish language newspapers have been weeklies. Some unsuccessful attempts to publish dailies have been made. In St. Paul, *Svenska Dagbladet* (Swedish Daily), was issued for a period of about six months in 1885.[16] *Skandia* in Chicago managed to keep alive for nine months (1890–1891), while *Dagens Nyheter* (Daily News) in Chicago in February, 1896, became barely two weeks old.

The Swedish-American newspapers have a long prior history. As early as 1851 the first paper, *Skandinaven,* was issued but lasted only two years.[17] On January 3, 1855, *Det gamla och det nya Hemlandet* (The Old and the New Homeland) was issued for the first time in Galesburg, Illinois. *Hemlandet* was for a long time – up to 1914 – one of the leading Swedish language papers in America. It was published by T.N. Hasselquist and in 1859 moved to Chicago. Toward the end of the 1850s several new Swedish-American papers were

[13] Joshua Fishman, *Language Loyalties,* p. 54.

[14] *Ibid.,* p. 56.

[15] Herbert Capps, *From Isolationism to Involvement,* p. 15; Oliver Linder, "The Swedish American Press," p. 340; Alfred Söderström's *Blixtar på tidningshorisonten* records that 1,158 papers had been published in America up to 1910. Of these, 290 (58 of them weeklies) were said to be still published in 1910.

[16] Ernst Skarstedt, *Svensk-amerikanska folket i helg och söcken,* (Stockholm, 1917), p. 180.

[17] J. Oscar Backlund, *A Century of the Swedish American Press,* (Chicago, 1952), p. 11 ff; Linder, *op. cit.,* p. 324 ff.

Diagram 7. Edition circulation of the Swedish, German, Italian and Norwegian-Danish newspapers in America, 1915—32. (Index: 1915 = 100)

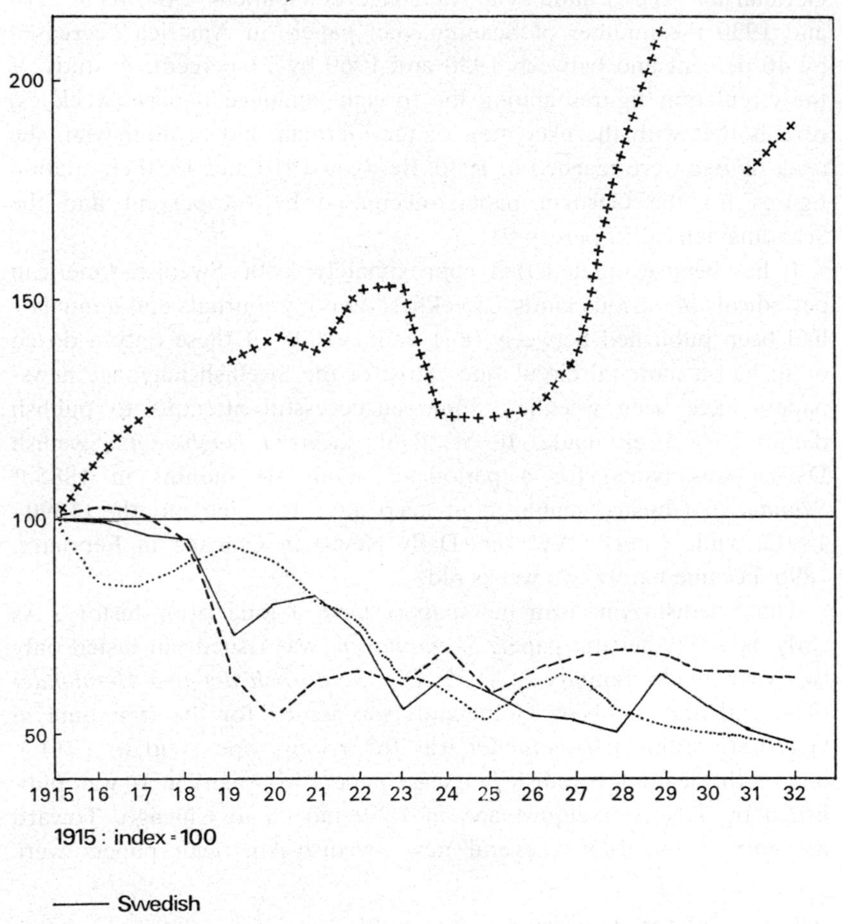

Source: N.W. Ayers, *Newspaper Annual and Directory*, 1915—32.

launched. Thus, between 1851 and 1886 no less than 173 newspapers had been published.[18] Of these 173, only ten remained at the beginning of the 1930s.

[18] Linder, *op. cit.*, p. 340.

Diagram 8. Number of Swedish, German, Italian and Norwegian-Danish newspapers in America, 1915—1932. (Index: 1915 = 100)

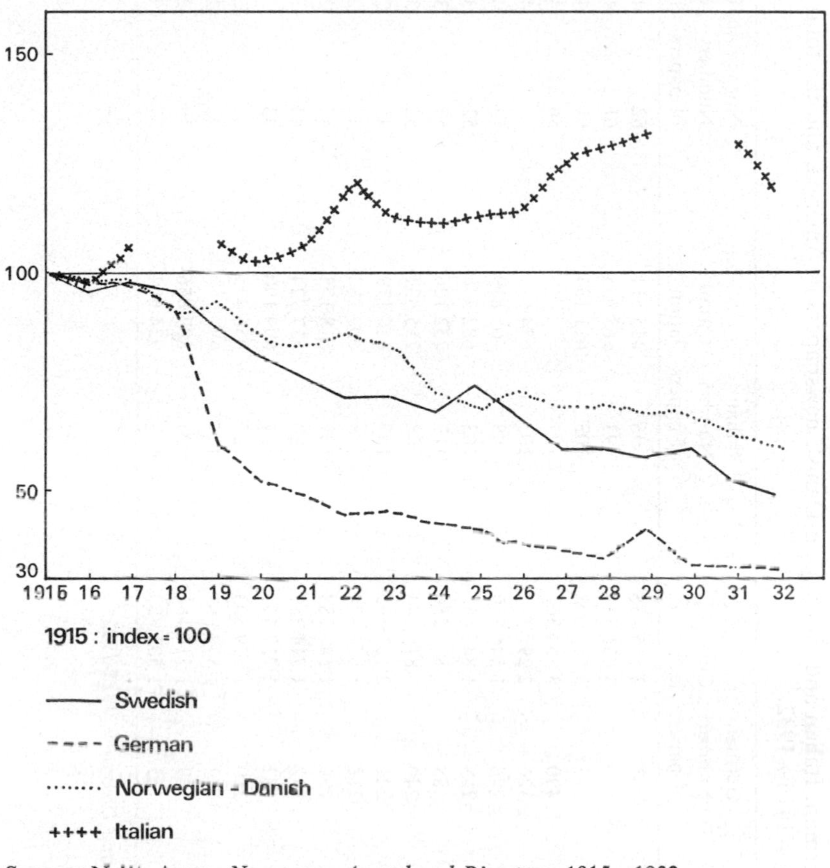

Source: N. W. Ayers, *Newspaper Annual and Directory*, 1915—1932.

An investigation of the Swedish, German, Italian and Norwegian-Danish papers in America shows that both the number of papers and their circulation decreased between 1915–1932, with the exception of the Italian. The latter recorded an increase both in the number of papers and in circulation up to 1930. On the other hand, indicated in Diagram 7 and 8, the growth of the Swedish, German and Norwegian-Danish papers consistently traced out a rather negative pattern. The graph curves follow each other very closely. The German-American papers experienced a sharp decline in 1918, undoubtedly caused by the animosity toward everything German during World War I. A

Table 26. Number of Swedish, German, Italian and Norwegian-Danish newspapers in America, and the total circulation for each nationality 1915—1932.

Year	Swedish Number of papers	Swedish Circulation	German Number of papers	German Circulation	Italian Number of papers	Italian Circulation	Norwegian-Danish Number of papers	Norwegian-Danish Circulation
1915	72	651 430	532	3 555 136	96	495 511	62	491 107
1916	69	647 384	520	3 631 339	93	568 933	61	416 506
1917	71	625 443	517	3 562 098	103	611 134	61	410 302
1918	69	614 004	490	3 354 367			56	437 878
1919	63	470 693	326	2 299 117	103	674 623	58	463 307
1920	58	523 598	276	1 546 889	98	705 819	53	440 711
1921	55	531 913	258	1 842 032	103	682 378	52	395 897
1922	52	472 440	238	1 883 286	117	752 126	53	361 805
1923	52	356 719	240	1 819 143	108	755 631	52	307 348
1924	49	410 297	221	2 107 365	107	610 179	45	288 392
1925	53	387 174	218	1 628 424	108	609 782	43	261 278
1926	48	352 966	196	1 548 788	109	618 173	45	298 750
1927	43	345 364	192	1 714 289	120	677 924	43	317 732
1928	43	384 213	182	1 727 911	124	899 190	43	273 583
1929	42	413 092	219	1 679 503	127	1 056 475	42	257 402
1930	43	363 185	172	1 573 869	125		42	245 348
1931	37	323 945	169	1 514 161	125	887 856	39	289 147
1932	35	309 369	163	1 502 720	115	934 654	37	227 019

Source: N.W. Ayers, *Newspaper Annual and Directory, 1915-1932.*

comparison of Diagrams 7 and 8 shows that both graph lines follow each other very closely, the difference being that the upward or downward trend in the number of papers was consistently a year after the corresponding circulation trend. In brief when the circulation of the Swedish-American press increased, for example, new papers were started – or just the opposite. The conclusion one may arrive at from a reading of the Diagrams and Table 26 is that the section of the foreign language press published by the "older" immigrants recorded a downward trend after 1910, while the section published by the "newer" immigrants noted an upward trend up to 1930, when even it began to experience a downward trend.

Between 1915 and 1932 the number of Swedish-American papers was reduced by *ca.* 50 percent and circulation by 52.5 percent. The circulation of the Norwegian-Danish papers declined 53.8 percent and the German-American 57.7 percent. The serious effect of World War I on the German-American papers is evidenced by the fact that practically the entire 56.5 percent decrease in circulation came during the years 1917–1920.

Finally, the Depression in the beginning of the 1930s brought on great difficulties for the Swedish-American papers. Newspaper columns constantly talked about "the hard times for the Swedish-American press." The year of the stock market crash, 1929, a total of 42 Swedish-American papers, either monthlies or weeklies, were published. The total was reduced from 42 to 35 during the years 1929–1932, and their circulation decreased from 413,092 to 309,369. As indicated in Table 27, circulation figures dropped in approximately the same proportion for the religious and the secular press. However, there was a regional difference; the circulation decreased more, for example, in Illinois than in the states on the Pacific coast – probably a reflection of the fact that the immigration into the Middle West was older and was becoming Americanized.

Besides the constant difficulties with which the Swedish language papers – as well as the entire immigrant press – had to wrestle, it was especially World War I, the decreasing immigration, and the Depression which created severe hardships for the publishers.[19] The distrust

[19] Maurice Davie, *World Immigration,* p. 489; Carl Wittke, *The German-language Press in America,* p. 274. Wittke writes: "World War I struck the German-language press a blow from which it has never recovered. The number of papers and their circulation had been declining for some years because of

Table 27. Circulation of some selected Swedish American papers, 1929, 1931, 1932 and 1933.

Name of Paper (State)	1929	1931	1932	1933
Augustana (Ill.)	16 454	14 805	14 077	13 971
California (Cal.)	2 100	2 000	1 888	1 890
Förbundets Veckotidning (Ill.)	8 000	7 200	6 480	–
Guldax (Nebr.)	–	12 000	10 800	9 720
Minnesota Stats Tidning (Minn.)	7 500	6 200	6 200	5 580
Omaha Posten (Nebr.)	12 864	13 500	15 000	13 500
Skandia (N.Y.)	3 000	2 700	2 430	–
Svenska Amerikanska Posten (Minn.)	40 000	42 000	42 000	40 000
Svenska Journalen (Wash.)	–	10 200	10 200	9 180
Svenska Pressen (Wash.)	3 450	3 200	3 400	3 400
Svenska Standaret (Ill.)	10 485	9 725	9 500	8 400
Svenska Tribunen Nyheter (Ill.)	60 174	58 922	52 078	45 613
Svea (Mass.)	35 109	35 642	35 296	35 648
Sändebudet (Ill.)	3 220	2 600	2 600	2 600
Texas Posten (Texas)	5 409	4 370	5 821	5 821
Utah Posten (Utah)	1 550	1 450	1 340	1 340
Vestkusten (Cal.)	4 500	4 800	4 800	4 800
Western Nyheter (Cal.)	2 225	3 201	3 201	2 880

Source: Ayers, N.W., *Newspaper Annual and Directory, 1929-1933.*

of immigrants during and after World War I had immediate repercussions on the Swedish language papers. Circulation dropped: the immigrants no longer dared to show that they subscribed to a non-English language paper. Agitation against immigrants expressed itself, for instance, in a conscious effort to suppress papers printed in a foreign language. The Swedish-American papers, however, stood the test relatively well. It was not until after the war that the downward trend began to be serious – a development that had more to do with the declining immigration than with any other factor. The incidental upswing in 1923–24 was undoubtedly a result of the large immigration wave from Sweden in 1923.

The number of discontinued papers hardly reflects all of the difficulties faced by the Swedish press in America. The anxiety expressed by the papers themselves gives perhaps a better view of the situation

falling immigration and the normal processes of Americanization, but it was the war and the hysterical reaction to all things German which precipitated a unique crisis in the history of America's foreign-language press."

than the press statistics. In their editorials, they often discuss their own problems in connection with World War I, the declining immigration, and the Depression. In the long run, the declining immigration naturally became the most serious cause for anxiety. The papers were well aware that their continued existence was directly dependent upon the extent of immigration. *Svenska Kuriren* was pessimistic about the development. Not only was immigration a closed chapter, but the Swedes were becoming Americanized faster than any other group – which nobody so far has proved – and as a result they lost interest in their own press.[20] When immigration ceased and the Swedes became Americanized, even the interest in the Swedish language waned. When *Lindsborg-Posten* was forced to discontinue publishing in 1930, it declared in its farewell issue that the Swedish people were retreating to an even greater extent from their native language and their Swedish-American papers.[1] When *Österns Veckoblad* ceased publication in 1929, the Mission Covenant thought that this indicated the direction in which the wind was blowing with regard to the Swedish language.[2]

The hardships encountered ever since the end of World War I were particularly aggravated by the Depression:

> The prevailing Depression in the United States is heavily felt by the Swedish-American press. Unemployment has contributed to the decline in the number of subscribers which, because of the on-going Americanization and the halt of immigration, has for several years been in a steady downspin. The Depression has also caused a considerable reduction in advertising revenues. As a result of the prevailing conditions, most of the Swedish-American papers have been compelled to reduce the size of their formats.[3]

The difficulties seem to have culminated in 1932. Even a paper as large as *Nordstjernan* was forced to reduce the number of pages from 16 to 12, beginning in July 1932. The same year *Omaha Posten* announced that "because of the economic Depression and the consequent reduction of the paper's income" it was compelled to reduce

[20] *Svenska Kuriren,* April 2, 1925, June 16, 1927 and August 22, 1929.

[1] *Lindsborg-Posten.* (It has not been possible to determine the date of the paper because the copy in question was completely worn ragged with age).

[2] *Minutes of the Mission Covenant Church Annual Meeting,* 1929—30, p. 5.

[3] *Allsvensk Samling,* No. 31, 1932, p. 13; Herbert Capps, *From Isolationism to Involvement,* p. 25. Capps says that "the depression of the 1930s hastened the decline of the Swedish-American press."

the size of its editions from 8 to 4 pages.[4] It is, of course, impossible to state definitely the role the Depression played, since the difficulties had accumulated for a number of years. As far as *Svenska Kuriren* and *Österns Veckoblad* are concerned both of which ceased publication in 1929, it may be said that at the time they closed down the Depression had not yet been felt. *Svenska Kuriren* stated that the unfortunate outburst of World War I was the cause of the dilemma in which the Swedish-American press now found itself.[5]

Svenska Amerikanaren discussed the problem of the Swedish-American press in several editorials. Toward the end of 1931, the paper declared that the Depression was as great a time of testing for the Swedish-American papers as for all other enterprises and that "*Svenska Amerikanaren* has received numerous forced cancellations."[6] A year or so later the same paper stated that as a matter of fact, a good many foreign language newspapers have been compelled to give up. The prevailing hard times have of course especially strangled the small local papers.[7] The difficulties, it was thought, had their origin in the diminishing immigration and were aggravated by the Depression. "When it was hard to get bread for the family, the newspaper subscription, as a rule, had to be sacrificed." However, the future looked considerably brighter, and it was hoped that the hardships were of a temporary nature.

Missionsvännen considered the crisis greatest in Chicago, "where our Swedes have lost their savings through failure of the banks."[8] An appeal was made to the readers to keep up their subscriptions so that the paper would be able to continue publication.

Of the papers that lived through the Depression it seems that *Ny Tid,* the communist newspaper in Chicago, had had the most difficult time. The delight which the editor expressed in November, 1929, when the size of the paper was increased to eight pages, was of short duration.[9] In less than a year the optimism had fallen considerably. In September, 1930, an announcement appeared under

[4] *Allsvensk Samling,* No. 33, 1932, p. 12.

[5] *Svenska Kuriren,* October 3, 1929.

[6] *Svenska Amerikanaren,* December 31, 1931.

[7] *Ibid.,* January 12, 1933.

[8] *Missionsvännen,* September 15, 1931.

[9] *Ny Tid,* November 25, 1929.

the heading "*Ny Tid* in serious distress."[10] The immediate reason was that Lake View State Bank had closed and the paper's assets had been frozen. A few weeks later the situation had further deteriorated, and the paper was compelled to issue an SOS – an appeal for help in the form of donations or loans.[11]

Ny Tid was able to withstand the crisis but was forced in the future to reduce its number of pages, at first to six[12] and later to four pages.[13] In spite of reduction of pages and other restrictions the situation was desperate, and in several issues it expressed anxiety for the future. The summer of 1931 was particularly distressing, and the publishers never knew in advance whether or not the next number could be issued.

As previously indicated, the Americanization process caused the Swedish language press great anxiety. In order to counteract this development, several English language papers were launched, some by the Augustana Synod, some by the Mission Covenant. It can be of interest here to see how these papers made out compared to the Swedish language papers. The preceding section has shown that in the period covered by the present study the English language papers of the Augustana Synod succeeded better than those in the Swedish language. While the circulation of the latter declined, the former experienced a continuous upswing and finally surpassed the Swedish language papers. Thus, from 1927 on *The Lutheran Companion* had a larger circulation than *Augustana* (Swedish language weekly). The Mission Covenant's English language paper, *The Covenant Companion,* also did well compared with the Covenant's Swedish language papers. *The Covenant Companion,* started in 1923, was published monthly with 16 pages.[14] The number of pages was later increased to 48, then to 52 and finally to 64 pages. In 1928 it began publishing twice a month, and in 1930 it took the final step to a weekly. But with the Depression the success was halted, and during 1933 the situation became so difficult that it was decided to combine it with *Förbundets*

[10] *Ibid.,* September 27, 1930, p. 1.

[11] *Ibid.,* October 4, 1930, p. 1.

[12] Beginning July 9, 1931.

[13] *Ny Tid,* July 23, 1931, p. 1.

[14] *The Covenant Companion,* November 10, 1930, p. 2; E. Gustav Johnson, "Periodicals Published by the Mission Covenant People in America," in *Covenant Memories* (Chicago, 1935), p. 213.

Veckotidning.[15] In January 1933 *The Covenant Companion* predicted that this year would be the most difficult in the history of the paper. The reason was explained by the paper: "*The Companion* is read by the younger generation in our churches. . . . Under such circumstances it becomes a difficult matter to find two dollars for the subscription."[16] Beginning with 1934 the paper was called *The Covenant Weekly* and was for a time bilingual. The difficulties of the Depression were suffered also by *The Lutheran Companion.*

3. *Influence of the Newspapers on Americanization*

The foreign language press in America has been looked upon with mixed feelings. Those who insisted that immigrants should adjust rapidly and immediately break with the past had difficulty in appreciating the hold vhich the newspapers had on the immigrants. The newspapers themselves denied every charge that they delayed Americanization. Even though research – as pointed out in our introduction – is unanimously agreed that the foreign language press facilitated Americanization while it also encouraged nationalism among the immigrants, there exists no thorough-going study aimed at more closely delineating the extent to which the papers were responsible for influencing the immigrants in either direction. Nor is there any more comprehensive investigation as to who were the readers of the foreign language press. Were they mainly the first generation, or did they include also the second and third generations? Albert F. Schersten has attempted to unravel the connection between the Swedish language papers and the assimilation of the Swedes by using Rock Island and Moline, Illinois, as a starting-point. The result was his book, *The Relation of the Swedish-American Newspaper to the Assimilation of the Swedish Immigrants.*

Albert Schersten believes he has found that those who read a Swedish language paper were less assimilated than the Swedes who did not. His theory is that those who read and subscribed to a Swedish language paper in the United States were those who felt a particularly strong affinity with Sweden.

Characteristic of those who subscribed to a Swedish-American

[15] E. Gustav Johnson, *op. cit.,* p. 213.

[16] *The Covenant Companion,* January 14, 1933.

paper was, partly, that they did not master English and, partly, that they did not wish to lose contact with Sweden or with their countrymen in the new homeland. Of the Swedish Americans who did not read a Swedish language paper, 41.6 percent used English as conversational speech in the home.[17] "These differences as to the use of English and Swedish show that those who do not read a Swedish-American newspaper much more closely approximate assimilation than do those who read such a paper."[18] Those who had a Swedish language paper had, as a rule, been in the United States a shorter time.

As indicated in Table 28, there is a connection between the choice of worship language and the choice of papers. Of the "readers" 76.7 percent preferred Swedish as the worship language against 40 percent of the "non-readers." Likewise, those who read Swedish language papers preferred to associate with their own nationality more than did the "non-readers." This may be explained by the fact that those who read Swedish-American papers were better informed about events in Swedish-American circles and were thus more easily absorbed by them. On the other hand, one may turn the problem around and say that they were forced to read Swedish language papers in order to keep track of the various activities among their own people. Whatever was cause and effect is, however, less interesting in this case. The important thing is the connection between "readers" and group solidarity.

Finally, it may be noted that "readers" on their arrival in America were on the average older than "non-readers." They had also on the average been in the new country a shorter time.[19]

[17] Albert Schersten, *op. cit.*, p. 66 Schersten's conclusions were based upon an investigation in Moline and Rock Island (Ill.) where, according to the census of 1930, there were 3,545 Swedish immigrants. Schersten gathered data from 415 persons, 11.7 percent of the total Swedish-born population. They were divided between "readers" and "non-readers" of Swedish language papers: 234 "readers" and 181 "non-readers." Schersten's problem was to determine whether or not there was, in respect to assimilation, any difference between a group of Swedish-born immigrants in a given community who read a Swedish-American newspaper and a group of Swedish-born in the same community who do not read one. The immigrants from whom data were collected were selected at random and were assumed to be representative of the various classes of Swedish immigrants in this community.

[18] Schersten, *op. cit.*, p. 67.

[19] Schersten, *op. cit.*, p. 98.

Table 28. Percentage of Readers and of Non-readers Attending Churches Using Swedish or English.

	Readers	Non-readers
English used most	67.2	73.0
Swedish used most	8.8	3.0
English and Swedish used half and half	24.1	23.8
Preference for Swedish in church	76.7	40.1
Preference for English in church	14.8	47.7
No language- preference in church	8.2	12.8

Source: Albert F. Schersten, *The Relation of the Swedish-American Newspaper to the Assimilation of Swedish Immigrants, p. 71.*

Table 29. Nationality- Contacts and Preferences Stated in Percentages.

Nationality contacts	Readers	Non-readers
Those who are with Swedes more than with others	81.0	53.6
Those who are less with Swedes than with others	6.6	25.5
Nationality preference:		
Preference for Swedes	74.0	48.5
Preference for others	0.1	—
No preference	25.9	51.5

Source: Albert F. Schersten, *The Relation of the Swedish-American Newspaper to the Assimilation of Swedish Immigrants*, p. 82.

The conclusion of the survey presented here, is: "... it appears that readers of a Swedish-American newspaper are in general less assimilated than the non-readers." This is perhaps what one would have expected – the very fact that an immigrant subscribes to a Swedish-American paper indicates that he does not wish to lose contact with Sweden and his countrymen in the dispersion. Nor is it surprising that those who read a Swedish language paper prefer Swedish as the language of worship and as the language of social intercourse to a higher degree than "non-readers." But these investigations reveal very little about the tendency of either "readers" or "non-readers" or even their children to become Americanized. That individual immigrants read a Swedish paper does not necessarily mean that they are less willing to be Americanized than those who read only American papers. Undoubtedly, other factors decide the matter: for example, the time of first arrival, the age at the time of emigration, economic circumstances, and so forth. It appears rather natural that the need for and the interest in a paper in the native language were greater during the first years in the new country than after a residence of ten or fifteen years.

4. *Summary*

The Swedish newspapers in America had two functions: on the one hand, they kept their scattered countrymen together by informing them about recent events in Sweden and the Swedish-American community; on the other hand, they promoted the Americanization of their readers by reporting to them in their own language about conditions in America.

Between 1915 and 1932 almost 50 percent of the pre-war Swedish-American newspapers discontinued publishing, while the circulation dropped 52.5 percent. The decline was especially sharp in 1918, undoubtedly caused by the anti-alien sentiment in America during World War I. Finally, the Depression in the 1930s caused great difficulties for the Swedish language papers.

Generally speaking, the Swedish-American press has had a remarkable tenacity for holding its own over the years. Approximately a half century has passed since the immigration to America from Sweden ceased, yet a number of good Swedish language papers still continue to be published in the United States.

XI. The Religious Denominations

1. *General*

Among the oldest organizations established by the Swedish people in America are the religious denominations, of which the following may first of all be mentioned: the Augustana Synod, the Swedish Mission Covenant, the Swedish Baptists, and the Swedish Methodist Church. Ever since the earliest period of immigration the churches were centers of the cultural and social life among the Swedes – gathering points where immigrants could meet their countrymen and receive assistance. The common bond among their members was that they spoke Swedish and that they directly or indirectly had come from the same country – Sweden. As a rule they were also proud of their ancestry. "The blood our parents gave us must not be blended with that of other races."[1]

In other words, one basic presumption for the existence of Swedish-American denominations was that they at all costs should be able to guard and defend whatever was "Swedish."[2] When they failed in this, they lost their legitimate right of existence, and this resulted in their fight against Americanization and, especially, the change-over to English. "The immigrants feel that the distinctive feature of their church is the language. Once it is gone, their church becomes like all other churches of the same denomination."[3] For the Methodists and the Baptists more than for the Augustana Synod and the Mission Covenant, it was a matter of safeguarding the Swedish language. The reason why the Swedish Baptists and the Swedish Methodists organized themselves in Swedish conferences was that they did not understand

[1] *The Covenant Companion,* August, 1925.

[2] George Stephenson, *The Religious Aspects,* p. 424.

[3] Carl M. Rosenquist, "Linguistic Changes in the Acculturation of the Swedes in Texas," *Sociology and Social Research* (January, 1932), p. 223.

English.[4] The more the Swedish language was shoved aside by English, the more watered down both of these denominations became.[5] "This is a matter of self-protection, for when a Swedish Baptist congregation becomes Anglicized, there is no longer any reason for its existence."[6] The Augustana Synod and the Covenant of course had Swedish connections beyond the linguistic bond.

The following pages provide an account of the general development within some of the largest Swedish-American churches and their relationship to the respective Swedish mother churches. One chapter will illustrate the efforts of the Augustana Synod to preserve its national identity, and another chapter will describe the transition from Swedish to English within the Augustana Synod, the Swedish Mission Covenant, the Swedish Baptist and the Swedish Methodist churches. Finally, the transition to English within the Augustana Synod will be compared with the transition within the German and Norwegian churches in America.

2. *Membership and General Development*

The development of all the Swedish-American denominations may conveniently be compared with the general development in the United States. High prosperity and a low rate of unemployment during the 1920s increased the posibilities of members to contribute extra funds to their churches. However, the Depression changed the situation. Church activities had to be curtailed. Appeals appeared regularly in every church newspaper asking for financial assistance so that institutions and mission projects would not be forced to discontinue.

Even though there were reasons for anxiety during the 1920s due to the fact that immigration from Sweden was ebbing out, and was

4 *Svenska metodismens allmänna konvent, 1914,* p. 28; K.H. Elmström, "Vår plikt att bevara svenskheten i vår kyrkliga verksamhet," pp. 39 and 43; George Stephenson has also pointed out (in *The Religious Aspects)* that as soon as the mother tongue was lost, the various denominations lost their identity. "When so-called "reformed" congregations became English, they were absorbed into the American synods and conferences, and it was thus a matter of self-preservation for them to retain the Swedish language" (p. 424).

5 *Svenska metodismens allmänna konvent, 1914,* p. 28.

6 Stephenson, *op. cit.,* p. 255.

threatening to successively weaken the foundations of Swedish immigrant churches, progress was nevertheless favorable. Membership figures increased in spite of the record low immigration from Sweden.[7] The Augustana Synod was the largest of the Swedish-American institutions. According to the *Census Reports of Religious Bodies of 1926,* there were 21 Lutheran synods in the United States. Augustana Synod was the fourth largest in terms of membership – only the United Lutheran Church of America, the Evangelical Lutheran Synod of Missouri, Ohio and other states, and the Norwegian Lutheran Church of America were larger. More than half of the Augustana Synod's members lived west of the Mississippi River. In all, it consisted of twelve conferences.[8] During the period 1906 and 1936 the membership in the Augustana Synod increased from 179,204 to 327,472.[9] In 1916 the Synod had 204,417 members; in 1926, 311,425 members. It is estimated that the total membership of all the Swedish-American denominations was between 350,000 and 400,000, or approximately 25 percent of the entire first and second generations of Swedes.[10]

7 The first Augustana Synod was organized in 1860, and it then included the Norwegian Lutheran churches. In 1870 the Norwegian element withdrew and organized its own synod. The Augustana Synod was re-organized and became that year (1870) an exclusively Swedish-American Lutheran church. In certain areas, congregations formed so-called conferences, which were the equivalent of the Swedish dioceses. The head of the synod was the President, who ordained the ministers of the synod and had approximately the same functions as those of a Swedish bishop. The President was elected for a four year term. Every congregation was represented in its conference by its pastor and an elected representative and in the synod by representatives, half of which was pastors and half of which was laymen, elected by the conference. In 1930 it had more than a thousand churches and approximately 1,200 congregations, seven colleges or schools of higher learning, and a large number of other institutions throughout the country such as homes for the aged and orphanages. In 1962 the Augustana Synod was absorbed into the Lutheran Church in America, and thus lost its identity.

8 Walter A. Lunden, "Some Statistical Facts of the Augustana Synod," in *The Lutheran Companion* (September 13, 1930), p. 1167.

9 *Census of Religious Bodies: Lutheran,* 1936, p. 27. Figures cited here do not correspond entirely with figures in the Augustana Synod yearbooks. However, there are no significant discrepancies.

10 The statement that only 25 percent of the Swedish Americans belonged to a religious denomination does not agree with the general opinion. The common conception among the Swedish Americans today is that there were extremely

It may be especially worth noting that membership in the Augustana Synod nearly doubled in the period 1906–1936 – that is, during a time when immigration from Sweden was strongly diminishing. (The number of Swedish-born in the United States was highest in 1910, after which it successively sank). The church's growth must have meant that either the Synod exerted a stronger power of attraction to the Swedish immigrants after 1910, than it did previously or the second generation of immigrants to an even greater extent than before sought affiliation with the church of their fathers. Regardless of whether members came from the first or second generation, the increased membership indicates that national affinity remained strong far into the 1930s. A contributing factor to the favorable rise in membership was the gradual change-over to English. This means that the second and third generations were not forced away because of their limited knowledge of the Swedish language. The transfer to English, on the other hand, did not influence Swedish speaking members to leave the Synod, since they had no other place to go. At the very most, they transferred to another congregation. In the larger cities there was usually more than one Augustana church, and it often happened that one of the congregations was more concerned for preserving the Swedish language than was the other.

Further statistics show that the Synod's Sunday school activities enrolled a consistently rising number of pupils, with the exception of the war years, 1916–1919, when the number decreased from 81,726 to 79,691 pupils. In the so-called "weekday schools" the number

few who did not belong to some religious organization. The Association of English Churches maintained, however, that by no means were all Swedes religiously active. In its report of 1922 the Association states: "Her [Augustana's] 300,000 members represent, however, only a small part of those whom it was her original purpose to serve, and if we add to this figure all those who belong to other churches we have accounted for only a small percentage of our Swedish people" (p. 34); *The Lutheran Companion,* in an article July 14, 1917, pointed out that one of every three Norwegians in America belonged to the Norwegian Lutheran Church, while only one of every eight Swedes belonged to the Augustana Synod. The paper believed this was largely due to the fact that the Norwegian church had a better understanding of the younger generation's need for English worship services than had the Augustana Synod.

Table 30. Statistical survey of the membership in the Augustana Synod, 1913—1932

Year	Augustana Synod members					Illinois Conference members
	Adults	Children	Totals	Sunday schools	Weekday schools	Totals
1915	—	—	187 834	81 144	18 004	58 480
1916	191 390	87 248	278 333	81 726	17 263	58 852
1917	193 545	88 662	282 207	81 447	15 383	58 596
1918	197 618	86 837	283 596	80 681	11 443	58 136
1919	200 253	87 223	287 476	79 691	9 025	58 925
1920	204 075	87 491	291 566	81 309	8 895	59 999
1921	206 477	87 300	293 777	85 872	8 622	60 271
1922	210 218	83 942	294 150	91 660	9 872	59 521
1923	213 658	83 738	297 396	95 918	10 927	61 110
1924	217 616	84 092	301 708	99 145	11 482	62 252
1925	222 183	83 860	306 043	103 584	12 331	63 380
1926	225 340	83 603	308 943	106 554	12 762	64 553
1927	226 932	83 715	310 647	109 779	12 624	65 437
1928	230 700	92 710	323 410	99 004	14 358	66 771
1929	234 434	83 160	317 594	110 745	14 993	68 224
1930	238 385	81 714	320 099	113 775	14 710	69 292
1931	239 611	85 262	324 873	117 013	15 608	71 622
1932	241 467	85 238	326 705	115 441	17 285	71 882

Source: *Minutes of the Augustana Synod, 1915-1932.* (Statistical supplements).

of pupils increased consistently up to 1903.[11] Thereafter it slowly declined up to 1915, and in the years immediately following the war the decrease was quite substantial. The number of pupils was reduced in 1915–1921 from 18,004 to 8,622. After 1922 it increased again, and in 1933 the number of pupils had risen to 19,912.

In 1926, 60 percent of the membership of the Synod lived in cities and 40 percent in rural areas.[12] The same year, 41.2 percent of the churches were located in cities and 58.8 percent in rural areas. This indicates that the city congregations had on the average 388 members

[11] Weekday schools were usually held a few weeks during the summer. (They were also called "summer schools.") The instruction centered mainly on Christianity and the Swedish language.

[12] Walter A. Lunden, "Some Statistical Facts about the Augustana Synod," in *The Lutheran Companion,* September 13, 1930, p. 1168.

Table 31. Development in ten "English" and ten "Swedish" congregations in Illinois, 1920—1930.

Members in "English" congregations			Members in "Swedish" congregations		
Congregations	1920	1930	Congregations	1920	1930
Immanuel, Chicago	1 418	1 091	New Windsor	417	467
Bloomington	251	402	Prophetstown	124	138
First, Kirkland	114	154	Salem, Moline	506	634
Fairfield	60	75	Knoxville	286	275
Emmanuel, Rockford	800	1 717	Salem, Peoria	403	371
Messiah, Chicago	580	440	Trinity, Waukegan	299	368
Immanuel, East Moline	82	281	Irving Park, Chicago	853	1 972
Trinity, Galesburg	970	1 175	Bethlehem, Chicago	950	1 037
Grace, Chicago	391	483	Ebenezer, Chicago	1 220	1 541
Trinity, Moline	455	1 086	Geneva, Rockford	467	609
	5 121	6 904 + 29%		5 525	7 417 + 29%

Source: *Minutes of the Illinois Conference, 1920-1930*. (Statistical supplements.)

and the rural congregations had 177.[13] In 1936, 64.1 percent of the members lived in cities, and 35.9 percent in the country; 42.5 percent of the churches were in cities, 57.5 percent in the country, which indicates that on the average city congregations had 436 members and rural congregations had 181. By way of comparison, it may be mentioned that in 1930 64.6 percent of the Swedish Americans lived in cities and 35.4 percent in country districts. This implies that the rural population and the city population were almost as regular in church attendance.

Of the Augustana ministers living in 1922 who had received their training within the Synod, 235 (31.5 percent) were born in the USA and 506 in Sweden.[14] In general, it may be said that most of those who graduated before 1914 were Swedish-born. After 1914, except for the year 1920, the majority of the graduates were born in the USA.

A comparison of a number of "English" and "Swedish" Augustana congregations in Illinois indicates no obvious differences.[15] It is completely impossible, on the basis of Table 31, to draw the conclusion that congregations which have wholly transferred to English or having been English speaking from the beginning have had a greater attraction than congregations that have strongly held on to the Swedish language. Nor does a comparison between the Association of English Churches and the Synod at large indicate any differences between "Swedish" and "English" congregations. In the ten "English" and the ten "Swedish" congregations selected (in Table 31) the membership increase was in both cases 29 percent for the ten-year period 1920–1930.

Between 1915 and 1928 the Synod's economic situation was strengthened. The favorable economic development enhanced the ability and willingness of its members to contribute more to the Church. During the same period the annual per capita contributions doubled from $11.99 to $24.41.[16]

[13] *Census of Religious Bodies, 1936 : Lutherans,* p. 26.

[14] Emeroy Johnson, "The Duty of the Augustana Synod in Regard to the Swedish Language," in *The Lutheran Companion,* February 9, 1924, p. 90.

[15] Selected for this comparison are ten Illinois congregations of the Association of English Churches and ten congregations in Illinois traditionally regarded as Swedish centers. The former were congregations that from the beginning had English as their main language or had completely transferred to English.

[16] *Minutes of the Augustana Synod, 1915—1932.* Statistical supplements.

Table 32. Membership in the Swedish Methodist Church and in the Mission Covenant Church, 1915—1932.

Year	Swedish Methodist Church	The Mission Covenant	
		Reported	Estimated
1915	20 587	19 868	29 147
1916	20 890	16 292	28 831
1917	21 105	—	—
1918	21 198	19 705	36 947
1919	20 800	25 637	34 402
1920	21 033	27 140	33 440
1921	20 522	28 919	34 827
1922	20 608	30 014	32 773
1923	20 347	30 550	34 570
1924	20 622	31 399	34 740
1925	20 856	32 011	37 097
1926	20 707	38 860	44 002
1927	20 673	41 133	44 832
1928	18 767	40 257	43 878
1929	16 877	40 852	43 243
1930	16 676	40 949	43 295
1931	16 674	41 838	43 088
1932	16 464	42 774	44 352

Sources: Lorraine R. Oblom, "Determining Factors in the Growth of the Evangelical Mission Covenant Church of America", p. 31 f. For the Swedish Methodist Church the figures have been gathered from the Annual Reports of the various conferences.

The other Swedish-American denominations – except the Swedish Methodist Church – could also register a rising membership during the period 1915–1932. The Evangelical Mission Covenant in 1932 had a total of 42,774 reported members.[17] The Swedish Methodists, on the other hand, reached their top figure in 1918 with a total of 21,198 members. In 1932 that number had decreased to 16,464.

[17] Lorraine Oblom, "Determining Factors in the Growth of the Evangelical Mission Covenant Church in the United States" *(The Covenant Quarterly*, May, 1943), p. 31; The Swedish Evangelical Mission Covenant of America dates back to 1885. Like the Augustana Synod, the Mission Covenant is administered by a president. According to the Constitution (revised in 1957) the Covenant Church is a body of "evangelical Christian churches united in faith and service, administratively organized into regional conferences." The Constitution further states that the Covenant Church has its roots in "historical Christianity as it emerged in the Protestant Reformation, in the biblical instruction of the Lutheran State

The Swedish Evangelical Mission Covenant of America dates back to 1885. Like the Augustana Synod, the Mission Covenant is administered by a president. According to the Constitution (revised in 1957) the Covenant Church is a body of "evangelical Christian churches united in faith and service, administratively organized into regional conferences." The Constitution further states that the Covenant Church has its roots in "historical Christianity as it emerged in the Protestant Reformation, in the biblical instruction of the Lutheran State Church of Sweden."

Table 33. Age distribution in the membership of the Mission Covenant and in the population as whole of the United States, 1941.

Ages	Covenant Percent	U.S. Percent	Ages	Covenant Percent	U.S. Percent
10–12	0.1	7.4	49–51	5.5	3.8
13–15	1.0	7.2	52–54	5.0	3.4
16–18	3.1	7.2	55–57	5.0	3.0
19–21	4.6	6.6	58–60	4.8	2.9
22–24	5.3	6.4	61–63	3.8	2.0
25–27	5.1	6.0	64–66	4.0	1.8
28–30	4.8	6.2	67–69	3.7	1.5
31–33	4.5	5.2	70–72	3.7	1.4
34–36	5.0	5.7	73–75	3.5	1.1
37–39	4.7	5.4	76–78	2.6	0.9
40–42	5.0	5.2	79–81	2.0	0.3
43–45	5.4	4.6	82–84	1.2	0.3
46–48	5.6	4.1	85 and up	1.0	0.4

Source: Lorraine Oblom, *op.cit.*,p.28.

Church of Sweden." The Swedish Methodist Church consisted of congregations within the Methodist Episcopal Church in America, whose members were Swedish immigrants and descendants and whose official language was Swedish. The Swedish Methodist Church was, in other words, a branch of the American Methodist Church. The Swedish conference existed, as did the other non-English speaking conferences, in order to "stimulate the Swedes to greater activity, give them greater influence and notice in the church as a whole, assure them of representation in the General Conference, and afford opportunity to discuss problems peculiar to themselves." (Sources: C.G. Wallenius and E.G. Olson, *A Short Story of Swedish Methodism in America;* George Stephenson, *The Religious Aspects,* pp. 256—263; and *Central Northwest Conference: Official Journal and Yearbook, 1942.*

Despite the constantly rising membership, the development in the Swedish Mission Covenant was not satisfactory. An investigation in 1941 regarding the age distribution of the Covenant members shows that the average age was high. A comparison with corresponding age groups in the American population indicates an uneven distribution. In relation to the whole population, the Covenant had a high percentage of members over 42 years of age.

The high average age has been ascribed to an unwillingness to adopt English in the churches. It is clear that if the transition to English had been made earlier, the Covenant would have retained the younger members who instead went over to other denominations. In New England particularly the linguistic transition was late. Even in the 1930s the numbers of English and Swedish worship services were about equally divided in the Swedish Congregational churches of New England.[18] "The retention of the Swedish language must be responsible to a good degree for this shortage of younger members."[19]

During the Depression favorable times came to an end for the Swedish denominations in the U.S. The effects of the Depression were felt early both economically and psychologically. The self-confidence of the 1920s, which had inspired new and venturesome goals both within and without the country's borders, was followed by uncertainty and a feeling of insecurity. During the Depression years of 1929–1932 the economy of the Augustana Synod was weakened alarmingly, as the income was reduced year after year. The local congregations, no longer able to fulfill their obligations, often indicated that prevailing unemployment among their members was the reason for deficiencies. An editorial in *The Lutheran Companion* even questioned the future existence of the Augustana Synod.[20]

From 1931 on the Depression was particularly severe, and congregations and conferences found it more and more difficult to collect funds to cover their respective obligations. The Augustana Synod and its institutions suffered great losses. The annual reports of the Synod and the conferences as well as the church papers expressed their anxiety. In 1931 it was pointed out in editorial columns of *Augustana* that the financial situation obviously concerned the Church, since

18 Lorraine Oblom, *op. cit.*, p. 28.

19 *Ibid.*, p. 29.

20 *The Lutheran Companion*, 1932, p. 612.

the existing unemployment made it impossible for church members to make sacrifices for denominational work.[1] In the annual report for 1931 the president of the Synod stressed the seriousness of the situation and stated that all of the Synod's institutions had been forced to reduce their expenditures.[2] The finance committee urged frugality and reported that only 59 percent of the 1931 budget had been collected.[3]

In 1932 the Synod's financial situation was further deteriorated, and the conferences could not meet more than 34 percent of the Synod's budget.[4] An editorial in *Augustana* said it was no longer a secret that all branches of activity, "as a result of the existing economic depression in our country, have come into inevitable financial difficulties."[5] In the beginning of 1932, the finance secretary of the Synod issued a call for help and asked: "Will it become necessary to discontinue work begun, close institutions and in many ways impair the efficiency of the work of the church"?[6] Similar distress appeals were voiced at the synodical meeting.[7] The same synodical meeting appointed a special committee, The Augustana Synod Control Committee, for the purpose of investigating the Synod's financial situation and of proposing emergency measures.

In order to reduce expenditures, the Synod lowered the salaries of the denomination's employees. In many of the Synod's congregations the pastors voluntarily reduced their salaries, which other congregations were forced to do.[8] Of the various institutions in the Synod, it seems that hospitals were particularly hard hit. While their income declined they faced increasing demands for the care of poor patients who no longer could pay for services. It became even more difficult for hospitals to collect fees from patients. "Hospitalization insurance was not in general use, and the need for surgery was considered a

[1] *Augustana,* January 22, 1931, p. 56.

[2] *Minutes of the Augustana Synod,* 1932, p. 14.

[3] *Ibid.,* p. 36.

[4] *Ibid., 1933,* p. 33.

[5] *Augustana,* March 17, 1932, p. 168.

[6] *The Lutheran Companion,* 1932, p. 471.

[7] *Minutes of the Augustana Synod, 1933,* p. 45.

[8] *Minutes of the Augustana Synod, 1932,* p. 17.

major calamity. Everything not life-and-death was postponed."[9] Augustana Hospital, which belonged to the Illinois Conference (Conference corresponds to diocese in Sweden), experienced serious effects of the depressed state of affairs.[10] During the year 1930, Augustana Hospital provided a large number of patients with free care or care at greatly reduced prices, to a value of $54,114. According to *Augustana* no branch of the Church's activities sustained greater hardships because of the financial Depression than the work of caring for the sick. "We cannot say that the depression caused fewer cases of illness, but those who were in need of hospital care were not able to avail themselves of it for financial reasons."[11]

Educational work was likewise affected by the Depression. The income of Augustana College and Theological Seminary was greatly reduced and the salaries of teachers and staff members had to be cut. For the academic year 1932–33 the faculty decided that salaries should be lowered five percent for the fall term and 10 percent for the spring term.[12] The other educational institutions were forced to adopt similar measures.[13] These depression cuts were almost standard for American colleges.

During the Depression the Synod's publishing house, the Augustana Book Concern, suffered an operational loss for the first time.[14] In 1931 expenditures exceeded incoming revenues by $548.[15] The loss was to a certain extent due to the loss of subscribers to the two official newspapers of the Synod, *Augustana* and *The Lutheran Companion*, and to the suspension of some local weekly church papers. In order to ease the financial burden, the Board of Directors for the publishing house decided that it would be necessary to begin reduction of salaries, which for certain employees would amount to 12.5 percent. Besides lowering wages, it was also necessary to lay off some of the employees and to cut the number of working hours for others.

The annual reports of separate congregations and conferences

9 Karl A. Olsson, *By One Spirit*, p. 401 f.

10 *Augustana*, April 30, 1931, p. 280.

11 *Ibid.*, May 4, 1932, p. 280.

12 *Minutes of the Augustana Synod, 1932*, p. 58.

13 *Ibid.*, p. 14.

14 *Ibid.*, p. 21.

15 *Ibid.*, p. 150.

reveal that the churches generally had difficulty in meeting financial obligations and that pastors often had a hard time to gather in the necessary funds. The Illinois Conference seems to have faced particular difficulty. In 1931 its president reported that the hardships had been the worst ever experienced by the Conference.[16] In 1932 the situation was further aggravated. "Individual congregations could not meet interest and capital obligations and were confronted with foreclosures."[17]

In an article in December, 1930, *Augustana* emphasized that the existing unemployment caused much difficulty for the churches, since thousands of the Synod's members were out of work and droves of others were employed on a short-time basis – two or three days a week.[18] In September, 1931, the same paper wrote that the lengthy unemployment had resulted in much poverty in the congregations and that "the situation was perhaps more serious than anyone could have surmised."[19]

The other Swedish-American denominations suffered as much distress as did the Augustana Synod, and, of course, even non-Swedish churches faced similar economic problems. The reports of the Covenant, the Methodists, and the Baptists speak for the material progress of the 1920s, and also the dire economic difficulties of the Depression years.

3. *Relationship to the Church of Sweden*

The relationship of the Augustana Synod to the State Church of Sweden was a sensitive subject. The Synod has often been characterized as a daughter-church but a completely independent one. While there were those who contended that the affinity which blood connections and inherited foundations of faith had established between the mother-church and her daughter-church in America ought to be deepened and further confirmed, there were, on the other hand, those who maintained that the Augustana Synod was a thoroughly American institu-

[16] *Minutes of the Illinois Conference, 1932,* pp. 20—21.

[17] *Minutes of the Illinois Conference, 1932,* pp. 14.

[18] *Augustana,* December 11, 1930, p. 808.

[19] *Ibid.,* September 10, 1931, p. 584.

tion.[1] An important reason why it was so sensitive a matter to talk about the Synod's relations to the State Church of Sweden was that the Synod was simultaneously the representative of the State Church of Sweden among the Swedish Americans and a direct protest against the restraints and shackles of the state church.

George Stephenson is among those who have maintained that it is a historical misconception to consider the Augustana Synod a daughter-church of the Swedish State Church.[2] He categorically denies that the Synod had been an effective promoter of Swedish culture. He admits, at the most, that it has meant much for the Swedish language but that the real motive was in the first place an effort to keep and recruit members and not a love for the Swedish language. "The appeal to the Swedish spirit, therefore, always had an empty sound; and when pastors awakened to the fact that the Swedish language was turning members away, it died to a faint echo."[3]

For the Americanization process it was of no consequence whether or not the Augustana Synod was formally a daughter-church of the State Church of Sweden. The interesting thing is that it was in many

[1] The relationship of the Synod to the Church of Sweden had been a sensitive question ever since the very beginning of the Synod. L.P. Esbjörn relates, for example, in 1858, that the detest of the State Church was so great that he dared not show the bound church record book he had taken along from Sweden (Conrad Bergendoff, "The Americanization of the Augustana Synod" in *The Lutheran Companion*, August 16, 1924, p. 522.)

[2] George Stephenson, "The Future of the Augustana Synod" in *Augustana Quarterly*, April, 1933, p. 129. Even in other connections Stephenson has maintained that the Augustana Synod was not a daughter-church of the Swedish State Church. In an article in *The Lutheran Companion* in 1930 he wrote: "With all due respect for the church of Sweden, nothing could be more un historical than to call the Augustana Synod the 'daughter' of the Swedish State Church.

In undiplomatic — and more accurate — language the Augustana Synod is a wayward 'daughter' who inherited the doctrine and language of the 'mother'. In polity, practice, spirit and, in those latter days, language there is little resemblance between 'mother' and daughter'." *(The Lutheran Companion,* May 10, 1930, p. 588.)

[3] George Stephenson, *The Religious Aspects,* p. 423. Stephenson writes: "It (the Synod) has been an important force in keeping the Swedish language alive; yet the underlying motive has been not so much a love for things Swedish as a desire to retain and recruit members."

details a direct copy of the Church of Sweden – but with the important difference that the Augustana Synod was not a state church. Furthermore, it had no bishops – a rather essential difference compared with the Swedish State Church. That the relationship to the Church of Sweden was a sensitive matter has also a psychological explanation. The Swedish Americans were by and large emphatic in claiming that they were not indebted to Sweden for anything and that the Augustana Synod was completely their own accomplishment. The Synod was established without any help from Sweden whatsoever, either economic or moral.[4]

> Still the Augustana Synod is historically and technically, if not actually, an American institution. It was born and bred on American soil. The early leaders of the Synod have time and again called our attention to this and also to the fact that from the very beginning it has developed independent of any aid, morally or financially, from the Church of Sweden. The Church of Sweden is not the mother church of the Augustana Synod. ... Why some of our leaders of today should insist on distorting the facts and make us a Swedish Church historically and otherwise is a deep mystery. ... A foreign stamp must hinder our progress.

The Lutheran Companion maintained that, even if the majority of its members were of Swedish extraction and the Swedish language was largely prevalent, it was not a Swedish church but an American Church.[5] The paper described the Synod as "an independent organization sprung into existence on American soil and as genuinely American in its spirit and purposes as any other church body in America. ... It would be more correct to call the Augustana Synod a sister church of the Church of Sweden."[6]

Even though there has never been any official and constitutional connection between the Augustana Synod and the Swedish State Church one cannot get away from the fact that they have been very close to each other. The Synod has always been intent upon serving the

[4] C.M. Olander, "What does the present situation demand of our Synod with regard to the language to be used in the upbuilding of God's Kingdom?" in *Augustana Quarterly,* January, 1930, pp. 1—2.

[5] *The Lutheran Companion,* May 11, 1918, p. 229.

[6] *The Lutheran Companion,* May 10, 1924, p. 289.

Swedes in religious, intellectual and moral matters.[7] Those who have wished to emphasize the close relationship of the Synod and the Swedish State Church have compared the situation with that of a mother and her daughter – the mother who stays at home while her daughter takes off for a strange country and matures there under different circumstances than those of the old country.[8] The Synod was organized by ministers trained within the Swedish State Church. From the beginning it had the same confession of faith and ritual of worship as the Swedish 'mother.'[9] The Synod almost exclusively used the Swedish prayer-book and hymnal far into the 1920s.[10] The kinship has also been strengthened by frequent pulpit exchanges and by visits to America by Swedish clergymen.[11] During the American visit of Archbishop Nathan Söderblom in 1923 the relationship was constantly emphasized.[12]

However, not much was needed to make the relationship tense. Misgivings and suspicions of the Swedish State Church were still extant. When, in 1930, Archbishop Söderblom presented a bishop's cross (a symbol of the episcopal office) to the Synod as a gift from the bishops of the Church of Sweden, suspicion flared forth. The rationality of accepting the cross was questioned. The symbol was discussed in the Synod's papers.[13] "The younger and more Americanized element was quick to resent any implication that the Synod was a Swedish body." Those who were opposed to accepting the cross gave as a reason that the Synod had no bishop and that their church was completely independent of the Swedish State Church. They also feared

7 P. Arthur Johnson, "National and International Relationships of the Augustana Synod." *After Seventy-Five Years, 1860—1935. A Jubilee Publication* (Rock Island, 1935) p. 89; G.A. Brandelle, "The Significance of the Augustana Synod to the Swedish Lutherans in America," *The Augustana Synod. A Brief Review of Its History, 1860—1910* (Rock Island, 1910) p. 238.

8 S.G. Youngert, "Augustana synoden och moderkyrkan i Sverige," *Minnesskrift med anledning av Augustana-Synodens femtioåriga tillvaro, 1860—1910*, (Rock Island, 1910), p. 411 f.

9 V. Berger, *Svensk-amerikanska meditationer,* p. 46.

10 Everett Arden, *Augustana Heritage,* p. 251.

11 George Stephenson, *The Religious Aspects,* p. 237 ff.

12 Emil Lund, *Minnesota-konferensens och dess församlingars historia,* p. 235.

13 George Stephenson, *op. cit.,* p. 240 ff.

that increased friendship with Sweden would render more difficult the collaboration with other Lutheran denominations in America.

The cross was presented in early February, 1930. At the annual meeting of the Synod held in June that year, the matter of the Swedish gift occasioned a long debate – "the most heated debate of all the issues before the convention."[14] The debate centered around the question of whether or not the Synod should accept the cross. When the meeting finally decided to accept the cross, it did so with the following reservation: "... we do not hereby adopt any episcopal insignia for the incumbent of the president's office."

Among the Swedish-American denominations the Mission Covenant occupied a unique situation, since, in contrast to the Augustana Synod, the Methodists and the Baptists, it could not merge with any other denomination without abrogating its basic principles. As a result, the Mission Covenant – or as it is now called the Evangelical Covenant Church of America – mainly has continued as a Swedish-American church even after Swedish has been replaced by the English language. In its revised Constitution in 1957 it states that the Covenant Church "has its roots in historical Christianity as it emerged ... in the biblical instruction of the Lutheran State Church of Sweden. ...") Even in 1931 the president of the Covenant urged the congregations that changed over to English to watch out for dangers "which they previously had not been threatened with."[15] The 'danger' he alluded to was that of being equipped with American preachers who were quite unfamiliar with the history of the Covenant and with the basic reasons for its existence alongside of, for instance, the Augustana Synod. To avoid this 'danger,' the congregations were advised to

[14] *The Lutheran Companion,* June 21, 1930, p. 783. Shortly before the close of the annual meeting, G.A. Brandelle re-introduced the question about the cross for additional discussion. His purpose was that he wanted to make a last attempt to soften the wording of the letter of acknowledgement. He did not succeed because the opposition was too strong. At the annual meeting of the Chicago District of the Association of English Churches, May 27, 1930, the pastor of the Maywood church, F.A. Johnson spoke on the topic: "The Bishop's Cross — Its Implications." Mr. Johnson said that an acceptance of the cross would mean that the Synod became a part of the Swedish State Church. "The Augustana Synod from its origin has not wanted and does not now want an episcopal system. Much less does it wish to become a diocese of a foreign state church" *(The Lutheran Companion,* June 7, 1930, p. 734.)

[15] *The Covenant Yearbook 1930—31,* p. 6.

include in their constitutions "a stipulation that ministers who would serve the congregation must belong to the Swedish Evangelical Mission Covenant Church of America."

4. *Relationship to American Denominations*

Even in its collaboration with Lutheran churches in the United States, the Augustana Synod strictly maintained its own national identity. In spite of continuous and energetic attempts to incorporate it in one of the Lutheran associations, it was not until 1962 that its fate was definitely sealed.[16] During the hundred years of its activity the Synod was a member of the General Council for 40 years – from 1870 to 1918. George Stephenson has called the Synod's membership in the General Council "an experiment in unionism."[17] Its joining of the Council has also been described as one of the Synod's most important decisions.[18] The General Council, organized in 1867, consisted at first of eleven synods and was a consultative association for its member synods – "the new organization functioned largely in an advisory capacity, confining its deliberations mainly to general prin-

16 Everett Arden, *Augustana Heritage*, p. 411.

17 George Stephenson, *op. cit.*, p. 314. The General Council was organized at a meeting in Fort Wayne, Indiana, in November, 1867. According to T.N. Hasselquist, the General Council — a body strongly German in character was to be a center of union for all Lutheran synods in America that adhered to "the revered and biblical confession of our church and wish to be the bond among them for mutual encouragement and strengthening in the truth for unity of cooperation in our common work." Erland Carlsson reported to the annual meeting of the synod in 1870: "The General Council has not only completely and unreservedly taken its stand on the confession of the Lutheran church, but has also drawn forth a new vitality, greater sacrificial giving, more eagerness to work for educational institutions and for establishing new churches, in the sending out of missionaries among the heathen, etc. — in one word: for home and foreign missions." (M.C. Ranseen, "Augustana-synoden och the General Council," *Minnesskrift med anledning av Augustana-Synodens femtioåriga tillvaro, 1860—1910* [Rock Island, 1910] p. 433 ff.). Concerning the decision of the Augustana Synod to join the General Council, Everett Arden wrote: "The decision was a deliberate and carefully considered move to identify the Synod with a particular type of Lutheranism in America" *(Augustana Heritage,* p. 143.)

18 Everett Arden, *op. cit.*, p. 143.

ciples, whereas the constituent synods retained the powers that were theirs in the old general body."[19] Within the General Council the Augustana Synod occupied a special situation in that it represented a nationality spread out geographically over the entire country. Otherwise the General Council was composed of district synods. One of the basic principles of the Council was that it could not organize a missionary activity of its own within the fields of member synods but only through co-operation with the missionary boards of the synods or after obtaining the separate synod's acquiesence.[20]

The co-operation of the Augustana Synod with the General Council reflected the existing fear that the Synod would be unduly influenced by or drawn into another denomination. The debate regarding the Synod's attitude to and situation within the General Council shows that the Synod as late as 1918 was quite determined to remain a Swedish immigrant church. The Synod would not renounce its stamp of national identiy, since it considered it had a function to perform among Swedish Americans.

As long as the Augustana Synod was an altogether Swedish speaking association, co-operation with the General Council went smoothly. Not until English speaking groups within the Synod became a strong factor did conflicts with the General Council arise. When English speaking congregations were organized, the question arose whether they should be a part of the Synod or of the General Council.[1] Suspicions that the General Council intended to by-pass the Synod caused irritation among the Synod's members. In the Minnesota Conference complaints were heard that the General Council started congregations which were outside of the influence of the Conference. In 1891, when some "English" ministers and their congregations, without the sanction of the Conference, withdrew from the Minnesota Conference and organized a new synod – the Synod of the North West – the co-operation with the General Council was seriously shaken at its foundations.[2] However, the co-operation continued without any serious intermezzo up to 1915, when the Synod at its annual meeting

[19] George Stephenson, *op. cit.*, p. 314.

[20] Carl J. Bengston, "The Association of English Churches" in *Korsbaneret*, 1923, p. 154 ff.

[1] George Stephenson, *op. cit.*, p. 319.

[2] Everett Arden, *op. cit.*, p. 156; Emil Lund, *op. cit.*, p. 199 ff.

decided to demand a change in the by-laws of the General Council so that the Augustana Synod would be recognized as a "General Body" and no longer be treated as only a district synod. The decision included, among other things the following: "That the Augustana Synod respectfully requests the General Council to revise the constitution of said body, so that the Augustana Synod no longer be placed in the relation of a district synod, but be recognized as a general body in order that the General Council may become both in principle and practic a deliberative and advisory body only."[3] At the General Council's annual meeting in 1915 a special committee was appointed to discuss the request of the Augustana Synod. No conclusion was reached and at its subsequent annual meeting in 1916, the General Council had to take a stand on a new and more important question in terms of structural solidarity, namely that of organizing a United Lutheran church in America. Leading to a definite break between the Augustana Synod and the General Council was a proposal, in 1917, of representatives of the General Council, the General Synod, and the United Synod to form the United Lutheran Church.[4] No merger could be considered until the member synods and their respective head synods had made up their minds on the proposal of a merger. Forty-four of the forty-five district synods had voted in favor of the proposal. The only synod that did not was Augustana. By an overwhelming majority it decided to remain without. The foremost reason was that it did not consider that the time was ripe for it to do so and that it still had a task to perform among the Swedish immigrants. The so-called declaration of independence of the Augustana Synod was proclaimed June 8, 1918. This action settled an issue that for a long time had been the subject of discussion in the publications of the Church, in the conventions of the conferences, at district meetings, and among the members of the congregations. The decision may be said to indicate that "there still was a general consensus that

[3] *Minutes of the Augustana Synod,* 1915, p. 161; Dorris A. Flesner, "The Formation of the United Lutheran Church in America," *Concordia Historical Institute Quarterly* (October, 1967), p. 153.

[4] S.G. Öhman, *Augustana-Synodens självständighetsförklaring,* p. 63 f; P. Arthur Johnson, "National and International Relationship of the Augustana Synod," p. 84 f.

the Synod had a mission to perform among the Swedish immigrants and their descendants."[5]

5. *"Declaration of Independence"*

Although the co-operation between the Augustana Synod and the General Council functioned well on the whole, there were many divided opinions regarding the appropriateness of belonging to an association of almost entirely German interests. In a book published the same year as the Synod withdrew from the General Council, S.G. Öhman explained why he thought the Synod ought to leave the General Council.[6] The pervading attitude of the author was his hostility toward the Germans. He said he bore no personal ill will whatsoever toward his fellow German-American Lutherans but only an antipathy toward the German propaganda which was unscrupulously carried on even in churchly matters. The book, however, gave the impression that the Germanophobia reached farther than he himself had intended. It reflects especially the rivalry between the Augustana Synod and the

[5] Karl E. Mattson, "The Theology of the Augustana Lutheran Church," *Centennial Essays. Augustana Lutheran Church, 1860—1960* (Rock Island, 1960), p. 44.

[6] S.G. Öhman, *Augustana-Synodens självständighetsförklaring,* p. 6 ff. It is difficult to ascertain whether the author's hostility toward the Germans was as marked before World War I as after. Everett Arden wrote *(Augustana Heritage,* p. 255, note) the following about Öhman: "The outstanding example of Swedish antipathy to merger, and the document which best summarizes the synodical determination to maintain synodical independence on nationalistic grounds is S.G. Öhman." *The Lutheran Companion* said in an editorial that Öhman ought to have been more generous in his judgment of persons who thought that the Synod's future lay in an intimate co-operation with the General Council. The paper maintained it was altogether too early now (1919) to decide whether or not that cooperation was the correct way. However, the paper thought the Synod had a future if it were called "Evangelical Lutheran Church of America" and not, as Öhman wished, "the Swedish Lutheran Church of America." It had no future as a Swedish church. It was further pointed out that the Synod, apart from its language, was from its very beginning an American institution. "The language has been accidental." The reason why Swedish was used as the worship language was that the majority of the Synod's members did not know English *(The Lutheran Companion,* January 4, 1919, pp. 1 ff.)

Missouri Synod – the German counterpart of the Augustana Synod. Öhman declared that "relatives are the worst." He did not want the Augustana Synod to unite with the United Lutheran Church, for "*Deutschland, Deutschland über alles* is too deep within the Germans even in America."[7] In the First World War, he said, the Germans had shown "the same ruthlessness and scandalous atrocities toward friend and foe alike." The Norwegians were complimented for never having joined the General Council.[8]

The attempt of the General Council to persuade the Augustana Synod to join the United Lutheran Church aroused an enormous storm of protest.[9] The Synod members were deeply disturbed by the inconceivable prospect that a Swedish synod, the only church without any German connections, should be swallowed up and disappear in a German-dominated federation.[10] The decision to remain outside the United Lutheran Church was preceded by a long and intensive debate, in papers such as *Augustana* and *The Lutheran Companion*. Both papers received a constant stream of letters from members of the Synod. In general, it can be said that both papers were hesitant. Above all, they doubted that the time juncture was the right one. *The Lutheran Companion* was in principle favorable to "the merger" but thought that an absolute premise ought to be that all potential member-synods accept membership on an equal basis – none should be able to demand any distinction.

> We believe that if the time is ripe for a larger organic union of all Lutherans in America, they should get together at once for their mutual good. But we cannot see that the time is ripe for such a union. . . . But we have become more and more convinced in later years, after giving the question more serious consideration, that the Augustana Synod is not yet ready to merge itself and its various interests into such a general body as the proposed United Lutheran Church in America. . . . It has had and still has its special mission and work to perform, that of gathering the immigrants from Sweden and their descendants into the Church, and also of preserving and developing that type of Lutheran

7 Öhman, *op. cit.*, pp. 13 and 85.

8 *Ibid.*, p. 54. "The Norwegians have not always understood us Swedes, but they have understood themselves and have had courage enough to adjust themselves accordingly, and that has been their strength."

9 *Ibid.*, p. 69.

10 *Ibid.*, p. 83.

> piety which has been characteristic of the Church of Sweden. When this work is done and our Synod has become American in its language as well as in all other respects, then and not until then should, in our opinion, the Synod enter into any larger organic union with the English-speaking synods. ... We repeat it again, if we are to join as a Synod in this union we should do so on the same basis as the other synods, and not expect to come in under a special dispensation.[11]

It was practical and not doctrinal obstacles that made "merger" difficult. *The Lutheran Companion* said only two alternatives remained, namely that of the Augustana Synod's joining the United Lutheran Church on the same conditions as the other members or that of remaining independent. The paper could not conceive of any other choice. *Augustana* tried to remain neutral regarding the merger but could not conceal its hesitation. In nearly every article it declared that a merger could come about only on the condition that the development of the Synod would not be curtailed – "otherwise we will not join."[12] The arguments which *Augustana* cited against the merger contained, among others, the phrases that the Synod would be "engulfed by" and "disappear in"and "lose its individuality." These three phrases show how unwilling the paper was to be absorbed by an American entity and give up the Synod's national characteristics. The essential difference between the papers' attitudes toward a merger was that *Augustana* was apprehensive of the Synod's welfare, while *The Lutheran Companion* did not believe that a merger would benefit either party as long as the Augustana Synod had not been completely Americanized.

One of the most ardent advocates of the Synod's joining the United Lutheran Church was its vice president, G.A. Brandelle. At the annual meeting in 1918, he urged the delegates to vote for a merger. "Sincerely and fervently we wish that the Augustana Synod which was active in organizing the General Council ... may be just as active in organizing the United Lutheran Church, which organization, if it is

[11] *The Lutheran Companion,* July 7, 1917, p. 321 f; January 12, 1918, p. 13; December 14, 1918, p. 635. Everett Arden has hardly interpreted *The Lutheran Companion's* stand correctly when he says that it was enthusiastic about the merger and urged the Synod to join the United Lutheran Church *(Augustana Heritage,* p. 254).

[12] *Augustana,* August 30, 1917, p. 576; January 24, 1918, p. 56, and February 14, 1918, p. 104.

constituted, will have the future before it."[13] Brandelle's appeal did not win favorable attention. An almost unanimous assembly voted against merger with the United Lutheran Church.[14]

After the declaration of independence, in 1918, the Augustana Synod continued its work as a wholly independent organization. It initiated no direct connections with other American Lutheran synods until 1930, when it formed the American Lutheran Conference together with the Norwegian Lutheran Church, the United Danish Church, the Lutheran Free Church, the Iowa Synod, and the Buffalo Synod.[15] The American Lutheran Conference signified a step on the way to an American Lutheran church. Its main purposes were to serve as an advisory organ in religious questions and to handle questions of common interests such as home missions, education and so forth.[16]

6. *The Swedish Language Submits to the Religious Message*

> At first we have great fuss to reach
> Some knowledge of this country's speech; And a lil' bit more!
> You cannot with some magic turning
> The English tongue at once be learning,
> Some cannot make a lucid sound
> Though twenty years they've been around, And a lil'bit more!
> (Ernst Skarstedt, "Svenskamerikanska – och lite till.")

The language question was the problem that overshadowed all other difficulties in the Swedish-American denominations during the period 1914–1932. The transition to English was for all of them a long and troublesome process. A review of the past will show that the language question is almost as old as the Augustana Synod. The Swedish immigrants were conservative in religious matters, and many of the older ones considered it almost unthinkable to participate in worship in the

13 *Minutes of the Augustana Synod,* 1918, p. 24.

14 Everett Arden, *Augustana Heritage,* p. 257.

15 P. Arthur Johnson, *op. cit.,* p. 87 ff; Everett Arden, *op. cit.,* p. 274 ff.

16 Fred M. Meuser, *op. cit.,* p. 249.

English language. The Synod, therefore, kept watch over the Swedish language and tried to persuade the second and third generations to attend the church of the fathers so as to uphold the contact with and feeling for Sweden.[1] Even though the Swedish language was for many of the members almost sacred, they yielded gradually to the increasing demand for more English. Sentiment gave way for the religious message. Each phase of the transition was determined by the development and the need: it was a matter of reaching as many as possible and taking into consideration both those who did speak English and those who spoke only Swedish. A frequent argument was that the churches had mainly to think of the future and the younger generation. However, on the other hand, it was necessary to act with caution and not hurt unnecessarily all of those who held the language of their fathers dear. Several of the Synod leaders early stressed that it would be necessary to change over to the use of English.[2]

As early as 1879, Eric Norelius called to the attention of the Synod the fact that the young people were leaving the church, which he thought was due to their rapid Americanization and their inclination

[1] V. Berger, *Svenskamerikanska meditationer,* pp. 47 and 54 ff. Berger was not alone in his ideas. S.G. Öhman maintained that if "Swedishness" had an obvious domiciliary right anywhere in America, it was within the Augustana Synod: The Synod was the principal seat of Swedish Christian life, Swedish culture and art, Swedish thought and Swedish speech (S.G. Öhman, *Augustana-Synodens självständighetsförklaring,* p. 113; "Vårt svenska arv," *Korsbaneret,* 1924, p. 117).

[2] I.O. Nothstein, "The Language Transition in the Augustana Synod,"*Augustana Quarterly* (July, 1945), p. 209; Oscar N. Olson, *The Augustana Lutheran Church in America* (Davenport, Iowa, 1956) p. 42; Nils Hasselmo, "Language Displacement and Language Influence in Swedish America," in *Swedish Pioneer Historical Quarterly,* Vol. XIV, No. 2 (April, 1963), pp. 62—84; As early as 1855, Erland Carlson introduced English in the Sunday School of his church in Chicago. In 1863, Eric Norelius wrote in a commentary to his translation of the Catechism: "The English language is progressing rapidly. Erl. Carlson is already using the English language in his confirmation classes and others ought to begin soon to do the same, especially in the towns.... Naturally, the need of English is not so urgent in Minnesota, Andover, etc. but it will come in time and we must be prepared for it." The Red River Valley Conference was engaged at a very early stage in solving the language question. In 1886 it appointed a committee consisting of one member from each district to study the matter and "report on the language question" (Edor Larson, *History of the Red River Valley Conference,* [Blair, Nebraska, 1953] p. 158).

to speak English rather than Swedish. He said he believed "that the Synod ought to take measures as far as the language was concerned to provide a remedy. If it is delayed too long we will suffer an irreparable damage."[3] A committee consisting of Olof Olsson, Eric Norelius and John Enander was appointed to study the problem.[4] In a report to the Synod in 1880 the committee said that, even though it was desirable that Swedes retain their mother tongue, one could not ignore the fact that those who have been born in this country, especially in the cities, gradually forgot the Swedish language. In rural areas the language was anticipated to live longer. The committee believed that church schools, Swedish literature, and Swedish language papers would stimulate interest in the Swedish language. To succeed in keeping the younger generation, two methods were indicated:

> One is to establish English Lutheran congregations alongside the Swedish ones where all religious instruction, sermons and everything would be in English. . . . The other is that in congregations where the young people need the English language in school as well as in church, pastors be called who are conversant in both languages, and that both languages be used in the congregation according to need. Thus one may have the sermon in one language in the forenoon and the other in the afternoon and for church functions use the language most appropriate for the occasion. In one word: one could make both languages of equal usage. In this way, it seems, our Swedish congregations need not die out but gradually become English congregations.[5]

In other words, the committee recommended a gradual transition to English. It was further recommended that as many of the candidates for the ministry as possible learn both languages.

In 1908 the Association of English Churches was organized, which was a federation of congregations within the Synod using English as their main language. When the AEC was started on November 13,

[3] *Protokoll hållet vid Skandinaviska Evangeliska Lutherska Augustana synoden, 1879,* p. 11.

[4] Oscar N. Olson, *The Lutheran Church in America,* p. 43.

[5] *Protokoll hållet vid Skandinaviska Lutherska Augustana synoden, 1880,* pp. 72 ff; Carl G. Bengston, "The Association of English Churches," *Korsbaneret,* 1923, p. 153.

1908 about fifteen churches and missions used English exclusively.[6] The initiative had been taken by the Messiah congregation in Chicago in 1907, when that church proposed at the annual meeting that the Synod establish an "English" mission board and that a committee be appointed to investigate and prepare the way for an English conference.[7] The synodical meeting approved the proposal and appointed a committee consisting of the pastors serving the English congregations and an equal number of laymen. The committee meeting in February, 1908, decided to recommend to the Synod that the English congregations be allowed to organize an Association of English Churches within the framework of the Synod and that of the officers of the organization be constituted an executive committee having the following functions: to approve the organization of English congregations in accordance with the same rules governing the organizing of other new congregations and to carry on the kind of church work that would directly promote the members' activity. The constitution adopted by AEC stipulated that the Association should consist of the ministers and congregations of the Synod whose official language was English.[8] Congregations having already made the transition to English were automatically considered members.[9]

When AEC was formed the decision was motivated by the necessity of keeping within the church the younger generation who lacked feeling for their fathers' church. Those who were most zealous for an association of English churches realized at an early stage that the Synod could not in the long run continue to be a Swedish church. They opposed those who battled against the trend of the times. Time and

[6] *Minutes of the Association of English Churches* (AEC), 1908, pp. 5, 6. The demand for an English conference was brought forth in connection with a request by some of the Synod's English speaking congregations for permission to leave the Augustana Synod and transfer to the Synod of the Northwest which was under the General Council. When St. John's Church in Minneapolis made this specific request the Augustana Synod denied it on the ground that the intention was evidently that of forming an English conference. St. John's Church was later allowed to withdraw from the Synod. Carl J. Bengston, "The Association of English Churches" in *Korsbaneret* 1923, p. 157 ff. Ira O. Nothstein, *op. cit.*, p. 332.

[7] Ira O. Nothstein, "The Language Transition," p. 332.

[8] *Minutes of AEC*, 1909, p. 25.

[9] *Ibid.*, 1926, p. 33.

again they pointed out that the main task of the Synod was not only that of serving Swedish immigrants but equally that of serving their children and grandchildren. They were ready for a long and serious agitation against pastors and members who, at all costs, defended the Swedish language and who seemed unable to appreciate the situation of non-Swedish speaking people.[10] Only reactionary elements were said to pretend that an overwhelming majority preferred religious worship in Swedish. As evidence that the Swedish language now belonged only to past history, it was cited that 86 percent of the Sunday school instruction was conducted in English in one of the Synod's conferences and that 96 percent of the members of the Luther Leagues used English.[11]

The existence of the AEC within the Synod created a great deal of tension. The leaders of the AEC had to proceed carefully and not be too provocative in the language question. Outwardly, therefore, they had to place more stress on the preparation for the transition to English than on measures aimed at forcing its adoption. The AEC was supported by *The Lutheran Companion,* which contended that the Synod ought to devote more attention to members who had no feeling for the Swedish language.[12]

In spite of suspicions and distrust, the AEC gradually managed to establish itself and thereby assist the transition to English.[13] Actions and statements that might be misinterpreted were avoided. It was even stressed in the request for establishing the AEC "that the forming of this organization does not intend to disrupt our relationship to the conferences of the Synod."[14] The aim was expressed in this way: "The faith of the fathers in the language of the children." The purpose was also to provide the pastors serving English congregations with a means for coming together to discuss common problems.[15]

10 *Ibid.,* 1920, p. 13; and 1921, pp. 26, 27.

11 *Ibid.,* 1921, p. 28.

12 *The Lutheran Companion,* November 3, 1917; and January 22, 1921, p. 56.

13 An additional reason why AEC remained passive in the beginning was also a lack of resources. "We are, it is true, only a few congregations, numerically weak, financially weak, weak in many ways." *Minutes of AEC,* 1908, p. 6.

14 Carl J. Bengston, *op. cit.,* p. 163.

15 E.E. Ryden, "What has the Association of English Churches Accomplished?" *The Lutheran Companion,* October 15, 1927, p. 1002.

In an address at AEC's first annual meeting, in 1908, A.T. Seashore, pastor of the Grace English Church, Minneapolis, spoke about the need for more English:

> We live in an age when the son does not speak the language of the father; but we look forward to the time when the son will speak the same language as the father. It is a period of language transition. It bothers us. We have been compelled to learn our Bible and Catechism in two languages. Thus it is, and we should make the best of it. . . . The children will not speak the language of the fathers unless this is the English. Now, the Faith is the essential, the language the non-essential. . . . We are today dealing with a generation that can not say that the language of the Church is the language of their preference. Our practical duty is plain. Speak in the language they love and use.
>
> The aim of this Association is then to promote the work of our Synod in the English language.[16]

A.T. Seashore defended those who actively promoted an increased use of English. It was not true, he said, that ministers who preached in English were presumptuous and over-ambitious visionaries. He maintained rather, that they were the ones who assumed a difficult and thankless task because reality demanded it. "It is not that we love Swedish less, but that we love souls more."[17]

Opposition to the AEC seems at first to have come from the rank and file members of the Synod. The leaders of the AEC became quite pessimistic.

> Thus, for instance, we have in mind the Swedish Church in a certain small country town where the language question is daily becoming more and more critical. . . . The Swedish language is gradually dying out, and one by one the young people drop away and join some other denomination . . . but the members of this church will not listen. The only thing they will do is to denounce the young people for being uppish.[18]

They deplored the dislike for English, when the young people left the Synod because they had lost interest in an activity which they did not understand because of the language barrier.[19]

16 *Minutes of AEC*, 1908, pp. 28—29.

17 *Ibid.*, 1908, p. 29.

18 *Ibid.*, 1908, pp. 33—34.

19 *Ibid.*, 1908, p. 50.

As the development within AEC has shown, the language had to step back in favor of the religious message. This was also the case for the entire Synod. At the Synod's meeting in 1921, concern was expressed for the first time over the Swedes who did not have a command of English. In his annual report, the president reminded the Synod that time was short and that it ought to take measures to insure that one or two exclusively Swedish speaking congregations were retained in those cities which have several churches and a high number of Swedes.[20] He also admonished the members not to neglect "in time to so arrange matters, even at the beginning of the language transition, that we shall be able to care for the religious concerns of those who come from Sweden and settle in commercial centers." At the synodical meeting in 1923 the president reported that the demand for more English was continuously increasing in all branches of the Synod's work.[1] At the annual meeting of the Synod in 1928, a resolution regarding the transition to English was adopted:

> In all our educational work as well as our church work in general, we must satisfy existing language needs. Our immigrants and our children are obliged to learn English ... but Swedish ought also to be preserved as far as possible as a valuable cultural heritage. The consensus of the Synod is that restricting the study of foreign languages is a lowering of national cultural ideals, and that prohibiting the public use of languages other than English is contrary to American principles of freedom for which the nation has bled and is bleeding.[2]

Judging only by the annual reports of the Illinois Conference, the transition to English occurred without jarring discord. Even the older people were said to be aware of the demand of the times. "They realize ... that the Lord can speak to their hearts even in the English language."[3] In Minnesota the transition did not occur

[20] *Minutes of the Augustana Synod*, 1921, p. 17; 1926, p. 19; 1928, p. 18. It is not indicated which conferences were concerned.

[1] *Ibid.*, 1925, p. 16.

[2] *Ibid.*, 1928, p. 29.

[3] *Minutes of the Illinois Conference, 1922*, p. 16. The same year it was reported that there was scarcely any area where church work could be carried on exclusively in Swedish (p. 44). Although in 1922 it seemed that old members were aware of the demands of the time, it was still evident that they had problems with the English language. In 1925 the following comment was made: "When we see the tear of homesickness in their eyes, we should not criticize them for shedding that tear. It is better to kiss that tear away." (1925, p. 15).

without some pain. "There were places where young people made fun of pastors who mispronounced English words. . . . Swedish was the language of the heart to the older generation, but sometimes it was a serious barrier between them and the Americanized newer generation."[4]

7. *Debate about the Language – the Sacred Swedish Language*

In the Augustana Synod, as in the other Swedish-American denominations, the language question was a continuously recurring subject of debate.[5] For the older people Swedish was the only conceivable language for worship: to listen to an English service was nearly unthinkable. Sharply delineated, one may say that worshippers did not believe salvation could be accomplished in any other tongue than Swedish.[6] This was the accepted conclusion in all the Swedish-American denominations. One of the leaders in the Mission Covenant, however, said he could not be persuaded that "the Swedish language had taken out a patent on the Gospel."[7] Vilhelm Berger maintained that the continuous preaching in Swedish year after year had even penetrated into those born in America to such an extent that no service in English made as comparably good impression as a Swedish Lutheran high mass.[8] The language was sacred and was not to be tampered with.

The most emotion-filled debates were carried on in the local congregations, where the members were directly confronted with the

[4] Emeroy Johnson, *God Gave the Growth,* p. 225 ff.

[5] Julius Lincoln wrote in "The Language Question," *The Augustana Synod. A Brief Review of Its History, 1860—1910* (Rock Island, 1910), that he did not minimize other problems the Synod faced when he designated the language question the dominating subject of contention (p. 202). The pattern was the same for all Swedish denominations in the USA. The president of the Mission Covenant declared in 1933 : "The language question has forced itself through great opposition, and in a number of places caused not a little disruption," *Annual Reports of the Swedish Evangelical Mission Covenant Church, 1932—33,* (p. 5.); Adolf Olson, *A Centenary History,* p. 597, wrote about the Baptists: "But the road of language transition was beset by many obstacles."

[6] Julius Lincoln, *op. cit.,* p. 204 ff.

[7] *Missionsförbundets ungdomstidning,* January 14, 1913, p. 13.

[8] Vilhelm Berger, *Svensk-amerikanska meditationer,* p. 48.

whole complexity of the problem. Minutes of congregations tell of bitter and grievous discussions which in some cases resulted in a group's withdrawal to form its own congregation within the bounds of the mother-church.[9] In Rockford (Ill.) a group of 54 Mission Friends withdrew from the First Mission Covenant Church to organize a completely English speaking congregation, the Bethesda Covenant Church. The reason for the extreme action was that the congregation had denied a request from a group of younger members that all Sunday evening services be held in English.[10] The Swedish Evangelical Lutheran congregation in DeKalb (Ill.) labored over the language question from 1914 to 1940.[11] The First Lutheran Church of Prophetstown (Ill.) found the period after 1914 particularly bothersome. The younger people left the church because they did not understand the language. When English was introduced on a trial basis it resulted in a fiasco, because the pastor did not have command of that language.

The division between younger and older members brought tensions and discord. In order to solve the language question, a "golden middle way" was recommended, namely that of using either of the languages as situations and needs required. "This is the fairest expedient and consistent with Christian love."[12] In spite of all appeals urging toleration and understanding, the differences of opinion broke into an open clash. In all the denominations there were those who insisted that the Swedish language should be preserved for all posterity, while there were others who desired an immediate transfer to English. There were

[9] This happened, for instance, in the Covenant in Rockford and in the Augustana Synod in Galesburg. *Allsvensk Samling*, May 3, 1932, contains an article that illustrates how many Swedes reacted to the transition: "A Swedish mood prevailed — which only lasted until the Swedish pastor of the church broke the beautiful feeling with his English speech. He said the mass in English: 'Holy, holy, holy,' etc., instead of the beautiful words: 'Helig, helig, helig.' The choir sang 'To God alone in heaven's realm' (Allena Gud i himmelrik) in English: — it was as if something precious were trampled upon. If ministers no longer use the language of the fathers in church, how can they truly respect the faith of the fathers, the faith which Gustaf II Adolf fought and died for?"

[10] *Prologue and Epilogue:* A Series of Talks Relating the History and Hopes of the Bethesda Evangelical Covenant Church on its Fortieth Anniverstry, 1926—1966.

[11] *Minutes of the First Lutheran Church, DeKalb and Prophetstown.*

[12] E.G. Hjerpe, "Att amerikaniseras." *E.G. Hjerpe Collection.*

many examples of this. Waldemar Skoglund, Editor of *Svenska Standaret,* said in 1923 that Baptists ought to safeguard their mother-speech.[13] In another place in the same paper another writer complained that the transition to English proceeded too slowly. He referred to his own congregation, where 86 percent of worship services were in Swedish. Since only three percent of the members understood Swedish, the church used according to his reckoning, Swedish 86 percent of the time in order to serve three percent of its members. Another common problem was that there was not a sufficient number of pastors and preachers able to preach acceptably in English.[14]

As a rule, the minutes of the congregations are written in very general terms and are content with noting that the language question caused an intensive and lively debate. However, there are many Swedish immigrants still living who can relate with keen recollection the heated meetings occasioned by the language question. There are those who still lament that Swedish has had to yield to English. The church service was for them more than a religious meeting – it was equally as well a reminder of Sweden, of kindred and friends in the old country.[15]

It was not only in the congregations that the stir of the debate was heard but also in the two periodicals of the Synod, *Augustana* and *The Lutheran Companion.* In December, 1916, *Augustana* made clear its stand concerning the language question. "The primary task of our church is to win our people for the evangelical Lutheran faith and thereby promote its highest interests for time and eternity, and in order to attain that goal, it must use the language in ways through which the best results may be reached."[16]

The prudence with which both papers, *Augustana* and *The Lutheran Companion,* expressed themselves shows how extremely controversial the matter was for them. It demanded much wisdom coupled with love, wrote *Augustana.*[17] The paper recommended a transition

[13] *Svenska Standaret,* November 2, 1923.

[14] Adolf Olson, *op. cit.,* p. 598.

[15] Selma Jacobson has studied the records of Nebo Lutheran Church, Chicago, and made the following resumé in 1968: "Loud voices and strong emotions cried out at annual meetings of the congregations. Some members transferred to churches having Swedish services."

[16] *Augustana,* December 7, 1916, p. 954.

[17] *Ibid.,* December 14, 1916, p. 972.

according to the following scheme: That in the larger communities congregations be organized in which the language of the land be used exclusively, and in smaller communities where existing possibilities are not sufficiently large to organize such congregations the language of the land be used along with Swedish until the time comes when a complete transition becomes possible.[18] The paper was categorically opposed to any forced Americanization, since this was proceeding fast enough already.[19] Any attempt to create an artificial need for English as the worship language would harm the Synod.[20]

In essence, there was no division of opinion between *Augustana* and *The Lutheran Companion.* Both maintained that the language most beneficial to the Synod should be used. The difference between them was in their judgment as to which language was most beneficial to the Synod. *Augustana* said there were clear indications that the Synod would lose more than it gained if the transition were accelerated.[21] As the demands for more English were intensified, *Augustana* heightened its tone of contradiction. It spoke of "a real danger" for the work of the Synod "in the manner by which one seeks to force the use of English."[22] The accusations that the Synod was trying to curb the development were rejected by the paper. It also said it was not convinced that the language question was the primary reason why the Synod was losing a portion of the younger members. As evidence of this it pointed out that even the congregations which had completely adopted English had difficulty in keeping its younger members.[23] This may be considered as a direct polemic against *The Lutheran Companion* which demanded more English. "The need of our young people of English . . . is real and acute."[1]

Symptomatic for *Augustana* during this entire period was a clearly marked anxiety that the transition was being forced too

[18] *Ibid.,* January 3, 1918, p. 8.

[19] *Ibid.,* December 14, 1916, p. 972.

[20] *Ibid.,* July 4, 1918, p. 432; February 20, 1919, p. 121; December 10, 1925, p. 793.

[21] *Augustana,* July 24, 1919, p. 484; July 8, 1920, p. 444 f; October 2, 1920, p. 652.

[22] *Ibid.,* June 2, 1921, p. 344.

[23] *Ibid.,* January 3, 1918, p. 8; June 2, 1921, p. 345.

[1] *The Lutheran Companion,* January 22, 1921, p. 49.

rapidly, and time and again it warned against this.[2] No show of force ought to be employed as long as the "elite troops" were composed of those who preferred to hear their mother-tongue or as long as the need for English was more "alleged than real."

As long as those who were anxious for a rapid transition to English did not show any discretion, there was no reason why *Augustana* should. When a motion to make English the official language was voted down in 1921, the paper could not conceal its joy and stated that the Synod had nailed down "the sound principle" that both languages would be used according to need.[3]

Augustana held its position to the very last. It insisted as late as 1926 that "particular situations demand that both languages be used."[4] The difference between its statements at this time and those made during World War I was that the paper had changed its position so much that it now demanded that both languages should be used. Earlier it had said that the transition to English was not to be forced.

A delicate question concerned the Synod's collegiate institution, which was described as "the center of strength" for the preservation of the Swedish language.[5] If Swedish colleges were to have a chance to compete with American institutions, it was imperative that they remain bastions and defenders of Swedish culture. If the Swedish language became an elective subject it would soon disappear from the curriculum. The paper received support in this matter from Conrad Bergendoff, who said that the educational institutions of the Synod showed slight regard for the Swedish language.[6] If they were to have some reason for existing, they ought in some respect to be different from American schools.

According to *Augustana* it was also not entirely impossible that immigration might again become active.[7] The Synod, it was said, was

[2] *Augustana,* January 3, 1918, p. 8; June 2, 1921, p. 345.

[3] *Augustana,* June 23, 1921, p. 392.

[4] *Ibid.,* May 25, 1926, p. 184.

[5] *Ibid.,* December 7, 1916, p. 954; December 14, 1916, p. 972; January 3, 1918, p. 8.

[6] Conrad Bergendoff, "The Americanization of the Augustana Synod," in *The Lutheran Companion,* August 16, 1924, p. 523.

[7] *Augustana,* July 8, 1920, p. 444; June 2, 1921, p. 345. Emeroy Johnson, "The Duty of the Augustana Synod in Regard to the Swedish Language" in *The Lutheran Companion,* February 9, 1924, p. 89.

responsible for newly arriving immigrants. If the Synod were not what it proclaimed itself to be, namely the "Swedish Lutheran Church in America," immigrants would turn to some other denomination.[8] Immigrants who came after the War were considered to offer "much wider opportunities" for the Synod than other nationalities ever would do.[9]

Förbundets Veckotidning (The Covenant Weekly) also expressed anxiety regarding newly arriving immigrants. The paper feared that American denominations would recruit Swedes for their churches by employing Swedish speaking preachers.[10] It wondered whether this ought not to be something for Mission Friend congregations to consider. As a direct result of increased immigration from Sweden in 1923, the Swedish Methodists in Chicago gave the language question great attention. The greatest waves of immigrants after World War I reached America in 1923. In order to assist the newcomers special instruction courses in English were arranged.[11] Some churches reintroduced Swedish evening services in the hope of winning new members. The result was not without problems: the young people of the churches protested. "In trying to win the one, we are in danger of losing the other."

The Lutheran Companion, in contrast to *Augustana,* was anxious to have the transition made as rapidly as possible. While *Augustana* was concerned about the older people, *The Lutheran Companion* showed great understanding of the young. It stated at an early stage that the Swedish language was bound to disappear, in spite of all the sentimental arguments to the contrary.[12] Like *Augustana* it urged the members of the Synod to show consideration and tolerance. It condemned the type of Americanism that did not tolerate any other language than English,[13] and at the same time it assailed those Swedes who wanted the second and third generations to learn Swedish. They

8 *Augustana,* September 15, 1921, p. 584.

9 *Ibid.,* April 10, 1924, p. 232; June 28, 1923, p. 392.

10 *Förbundets Veckotidning,* October 11, 1921, p. 4.

11 *General Swedish Methodist Conference's Minutes,* 1923, p. 218 ff.

12 *The Lutheran Companion,* July 12, 1919, p. 359; January 4, 1919, p. 2.

13 *Ibid.,* February 1, 1919, p. 54.

were Americans the newspaper stated, and consequently they ought to have English as their language for worship services.[14]

Characteristic for Swedish Americans in general has always been an over-sensitivity when confronting homeland-Swedes. When *All-svensk Samling* criticized the Augustana Synod for not having sufficiently guarded the Swedish language, *The Lutheran Companion* reacted sharply.[15] The problem with a part of the Swedish-American journalists, as well as the greater part of the Swedish people, was that they were unable and unwilling to understand American conditions.[16] The reason why the Synod gradually transferred to English was that such a change was really needed. ”In the great majority of cases the churches of our Synod in Iowa are ripe for a complete transition at any time to the use of English in their work.” The paper even went so far as to defend the language restriction that followed in certain states immediately after World War I. The war had thought America that ”much of the activity on the part of European nations to keep alive and strong nationalistic ties in their people abroad had ulterior motives that were not altogether unselfish.” If the Swedish Americans could not maintain contact with Sweden unless the

[14] *Svenska Amerikanaren* (The Swedish American) shared the opinion of *The Lutheran Companion* that it was useless to work for the preservation of the Swedish language among the second and third generations, since ”it would be contrary to the nature of the Swedish language if it were retained among Swedish descendants beyond the second generation” *(Svenska Amerikanaren,* December 25, 1914). A. Serenius maintained in an article in *Missionsförbundets ungdomstidning* (May 21, 1912, p. 6) that it was pure nonsense to say that Swedish-American children cannot learn Swedish. The president of the Mission Covenant, 1910—1927, E.G. Hjerpe, commenting on the problem within the Covenant, declared that people ought to understand that the younger generation, having learned English from the very start, could not become ”a promising mission field” for Swedish (E.G. Hjerpe, ”Att amerikaniseras” — typescript, unpaged.); *Augustana,* on the other hand, maintained that even the second and third generations could easily learn Swedish if parents and pastors wanted them to *(Augustana,* January 10, 1924, p. 25).

[15] When two congregations in Fort Dodge, Iowa, decided to change to English, *Allsvensk Samling* (May 1, 1918, p. 3) made the following comment: ”One surely stands speechless before such displays of cowardice and brash flirtation with Americanism! If the Fort Dodge Swedes think they can win the respect of Americans by so deeply denying and degrading themselves, their nation and their language, they are certainly mistaken!”

[16] *The Lutheran Companion,* July 20, 1918, p. 362.

Swedish language were preserved, it might be just as well to break the contacts. It sounds hard, but it must be said, wrote the paper.

The transition to English was a matter of discussion for both the editorial pages of the newspapers as well as the individual members of the Synod. During the period with which we are concerned, both *Augustana* and *The Lutheran Companion* contained numerous contributions in which the language question was discussed. In general, it may be said that most of the writers of articles defending Swedish as the language of religious worship wrote for sentimental reasons. Emeroy Johnson describes the language debate as narrow-minded.[17] "This narrow-mindedness among people on both sides of the language problem constitutes a greater problem for our Synod than the language problem itself." Those he refers to are partly those who understood English very well but insisted that a worship service must be in Swedish and partly the "one hundred percent Americans" who found it disgraceful to use any other language than English.

Conrad Bergendoff thought that ultimately the Synod ought to unite with other Lutheran churches in the United States and form a single, large Lutheran entity, but he said that as long as this could not be realized the Synod ought to safeguard the Swedish language.[18] If it lost its identity it would no longer have a right to exist. Bergendoff had difficulty in reconciling himself with the idea that theological students should learn Latin, Greek and Hebrew but not Swedish. He did not want either the individual immigrant nor the Swedish-American organizations to appear as colorless neutrals. The Swedes ought instead to show self-confidence, be proud of their origin, and maintain that Swedish culture is as good as that of any other nationality. "Gustavus Adolphus belongs as much to us as to our brethren in Sweden, and we are as much the heirs of Wallin and Rosenius as

[17] Emeroy Johnson, "The Duty of the Augustana Synod in Regard to the Swedish language" in *The Lutheran Companion*, February 2, 1924, pp. 75 ff; *Augustana* wrote (December 14, 1926, p. 972, and January 3, 1918, p. 8 ff.) that it was more a matter of the heart than a question of language.

[18] Conrad Bergendoff, *op. cit.*, *The Lutheran Companion*, August 16, 1924, p. 523; In studying the Texas Swedes, Carl M. Rosenquist found that language constituted the identity of the church for the immigrants. "Once it is gone, their church becomes like all other churches of the same denomination" (Carl M. Rosenquist, "Linguistic Changes in the Acculturation of the Swedes of Texas," p. 223.)

they."[19] Even though the Augustana Synod did not have as its main task the preservation of Swedish culture, there was, according to Bergendoff, a great deal in that culture that should be preserved. By this he did not wish to imply that the Americanization of the Synod would mean that America re-shaped the Synod, but that the Synod was re-shaping America. If the Synod wanted to exert any influence, it could not compromise that which it considered essential. The moment the Augustana Synod did not differ from other denominations there was no reason for it to continue its work.

S.G. Hägglund, one of the most vigorous champions of Swedish culture, declared that his heart bled at the thought of how the transition to English proceeded. The reason was that it did not advance openly and honestly.[20] "That our old mother tongue has been shunted aside is lamentable, but that it has been done so coldly and unfeelingly is grievously painful to all friends of Swedish culture."

For his part S.G. Hägglund called for loyalty to the past – the history of the Swedish Americans.[21] He was also of the definite opinion that a worship service never could be the same in English as in Swedish; the language is for people as the bark is for the tree. Hägglund was supported by S.G. Öhman, who deplored the fact that pastors neglected to study Swedish because of indolence and love of ease.[22] The Swedish heritage was jeopardized through the Synod's self-isolation from the Swedish mother-church. Andrew Stomberg considered the transition an inevitable and sad development. He had difficulty in condoning the intolerance toward the old people "who had shouldered the heaviest burdens."[23]

A lively debate on the language question was also carried on in the Mission Covenant, especially during and after World War I. In 1918 *Förbundets Veckotidning* stated that "the language question has

[19] Conrad Bergendoff, *op. cit.*, in *The Lutheran Companion,* August 16, 1924, p. 523 ff, and August 23, 1924, p. 539.

[20] S.G. Hägglund, "Svenska Språket vid Sydnodalmötet i Minneapolis" in *Augustana,* July 9, 1925, p. 442.

[21] S.G. Hägglund, "The Swedish Demand" in *Augustana Quarterly,* January 1925, p. 442.

[22] S.G. Öhman, "Vårt svenska arv" in *Korsbaneret* 1924, pp. 120—22.

[23] Andrew Stomberg, *Den svenska folkstammen i Amerika* (Stockholm, 1928), p. 59.

become acute."[1] E.G. Hjerpe, President of the Covenant, said in an address in 1919 that the war had forced the Covenant "into this situation" more rapidly than had been anticipated.[2]

The problem that particularly worried *Förbundets Veckotidning* was the lack of pastors who had a sufficient command of English.[3] This anxiety prevailed during the greater part of the 1920s. The paper also feared that the younger generation of preachers would not be able to transmit the specific aspects of the Covenant.[4] "It is by no means an easy matter to preach the evangelical truths of the gospel in English and to give them the same emphasis as in Swedish."

The argumentation of *Förbundets Veckotidning* generally followed the same line as that of *Augustana.* Like *Augustana, Förbundets Veckotidning* stated in 1921 that the overwhelming number of members still preferred a Swedish sermon.[5] It is urgent, said the paper, that the importance of the Swedish language for the preservation of Swedish culture be continuously stressed, because otherwise the next generation would be deprived of its precious Swedish heritage of cultural and spiritual content. None of the papers believed that all denominations would gain by a transition to English. They insinuated that it was less a matter of an acute need than a wish to be up-to-date. "The idea that by preaching in English one may be able to win young people for Christ has not yet been demonstrated. Contrariwise, it has been shown that Swedish preaching has a greater impact on the heart and feelings of the young."[6] In a later editorial, *Förbundets Veckotidning* claimed it had proof that "nowhere can anything be gained by using only English." *Missionsvännen* shared the concern of *Förbundets Veckotidning* over a far too rapid pace of Americanization by saying that it was dangerous to become Americanized "superficially in thought and principles so that we follow along into worldly

[1] *Förbundets Veckotidning,* June 4, 1918, p. 4.

[2] *Ibid.,* May 6, 1919, p. 5.

[3] *Ibid.,* February 4, 1919, p. 4, and March 4, 1919, p. 4. In an editorial on July 5, 1921, an article was reprinted from *Augustana* warning against a forcing of the transition. It was reprinted because the paper thought the matter was applicable to conditions in the Covenant as well.

[4] *Ibid.,* February 28, 1922, p. 4.

[5] *Förbundets Veckotidning,* September 13, 1921, p. 4.

[6] *Ibid.,* March 4, 1919, p. 4; and November 11, 1919, p. 4.

and shallow American churchliness."[7] Those who would accelerate the transition were described as vain and stupid.[8] "Do not make the mistake of thinking that the language change will to a greater degree give the congregation new members," warned *Förbundets Veckotidning*. When local conditions do not absolutely crave English services, one ought to continue with exclusively Swedish services.[9]

As the transition to English progressed, the Swedish schools were urged to keep the Swedish language alive.[10] After 1924 a change was noted, and the "nervous swing to English" was explained by the claim that preachers had not been zealous enough in learning Swedish.[11] Professor N.W. Lund of North Park Theological Seminary answered the critics by saying it was preposterous to demand that young ministeral students should be able to preach in mellifluous Swedish.[12] He called to mind the fact that all ministerial students were obliged to take courses in Swedish. "But one should, in the name of fairness, remember that a theological seminary in America is something more than just a school of instruction in Swedish."

When the Mission Covenant adopted English as its official language in 1929, *Förbundets Veckotidning* made the following acidulous comment: "To be sure, it was said that those who wish to speak at the conferences may use the language they prefer – a concession not quite amiss in a land where liberty is so abundantly praised."[13] However, interestingly enough the paper made a complete reversal in the following issue. The first comment was made because "a colleague in the editorial office had compassion for the old."[14] Now the paper said it did not feel the transition had come too early.

8. *The Transition in the Denominations*

The Augustana Synod: In the following pages the transition to English will be described in more detail. The first part deals with the

[7] *Missionsvännen,* October 18, 1927.

[8] *Förbundets Veckotidning,* February 8, 1921, p. 4; and February 21, 1922, p. 4.

[9] *Ibid.,* March 14, 1922, p. 4.

[10] *Förbundets Veckotidning,* September 25, 1923, p. 4.

[11] *Ibid.,* October 21, 1924, p. 4; and October 4, 1927, p. 4.

[12] *Ibid.,* October 18, 1927, p. 4.

[13] *Ibid.,* July 2, 1929, p. 4.

[14] *Ibid.,* July 9, 1929, p. 4.

different stages of the transition in the denominations. This is followed by an account of the transition in the individual congregations in Illinois.

Although the Synod's minutes do not have much information about the language transition, they at least have some important data which show that English forced out the Swedish language in the 1920s.

AEC made little progress, for instance, during its first decade. At the second convention in 1909, the president of the AEC states that the progress of the Association consisted in gaining only seven new member-congregations.[1] But more important than new members was the increased understanding of the AEC's activity. In 1910 AEC was given the same rights as the conferences in the Synodical Council.[2] The Synod also approved the proposal that an abstract of the synodical minutes be printed in English. The separate conferences were advised to do likewise. In 1911 the appointment of an "English Field Secretary" was approved. In a letter to G.A. Brandelle, the president of the English organization pointed out that the War had brought about an "unprecedented upswing" in favor of English, even though this was not noticeable as far as the number of new members was concerned.[3] As time went on, however, optimism in the AEC increased. The annual report of 1922 stated: "The outlook and even the spirit of the congregations comprising the Association have changed greatly in recent years."[4]

The Association of English Churches looked not only to the Swedes in the U.S. but also to other nationalities. One congregation in Iowa reported in 1923 99.2 percent non-Swedish members; Calvary, Moline, reported 80 percent were non-Swedish; others reported 75 percent, 50 percent and 30 percent. In the remaining congregations of the Association the number of non-Swedish members was approximately 25 percent. Compared with the membership increase in the Synod as a whole, the English congregations claimed a more rapid growth. In 1924 the English organization had approximately 15,000 members, in fact more members than had eight of the Synod's conferences.[6]

1 *Minutes of AEC,* 1909, p. 27.
2 Ira O. Nothstein, *The Language Transition,* p. 336.
3 The letter is dated May 5, 1918.
4 *Minutes of AEC,* 1922, p. 11.
5 *Ibid.,* 1923, pp. 10—11 and 50.
6 *Ibid.,* 1924, pp. 14—15.

In his annual report for 1923, the president of AEC said that on the average its congregations had increased in membership by 19 percent in 1922–1923, while the Augustana Synod had grown by 1.1 percent. It is true that the Synod's membership increased by 1.1 percent. However, it seems that the figure of 19 percent for AEC was purely invented. According to recorded statistics, AEC had 13,235 members and 46 congregations in 1922; in 1923 the figures were 14,267 members and 55 congregations. This implies that the membership increased by about 8 percent, but the figure also includes the nine congregations that joined during the year. If these are left out of the reckoning, the increase for AEC was approximately the same as that for the whole Augustana Synod.

At the same time that its number of non-Swedish members increased, AEC avoided presenting itself as a Swedish church. "We do not blame anyone for being proud of his ancestry, but in our Association churches where Irish, and German, Greek and Jew, Austrian and Italian, Dane and Swede work and worship together, it is at least poor taste to take it for granted that they all come from the same European stock."[7] Even if non-Swedes joined the Augustana Synod, it is not likely that Irishmen, Italians, Greeks and Jews came in any appreciable numbers.

About 1927 Americanization had made such progress that there was talk about whether the AEC had any longer a function to perform.[8] In an article in *The Lutheran Companion* in 1927, C.O. Bengston, President of AEC, joined issue with those who contended that the organization of English churches had finished playing its role.[9] He was of the opinion, namely, that it still had a large task ahead

[7] *Minutes of the AEC,* 1926, pp. 8, 10, and 36.

[8] *Op. cit.,* 1927, pp. 9—11. At the annual meeting in 1928 a resumé of the activity of the past 20 years was noted: "When the Association was organized the sessions of the Synod as well as all Conferences were conducted exclusively in Swedish. Now the Synod and all Conferences conduct their business almost entirely in English" *(Minutes of AEC,* 1928, pp. 7, 8.)

[9] C.O. Bengston, "The Future of the Association of English Churches," in *The Lutheran Companion,* October 15, 1927, p. 1010. Bengston's observations coincide well with M.L. Hansen's theory that the third generation was more conscious of its ancestry than the second generation. Those who were eager for more English in the work of the Synod in 1908, when the AEC was formed, were children of immigrants. In 1927 they had children of their own who were perhaps not ashamed of their origin.

of it because of a growing nationalism among the Swedes concomitant with their Americanization. "In fact, hand in hand with the tendency to put away the Swedish language there has been growth in appreciation of Swedish ancestry and Swedish culture. The Augustana Synod was never closer to the state church of Sweden than it is today. The surprising fact is that the English language lends itself well to Swedish propaganda." Even though English made certain progress, the Synod remained basically the same. In 1928 a committee was appointed by the Synod for the purpose of planning its future activity. In its report prepared for the 1929 synodical meeting the committee recommended, among other stipulations, that AEC continue, as long as a large part of the Augustana Synod's members gave the impression that the Synod was exclusively a Swedish organization.[10] It was pointed out that in view of what appeared to the committee to be the tendencies in the Synod to revive the use of the Swedish language in the church work, the Association should therefore continue its work. A new committee was elected in 1930 to investigate the possibility of reorganizing AEC into a separate conference.[11] In such a conference all congregations having completely transferred to English would be gathered. That plan was never consummated. Instead, AEC ceased to exist the following year. The synodical meeting in 1931 decided to dissolve it. This was done, it was said, because English had now become the official language of the Synod, and the English organization had no longer any purpose to fulfill.[12] The decision was made in spite of the expressed protest of the AEC. Its work was far from finished, its proponents said.

> Not by the wildest stretch of the imagination can it truthfully be said that the Augustana Synod is an English speaking body. It is true that the business of the synodical meetings is conducted in English, but an overwhelming number of the synod's churches are still bilingual and some of them still use only Swedish.[13]

To judge by the minutes of the annual meeting of 1931, opinions were divided regarding the AEC. There was even uncertainty whether or not an annual meeting ought to be held. The president of AEC

10 *Minutes of AEC,* 1929, pp. 18, 19. See also Ira O. Nothstein, *The Language Transition,* p. 343 f.

11 *Minutes of AEC,* 1930, p. 21.

12 *Minutes of the Augustana Synod,* 1931, pp. 230—31.

13 *Minutes of AEC,* 1930, pp. 24—25.

therefore sent a questionnaire to the member-congregations.[14] The questionnaire was sent to 96, and 51 responded: 27 did not want an annual meeting to be held, six were undecided, and 18 favored the holding of a meeting. Of the 18 who wanted a meeting to be held, 11 declared that AEC ought to continue its work. While a minority voted No, a final annual meeting was held in 1931. At the meeting the opinion was unanimous that AEC should be allowed to continue its work in the Synod. A special resolution was adopted which was to be submitted later to the Synod:[15]

> Resolved, that in view of the endeavors and accomplishments of the Association in the past, as well as its loyalty to the Synod and its work, and in view of the fact that the Association is convinced that it is a matter of vital importance that the Association be permitted to continue to function as in the past, we respectfully memorialize the Synod to reconsider the action of the 1931 convention.

In spite of the appeal the AEC was dissolved. "Whereas English being now the official language of the Synod, said Association now has no specific purpose, therefore, be it resolved that the English Association be dissolved."[16] At its last annual meeting in October, 1931, the AEC had 124 member-congregations; when it was started it had eleven.

Several discussions and decisions at the different annual meetings of the Synod and Conferences also show that the transition to English chiefly took place after World War I. In 1919 the President of the Synod, G.A. Brandelle, stated that English had been made the official language in several congregations and that some churches had changed their names or had eliminated the designation "Swedish."[17] In 1921 in one of the Synod conferences, half of the high mass services were held in English.[1] In the same conference 75 percent of the evening services were in English. Two conferences reported that English was their official language. In 1923 five conference presidents presented their annual reports in English.[2]

14 *Ibid.*, 1931, p. 6.

15 *Ibid.*, 1931, pp. 7, 8.

16 *Minutes of the Augustana Synod,* 1931, p. 230 f.

17 *Ibid.*, 1919, p. 20.

1 *Ibid.*, 1921, p. 17.

2 *Ibid.*, 1923, p. 16.

Table 34. The transition to English in the Augustana Synod.

1919	The Illinois Conference began printing its minutes in both Swedish and English.
1919	The Minnesota Conference began printing its minutes in both Swedish and English.
1920	English became the official language of the Iowa Conference.
1923	The president's annual report was, for the first time, written in English.
1924	The minutes of the Synod were, for the first time, printed in English.
1924	The graduates of Augustana Theological Seminary, were for the first time, ordained in English into the ministry. *)
1924	English became the official language of the Kansas Conference.
1925	The complete order of divine worship was published in English.
1928	The Synod's constitution was translated into English.
1928	The Red River Valley Conference discontinued printing its minutes in Swedish.
1929	The Minnesota Conference began printing its minutes in English.
1929	An English translation of the Minnesota Conference's constitution was presented for consideration. It was adopted in 1931.

*) *Minutes of AEC*, 1924, p. 15.

No official decision has ever been made making English the official language of the Synod. The year 1931 – the year when the Association of English Churches was dissolved – has, however, been considered the demarcation year when English became the official language.[3] As indicated, the transition proceeded slowly. According to C.M. Olander, in 1930 only 150 congregations of a total of 1,250 used English exclusively.[4] A few continued as wholly Swedish speaking congregations, while the great majority was bilingual. In the bilingual congregations the young people spoke English, and the older people who were born in Sweden, spoke Swedish. Olander's conclusion was: "Though a transition is going on from the use of Swedish to English, it is not nearly as strong or rapid as some would lead us to think . . . church work as a whole, is in both language and spirit, in spite of our English work, quite Swedish."

[3] A.D. Mattson, *Polity of the Augustana Lutheran Church* (Rock Island, 1952), p. 145.

[4] C.M. Olander, "What does the present situation demand of our synod?" in *Augustana Quarterly*, January 1930, p. 1; *Minutes of the Illinois Conference, 1924*, p. 18.

Within the separate conferences the transition followed the same pattern as in the Synod. The conferences also discussed the language transition at their annual meetings. At the annual meeting of the Illinois Conference in 1919, it was reported that the use of English had increased considerably during the fiscal year 1918–19. The reason for this was thought to be "a kind of nervousness some people displayed when they seemed to fear a person would be considered less loyal if he revealed by his pronounciation that he was Swedish."

According to the minutes of the Illinois Conference the transition to English proceeded quietly and unnoticed. In 1921 English and Swedish had approximately equal standing in the Conference.[5] In 1925 it was reported the English services were generally better attended than the Swedish. At any rate, however, it took time even in the Illinois Conference for the language question to be solved completely. The president of the Conference stated in 1930 that "the language question presents difficulties. . . ."[6] Even by 1932 the matter had not been entirely unraveled.[7]

In the Minnesota Conference, as in Illinois, the transition proceeded slowly.[8] Swedish services were held in a number of churches up to World War II.

The New England Conference had opposed the transition to English longer than any other Augustana conference.[9] Not until 1932, for example, did the New England Conference print its minutes completely in English. Even in 1930 all Augustana congregations in the Boston area used Swedish to some extent as the worship language.[10] Of the eighteen congregations, twelve of the pastoral reports were written in the Swedish language as late as 1930. The reason why the

[5] *Minutes of the Illinois Conference, 1921,* p. 14, and 1925, p. 15.

[6] *Minutes of the Illinois Conference, 1930,* p. 14.

[7] *Ibid.,* 1932, p. 14. In 1931 the president gave an account of the main reasons why church attendance was not what it should be. According to information gathered from pastors, the reasons were: 29, long distance to the church; 2, lack of transit means; 24, language difficulties; 17, absent-mindedness; 42, indifference; and 34, secularization *(Minutes of the Illinois Conference, 1931,* p. 13).

[8] Emeroy Johnson, *God Gave the Growth,* p. 224 f.

[9] E. Eklund, "Acculturation in the Swedish Lutheran Congregations of the Boston Area, 1867—1930," p. 3 ff and p. 175.

[10] *Ibid.,* p. 175.

New England Conference held on to the Swedish language longer than the other conferences seems to be that it was considerably younger than the others. Thus it is not quite correct to say that the linguistic transition proceeded more slowly here than in other places. "The rate of acculturation for the Boston area churches was just as rapid, possibly more so. The period of time between the organization of the Augustana Synod's first congregation (1848) and that of the first Boston area (1867) was nineteen years."[11] The difference between the year when the first conference printed its minutes entirely in English (1921) and the year when the New England conference did so (1932) was only eleven years.

The Swedish Methodist Churches: The other Swedish-American denominations also gave much time at their annual conventions for discussion of the language question. In 1920 the American Methodist Church appointed a special committee, The Foreign Language Commission, to investigate the need for non-English-speaking conferences and to propose effective ways of organizing immigrants.[12] In 1924 the committee submitted a report together with suggestions for formulating measures. These included an appeal to the Methodists to continue working among new settlers in their own language in order to enable them to change over to English as soon as possible.[13] The tacit intent was that the non-English-speaking conferences ought to be perpetuated as long as there was an actual need of them. In other words, the transition should not be forced. Of the 817 non-English-speaking congregations the committee investigated, 50.7 percent of the members used English predominantly, while 49.3 percent did not. In German congregations 57 percent of the members used English predominantly; in the Swedish congregations 39.7 percent, and in Danish-Norwegian congregations 39.8 percent. The Swedish Methodists showed strong resistance and were not Americanized over night. The annual report of 1927 stated that instruction in Swedish at the theological seminary in Evanston had to continue because there would always be people in the United States who preferred Swedish worship services to English ones.[14] However, the trend of the times had its way, and in

[11] *Ibid.*, p. 288 f.

[12] *Report of the Foreign Language Commission to the General Conference of the Methodist Episcopal Church*, pp. 4 ff.

[13] *Ibid.*, p. 9.

[14] *Central Swedish Conference's Yearbook 1927*, p. 248 ff.

1928 the Central, Northern, and Western Swedish Conferences were consolidated to form the Central Northwest Conference of the Methodist Episcopal Church, the final annual meeting of which was held in 1942.[15] This signified the end of Swedish Methodism in America: "... we are about to dissolve the last of our Swedish speaking conferences and return the churches and pastors to the English speaking conferences where they originally began." The previous year, the Eastern Swedish Conference had merged with neighboring American conferences. *Sändebudet* (The Messenger), the official newspaper of the Swedish Methodists, ceased publication in 1948.[16]

Though it is impossible to determine the exact year when English and Swedish were of equal status, one may, nevertheless, quite safely designate the period 1925–1930 as the time in which the language question was resolved. The following statement was made in 1925: "The problem of language is gradually being solved according to local needs."[17] In 1930 the Galesburg district reported that work carried out in Swedish among the Swedish Methodists could be considered concluded.[18]

The Mission Friends: If one is to judge by the annual reports of the Mission Friends, the resistance to the change to English was stronger in the Mission Covenant Church than in the Augustana Synod. In 1917, 63 percent of the Covenant Sunday Schools used Swedish exclusively, and 37 percent used Swedish in varying degrees.[19] In 1918 certain measures were introduced for making the transition easier. A Sunday school committee requested that the instruction material be published in both languages. A resolutions committee recommended, the same year, that the Covenant devise ways and

[15] George Stephenson, *The Religious Aspects,* p. 262; *Central Northwest Conference, 1942, Historical Edition,* p. 205; In 1912 the Southern Swedish Conference was organized and in 1926 merged with the American Southern Conference. The Pacific Swedish Conference was organized in 1908 and dissolved in 1928.

[16] O. Fritiof Ander, *The Cultural Heritage,* p. 172.

[17] *Central Swedish Conference's Yearbook 1925,* p. 87.

[18] *Ibid.,* 1930, p. 224.

[19] Karl A. Olsson, *By One Spirit,* p. 490; *Missionsförbundets årsberättelse,* 1917, p. 113; 1918, pp. 136—137.

means by which the transition to English could be facilitated.[20] The committee said the need of transferring to English had come more rapidly than had been anticipated. The young and the old were admonished to hold firm. "The older people ought, even if they do not know English well, still to attend English meetings, just as they had expected the young people to attend when Swedish was used." Karl A. Olsson has called the resolution a "crash program of Americanization," which in many respects was a failure.[1] The Swedish language was so deeply rooted in the older ministers that they could only comply with the demand for English sermons only by translating published Swedish sermons.

Table 35. The transition into English in the Evangelical Covenant Church.

1921	The Covenant published its first hymnal in English. *)
1929	English was made the official language of the denomination, while the minutes and proceedings were also issued under the heading "Årsberättelser" up to 1931.
1931	The name of the denomination was changed from the Swedish Evangelical Mission Covenant to Evangelical Mission Covenant.
1932	"Årsberättelser" became "Annual Reports."
1932	The president's annual report was in Swedish up to and including this year.
1933	Theodore W. Anderson became president, which meant that the Covenant got its first American-born president 22 years later than the Augustana Synod.
1934	The official Swedish language newspaper of the Covenant, *Förbundets Veckotidning*, had served its time. That paper and *The Covenant Companion* were merged to form *The Covenant Weekly*.
1955	*The Covenant Weekly* transferred completely to English. This meant that the Covenant's publishing activity from 1955 on was entirely in English.

*) The first all-English hymnal, called *Mission Hymns*, was published in 1921. It contained 223 hymns, many of them translated from the Swedish, and was intended for use by the younger people. The official hymnal of the Covenant, *Sions Basun*, which was published in 1908 and contained 731 hymns, included 27 hymns in English.

As the need for English increased the ministers who could handle both English and Swedish had the best opportunities for finding work.[2]

[20] *Mission Covenant Yearbook*, 1918, p. 132 f; Theodore W. Anderson in *Covenant Memories*, p. 99 f.

[1] Karl A. Olsson, *op. cit.*, p. 508.

[2] *Missionsförbundets ungdomstidning*, November 3, 1914.

In 1929 the transition to English had advanced so far that preachers who were unable to use English in the pulpit did not receive appointments. "Many a small congregation would rather be without a pastor than call one whose English is faulty. It is a highly lamentable situation."[3]

The Covenant Weekly was bilingual, but as the Swedish language lost territory the interest for the Swedish section of the paper decreased. However, it was not until 1955 that the paper made the full transition to English. This meant that the Covenant's publishing activity from 1955 on was entirely in English.[4] Even though the Swedish section of the paper was kept alive so long, the Swedish language was by that time a relic of the past. At the annual meeting in 1935 it was stated that "the old guard of Covenanters is rapidly dropping off. 'Oscar Peterson,' the typical immigrant, no longer sits in our churches during the English services with a slightly puzzled expression on his kind face. He has left his dialect and gone to use fluently the universal language of Heaven."[5]

The Swedish Baptists: In the Swedish Baptist churches the language question became acute toward the end of the 1920s. As early as 1917 the official newspaper, *Svenska Standaret,* found the time ripe for the introduction of a separate English section, the "Young People's Department."[6] In 1925 an English hymnal was published,[7] and in 1931 a new paper in English, *The Baptist Evangel,* was started. When it was found too expensive to publish two papers, a merger of the two, *Svenska Standaret* and *The Baptist Evangel,* took place in 1940 under the name of *The Standard.* In 1933 the annual conference records were printed in English for the first time.[8] In the Swedish Baptist Seminary – Bethel Academy and Seminary – the transition occurred gradually between 1916 and 1930. After 1930 the educational work was carried on in English entirely. Over the years, one congregation after another eliminated "Swedish" from its name, and in 1945 the Swedish Baptist General Conference in America became the Baptist General Conference of America.

[3] *Mission Covenant Yearbook,* 1928—29, p. 6.
[4] Karl A. Olsson, *op. cit.,* p. 565.
[5] *The Covenant Conference Review,* June 21, 1935.
[6] Adolf Olson, *A Centenary History,* p. 502.
[7] *Ibid.,* p. 510.
[8] *Ibid.,* p. 600.

9. *The Transition in Different Congregations in Illinois*

The general pattern: The transition to English also proceeded gradually in the individual congregations. A beginning was made with the introduction of, for instance, one evening service a month in English. If the attempt proved satisfactory, more English services were repeated little by little. After a time, alternating services were held or so-called "double services" – that is, both a Swedish and an English service were held each Sunday. When a congregation had reached the stage of having alternating or double services, it could roughly be said that both languages had gained a position of equal importance. After a time, the use of Swedish began to diminish until it finally ceased altogether.

The Evangelical Mission Covenant Church of Hinsdale, Illinois, and Chisago Lake Lutheran Church, Center City, Minnesota, provide illustrations of how the process developed.[10] With few exceptions, the pattern was the same for other denominations. On January 2, 1922, the congregation in Hinsdale decided to introduce one English evening service a month; on May 6, 1924, the number was increased to two; on May 4, 1925, two morning services in English a month were introduced; on May 1, 1928, the congregation voted to have the minutes kept in English; a meeting on December 31, 1931, discussed whether to transfer entirely into English. Since opposition to this proposal was strong, it was decided that members should have a chance to express their views. The response to the questionnaire showed an overwhelming majority in favor of continuing the alternating set-up. On December 31, 1934, a motion was again made that the congregation transfer entirely to English. Fifteen voted yes, seven no, and two abstaining. This meant that, as far as this church was concerned, the Swedish language, on and after December 31, 1934, belonged to the past. The process had taken a total of twelve years to accomplish.

Nils Hasselmo, who has been studying the language question in the churches in Chisago County, Minnesota, has come to the conclusion that the transition question emerged around 1915 and that the debate

[10] Evangelical Mission Covenant Church, Hinsdale, Illinois: *Golden Jubilee Anniversary, 1892—1942*. Very few congregations have been able to present such a detailed record as this of the transition from Swedish to English.

reached its climax during the 1920s.[11] The issue was finally resolved in the 1930s.

Information taken from the records of Chisago Lake Lutheran Church, Center City, Minnesota, summarized in Appendix B, shows the gradual displacement of Swedish by English in various activities of the church. The language question emerged in 1915, when the English Bible class requested the use of the chapel for its meetings. The request was granted. At this time all other activities of the church were conducted in Swedish. Nils Hasselmo pinpoints that the minutes of the 1916 annual meeting in Chisago Lake Lutheran Church indicate "that the outside English speaking world was indeed impinging on the community, if not in spiritual matters at least in financial ones. The impact of finances and youth makes itself felt in the corresponding minutes for 1917 in the form of financial report in English from *Ungdomsföreningen.*"

The growing problem of the new generation which did not know Swedish is underscored in the pastoral report of 1920. "The English language has been used exclusively in some classes in the Sunday school and partly in the confirmation school. It now seems to be a matter of time also in this Swedish speaking area, when the English

Table 36. Language used in the Sunday school at Chisago Lake Lutheran Church, Center City, Minnesota, 1920–1928.

Year of report	Number of classes		Number of children	
	Swedish	English	Swedish	English
1920	17	4	106	46
1921	12	7	105	66
1922	11	10	87	82
1923	12	11	80	93
1924	9	18	51	159
1925	10	18	56	168
1926	5	20	44	131
1927	5	24	27	184
1928	4	22	–	–

Source: Nils Hasselmo, "The Swedish Language in Chisago County, Minnesota."

[11] Nils Hasselmo, "The Swedish Language in Chisago County, Minnesota." I have been allowed to quote from his manuscript, and I cannot refer to the page. The information given here is from Chapter 2, "The Language Question in the Churches."

language must be used more in giving instruction in Christianity." Table 36, which includes statistics in terms of language used in the Sunday school from 1920 to 1928, shows the rate of transition.

The trend in Chisago Lake Lutheran Church is the same as in the Synod at large. The language shift began in the Sunday school and the confirmation classes, and a couple of years later it asserted itself in regard to Sunday services. The report from 1926 states: "It is absolutely necessary for this congregation to use the English language more or less, if it is satisfactorily to take care of the younger generation and those older members who do not at all understand the Swedish language." The transition from Swedish to English took a long time at Chisago Lake Lutheran Church. Reference is made, for example, to services in both languages from 1927 to 1945 The following combination of facts compiled by Nils Hasselmo gives a clear conception of language transition in a single Swedish-American church. The pattern in Chisago is very much the same as for the Augustana Synod at large.

Lutheran and Covenant congregations: An investigation of Lutheran congregations in Illinois indicates that 34 congregations of 49 introduced at least one regular service in English a month during the ten-year period 1917–1926.[12] Of the remaining congregations, six initiated

[12] In 1925 the Illinois Conference consisted of 160 member-congregations. But 47 of these were not in the state of Illinois: thus, there were 113 Augustana congregations in Illinois. The reason why only 49 congregations are recorded is that in most cases it is impossible to find any information as to when English began to be used in the Churches' work. In other words, it is not a sample. This means that the selection in a statistical sense cannot be considered completely representative. In spite of this, certain interesting tendencies can be distinguished. The congregations included here are the most stable and most interesting ones. Those which are omitted are mainly smaller congregations which struggled for their existence. In many cases these are congregations which did not have their own pastor but from time to time had to share pastors with the neighbouring congregations. The language of worship could in these cases change from Sunday to Sunday depending on the language each pastor preferred. In the 49 congregations included here it has been possible to show, on the basis of the minutes of the individual congregations, when the transition was made. In some cases the information has been gleaned from so-called "jubileum-albums." In situations where the Lutheran School of Theology in Chicago has not had information on the Illinois congregations, I have personally by letters gathered the necessary data, questionnaires, or through visits. Only those congregations where the year for the introduction of English is definitely known have been included.

English worship services before 1917 and nine after 1926. Even if one cannot, on the basis of these figures, make any far-reaching conclusions regarding the whole Augustana Synod, they nevertheless clearly show that the transition to English started in earnest after 1917.

In the Mission Covenant congregations in Illinois, 61 percent – or 17 of 28 – introduced at least one regular church service in English per month in the period 1917–1926.[13] From 1929 to 1935 an additional 10 congregations – or 36 percent – initiated English services. These figures show that Americanization began in earnest only after the end of the war.

In 39 Augustana congregations in Illinois it has been possible to ascertain what year alternating or double services were first introduced. Twenty-nine congregations, or 73 percent, initiated one or the other of these practices during the period 1917–1926. As far as the Mission Covenant congregations in Illinois are concerned there is information as to when 21 congregations began alternating or double services. Not until 1925 did three congregations accord both languages equal standing. In 1929 an additional seven followed suit.

After World War I demands increased for the elimination of the nationality designation "Swedish" in names of congregations. Instead of the Swedish Salem Lutheran Church, for instance, the name became Salem Lutheran Church. For 64 of the Augustana Synod congregations in Illinois and in 18 of the Covenant churches it has been possible to determine when the name change was decided. During the years 1915 to 1919 seven Augustana churches dropped the designation of origin; between 1920 and 1929, 27 churches; between 1930 and 1939, 15; in 1940 and later, 15. This means that 53 percent of the congregations had eliminated the word "Swedish" in their names before 1930 and 77 percent before 1940. It also indicates that the churches were not gripped by the war-hysteria and hastened to eradicate any signs of their national origin. Not until 1925 did any Covenant church erase the word Swedish, and not until 1936 did the

[13] With respect to 28 of the 43 Covenant congregations in Illinois, it has been possible to ascertain the year when the first regular worship service in English was held. In the Covenant the same situation prevails as in the Augustana Synod, namely that for most churches it is difficult to obtain exact information about the transition from Swedish to English. The procedure has been the same for both the Covenant and the Augustana Synod. (See the previous footnote.)

Covenant seriously begin to rid itself of the nationality designation. Between 1936 and 1940 "Swedish" disappeared in 56 percent of the congregations.

For a total of 74 of the 113 Augustana congregations in Illinois and in 29 of 43 Covenant congregations it has been possible to determine the time when all regular services were first held in English.[14] As indicated in Diagram 10, half of the Augustana congregations had made a complete transition to English by 1935. In 1939, 76 percent and in 1948 90 percent had completely abandoned the Swedish language. In this connection it may be pertinent to note that 85 percent of the worship services in the Missouri Synod were held in English in 1946.[15] In the Norwegian Lutheran Church 90 percent of the services were held in English in 1942.

The Mission Covenant held more stubbornly to the Swedish language than did the Augustana Synod. As late as 1935, only 17 percent of the congregations had completely transferred to English. Between 1936 and 1940, 52 percent made the transition completely to English.

The constitution and the minutes of each of the Swedish speaking congregations in the Augustana Synod were written in Swedish. When English gained acceptance in the work of the congregations, the need arose for by-laws in English. The various years in which decisions were made to have the by-laws translated is recorded by 57 congregations. Prior to 1920 only four churches in Illinois had their by-laws in English, churches using English since their inception are not included. From 1923 on the number increased rapidly. In the period 1923–1932, 44 congregations – or 77 percent – decided to have their by-laws in English. A survey of 58 congregations where minutes were originally kept in Swedish, shows that 49 decided to change to English in 1923–1930. Out of 20 Covenant congregations surveyed in this connection, four started to keep their minutes in English before 1930 and 15 between 1930 and 1940. The figures cited

[14] These 74 congregations do not include those that from the beginning were entirely English. This applies to the Covenant as well. It also concerns only the so-called regular services. In some churches it can even happen today that a Swedish service is held on special occasions, for instance, the early morning service on Christmas Day (*Julotta*).

[15] See further the specific chapter on the development of German, Norwegian, and Danish churches.

Diagram 9. Number of Augustana and Convenant churches where English and Swedish had an equal standing as the language of religious services --- i.e., the year when alternating or double services were initiated.

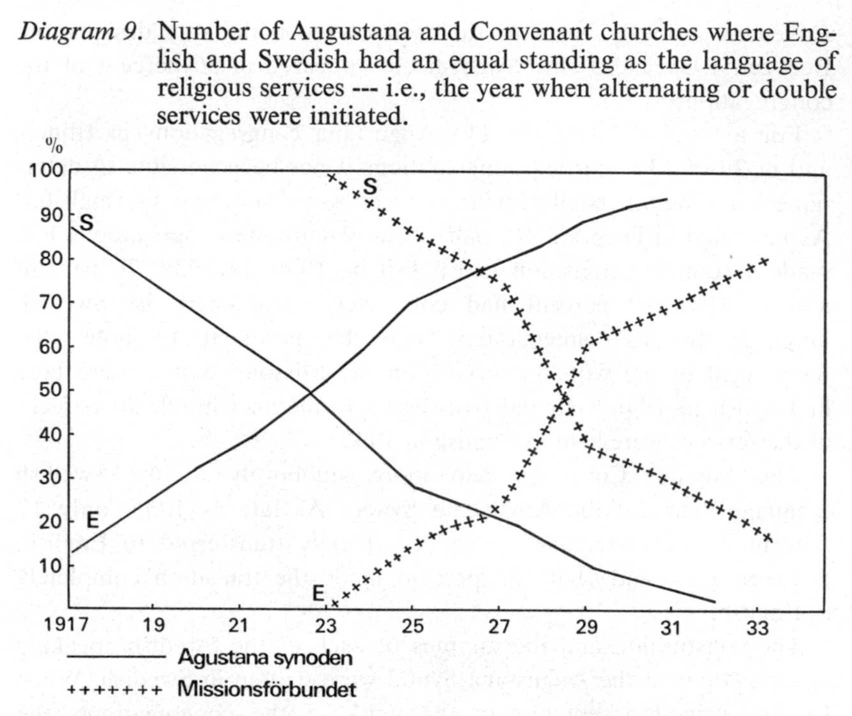

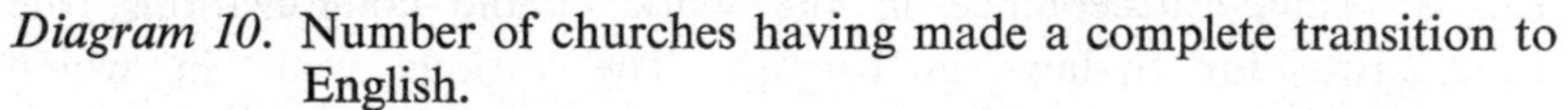

Diagram 10. Number of churches having made a complete transition to English.

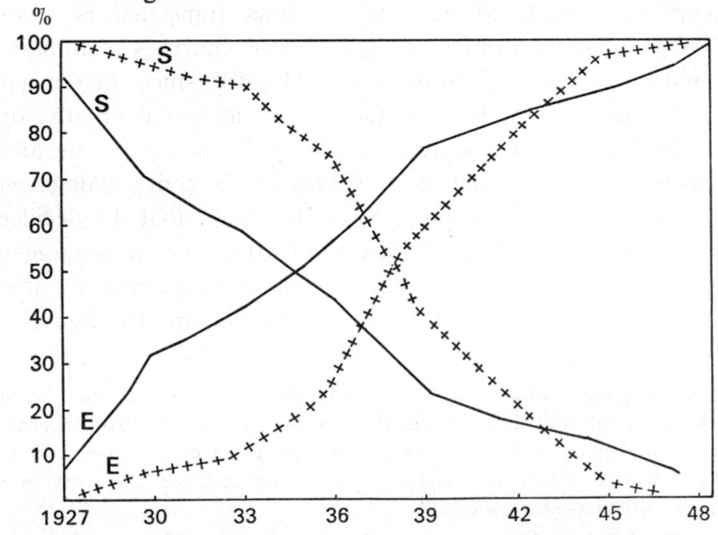

Churches having used English since their inception are not included. In Illinois there were eleven such churches during the time under consideration.

Table 37. Swedish Methodist congregations in the Chicago District using Swedish or English in worship services, 1925.

Language	Morning services	Evening services
Swedish	18	3
English	3	17
Swedish once a month	1	2
English once a month	1	1
Alternating	1	1
Other	2	2

Source: Henry Nylin, "History of Swedish Methodism in Chicago,"p.158.

here show clearly that in all aspects the transition went more rapidly in the Augustana Synod than in the Covenant.

An investigation of the Swedish Methodist congregations in the Chicago District in 1925 shows that no congregation conducted its work exclusively in Swedish. In spite of this, the Swedish language was predominant. Of the 26 congregations in the District, three used English exclusively, but they were not in the city of Chicago.

Swedish dominated in the morning services, English in the evening services. Compared with the situation in the Augustana and Covenant congregations in Illinois, the transition to English among the Methodists proceeded more slowly. There was a larger percentage number of English morning services in both the Augustana Synod and the Covenant than in the Swedish Methodist Church.

Summary. In *Augustana Heritage* Everett Arden says:

> Virtually over night the congregations of the Augustana Synod made the transition from Swedish to English, even though in some parishes neither the pastors nor the people were adequately prepared for the sudden change. In spite of such hardships, it may nevertheless be said that one of the few benefits of the period of 1917–1918 was the powerful impetus which it gave to the quick and relatively easy transition which many nationalistic groups in America, including the Augustana Synod, made to the English language.[16]

16 Everett Arden, *op. cit.*, p. 246 ff.

One may conclude from the reports on the transition to English given by the denominations' minutes and the statistical examples from Illinois congregations that the 1920s were more important than World War I in effecting the course of the language question. Most of the evidence indicates that the War was not as directly responsible for the transition to English as Everett Arden seeks to show.

Arden's comments are delusive, for it was not "a quick and easy" transition. They are also delusive in that they give the reader the conception that the war provided the necessary "push." Nor was the transition as smooth as Arden maintains. He has, among other things, disregarded the recoil effect after the war. When the Swedish Americans as all immigrants no longer feared to display outwardly that they were "hyphenated Americans," a reaction ensued against the coercive measures of federal and state authorities. History records numerous examples of how pressure from without welds a group together and makes it contumacious.

Even though World War I on the whole hardly influenced the transition to English, one must not lose sight of the problems facing the religious denominations, among others those which were caused by the many language restrictions.[17] It is quite probable that "the cruel and indefensible language restriction"[18] – this applied primarily to Iowa – actually aided the difficult transition, which had for a long time been shunted aside. One became accustomed to the thought of an inevitable transition and of accepting the Swedish language as a highly valued treasure, "as a drinking-vessel but not the beverage itself." The war meant that the young had to leave their parents and Swedish connections. "The young man ... was faced for the first time with the strange, frightening, and alluring world of America."[19]

Even though it is impossible to indicate exactly the importance of AEC for the transition to English, it is clear that it helped to prepare the way by softening up the worst opposition. The very fact that there was within the Synod an organization which had as its only purpose the unification of the English congregations and the protection of their interests meant much from a purely psychological standpoint for promoting Americanization. The Synod and its members

17 See separate chapter: "The language question during the War."

18 *Mission Covenant Yearbook,* 1918, p. 22 f.

19 Karl A. Olsson, *op. cit.,* p. 487.

were gradually made aware that sooner or later a transition had to take place.[20] After repeated requests from the AEC, the Synod began printing its minutes in English in 1924. The annual meeting of AEC in 1923 recorded: "We believe it will also be quite generally admitted that every forward step taken by the Synod in the language question has been made as the result of persistent appeals from the Association."[21] Not only the positive influence of AEC on the transition to English is of interest but also the mistrust it engendered. Every step in the Americanization process was accepted only with reluctance.

10. *A Comparison with Some Lutheran Immigrant Churches*

The Danish, Norwegian, and German Lutheran churches had largely the same problem with the transition to English as the Augustana Synod. The older generation resisted it as long as possible, while the younger accelerated it. The pastors held out against it because of their difficulty in preaching in English. Both the Norwegian Lutheran Church and the Missouri Synod had, like Augustana, a separate organization for churches which had transferred entirely to English. For all of the denominations the year 1917 became a turning point – Americanization could no longer be halted. "The NLCA [The Norwegian Lutheran Church of America] was not immune to this pro-American feeling and almost at once some leaders began agitation to eliminate the word 'Norwegian' from the name of the Church."[1] "At this time [the Missouri] Synod found it wise to drop the word 'German' from its name."[2]

At the annual meeting of the Missouri Synod in 1917 the word "German" was erased from its name and thereafter it was called the Evangelical Lutheran Synod of Missouri, Ohio, and Other States.

[20] E. Ryden, "What Has the Association of English Churches Accomplished?" *The Lutheran Companion,* October 15, 1927, p. 1003.

[21] *Minutes of the AEC,* 1923, p. 9.

[1] Clifford Nelson and Eugene Fevold, *The Lutheran Church among Norwegian-Americans. A History of the Evangelical Lutheran Church* (Minneapolis, 1960), Vol. II, p. 248.

[2] Paul T. Dietz, "The Transition from German to English in the Missouri Synod from 1910 to 1947," *Concordia Historical Institute Quarterly* (October, 1949), p. 103.

In a report to the annual meeting of the Danish Synod, Professor P.S. Vig, Dean of Trinity Seminary, proposed that all future graduates of the Seminary would have to have a command of both Danish and English.[3]

For these Synods the language question was a difficult internal problem. According to Eugene Fevold, the whole Americanization problem was focused on the language question.[4] The transition from Norwegian to English was painful, particularly for the older people who were unable to cope psychologically with the process of adjustment. Einar Haugen, like Eugene Fevold, has stressed the difficulties in the wake of the language question.[5] It was a shock for the older members to discover that the "enemy" existed in their own ranks.

During the post-war years the language question was intensively discussed among the Norwegians.[6] In 1918 a special committee was appointed – 533 voted in favor of appointing the committee, 61 against – for the purpose of proposing means by which the younger members might be persuaded from leaving the Synod and of investigating the possibility of eliminating the word "Norwegian" from the name of the church. The result was not what had been anticipated. At the annual meeting in 1920, the pendulum had turned: 377 voted for retaining "Norwegian" and only 296 for a change. Not until 1946 – in spite of repeated attempts – did those who wanted to eliminate the word "Norwegian" get their way.

In the Missouri Synod the transition to English significantly increased after 1918.[7]

The foremost causes for the Americanization of the Synod have been ranked as follows: 1) World War I; 2) The gradual superiority of the third and fourth generations; 3) The rise of new congregations; and 4) The urbanization of the Synod's members. A motion to make English the official language was made at the annual meeting in 1923

[3] Paul C. Nyholm, *The Americanization of the Danish Lutheran Churches in America,* (Copenhagen, 1963), p. 176 ff.

[4] Eugene Fevold, "The Norwegian Immigrant and His Church," *Norwegian-American Studies and Records,* Vol. 23 (Northfield, Minn., 1967), p. 15.

[5] Einar Haugen, *The Norwegian Language in America. A study in Bilingual Behavior* (Philadelphia, 1953), p. 238. The transition from Danish to English caused "many heated controversies," writes Paul Nyholm, *op. cit.,* p. 308.

[6] Clifford Nelson, *op. cit.,* (Vol. II), pp. 249 and 252.

[7] Paul T. Dietz, *op. cit.,* p. 101 ff.

but was defeated on the grounds that time was not yet ripe for such a move. In 1927 it was decided to have the minutes printed in both German and English, but after 1938 they were printed only in English.[8]

In the Norwegian Lutheran Church as well Americanization progressed uninterruptedly during all of the 1920s. By 1928 religious instruction of the young in Norwegian had ceased entirely. The transition in this church, as in the Augustana and the Missouri Synods and the Danish Lutheran Church, followed the same pattern, "with each change fought through by the younger members against a certain opposition from the older ones."[9] From 1928 on the minutes of the Norwegian Lutheran Church were issued in English. The English Association was dissolved in 1935 – four years after its Swedish equivalent had met the same fate. In 1930 practically all Norwegian instruction of theological students was discontinued.[10]

In the case of the Norwegian Lutheran Church, it has been possible to establish a direct connection between its growth and its tendency to accept English.[11] It was found rather difficult to recruit new members in a congregation where more than 50 percent of the services were conducted in Norwegian. "In fact, we may put it even stronger and say that according to the above facts, we drive people away from the Church if we use too much Norwegian."

In the Danish Lutheran churches – the United Church and the Danish Lutheran Church in America – the transition to English proceeded somewhat more slowly than in the other Lutheran churches mentioned here. In the Sunday schools, English became the dominant language of instruction in the United Church about 1921 and in the Danish Lutheran Church in 1929; as for the Sunday services, the respective years are 1934 and 1940.[12]

[8] W. Baepler, *A Century of Grace* (St. Louis, 1947), p. 276. Baepler gives the following summary of the Americanization: "During this period (1922—1947) the transition from German to the English language was practically completed in Synod's congregations, at the meetings of its Districts, and at conventions of the General Body. Since 1917 the proceedings of the Delegate Synods appeared in the English language."

[9] Einar Haugen, *op. cit.*, p. 264 ff.

[10] Clifford Nelson, *op. cit.*, p. 247 f.

[11] Philip S. Dybvig, "Facts About the Language Question," *Lutheran Church Herald* (May 20, 1930), p. 700.

[12] Paul Nyholm, *op .cit.*, pp. 478.

Diagram 11. Number of English, Norwegian and German services in the Missouri Synod and the Norwegian Lutheran Church.

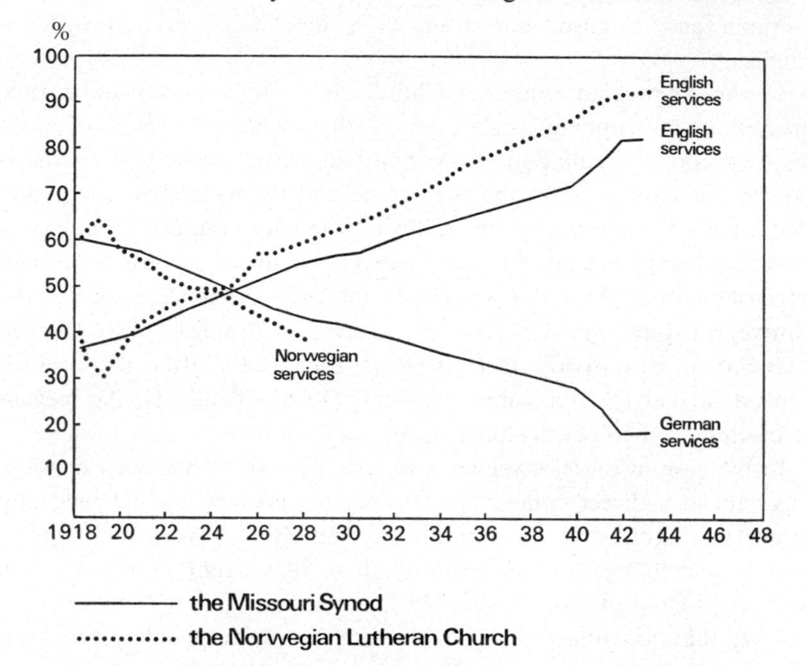

Sources: Paul T. Dietz, "The transition from German to English in the Missouri Synod from 1910 to 1947," p.126.
Clifford Nelson, *The Lutheran Church Among Norwegian-Americans.* Volume II, p.251.

A particularly striking aspect of the transition in the different Lutheran churches is its synchronization. As indicated in Diagram 11, the development in the Missouri Synod and the Norwegian Lutheran Church is largely identical. Unfortunately, it has not been possible to sketch into the same diagram the development in the Augustana Synod, since the figures on the number of English and Swedish services are not at hand. However, on the basis of the diagram one may ascertain a marked similarity of development both as to the trend and the time. In other words, one may quite definitely say that the English language attained an equal footing with Swedish, Norwegian, and German around 1925.

In the Missouri Synod 54 percent of the worship services in 1923 were in German and 46 percent in English. By way of comparison it may be mentioned that in 1919, 62 percent were conducted in German. The year 1925 was the boundary year when the two languages had an equal position. In 1930, 58 percent and in 1946, 85 percent of the services were held in English.[13]

For the Norwegian Lutheran Church the year 1925 was also a demarcation year. For the first time the number of English services surpassed the Norwegian. In 1928, ten percent of the congregations had only Norwegian services, 19 percent were entirely English speaking, and 71 percent were bilingual. Among the Augustana congregations in Illinois, 12 percent had transferred completely to English in 1928. On the average the number of Norwegian services was reduced by 2.3 percent annually after 1918.[14]

11. *Summary*

From the beginning of immigration the Swedish-American denominations were centers of the cultural and social life among the Swedes in the United States. Among the religious denominations the first to be mentioned are the Augustana Synod, the Mission Covenant, the Swedish Methodist and Baptist Conferences. These four denominations were of enormous importance for "Swedishness" and the unity of the Swedish Americans. In the churches the Swedish language was kept alive, which to a great degree was due to their conservatism in religious matters. In other words, they had difficulty in accepting an English service, and when they were obliged to do so they did it reluctantly.

The Augustana Synod, the largest Swedish organization in the United States constituted by far the strongest bulwark for the Swedish language and Swedish culture. More than any other Swedish-American organization the Synod offered abundant opportunities for immigrants to meet countrymen and to speak Swedish. It made no difference whether or not the Synod was looked upon as a daughter-church of the Swedish State Church. The main thing was that it adhered strongly to the idea that it was a "Swedish" immigrant church, that it worked among Swedes and their descendants, and that Swedish was its official

[13] Paul T. Dietz, *op. cit.*, p. 104.

[14] Clifford Nelson, *op .cit.*, (Vol. II), p. 252.

language. George Stephenson underrates its importance when he says it was not an effective promoter of Swedish culture. Even if its task – like that of the other denominations – was not primarily that of nurturing the Swedish cultural heritage, it did indirectly do so to a very high degree.

In spite of the hysteria during and immediately following World War I and in spite of the difficulties unleashed by the Depression, the Swedish-American denominations registered a continuous period of growth between 1915 and 1932. The only exception was the Methodist Church, which reached its top membership figure in 1918. In the main, the work of the churches may be compared with the general national development in the United States during the same period: expansion during the 1920s and far-reaching retrenchments during the Depression years. One may also say that up to the Depression the denominations were characterized by a firm determination to enlarge their fields of activity, while after 1930, their work was mainly devoted to preserving that which had already been accomplished. A common strength of the four largest church bodies was also their national affinity, which helped them to withstand the severe strains following the war and the Depression.

While the churches shared in the material prosperity of the 1920s, they simultaneously wrestled with a difficult internal problem, namely the transition from Swedish to English or, in a word, the Americanization process. Parallel with the reduction in immigration, the demand for the use of English increased, which in turn intensified the debate on the language question.

A premise for the continued existence of the denominations was the preservation of the Swedish language. When there was no longer any real need for Swedish services, the Augustana Synod as well as the Swedish Methodist and Baptist Conferences had difficulty in justifying their existence. This applied to a lesser degree to the Covenant which, because of its particularity, has remained a Swedish-American denomination even after the transition to English.

The Augustana Synod was from the beginning a wholly Swedish church, something which it rigidly maintained through the decades. During the fifty years the Synod belonged to the General Council, it was constantly alert over its integrity and never entered any compromise limiting its freedom of movement. The so-called declaration of independence of 1918 signified in practice that the Synod would not allow itself to be "swallowed up." Characteristic of that decision was its motivation: the Synod still had a mission to perform among the Swedish Americans.

The most intensive phase of the Americanization process came between 1918 and 1930 as a direct result of the cessation of immigration and the increasing influence of the second and third generations. On the other hand, it is difficult to determine the importance World War I had for the Americanization of the Swedish-American religious denominations. Even though it is quite clear that the War and the war hysteria briefly hastened the transition to English, it is not so clear that in the long run it meant very much. Its influence was undoubtedly more indirect in its robbing the most recalcitrant of their notions that a transition was impossible. Satirically speaking one may say the war had taught them that God also understood English. When the war hysteria had subsided, a reaction set in: people spoke of a person's right to use the language he preferred.

After the World War and up to 1930 the English language constantly made new conquests. In most fields of activity the Swedish language had to give way: the number of English services increased; records and minutes began to be written in English; by-laws and regulations were translated into the speech of the land; and "Swedish" was eliminated from the name of churches. Prior to 1921 the leaders of the Augustana Synod worried about the young people; after 1921 the older ones were feeling the pinch. By 1928 the transition had advanced so far that one no longer talked about the immigrants' need of Swedish services but referred instead to the cultural values of the language.

An investigation of Augustana and Mission Covenant congregations in Illinois shows that the transition gained momentum after the war. Opposition to English was stronger in the Covenant than in the Augustana Synod. On the basis of records from Illinois congregations, 69 percent of the Augustana churches and 61 percent of Covenant churches introduced one regular service in English per month, between 1917 and 1926. Augustana was faster than the Covenant in eliminating its national titles: 53 percent of its churches had erased the word "Swedish" before 1930, as compared with 17 percent of the Covenant churches. By 1935 half of Augustana churches in Illinois had completely transferred to English as against 17 percent of the Covenant churches.

The American Association of English Churches may simply be

described as a type of *avant-garde* for the Americanization process. It prepared for the transition by constantly accentuating the Synod's inability to remain a Swedish church in the long run. The English organization was of purely psychological importance in making the transition go smoothly. It gradually softened the worst opposition. It addressed itself as much to non-Swedes as to Swedes in general. As the transition progressed, however, the AEC lost its function, and in 1931 it ceased to exist, although against its own will. It denied the allegation that it had no longer any task to fulfill.

The language question was the great subject of debate after World War I. Opinions clashed against opinions. First generation immigrants were reluctant to think or speak of a transition to English. The denominational papers engaged in vigorous debate. They agreed that discretion and tolerance were required to solve the question without hurting the separate churches. They also concluded that the language best suited for the individual churches ought to be their official language. In this they agreed no matter which side they favored in the language matter.

While *Augustana* was against every form of coercion *The Lutheran Companion* complained that the transition proceeded too slowly. The younger members threatened to transfer to other denominations where they could understand the language. *Augustana* warned against what it called "artificial needs" and called to mind that the main stalwart body of the Synod still consisted of Swedes. The paper also believed that if immigration got under way again the Synod could not avoid its responsibility. *Förbundets Veckotidning* and *The Covenant Companion* argued along the same lines as the Synod's two papers. The former warned that the transition was going too fast, while the latter complained that it did not go fast enough. Americanization followed the same pattern in the Danish, Norwegian, and German synods as in Augustana. The transition occurred gradually.

In conclusion, it may be said that the loyalty and solidarity of the Swedish churches in America and its leaders was not disturbed either by World War I, or by the strains of the Depression. Instead, people gathered around their own churches in order to get them on their feet again and to assist each other. The work of the religious denominations during the Depression demonstrates perhaps better than anything else the strengh of the national affinity. Not until 1962 was the Swedish bastion of the Augustana Synod forced to capitulate. At the final convention in Detroit, June 25–27, the Augustana Lutheran Church ended its existence by merging with the Lutheran Church of America, which also included German, Finnish and Danish Lutherans. At the Detroit convention the Swedish-American Lutherans drew to a close a century-old Swedish tradition.

XII. Activities of the Secular Societies

1. *The Sick Benefit Societies*

The complex of Swedish-American organizations was dominated by the large sick benefit societies, which, along with sick and death benefits, provided for the enjoyment of their members through social gatherings with singing, music, and lectures – all in Swedish. The largest of these organizations were the Vasa Order of America, the Order of Vikings, and the Order of Svithiod. There were also singing societies, folk dance organizations, athletic clubs, and provincial societies. Together they played an important role in strengthening the national ties among Swedish Americans and the cultural ties with Sweden. While striving to preserve Swedish culture, they eased the process of accommodation for the immigrants. The constitution for the District Lodge Illinois, Vasa Order of America, states that the members should, to the best of their ability, "preserve the Swedish language and Swedish culture in general, and assist members in achieving American citizenship."[1]

It was natural that the secular organization should have as a primary goal to provide internal help and benevolence for their members, since the immigrants as a rule lacked the resources to meet emergency situations. Many of the Swedish societies can trace their origin to a temporary act of assistance for some needy countryman.

The profile of the Swedish-American organizations is dominated by the three large benefit societies, all of which show an almost uninterrupted growth up to 1930, when a turning point occurred. The Vasa Order, which serves us here as a model, grew consistently until 1930, when it reached its peak with over 72,000 members distri-

[1] *Statutes for Illinois District Lodge No. 8, Vasa Order of America,* 1937, p. 1.

Table 38. Summary of activities of Vasa Order, Dec. 31, 1914— Dec. 31, 1934 (dollars).

	Dec. 31 1914	Dec. 31 1916	Dec. 31 1918	Dec. 31 1920	Dec. 31 1922	Dec. 31 1925	Dec. 31 1928	Dec. 31 1931	Dec. 31 1934
Members	35 374	41 458	43 166	48 620	55 551	68 027	72 261	68 264	56 910
Paid in sick benefits	174 747	231 671	274 314	265 840	315 952	624 361	811 173	932 330	787 949
Paid in death benefits	34 669	47 550	77 857	65 313	64 565	—	130 032	158 098	186 227
Total assets	270 543	330 740	384 185	493 112	760 354	1 092 924	1 384 196	1 524 617	1 861 014

Source: *Minutes of Proceedings and Actions Approved at Meetings of the Grand Lodge, Vasa Order of America, 1915-1935; Vasa Orden av Amerika, Historik, 1896-1946*, p 17.

buted over 17 districts and 438 local lodges.[2] Since the membership in 1915 was 35,374, it more than doubled during the period from 1915 to 1929. The increase was especially great from 1923 to 1926. One factor contributing to this growth was that English speaking lodges were permitted where situations demanded them.[3] During the Depression the membership was sharply reduced. In January, 1932, the membership had dropped to 68,264, and in December, 1934, to 56,910. Income from membership fees reached its peak in 1929 with $14,462.00 but then dropped steadily to $9,003.00 in 1934.[4]

The restraining influence of the Depression on the Swedish lodges is evident in the minutes of the Vasa Order for the seventeenth meeting of the Grand Lodge in June, 1932:

> The economic conditions which have prevailed during this period have had a detrimental effect on the lodge's growth, numerically as well as financially. Many of our lodges, especially in the Midwest, have suffered heavy losses in both respects. With a large part of the membership deprived of income through unemployment for nearly two years, great losses have occurred as a result of bank closings and losses in funded assets, many of our lodges have been seriously questioned.[5]

In spite of this pessimistic note, the meeting discovered that the situation still gave cause for "a certain measure of satisfaction," since the numerical decline in relation to the serious character of the crisis was hardly cause for wonder.

[2] The Vasa Order was founded in New Haven on September 18, 1896. An excerpt from the Statutes of the Order illustrates its aim and purpose: "By means of income from entrance fees, monthly dues, donations, interest on deposits and other sources, to raise and maintain funds for the disbursement of financial aid to its members, if through illness or other misfortune they should be incapable of working or providing their own livelihood; to raise and maintain funds for disbursement of death benefits to authorized relatives of deceased members in accordance with regulations issued especially for this purpose; to seek to educate its members in moral, intellectual, and social aspects and to increase their esteem as representatives of the Swedish nation," (*Constitution for the Vasa Order of America,* revised edition, 1962).

[3] *Vasa Orden av Amerika. Historik 1896—1946* (Worcester, 1946), p. 11.

[4] *Minutes of proceedings at Meetings of the Grand Lodge,* 1928—1934.

[5] *Minutes of proceedings and actions taken at Vasa Order's Seventeenth Meeting of the Grand Lodge,* June 20—24, 1932, p. 12.

At the next meeting of the Grand Lodge, the difficulties had become even more severe. To a great extent the work of the Order during the period had been restricted "to already existing districts, inasmuch as it seemed almost worthless under present economic conditions to try to break new ground."[6] In order to lighten the financial burdens of the local and district lodges, the executive committee of the Order decided not to levy the customary fees for the fund for aged and for relief during the year 1933. Instead, it was recommended that the respective lodges distribute this amount to those members who, because of unemployment or similar reasons, could not pay the fee themselves.

When the Vasa Order was founded it was understood that it should not only be a sickness and aid association but also a connecting link culturally between the Swedes in Sweden and those who had emigrated to the United States. In its constitution, the Order ruled that in "moral, intellectual, and social aspects" it should "seek to educate its members and to increase their esteem as representatives of the Swedish nation."[7] One of the purposes of the lodge was to do everything in its power to preserve the Swedish language.[8] The Vasa Order was from the beginning entirely a Swedish organization. Only "men and women who belong to the White race, have reached the age of sixteen but have not exceeded 50 years, possess good health and moral character and are able to speak and understand the Swedish language or are the offspring of Swedish parents" could become members.[9]

Since the beginning of the Twenties the Vasa Order attempted to stimulate the younger generation's interest in the ancestral country, its history, its culture, and its language. The constitution contained the following directive: "The Order shall by instituting organizations for children and young people interest the younger generation in the purpose and work of our Order."[10] The first children's club was formed in New York in 1921.

[6] *Ibid.*, June 25—29, 1935, pp. 10 ff.

[7] *Constitution for Vasa Order of America.*

[8] *Vasa Orden av Amerika, Historik*, p. 20.

[9] *Minutes of the Fourteenth Meeting of the Grand Lodge*, 1923.

[10] *Vasaorden i Amerika under 30 år*, p. 166; *Vasa Orden av Amerika, Historik*, pp. 11, 26.

The language question was first discussed at the meeting of the Grand Lodge in 1917, when a proposal was made that the English language be used at the installation of new members who did not know Swedish. The proposal was defeated. On the other hand, the meeting adopted another proposal for the translation of the ritual into English.[11] Language problems for the Vasa Order as for the religious denominations, arose with World War I. The Minnesota District describes the year 1918 as unfavorable in all aspects, since "we all know what the War did for those who did not use the English language at their meetings."[12]

The language question was actualized seriously in the Twenties. According to a decision at a meeting of the Grand Lodge at the beginning of the decade, certain lodges could request permission to use the English language where conditions required it. At the meeting of the Grand Lodge in 1923 this privilege was extended so that consent to use English at lodge meetings was granted by the respective district lodge and not by the Grand Lodge as formerly. The district lodge was even given the right to determine for itself which language would be used at its own meetings.

Despite this liberalization on the language question, the transition was slow. Between 1926–29 only "a dozen lodges" were organized with English as the official language.[13] These lodges were said to be comprised chiefly of young people who undoubtedly, if consent had not been given for organizing them, would have taken a passive attitude to the work of the Order, if in fact they would have participated at all. Judging from the minutes, the District was reluctant to give consent for the use of English. When the Danville, Illinois Lodge requested in 1941 to change to English, the district lodge decided to give the local lodge six months in which to experiment with English. If fifteen new active members were not received during that period or if "some other shake-up could not be demonstrated, the lodge must return to Swedish."[14] When Thor Lodge petitioned to introduce English, the district lodge said that the time was not yet ripe to reject the Swedish

[11] *Vasa Orden av Amerika, Historik,* p. 10 f; *Minutes of the Grand Lodge Meetings,* 1917 and 1929.

[12] *Historik över distriktslogen Minnesota, 1908—1935,* p. 16.

[13] *Minutes of the Grand Lodge Meeting,* 1929.

[14] *Minutes of Illinois District Lodge No. 8,* 1941, pp. 6, 17.

language, inasmuch as Thor Lodge was "one of the oldest and best lodges in the district."

Even in 1946 only about twenty-five percent (25 percent) of the lodges were officially English speaking.[15] The Grand Master stated at the twenty-first meeting of the Grand Lodge in 1946 that he found it gratifying that the lodge meetings always opened and closed in Swedish, "by which means the meeting's Swedish character was emphasized."[16] He was convinced that the Swedish language was being used more in 1946 than before. As evidence of the strong hold that the Swedish language had on the order, it can be pointed out that the same meeting defeated a proposal to use English in the business sessions of the Grand Lodge.

In Connecticut, seventy-six percent (76 percent) of the lodges had officially changed to English by 1946 – a higher percentage than in any of the other larger districts.[17] In Massachusetts approximately one-fourth of the lodges were English speaking. According to the history of the Illinois District Lodge, the first English lodge was formed in 1926.[18] The second English lodge in Illinois was formed in 1927. By 1946 approximately 25 percent of the local lodges in the same district used English.[19] The Illinois District Lodge also decided in 1937 to print the constitution in both Swedish and English. In 1938 for the first time the District Master greeted those in attendance at the annual meeting in English. In 1939 it was decided to stimulate the formation of English lodges.

The transition to English followed the same pattern as in the religious denominations, namely that the older generation opposed every form of transition while the younger generation demanded a quick change.[20] Long and divisive debates occurred in the local lodges as a result of the language question. Scandia Lodge relates in 1946 that the question of the transition to English was discussed several times, but each time the proposal was made it was defeated in respect for

15 *Vasa Orden av Amerika, Historik,* p. 11.

16 *Minutes of Grand Lodge Meeting,* 1946, pp. 20, 57.

17 *Vasa Orden av Amerika, Historik,* pp. 45—75.

18 District Lodge Illinois No. 8, *Historical Review, 1908—43* (Chicago, 1943), pp. 233 and 235.

19 *Ibid.,* The statistics are based on the number of lodges which had written their histories in English rather than Swedish.

20 *Vasa Orden av Amerika, Historik,* p. 22.

"the language of honor and heroes."[1] Tuna Lodge reported triumphantly in the same year that the Swedish language still sounded "noble and proud." Lodges explained that they had always "worked in behalf of Swedish culture and had always attempted to cultivate our Swedish traditions." A recurring problem for the local lodges was the mobility of the population. Forward Lodge *(Logen Framåt)* in Illinois was forced to move around 1920 when the population began "to change skin color."[2] Bernadotte Lodge also complained that its area was "populated by Bohemians, Jews, and other elements that are not appropriate for a respectable Vasa Lodge."

With time, Vasa Order has become more and more a gathering place where people meet to observe some Swedish festivity or special event. At Vasa Order's Grand Lodge in 1938 it was decided to broaden the cultural activities within the Order along the following lines:

1. Encourage and foster instruction in the Swedish language.
2. Institute a systematic study of Swedish literature, et al.
3. Observe special festive days.
4. Arrange exhibits or lectures.[3]

In spite of this ambitious program, Vasa Order has met the same fate as other Swedish-American organizations, namely a languishing existence.

The development within the two other Swedish sick and death benefit societies, the Order of Vikings and the Order of Svithiod, followed that for the Vasa Order: expansion up to 1930.[4] One of the record years for the Order of Vikings was 1928, when no less than 2,100 new members were received.[5] During 1929 it achieved a "magnificent" result of 2,658 new members, but during 1930 the membership was reduced. After 1929, even the reports for the Order of Svithiod were pessimistic. Between 1929 and 1933 the membership was reduced by twenty percent – from 15,807 to 12,750. In comparison with the religious denominations, whose membership consistently

[1] District Lodge Illinois No. 8, *Historical Review*, pp. 91, 269.

[2] *Ibid.*, pp. 86, 136.

[3] *Minutes* of Swedish American Conference arranged by Augustana Institute of Swedish Culture, November 15, 1941, p. 15.

[4] The Order of Vikings was founded 1892 and the Order of Svithiod 1880.

[5] *Vikingen*, Golden Jubilee number, 1890—1949, p. 32; *Svithiod Journal*, September, 1929.

increased during the period in question, it should be noted that in all three of the above named orders the development was the opposite: the membership decreased after 1929. It is difficult to find a tenable explanation for this fact. Factors which conceivably could have had some effect are partly that the difficulties in connection with the Depression increased the need of belonging to a religious group, and partly that the orders required established fees while contributions to the churches were voluntary.

The economic Depression struck the Orders of Vikings and of Svithiod equally as hard as it did the Vasa Order. *Vikingen,* the newspaper of the Viking Order, noted as early as February, 1930, "that the benefit societies – at least this is true in the Order of Vikings – have a feeling that it is not as prosperous on the job market, because there are many members who cannot pay their dues."[6] Of all the Svithiod's local lodges, the Chicago branches felt more seriously the effects of the Depression. The largest lodge in Chicago, Verdandi, reported serious trouble as early as the first half of 1930. "The first six months of the current year have in many respects been a time of trial for Verdandi. Many of our members have been without work for a long time, some as much as a year. As a result of the prevailing unemployment, many of our members have been unable to pay their dues."[7] Neither of the two orders has recovered from the Depression. Both still exist but they have lost their importance as meeting places for Swedish immigrants.

Not only were the Swedish benefit societies affected by the Depression but to a similar extent other voluntary organizations. The Swedish Engineers' Society talked about "hard times and years of hunger." "We are certainly undergoing hard times in America; we Swedes, not least we Swedish Engineers, have felt it perhaps more than other nationalities."[8] The year 1932 was especially difficult for the organization and it was summed up in the following manner: "We read in our history books about times of want and hunger and how the oldtimers mixed tree bark into their bread. For them it was a reasonable substitute, but where is a poor fellow in an urban asphalt jungle going to find any bark."[9]

[6] *Vikingen,* February, 1930, p. 4.
[7] *Svithiod Journal,* July, 1930, p. 3.
[8] *Trasdockan,* 1931, p. 1.
[9] *Ibid.,* 1932, p. 6.

Among the organizations which completely collapsed was the Cooperative Temperance Café Idrott in Chicago, which was founded in 1913 with the idea of "being a place where Swedish youth can gather for more refined and better leisure-time activities than can be provided by the saloons and the pool halls."[10] As long as there was a great deal of interest, Idrott expanded its activities by buying up new buildings.[11]

The expansion continued until the Depression intervened. "The Depression years swept away Café Idrott as they did many of the businesses on Belmont and elsewhere."[12]

The Café sponsored a comprehensive lecture program and offered its members access to a large library and reading room. It was emphasized that the Café not only offered physical food but even spiritual. In 1932 the Café appealed to all Swedish societies, especially those whose goal was the promotion of Swedish culture, to support as much as possible "this voluntary and, for us Swedes, honorable undertaking."[13]

At the annual meeting in December, 1916, Café Idrott decided to start a loan library, "which in the future should pay its own way and from the standpoint of education supplement our whole undertaking as a milestone of Swedish culture in America."[14] In 1927 Café Idrott declared in its annual report that the library had developed into a "unique cultural project."[15] The library activies were said to qualify the Café as one of the true sponsors and conservers of Swedish culture. At the annual meeting in 1930 provision was made for a salaried librarian.[16] But the Depression was setting in and it was the beginning of the end for Café Idrott.

10 Café Idrott, *Årsrevy,* 1918.

11 *Ibid.,* 1925.

12 Henry Bengston, "Chicago's Belmont and Clark," *The Swedish Pioneer Historical Quarterly* (October, 1962), p. 159.

13 *Svenska Tribunen Nyheter,* March 16, 1932, p. 13.

14 Café Idrott, *Årsrevy,* 1916.

15 *Ibid.,* 1927, p. 17.

16 *Ibid.,* 1930, p. 10.

2. *Organizations for Preserving Swedish Culture*

It was characteristic that the religious denominations and the secular lodges should be founded for the purpose of ministering to the religious intesrests of the Swedish immigrants and assisting them in times of need, while also indirectly becoming national centers and important carriers of Swedish culture. In addition to these organizations there was a long list of societies which arose only for the purpose of preserving "Swedishness" and watching over Swedish culture in the United States. As a rule, these societies appeared rather late, which can partly be explained by the fact that they more or less took over from the religious groups and the lodges. When the churches no longer functioned as Swedish centers, special organizations were started which functioned as connecting links between the old country and the adopted land. The leadership in these societies consisted often of the same persons who, in the churches and the lodges, persisted to the end for the preservation of the Swedish language. There are primarily two categories of societies that are of importance here, namely the so-called provincial societies or local historical societies which were formed locally, and the Swedish Cultural Society in America *(Svenska Kulturförbundet)*, whose parent organization was The Swedish Society for the Preservation of Swedish Culture Abroad and which had many branches in the United States.

The Swedish provincial societies *(hembygdsföreningar)* had only one interest: Swedish culture. They arose relatively late. Most of them were founded in the 1920s, a period when they "sprang up like mushrooms."[17] The occasion would often be a temporary one: for example, a collection of funds for some cultural purpose in the local community in Sweden. These societies would represent a certain town or provinces. In Chicago there was even an organization, "Norrlänningarna" (The Norrland Association), representing the northern provinces of Sweden.

New local societies arose even during the 1930s. In 1938 A.G. Witting wrote: "We have an ever increasing number of provincial societies . . . founded on the idea of localized Swedishness, nurtured by childhood memories and a love for the ancestral soil."[18] In Chicago

[17] Einar Andersson, "Våra hembygdsföreningar," *Svenska kulturförbundets minnesskrift* (Chicago, 1938), pp. 42 ff.

[18] A.G. Witting, "En allmän svenskamerikansk samling," *Svenska kulturförbundets minnesskrift*, p. 53.

at the close of the 1930s there were approximately 25 local societies representing all of the provinces with the exception of Uppland. These societies are still found in most of the larger Swedish centers. As a rule they have had strong support from the Swedish-American press, and several of the newspapermen have been among the leaders within this movement.[19] By comparison with the large Swedish organizations, the local societies, if considered singly, have been of little consequence, but taken together they comprise a considerable strength in behalf of Swedish culture.

In 1929 "Svensk-Amerikanska Hembygdsförbundet" (The Council of Swedish-American Local Societies) was formed in Chicago to serve as a mediating link for the separate societies. Its constitution reads:[1]

> In order to commemorate and to preserve for coming generations the rich Swedish memories, which are so closely and inseparably connected with American development, it is extremely important to nurture and maintain among the American people of Swedish origin a lively interest in the great deeds of our ancestors and a natural and rightful pride in our stock and its peculiar qualities.
>
> This lofty goal can be achieved only by bringing all Swedes and descendants of Swedes in America into a unitary organization, which, free of all political, religious, and social interests, can work only in the above direction and contribute to preserving for the nation the best and most desirable in Swedish culture.

The local societies have first of all attempted to keep watch over Swedish customs and traditions. They have taken the initiative in planning Midsummer and Lucia festivals. They have also devoted themselves to cultural activities in general. They have kept in touch with their own local communities in Sweden. By coming into the picture relatively late their task has been more to preserve than to originate. They have reminded the second and third generations about Swedish culture and its importance. Many of these local societies can still be found, but in general they lead a languishing existence in which the activities are limited to observance of special days and

[19] Raine, "Svenska hembygdsföreningar i Amerika," *Julbrasan,* 1943, p. 46.

[1] *Constitution of Svensk-Amerikanska Hembygdsförbundet,* adopted 1929.

social events in connection with visits from Sweden, and then, for the most part, from their own local communities.[2]

The Swedish Cultural Society of America, an offspring of the Swedish Society for the Preservation of Swedish Culture Abroad, has played a predominant role in the debate on Swedish culture. The Society was founded in 1910 in connection with the fiftieth anniversary of Augustana College. The Reverend Per Pehrson came to the United States on an official visit to form a branch of the parent Society.[3] Its purpose would be to provide an organization for the Swedish element in America to maintain Swedish ties with regard to customs, memories, and language.[4] The first paragraph of the Society's constitution states the objectives:[5]

> . . . in close connection with the Swedish Society for the Preservation of Swedish Culture Abroad and in all possible ways to support and to pursue the task of preserving the Swedish language and Swedish culture among Swedes and Swedish descendants in America, especially through co-operation with the Swedish-American press as well as with Swedish organizations, church denominations, benefit societies, and singing societies.

[2] For those interested in the various local historical societies and their activities, a good summary is *Hembygden. Historik av Chicagos svenska hembygdsföreningar* (Chicago, 1933).

[3] Per Pehrson, D.D. (Augustana College), Member of Parliament 1906—08 and 1921—36. He was the general secretary of the central committee of the all-Swedish association of parish priests *(Allmänna Svenska Prästföreningen)* 1927—42. He was also active in the Swedish Society for the Preservation of Swedish Culture Abroad and in the National Society Against Emigration.

In a brochure sent out in 1911 by Editor Anders Schön, the American Society's first secretary, it is stated: "At the fiftieth anniversary of Augustana Synod and Augustana College in Rock Island, Illinois in June of last year (1910), on the initiative of the Reverend Per Pehrson of Gothenburg a priest of the Church of Sweden on a visit to our country, the Society for the Preservation of Swedish Culture in America was formed with the intent that it not be a subordinate part of, but a sister-organization to, the Swedish Society for the Preservation of Swedish Culture Abroad, which has existed in Sweden for several years. Almost 100 persons joined the Society, a constitution was adopted, and a board of twelve members was elected." *Svenska kulturförbundets minnesskrift,* 1938, p. 11.

[4] *Svenska kulturförbundets kvartalsskrift,* Vol. I, No. 1—2, June, 1946, p. 1.

[5] *Constitution of Swedish Cultural Society in America in force 1924—1927.*

The Society had a period of expansion up to the time of World War I, which more or less put an end to its activities.[6] To declare publicly that one was working for the preservation of Swedish culture was, during the war years, hardly the proper note. "The events of 1914 . . . wrecked almost all plans in behalf of Swedish culture and led to the worst humiliation we have ever experienced."[7] At the outset the Society's members entertained bold plans. The officers assumed leadership for a fund-raising effort whose goal was "at least" $10,000, the earnings of which should be used to provide scholarships for students who demonstrated competence in the Swedish language and Swedish literature at any one of the Swedish-American colleges or secondary schools.

The work resumed after the War but without any significant growth. At the meeting in Minneapolis in 1918 "the spirit of timidity prevailed" and the few members who attended decided to wait for better times.[8] At the 1923 annual meeting the Society's working regulations were restructured so that their annual meeting in 1924 did not meet simultaneously with the annual conference of the Augustana Synod. A constitution was adopted for the first time, and this meant a more stable organization in that the local branches fell under a common governing board. The name was changed from "The Society for the Preservation of Swedish Culture in America" to "The Swedish Cultural Society in America." Local branches were located, among other places, in Minneapolis, Detroit, Lindsborg (Kansas), and Kenilworth (New Jersey).[9] The Chicago branch, organized in 1923, was given the responsibility of serving as an executive committee for the purpose of managing general matters. Under the new designation, the Society continued, as before, to distribute Swedish literature and

[6] N.G. Swan, "Svenskhetens bevarande," *Augustana,* December 22, 1921, pp. 818 ff.

[7] *Svenska kulturförbundets minnesskrift,* p. 12.

[8] *Ibid.,* p. 13.

[9] G.N. Swan, *op. cit.,* pp. 818 f. The local branches named herein are only a few. Branches were later formed also in Boston, Worcester, Milwaukee, Seattle, St. Louis, Jamestown, and elsewhere.

Among the more active branches was the Northwestern branch with headquarters in Minneapolis. In a circular dated July, 1922, in Minneapolis, Swedes who considered Swedish culture "worthy of being preserved" were invited to become members. The Constitution for the Northwestern branch gives a detailed statement of the Society's purpose.

arrange lectures on subjects with Swedish emphasis. In *Svenska Tribunen Nyheter,* April 11, 1923, "every upright Swede, man or woman," was urged to become a member and support the Society's work for the preservation of "the Swedish language, our glorious Swedish song, our lofty Swedish ideals, and our proud Swedish memories."

The Depression had a detrimental effect on the Society and its activities. A turning point came with the "Allsvenska tinget" (The All-Swedish Council) in 1933 in connection with the Chicago World's Fair. A large number of delegates from Sweden, among whom was Folke Bernadotte, attended the Council. The Council was thought to have strengthened considerably the sense of solidarity between the members of the Cultural Society and friends in the old country and "to have given to our movement an image it did not have previously."[10] In spite of this temporary stimulus, the Society was not successful in making any permanent contribution to the preservation of either the Swedish language or Swedish culture in America. As the first-generation Swedes thinned out, the interest in Sweden and Swedish culture declined. Because of this and also because of the great distances between the various branches, the Society had severe difficulties in holding the organization together.

During World War II the Swedish Cultural Society's activities became dormant, as the War almost paralyzed all voluntary efforts. When the Society took on new life after the War, it began looking for new directions. Among other things it started a quarterly, *Svenska kulturförbundets kvartalsskrift* (Swedish Cultural Society Quarterly).[11] The first number appeared in June, 1946. The quarterly was intended to be a connecting link between the widely separated local branches.

Simultaneous with the end of immigration and the thinning out of the first generation, the Society lost its importance. At the meeting of March 26, 1949, the language question was discussed. Among other things the objection was raised that the use of Swedish as the official language had limited recruiting "to a certain category," which had a lesser impact as long as there was access to a large source for recruitment."[12] This situation, meanwhile, is being altered, inasmuch as the number of Swedish speaking people in the United States is being greatly decimated every year." The meeting therefore went on

[10] *Svenska kulturförbundets minnesskrift,* p. 19.

[11] *Svenska kulturförbundets kvartalsskrift,* June, 1946, p. 1.

[12] *Svenska kulturförbundets kvartalsskrift,* editorial, Spring, 1949.

record as favoring provision for English alongside of Swedish. It was further declared that the quarterly should, in the future, even include articles in English. Today the Society leads a languishing existence. Its gatherings are now limited to the celebration of Gustaf II Adolf's Day on November 6. The Society continues to publish *Kulturarvet* (Cultural Heritage) once a year.

Even if the development within the Swedish Cultural Society after 1932 does not fall within the time period established for this study, it would be of interest to follow the Society a few decades longer when the development of the Society illustrates very well the general situation among Swedish Americans. Symptomatic for the Society's activities during the 1930s and after is the fact that the attempt to maintain Swedish culture has become more and more strained. The interest has successively been narrowed down to a small group of well established Swedish Americans. The three major attempts to stimulate interest in Swedish culture – the Swedish American Day at the Chicago World's Fair in 1933, the 300th anniversary in 1938 of the first Swedish immigration, and the pioneer centennial in 1948 – hardly affected the broader strata of Swedish descendants.

Even if the ranks of Swedish Americans thinned out over the years and the interest for the Swedish language diminished among the general Swedish-American public, it is interesting to take note of all the annual events which continue to be held in the so-called "Swedish Centers" with the purpose of commemorating the Swedish cultural heritage.[13]

3. *Summary*

The Swedish-American organizations have exercised a strong attraction for Swedes long after immigration ceased. Their interest for them and their attempt to keep them Swedish as long as possible indicate that there was need for contact with Sweden. Even if the sick benefit societies, like the religious denominations, primarily had other objectives than preserving Swedish culture and maintaining contact with the old

[13] "Swedish-Day" is still celebrated both in Chicago and Minneapolis. In Chisago Swedes celebrate "Karl Oskars-Day." One can also mention the many activities of the Swedish Pioneer Historical Society and the Lucia-celebration which is held wherever one can find a Swedish organization.

country, they have nevertheless provided strong foot holds for Swedish culture. The history of all Swedish-American organizations shows that the accommodation of the first-generation's immigrants was never total. Even those members who accommodated themselves socially and economically in order to do a job and to mix with their fellow workers when the day's work was done, sought out their own countrymen by identifying with a Swedish congregation or some other organization.

A prevading ambition for the secular organizations was to keep watch over everything Swedish. Even if it can appear unimportant whether a sick benefit or death benefit society uses Swedish or English, it was not so for the individual members. For them it was a matter of profound urgency. The proceedings of the various organizations clearly show that the Swedish language had deep roots and that there was much to-do before the transition to English was accepted. A common perception within the Swedish-American organizations was that they felt an obligation to guard Swedish culture not only against their own kind but even against the United States. They also worked intensively to impress the American consciousness with the contributions that the Swedish nationality had made in the United States.

In contrast to the religious denominations, the language question did not become a major bone of contention within the non-religious organizations. It was first during the Depression that they confronted almost overwhelming difficulties. The decline which began at that time was halted. For the religious groups the message was primary and the language only a medium. When the transition to English became necessary, they accepted it. The situation with the non-religious groups was almost the opposite. As the interest in, for example, the sick benefit socities declined, they saw their main task as revitalizing Swedish culture and becoming centers for Swedish immigrants.

The importance of the organizations with respect to accommodation is difficult to measure. Even if they did not strive directly to enfold the immigrants in the new community, the mingling with Swedish men and women, all of whom were in the same situation, must have meant a great deal. At the meetings of these organizations they could discuss their problems and perhaps get advice. Psychologically it was supportive just to belong to an organization where one could meet his countrymen, speak his native language and celebrate the holidays and holy days which otherwise were not observed in the adopted land.

It is likewise difficult to determine the importance of the organizations whose only object was to preserve Swedish culture and maintain Swedish traditions, since neither the Swedish Cultural Society nor the local historical societies were successful in taking deep root in the lives of Swedish Americans.

XIII. Conclusion

The aim of this investigation has been to illustrate the mutual cohesiveness of the Swedish Americans and the factors which tended to preserve Swedish ideals – the Swedish institutions, the Swedish language, and whatever was characteristically "Swedish" in general. In short, interest has been concentrated around what one may call "maintenance phenomena." Since the Americanization process, on the other hand, is directly connected with the immigrants' tendency either to abandon or preserve that which is Swedish and their own identity, it has naturally been difficult to speak only of those elements which tended to preserve Swedish characteristics.

The efforts of the Swedish Americans to preserve their national characteristics have only had passing attention in scholarly connections. The earlier Swedish historical research has, in the first place, interested itself in the background of the emigration and in the Americanization of the immigrants and less in their efforts to preserve the Swedish heritage. These historians have rarely recorded what happened to the approximately one and a third million Swedes who sought their livelihood in America.[1] This applies likewise to the historians who have studied other nationalities as well as immigration as a whole, for they have, as Joshua Fishman and Rudolph Vecoli point out, been most interested in "disappearance phenomena" and less in "maintenance phenomena."

The period we are considering stretches from 1914 up to and including 1932. It concerns a period when immigration from Sweden was more or less a closed chapter. The investigation has been on two

[1] A series of projects for the study of the Swedish immigrants in America continues at the Historical Institute at Uppsala University. Ulf Beijbom has studied the history of the Swedes in Chicago; Hans Norman, the Swedes in Wisconsin; and Kerstin Hallert, the settlers in Chisago in Minnesota. Lars Ljungmark, in the spring of 1971, presented his graduate disseration in Gothenburg, entitled *For Sale — Minnesota; Organized Promotion of Scandinavian Immigration, 1866—1873* (Göteborg and Chicago, 1971).

planes, partly on the national scale, partly on a regional basis, the latter concerned mainly with Illinois and Minnesota. The reason for the geographic restriction is that in order to make specific investigations I have found it most suitable to choose two so-called "Swedish states." Most of the Swedish language papers were published in either Illinois or Minnesota. The headquarters of the various religious denominations and secular associations were located there and so were the different archives. Furthermore, because of the long distances involved in travelling, it was necessary for practical reasons to limit the geographic spread.

One difficulty is that the source material does not cover the entire Swedish-American community but only that part which in some way has identified itself with "Swedish America." In this connection, "Swedish America" means collectively the Swedish language press, the churches and societies established in America by Swedish immigrants, and the people who belonged to any or several of these institutions or in some way actively sustained the Swedish nationality in America. The large number of Swedes who have disappeared in the melting-pot have left only faint traces behind, and these are almost impossible to analyze or evaluate.

It has not been possible to ascertain exactly how many Swedish immigrants entered "Swedish America." Yet the number of members in the Swedish-American churches and in various associations, and the number of subscribers to Swedish language papers can give a certain indication of the numerical extent of "Swedish America." The usual estimate is that about 25 percent, or 400,000, mainly first-and-second generation Swedes, belonged to one or another of the Swedish denominations. Moreover, the Swedish language newspapers had a circulation of approximately 650,000 (in 1915). At its peak, the Fraternal Order of Vasa had somewhat over 70,000 members.

The final conclusions of the dissertation are based partly on various opinions set forth in the Swedish language press and in the recorded minutes and publications of the denominations and societies and partly on an attempt to enumerate factors which in one way or another influenced Americanization. The transition from Swedish to English in the religious denominations may, for instance, be determined quite exactly through a comparison between the number of Swedish and English worship services. There are also records of decisions on the various phases of the transition in denominational protocols. Even though worship services were the last to be changed, one must remember that the choice of language in worship to a particularly high degree concerned the individual members of the congregations, and thus it reflected not only the leaders' view of the transition to English but also that of the majority of the individual members. Many difficulties have been encountered in measuring Americanization because official statistics are faulty and personal information on immigrants sparse. There is no official record of intermarriages, of trades and occupations, of immigrants' income, etc. This means that the research relies for the most part on Swedish-American sources.

This investigation may reveal – even if it chiefly concerns those Swedes who made up "Swedish America" – that the idea that the Swedes were easily assimilated and quickly Americanized may be open to question. The idea that the Swedish Americans were easily adaptable to American society has prevailed for a long time. Both Swedish and American historical literature have characterized them as easily assimilated. Instead of cutting the bonds that tied them to Sweden, they were anxious to preserve not only the Swedish institutions but also the Swedish language and Swedish manners and traditions. Immigration aroused a feeling of nationalism that undoubtedly was alien to the immigrants prior to immigration. Mutual cohesion and solidarity was strong. The Swedish immigrants were eager to keep their identity and compensated for their estrangement in America by clinging fast to their own country's history and culture. The feeling of national identity was symbolized first of all by the Swedish language which constituted a stable factor in their existence and a psychological strength for those who in any way associated themselves with "Swedish America." Instead of exhorting their countrymen to become quickly Americanized and rid themselves of the heritage from Sweden, the Swedish organizations worked for the preservation of "Swedishness" and for their own existence. The national cohesion naturally became a check on Americanization which implied wide contacts with people outside of the homogeneous group. The Swedish-American press was, however, an exception, inasmuch as it not only helped to preserve the Swedish-American identity but also promoted the Americanization process by providing its Swedish speaking readers with information on America.

The Swedish Americans have been said to have become more rapidly naturalized than most other nationalities in America. They had one of the highest shares of naturalized immigrants in 1910, 1920 and 1930. This may be explained by the fact that they were early arrivals in America. If the time of arrival is taken into consideration, there is nothing that would substantiate the idea that Swedes became naturalized more rapidly than other immigrants.

Intermarriage, which like naturalization is thought of as a measure of the progress of Americanization, was unusual among the Swedes. Records of intermarriage indicate that it became more common the longer a nationality had been in America. It occurred more often among the second generation than among the first-generation immigrants. When intermarriage occurred among the Swedes, the opposite party was most often from Norway, Denmark, Germany or Finland. They married almost exclusively with immigrants from Protestant countries, which indicates that religious obstacles were more difficult to overcome than national. It was, for instance, unusual that a Protestant married a Catholic. As a rule, Protestants married Protestants, Catholics married Catholics, Jews married Jews. This gave rise to the talk about "the triple-melting-pot." There are also factors which indicate that in-marriage was more common in places where the same nationality predominated. The consistently low frequency of intermarriage shows that the Swedes kept together and that group consciousness was strong. It should be pointed out that this term, "the triple-melting-pot," did not include all American minority groups of people – for example, Negroes, Mexicans, Chinese, and others – who have generally been excluded from all three melting pots. It can also be maintained that the Swedish Americans wound up in that particular melting pot (Protestant) which was most easily identified with typically "American society." This may explain why Swedish Americans were considered to be more easily adaptable to the Americanization process than, for example, Italians and other South Europeans.

Group coherence was strong during World War I and during the economic Depression in the first part of the 1930s. On both occasions attention was directed toward the immigrants. Even in connection with the enactment of the quota laws the Swedes kept watch on their own national quotas and interests. Circumstances connected with the war, the Depression, and the enactment of quota laws show that every threat to the immigrants and that which they conceived as their rights according to the American constitution welded them together.

The war revealed that America had a heterogeneous population in which the bonds with the old world were still strong. The discovery that certain immigrants showed loyalty to the land of their origin incensed many Americans. The war enhanced the demand for Americanization all over America. In certain states the immigrants were forbidden among other things to conduct church services and provide instruction in their own native languages.

At the beginning of the war several of the Swedish-American papers openly showed their sympathy for Germany, thus giving the Swedish Americans the reputation of being pro-German. When the papers discussed the war they often referred to Sweden and its attitude toward the belligerents. The Swedish-American press was unanimous in insisting that America ought to remain neutral. It thought that the neutral policy of Sweden could well serve as an example because it was more honorable than the American. When war became a reality even for America, the Swedish Americans avowed their loyalty to the country and offered their full support. They tried with all available means to show that any suspicion that they lacked loyalty was groundless. In those parts of the United States where larger concentrations of Swedes lived loyalty demonstrations were arranged. The accusations against the Swedish Americans of lacking loyalty were as a rule poorly conceived and exaggerated. Scarcely any examples of disloyal actions exist.

The pressure imposed on the immigrants and the intolerance of any dissenting opinions make it impossible, however, to determine to what extent the assertions of loyalty made by Swedes were genuine or merely expressions of fear of reprisals. In light of the pressure under which the foreign language papers worked, it is impossible, when relying on them as the main source material, to determine the real attitude of the Swedish Americans toward the war. Those papers that desired to criticize the American war policy could not do so, for their papers would have been confiscated. For this reason the Swedish-American papers did not risk publishing articles or editorials on the war which could jeopardize the papers' existence.

It was characteristic of the Swedish-American press, in making repeated appeals to Swedes to buy Liberty Bonds, to place emphasis more on maintaining the reputation they had as Swedes than on lending financial support to the war effort. Swedes were urged to indicate their nationality when buying bonds. Advertisements called to their attention the fact that the war was being fought more for Sweden, its institutions, independence, and political existence than for any other country in the world. The dominant impression is that Swedish Americans attempted to show that they were good patriots, that their unity was good, and that they consciously tried not to discredit the Swedish reputation.

The enactment of the quota laws, which aimed to limit and selectively restrict immigration, was accepted by the Swedish Americans as long as it did not discriminate against them in particular. They thought it was proper to curtail immigration from South and East Europe. The immigrants from Northern Europe were praiseworthy because they were industrious. When the National Origins Act came up for discussion the Swedish Americans were critical and completely unsympathetic to the prospect that immigrants of Scandinavian birth would be the special targets of discrimination. The law was described as an insult to "the best citizens." The reduction of quotas for Swedish and Irish immigrants was said to be due to the fact that they were suspected of pro-German sympathies during the war.

During the Depression the Swedish community received new strength. Unemployment and the severe economic conditions made it necessary for the Swedish immigrants to keep together and to assist each other. They showed their solidarity with needy countrymen who had become unemployed or were in other ways affected by the Depression. The work carried on by business associations and the temporarily organized relief committees indicate that the Americanization process of the 1920s had not noticeably weakened the feeling of national unity. However, the Depression had far-reaching consequences for the Swedish-American institutions. During the 1920s members of these societies worried about the future and what it might bring. After 1930 they were suddenly faced with a host of problems, and the period was characterized by energetic attempts to conserve what the previous decades had built up.

The Swedish language papers probably meant a great deal to the efforts of unifying and preserving a distinctive "Swedishness" in America. The papers continually exhorted their readers to preserve their Swedish heritage and at the same time disseminated information about conditions in "Swedish America." They functioned also as a natural link with Sweden and the old home districts. Even though the Swedish press had been forced to battle with great difficulties ever since World War I, it proved to have far more vitality and persistence than had been anticipated. Between 1915 and 1932 the number of Swedish language papers was reduced by approximately 50 percent and the circulation by 52.5 percent. The papers fared relatively well during World War I. It was only after the war that their decline began to be seriously noticed as a result of the diminishing immigration. Finally, the Depression caused more difficulties for the papers. In 1929 a total of 42 Swedish language papers were still in existence. By 1932 the number had diminished to 35; circulation figures during the same period dropped from 413,092 to 309,369.

The language question occupied a central place in the life of Swedish America. It was a widespread belief among those who participated in the debate on the transition to English that "Swedishness" could not be preserved without a knowledge of the Swedish language. Only in exceptional cases was there talk of "Swedishness" without knowledge of the language. The reason why so much weight was attached to the mother tongue was that it symbolized the Swedish cultural heritage. It served as a living link with the fatherland. Swedish churches, societies, and newspapers were started because the immigrants did not understand English. It was then quite natural for them to safeguard the Swedish language, since it more or less constituted the basis for the existence of the institutions. A change-over to English would, for instance, cause the Swedish churches to lose their national uniqueness. When the real necessity for Swedish language institutions no longer existed, the more rational reasons were abandoned for the purely sentimental ones.

The Swedish-American denominations were strong centers of both religious and cultural life. The common reason for their coming into being was first of all that of serving those who did not understand English. While the Augustana Synod and the Covenant Church were wholly Swedish denominations, the Swedish Methodist and Baptist churches were a part of the American denominations. This implied that Methodist and Baptist churches more than the Augustana Synod and the Covenant Church were obliged to safeguard the Swedish language.

The Swedish-American denominations showed a steady growth in the period between 1915–1932, with the exception of the Methodist Church which reached its largest membership in 1918. Characteristically enough, the churches were quite determined to widen their sphere of activity. However, the Depression put a spoke in their wheels, and after 1930 they were mainly concerned with saving as much as possible of that which had already been built up.

As far as internal problems were concerned the language question overshadowed all other difficulties. Opposition to the change-over to English was strong among members of the churches, and the matter demanded great caution. Each change had to be accepted before the next step could be taken. The usual pattern was that of trying out innovations such as, for instance, the holding of one evening service a month in English. If this proved successful, the number of English services could gradually be increased. It is important to remember that the reason why the churches made the transition over to English was mainly in order for them to survive. The development was settled on the basis of existing conditions and by a desire to reach out to as many people as possible. When all is said and done, the language was a means of communication for the various churches. Even those who in the beginning of the transition claimed that the intrinsic value of a worship service was its being held in Swedish gradually succumbed to the demand for English, especially when they noticed that the younger members began to draw away from the congregations. This implied that they abandoned the Swedish language in order to save the Swedish immigrant church in America.

It is difficult to determine what significance World War I had for the Americanization of the Swedish-American churches. In the long run the war seems not to have hastened the transition to English. It is possible that the churches did not change the language of worship earlier because of the animosity toward everything foreign which followed on the heels of the war. The effects of the war appear to have been more indirect. It softened the worst of the opposition and shook up those who were most stubbornly convinced that a transition was unthinkable. Many discovered that the language did not mean as much as it was first thought. The great transformation came during the 1920s when Swedish was crowded out by English, which in the first place was the result of the discontinuation of immigration from Sweden. When no new blood flowed into Swedish America the interest and need for the Swedish language declined.

After the war and up to 1930 English constantly won new ground in spite of protests. In most branches of activity the Swedish language had to retreat. The number of English services in the churches increased, minutes and records were kept and printed in English, and the word 'Swedish' was eliminated from the names of the congregations. In 1931 the Association of English Churches was dissolved on the grounds that English was now the Synod's official language and the separate association of English speaking churches within the Synod had no longer any function to perform.

Characteristic for the Augustana Synod was its dread of and aversion to entering any of the larger combinations of Lutheran churches in America. The Synod was absolutely determined to remain an immigrant church. It was particularly suspicious of the German Lutherans. The reason why the Synod did not affiliate with the United Lutheran Church was that being the only synod without German connections it would be engulfed and disappear in a German dominated federation.

A comparison of the Augustana Synod and the Covenant Church shows that the transition to English progressed considerably slower in the Covenant, where the opposition to English was strong.

Conclusively the research indicates that a definite ambition existed among the Swedish Americans to preserve their national identity, their cultural heritage, and their institutions. The strong unity, not least in connection with the war, the enacting of quota laws, and the Depression, shows that there was a deep feeling of national identity even on foreign soil. The research has not corroborated the idea that the Swedish Americans were more prone to assimilate or became assimilated more easily than other nationalities.

XIV. Appendices

A. *The Swedish-American Newspapers – an Introduction*

A large number of Swedish-American newspapers, chiefly Swedish speaking and almost exclusively published in Illinois and Minnesota, have been used. The papers which have been systematically perused and which have been cited are here introduced in brief. Statistics on circulation – when available – are given in parenthesis.

Augustana (1915 – 21,102; 1932 – 12,038) appeared in Rock Island. The newspaper, which was founded in 1889, was the official Swedish language medium of the Augustana Synod. In 1950 it assumed the name, *Augustana Lutheranen,* the Swedish edition of Augustana *Lutheran,* and in 1952 it was called *Augustana Lutheranen.*

Covenant Companion (1932 – 4,085) Chicago, 1923–1934. The newspaper was the official voice of the Swedish Evangelical Mission Covenant Church of America. When it merged with *Förbundets Veckotidning* in 1934 the new name became *Covenant Weekly.*

Förbundets Veckotidning (1915 – 11,200; 1932 – 6,480) Chicago, 1915–1934. In 1934 the paper merged with Covenant Companion, which was then called *Covenant Weekly.* It was published by the Swedish Evangelical Mission Covenant of America, which was originally called "Svenska Missionsförbundet" (Swedish Mission Covenant).

Hemlandet, det gamla och det nya Galesburg and Chicago, 1855–1914. *Hemlandet* merged in 1914 with *Svenska Amerikanaren.* Founded by T.N. Hasselquist, the newspaper was closely identified with the Augustana Synod. Few Swedish-American newspapers have been so closely associated with the Swedish emigration to America as *Hemlandet.*

Lindsborgs-Posten was published in Lindsborg, Kansas, 1897–1930.

The Lutheran Companion (1915 – 6,917; 1932 – 12,466) Rock Island. The paper was founded in 1911 and became the official English organ for the Augustana Synod. In 1949 the paper merged with

Augustana and became *Augustana Lutheran.* In 1952 it again appeared as *The Lutheran Companion.*

Minnesota Stats Tidning (1915 – 12,513; 1932 – 6,200) St. Paul and Minneapolis, 1877–1939. The paper was closely allied with the Augustana Synod. It was founded by Hans Mattson.

Missionsvännen (1915 – 18,667) Chicago, 1887–, was published by the Mission Covenant and was its oldest paper in America. In 1882 it was taken over by a private publisher, The Mission Friend Publishing Company.

Nordstjernan (1915 – 12,500) was published in New York, 1872–. It was first published in 1872 by *Svenska Tryckföreningen* which in 1875 became the Publishing and Printing Company. Among the newspaper's more noteworthy editors have been Vilhelm Berger, Johan Person, Ernst Skarstedt, and Gerhard Rooth, who still edits the paper.

Ny Tid (1928 – 5,000) was a communistic paper published in Chicago 1922–1931 as a continuation of *Facklan* and *Folket.* It was published by the Scandinavian Workers Educational Society. After March, 1931, it was published in New York.

Stridsropet New York, 1891–. The official organ of the Salvation Army in Swedish.

Svea (1915 – 18,987; 1931 – 35,642), which appeared in Worcester, Massachusetts, in 1897, merged a few years ago with *Nordstjernan.* At the outset *Svea* appeared twice a month but in 1901 began to appear weekly.

Svenska Amerikanaren (1915 – 75,847; 1932 – 61,108) was founded in 1896 under the name of *Svenska Posten,* which the following year was changed to *Svenska Amerikanaren.* In 1936 it absorbed *Svenska Tribunen Nyheter* (1915 – 65,006; 1932 – 52,078). The name was changed at that time to *Svenska Amerikanaren Tribunen.* Other newspapers which merged with *Svenska Amerikanaren* are: *Svenska Världen* (1908), *Hemlandet* (1914), *Svenska Kuriren* (1929), and *Svenska Amerikanska Posten* (1940). Among the more prominent writers have been Jacob Bonggren, Ernst Skarstedt, and O.A. Linder. The paper is still being published in Chicago.

Svenska Amerikanska Posten (1915 – 56,427; 1932 – 42,000) Minneapolis, 1885–1940. In 1887 Swan J. Turnblad took over the newspaper. He doubled the newspaper's subscription list in a short time. In 1935 it had an edition of 38,000. In 1940 it was absorbed by *Svenska Amerikanaren.*

Svenska Kuriren (1915 – 42,400) Chicago, 1888–1929, has been one of the most respected newspapers in Swedish America. It is a continuation of the comic paper, *Kurre,* which was founded in 1884 and purchased in 1888 by Alex J. Johnson, who remained from that time as the newspaper's publisher and editor-in-chief. Alex Johnson is one of the best known personalities in the Swedish-American newspaper world. He was editor during the entire life of *Svenska Kuriren.*

Svenska Socialisten (1915 – 3,900) appeared first in Rockford, Illinois, and later in Chicago. The newspaper existed between 1905 and 1921, when the name was changed to *Facklan.* It encountered great difficulties during World War I, when it was repeatedly denied circulation by the United States Post Office. Since those who were employed at the newspaper feared reprisals, almost all of the material was destroyed. As far as is known, no complete collection of all volumes is to be found.

Svenska Standaret (1932 – 9,500) Chicago, 1911–1940, was the official organ of the Baptist General Conference – the Swedish conference within the American Baptist denomination. In 1940 the name was changed to *Standaret.*

Next oldest after *Sändebudet* was *Svenska Tribunen Nyheter* (1915 – 65,006; 1932 – 52,078), which was published in Chicago from 1876 to 1936. It was the successor to a newspaper started in 1869 as *Illinois Swede,* whose name was changed to *Nya Världen* in 1870 and to *Svenska Tribunen* in 1876. It finally came to be known as *Svenska Tribunen Nyheter* in 1906. In 1936 it was absorbed into *Svenska Amerikanaren Tribunen. STN* was one of the best known and largest Swedish language newspapers in Chicago.

Sändebudet (1932 – 2,600) Chicago, 1862–1948, the official medium of the Swedish Methodists, was one of the first Swedish-American newspapers.

Ungdomsvännen (1915 – 7,693) Rock Island, 1902–1918. It was published by the Augustana Synod and is considered to have been one of the best representatives of Swedish-American culture. It was forced to cease publication in 1918 because of its strong sympathies for Germany.

Veckobladet (1915 – 18,957) Minneapolis, 1906–1935. The newspaper was a continuation of *Minneapolis Weckoblad.* It belonged to the Swedish Evangelical Mission Covenant. Erik Dahlheim, a prominent person within the Mission Covenant, was editor for *Veckobladet* from 1910 to 1930.

B. Chisago Lake Lutheran Church, Center City, Minnesota (founded in 1854)
The transition to English: The language of Sunday school, Summer School, Confirmation classes, Bible classes, and Services.

Year	Sunday services	Summer school	Confirmation classes	Sunday school	Bible classes	Comments
Before 1915	S	S	S	S	S	
1915	S	S	S	S	E S	Stated in minutes of annual meeting that English Bible class had been granted permission to use the chapel.
1916–1918	S	S	S	S	E S?	
1919	S	S	S	E S	E S?	Stated in report for the Sunday school that 'some children who have been more at home in the language of the land have been taught in English...'
1920	S	S	E S	E S	E S?	Some classes of Sunday school used only English; English used 'partly' (*delvis*) in confirmation instruction. In 'branch' Sunday school in Shafer, apparently 50 children taught in Swedish, 14 in English.
1921	S	S	E S	E S	E S?	Shafer Sunday school: 44 in Swedish, 18 English.
1922	S	S	E S	E S	E S	Specific mention of Bible class in English.
1923	S	S	E S	E S	E S	Specific mention of Bible class in English for those who have been confirmed in English.
1924	S	S	E S	E S	E S?	Mentioned in Sunday school report that the beginners 'desire most' (*vilja helst*) to read in English.

1925	E S	E S	E S	E S	E S?	English services Sunday afternoon during summer and fall: both languages in Summer school. *Pastoral Report* (then still called *Kyrkorådets rapport*) *1925*, p. 301.
1926	E S	E S	E S	E S	E S?	Double services: decided at annual meeting to purchase English Hymnal for use in Sunday school and at English services: assurances given by minister that 'Swedish service will nevertheless be celebrated every Sunday in Chisago Lake Church as long as some remain who prefer to worship God in that language'. Sunday school mainly English; only the English magazines *Olive Leaf* and *Our Young People* will from now on be given to Sunday school children and confirmands.
1927	E S	E ?S	E S	E S	E S?	New books in Sunday school lessen need to use Summer school 'only for teaching Christianity'. Suggested that Summer school be made 'mainly a language school for learning the Swedish language' (*övervägande en språkskola för inlärandet av det svenska språket*). In Sunday school 27 children took instruction in Swedish, 184 in English.
1928	E S	E ?S	E S?	E S	E S?	Of the 26 classes in the Sunday school, four had instruction in Swedish.
1929	E S	E ?S	E	E S	E	Mentioned that 'all Sunday school children' come to the English service: decision by *Kyrkorådet* (Board of Deacons) April 7, 1929, that no Summer school (*hvardagsskola*) be held.
1930	E S	E?	E	E	E	Most baptisms at the English service: discussion of alternation between Swedish and English services - on alternate Sundays or double services. Summer school called Vacation Bible School.

1931	E S	E	E	E	E	Discussion indicates that some thought the Swedish services hurt by arrangement with double services. English at 10 and Swedish at 11:30: arrangement with alternate Sundays would be preferable some thought.
1932	E S	E	E	E	E	Alternate Sunday system recommended as being more satisfactory.
1933–1945	E S	E	E	E	E	Change gradually to double services only on 1st and 3rd or 2nd and 4th Sunday: Swedish Easter service dispensed with in 1943.
1946	E	E	E	E	E	No mention is made of Swedish services. One Swedish service a year has been customary.

Source: Nils Hasselmo, "The Swedish Language in Chisago County, Minnesota."

Bibliography

I. Unpublished Sources.

National Archives, Washington D.C.:

Documents of the War Loan Organization – information about the foreign-born and the Liberty Bonds.

Committee on Public Information (CPI):
- Pamphlets
- Correspondence
- Official reports
- Publications
- Articles distributed by CPI
- Liberty Bonds
- Edwin Björkman papers
- John Ericsson League of Patriotic Service

The Evangelical Covenant Church of America Historical Library and Archives, North Park College and Theological Seminary, Chicago:
- David Nyvall collection:
  - The Swedish Liberty Bond Committee papers and leaflets
  - The American Embargo Conference
  - Leaflet distributed by *Nordvästernavdelningen av Föreningen för Svenskhetens bevarande i Amerika*, Minneapolis, July, 1922.
- E.G. Hjerpe collection

The Lutheran School of Theology at Chicago, Chicago:
- G.A. Andreen collection
- G.A. Brandelle collection
- Information about Augustana Synod:
  - Letters from prominent persons
  - Committee reports
  - Minutes
  - Proceedings of synodical and conference conventions

Swedish Pioneer Historical Society Archives at North Park College, Chicago:
- Carl Hjalmar Lundquist collection:
  - Proceedings of the Swedish National Society (Svenska Nationalförbundet i Chicago).
  - Leaflets and pamphlets
  - Clippings

Speeches from different activities within the Swedish National Society

The American Embargo Conference – articles written by Carl Hjalmar Lundquist and published by the American Embargo Conference

The Swedish Pioneer Historical Society's papers

Minnesota Historical Society, St. Paul:

John Lind Papers

Minnesota State Commission on Public Safety

United Charities, Chicago:

List of persons registered at the different local bureaus of the United Charities, 1929–1934

Socialstyrelsens Arkiv, Stockholm:

Yttrande från Socialstyrelsen till socialministern, 1:a byrån, June 24, 1930

Illinois State Historical Library, Springfield:

The State Council of Defense papers

II. Information given by persons in letters or interviews

Albers, Charles, manager and chief examiner, Chicago Clearing House Association (Spring 1965).

Bengston, Henry, former Editor of Svenska Socialisten (Spring 1965 and Spring 1968).

Carlson, Adde, President of Baltic Lodge, Independent Order of Vikings, Rockford (Summer 1965).

Eckerson, Helen, Director of the Immigration Naturalization Bureau, Washington D.C. (Fall 1964).

Hedman, Herbert, President of the Swedish American Relief Committee in Chicago (Spring 1965).

Johnson, Emil, Pastor in the Augustana Synod (Houston, Summer 1965).

Loreen, Albert, Pastor in the Augustana Lutheran Church in Rockford (Summer 1965).

III. Published Sources.

1. Official Publications:

The Alien and Public Employment. U.S. Work Projects Administration (New York, 1937).

Annual Report of the Commissioner General of the Immigration. U.S. Department of Labor (Washington D.C.).

Census of Religious Bodies, 1936. Lutherans. U.S. Department of Commerce (Washington D.C., 1940).

Complete Report of the Chairman of the Committee on Public Information, 1917, 1918, and 1919.

Congressional Records (Washington D.C.).

Emigrationsutredningen. Betänkande med bilagor I–XX (Stockholm, 1908–1914).

Fifteenth Census of the United States, 1930. Age of the Foreign Born Population by Country of Birth. U.S. Department of Commerce (Washington D.C., 1933).

— *Foreign Born White Families by Country of Birth of Head* (Washington D.C., 1933).

— *General Report on Occupations* (Washington D.C., 1933).

— *Population* (Washington D.C., 1933).

First Annual Report of the Illinois Emergency Relief Commission (Chicago, 1933).

Foreign Language Information Service. "Hur arbetslösheten drabbat icke medborgare." *Svenska Amerikanaren,* May 28, 1931.

Fourteenth Census of the United States, 1920, Population. U.S. Department of Commerce (Washington D.C., 1921).

Historisk Statistik för Sverige, befolkning, 1720–1950 (Stockholm, 1955).

Historical Statistics of the United States – Colonial Times to 1957 (Washington D.C., 1960).

Immigration. Hearings before the House Committee on Rules. 72nd Congress, 2nd session.

The Immigration Work of the Department of State and Its Consular Officers. U.S. Department of State (Washington D.C.).

Men in the Crucible. Illinois Emergency Relief Commission (Chicago, 1931).

Myers, William, *The State Papers and Other Public Writings of Herbert Hoover.* Volume 1–2 (New York, 1934).

Proposed Deportation of Aliens Who Surrendered Their First Papers in Order to Escape Military Service. Hearings before the Committee on Immigration and Naturalization 66th Congress, 1st session (Washington D.C.).

Report of the Ellis Island Committee. U.S. Department of Labor (Washington D.C., March, 1934).

Report of the Provost Marshal General to the Secretary of War on the First Draft under the Selective Service Act (Washington D.C., 1918 and 1919).

Riksdagstrycket med Bihang (Stockholm).

Rockford. Compiled by the Workers of the Writers Program (Rockford, 1941).

Segner, Paul, *Minneapolis Unemployed. A Description and Analysis of the Resident Relief Population of the City of Minneapolis from 1900 to 1936.* U.S. Works Projects Administration (Minneapolis, 1937).

Sixteenth Census of the United States, 1940, *Population.* U.S. Department of Commerce (Washington D.C., 1943).

Statistical Abstracts of the United States. U.S. Department of Commerce (Washington D.C.).

Statistiska Meddelanden, Serie F, Sociala Meddelanden. Publ. by Kungl. Socialstyrelsen (Stockholm).

Statistisk Årsbok (Stockholm).

Statistics. Council of Social Agencies of Chicago.

Sveriges Officiella Statistik. Ut- och Invandring (Stockholm).

Utlandssvenskarna. Statens Offentliga Utredningar (Stockholm, 1941: 36).

Visa Work of the Department of State and the Foreign Service. U.S. Department of State. Publication 6510 (Washington D.C., June 1, 1957).

Vissa åtgärder beträffande emigrationen. Statens Offentliga Utredningar (Stockholm, 1928:8).

Vital Statistics. Special Report. Bureau of Census (Washington D.C.).

2. *Statutes:*

Svensk-Amerikanska Hembygdsförbundet. *Stadgar* (Chicago, 1929).

Svenska Kulturförbundet i Amerika. *Stadgar* (Chicago 1924—1927).

Vasa Order of America. *Constitution for Vasa Order of America* (1962).

Vasa Orden av Amerika. *Stadgar för Distriktslogen Illinois No 8* (1937).

3. *Pamphlets:*

Svenskhetens berömmelse. Två märkliga tal översatta från engelska. President Calvin Coolidge's tal om John Ericsson och överdomare Harry Olson's tal om Abraham Lincoln. Publ. by Erik Sjöstrand (Chicago, 1926).

Swedish American 300th Anniversary. Workers and Speakers Manual (1927).

4. *Annuals, Souvenir Albums, Catalogues, and Minutes:*

Annual Report of the Year. United Charities of Chicago (1930–1934).

Golden Jubilee Anniversary, 1892–1942. Evangelical Mission Covenant Church, Hindsdale, Illinois.

Minutes. The Augustana Synod (1914–1933).

Minutes. From the Different Conferences of the Augustana Synod (1914–1933).

Proceedings of the Association of English Churches. The Augustana Synod (1908–1931).

Protokoll fört vid Svenskamerikanska konferensen anordnad av Augustana Institute of Swedish Culture (Chicago, November 15, 1941).

Protokoll över förhandlingar fattade vid Vasa Ordens Storlogemöten (1914–1935).

Report of the Foreign Language Commission to the General Conference of the Methodist Episcopal Church (Springfield, Mass., 1924).
Social Service Yearbook. United Charities of Chicago (Chicago, 1930–34).
Svenska metodismens allmänna konvent 1914 (Evanston, 1914).
Yearbooks. Central Swedish Conference of the Methodist Episcopal Church.
Årsberättelser. Svenska Evangeliska Missionsförbundet i Amerika.
Årsbok för Riksföreningen för svenskhetens bevarande i utlandet (Göteborg).
Årsrevy. Kafé Idrott (Chicago, 1918–1932).

5. *Newspapers and periodicals:*

Allsvensk samling. Publ. by Riksföreningen för Svenskhetens Bevarande i Utlandet (Göteborg).
The American Scandinavian Review (New York).
Augustana, tidning för den svenska lutherska kyrkan i Amerika (Rock Island).
Augustana Observer (Rock Island).
The Bohemian Review (Chicago).
Chicago Examiner (Chicago).
Chicago Herald (Chicago).
Chicago Tribune (Chicago).
The Covenant Companion. Official Organ of the Swedish Evangelical Mission Covenant of America (Chicago).
The Covenant Conference Review (Chicago).
Dagens Nyheter (Stockholm).
Förbundets Veckotidning (Chicago).
Gamla och Nya Hemlandet (Chicago).
Interpreter Releases. Publ. by the Foreign Language Information Service (New York).
Lindsborgs-Posten (Lindsborg, Kansas).
The Lutheran Companion. Official Organ of the Evangelical Lutheran Augustana Synod of North America (Rock Island).
The Minneapolis Tribune (Minneapolis).
Minnesota in the War. Minnesota Commission of Public Safety's Official Bulletin. Publ. from September 1917 to February 1919.
Minnesota Stats Tidning (Minneapolis).
Missionsförbundets Ungdomstidning (Chicago).
Missionsvännen (Chicago).
Monthly Bulletin. Publ. by the Swedish Engineers' Society (Chicago).
New York Times (New York).
Nordstjernan (New York).
Ny Tid. Publ. by the Scandinavian Workers Educational Society (Chicago).

Omaha Posten (Omaha).
Press Releases. U.S. Department of State (Washington D.C.).
Saturday Evening Post (Philadelphia).
Skandia (Jamestown).
Stridsropet. Officiellt Organ för Frälsningsarméns Skandinaviska arbete i Förenta Staterna (New York).
Svea (Worcester).
Svenska Amerikanaren (Chicago).
Svenska Amerikanska Posten (Minneapolis).
Svenska Kulturförbundets Kvartalsskrift (Chicago).
Svenska Kuriren (Chicago).
Svenska Socialisten (Chicago).
Svenska Standaret. Official Organ for the Swedish Baptist Church of America (Chicago).
Svenska Tribunen Nyheter (Chicago).
Svithiod Journal. Månadsskrift för Independent Order of Svithiod (Chicago).
Svithiod Life. Publ. Monthly by Svithiod Singing Club (Chicago).
Swedish American Bulletin. Publ. by the Swedish American Historical Society (St. Peter, Minnesota).
Swedish Pioneer Historical Quarterly (Chicago).
Sändebudet. Official Organ of the Methodist Episcopal Church (Chicago).
Trasdockan. Svenska Ingenjörsföreningen i Chicago Årsskrift (Chicago).
Ungdomsvännen (Rock Island).
Veckobladet (Minneapolis).

6. Books and Articles:

Adamic, Louis, "Aliens and Alien-Baiters," *Harper's Magazine* (November, 1936).
Amerika-svensk lyrik genom 100 år, 1848–1948. Ed. Martin S. Allwood (Mullsjö, 1949).

Ander, Fritiof O., "The Effects of the Immigration Law of 1924 upon a Minority Immigrant Group," *Annual Report of the American Historical Association,* Volume III (1942).
— *The Cultural Heritage of the Swedish Immigrant. Selected References* (Rock Island, 1956).
— "An Immigrant Community during the Progressive Era," *The Swedish Immigrant Community in Transition*. Essays in Honor of Dr Conrad Bergendoff (Rock Island, 1963).

Anderson, Charles H., *White Protestant Americans. From National Origins to Religious Group* (Englewood Cliffs, New Jersey, 1970).

Anderson, Einar, "Våra hembygdsföreningar," *Svenska Kulturförbundets Minnesskrift* (Chicago, 1938).

Anderson, Laurence A., "The Swedes of Lindsborg, Kansas, and Their Cultural Institutions: Bethany College and the "Messiah Chorus." M.A. thesis, University of Chicago (Chicago, 1953).

Andreen, Gustav, *Det svenska språket i Amerika* (Stockholm, 1900).

Arden, Everett, *Augustana Heritage. A History of the Augustana Lutheran Church* (Rock Island, 1963).

Babcock, Kendric C., *The Scandinavian Element in the United States* (Urbana, Illinois, 1914).

Backlund, Oscar J., *A Century of the Swedish American Press* (Chicago, 1952).

Baepler, W., *A Century of Grace* (St. Louis, Mo., 1947).

Bengston, Carl J., "Varen amerikanske," *Ungdomsvännen* (October, 1918).
— "The Association of English Churches," *Korsbaneret* (1923).

Bengston, Henry, "Chicago's Belmont and Clark," *Swedish Pioneer Historical Quarterly* (October, 1962).
— *Skandinaver på vänsterflygeln i USA* (Stockholm, 1955).

Bengtson, C.O., "The Future of the Association of English Churches," *The Lutheran Companion* (October 15, 1927).

Bennet, Marion, *American Immigration Policies* (Washington D.C., 1963).

Benson, A.B., and Hedin, Naboth, *Americans from Sweden* (Philadelphia, 1950).
— "The Assimilation of Swedes in America," *Swedish Pioneer Historical Quarterly* (October, 1956).
— "Det svenska kulturproblemet i Amerika," *Årsbok utg. av Samfundet S:t Erik* (Stockholm, 1920).

Benson, Oscar A., "Problems in the Accomodation of the Swede to American Culture." Ph.D. thesis, unpublished (Pittsburgh, 1933).
— "Problems in the Accomodation of the Swede to American Culture," *University of Pittsburgh Bulletin* (November 15, 1933).
— "Studies in Americanization," *The Lutheran Companion* (October 14, 21, 28, and November 11, 1922).

Bergendoff, Conrad, "The Role of Augustana in the Transplanting of a Culture across the Atlantic," *The Immigration of Ideas. Studies in the North Atlantic Community*. Essays to Fritiof Ander (Rock Island, 1968).
— "The Swedish Immigrant and the American Way," *Swedish Pioneer Historical Quarterly* (July, 1968).

— "The Americanization of the Augustana Synod," *The Lutheran Companion* (August 16, 1924 and August 23, 1924).
— "The Future of the Augustana Synod," *Augustana Quarterly* (April, 1933).

Berger, V., "De svenskes villighet att ge efter," *Allsvensk Samling* (November 15, 1919).
— "Några svenska karaktärsdrags amerikanisering," *Valkyrian* (New York, 1908).
— *Svensk-Amerika i målbrottet* (New York, 1933).
— *Svensk-amerikanska meditationer* (Rock Island, 1916).

Bernard, William S., *American Immigration Policy – A Reappraisal* (New York, 1950).
— "Cultural Determinants of Naturalization," *American Sociological Review* (Volume I, No 6).

Bogardus, Emory, *Immigration and Race Attitudes* (New York, 1928).
— *Essentials of Americanization* (Los Angeles, 1923).

Bonggren, Jacob, *Sånger och sagor* (Rock Island, 1902).

Bossard, James H.S., "Nationality and Nativity as Factors in Marriage," *American Sociological Review* (December, 1939).

Brandelle, G.A., "The Significance of the Augustana Synod to the Swedish Lutherans in America," *The Augustana Synod. A Brief Review of Its History, 1860–1910* (Rock Island, 1910).

Brandt, Lillian, *An Impressionistic View of the Winter of 1930–1931 in New York City* (New York, 1932).

Brunner, Edmund de S., *Immigrant Farmers and Their Children* (New York, 1929).

Capps, Finis Herbert, *From Isolationism to Involvement. The Swedish Immigrant Press in America, 1914–1945* (Chicago, 1966).

Carlson, J.S., *Hvarför böra vi behålla och bevara, vårda och bruka svenska språket i Amerika?* (Minneapolis, 1923).

Carlsson, Sten, "Från Värmland till Minnesota," *Emigranten* (1970:2).

— *Skandinaviska politiker i Minnesota 1882–1900. En studie rörande den etniska faktorns roll vid politiska val i en immigrantstat* (Uppsala 1970).

Carpenter, Niles, *Immigrants and Their Children, 1920. A Study based on Census Statistics Relative to the Foreign Born and the Native White of Foreign or Mixed Parentage.* Census Monographs VII (Washington D.C., 1927).

Clark, Jane, *Deportation of Aliens from the United States to Europe* (New York, 1931).

Cohen, Felix, *Immigration and National Welfare* (New York, 1940).

Covenant Memories, 1885–1935. Golden Jubilee, Swedish Evangelical Mission Covenant Church (Chicago, 1935).

Creel, George, "Our Aliens – Were They Loyal or Disloyal? "*Everybody's Magazine* (1919).

— *How We Advertised America. The First Telling of the Committee on Public Information That Carried the Gospel of Americanism to Every Corner of the Globe* (New York, 1920).

Davie, Maurice, *World Immigration. With Special Reference to the United States* (New York, 1949).

Davis, Jerome, "The Assimilation of Immigrants and Our Citizenship Process," *Social Forces*, Volume XII (May, 1934).

Dietz, Paul T., "The Transition from German to English in the Missouri Synod from 1910 to 1947," *Concordia Historical Institute Quarterly* (October, 1949).

Divine, Robert A., *American Immigration Policy, 1924–1952* (New Haven, 1957).

Drachsler, Julius, *Democracy and Assimilation* (New York, 1920).

— *Intermarriage in New York City. A Statistical Study of the Amalgamation of European Peoples* (New York, 1921).

Duncan, Hannibal, *Immigration and Assimilation* (New York, 1933).

Dybvig, Philip S., "Facts about the Language Question," *Lutheran Church Herald* (Minneapolis, May 20, 1930).

Eckerson, Helen F., "Immigrants and National Origins," *Monthly Review*. Immigration Naturalization Service (Washington D.C., August, 1945).
— "Nonquota Immigration. Fiscal years 1925–1944," *Monthly Review*. Immigration and Naturalization Service (Washington D.C., August, 1945).

Eckler, Ross and Zlotnick, Jack, "Immigration and the Labor Force," *The Annals of the American Academy of Political and Social Science* (March, 1949).

Eklund, E.E., "Acculturation in the Swedish Lutheran Congregations of the Boston Area." Ph.D. thesis, unpublished (Boston University, 1964).

Elmström, K.H., "Vår plikt att bevara svenskheten i vår kyrkliga verksamhet," *Svenska metodismens allmänna konvent 1914* (Evanston, 1914).

Enzler, Clarence, *Some Social Aspects of the Depression, 1930–1933* (Washington D.C., 1939).

Erikson, Martin, *Baptist General Conference of America. Centenary Glimpses, 1852–1952* (Chicago, 1952).

Fairchild, Henry P., *The Melting-Pot Mistake* (Boston, 1926).
Fellman, David, "The Alien's Right to Work," *Minnesota Law Review* (January, 1938).

Fevold, Eugene, "The Norwegian Immigrant and His Church," *Norwegian-American Studies and Records,* Volume 23 (Northfield, Minnesota, 1967).

Fields, Harold, "Where Shall the Alien Work?" *Social Forces* (December, 1933).
— "The Unemployed Foreign-Born," *The Quarterly Journal of Economics* (May, 1935).

Fishman, Joshua, *Language Loyalty in the United States* (The Hague, 1966).

Fleshner, Dorris A., "The Formation of the United Lutheran Church in America, 1918," *Concordia Historical Institute Quarterly* (October, 1967).

Franzén, Gösta, "The Development of Scandinavian Studies in the United States," *Scandinavica,* Volume 3 (May, 1964).

Frazier, E. Franklin, "Ethnic and Minority Groups in Wartime, with Special Reference to the Negro," *The American Journal of Sociology* (December, 1942).

Gavit, John, "American by Choice," *Immigration an American Dilemma. Problems in American Civilization* (Boston, 1953).

Gerson, Louis L., *The Hyphenate in Recent American Politics and Diplomacy* (Lawrence, 1964).

Glazer, Nathan, "Process and Problems of Language Maintenance. An Integrative Review," Joshua Fishman, *Language Loyalty in the United States* (The Hague, 1966).
— and Moynihan, Daniel, *Beyond the Melting Pot* (Harvard University, 1963).

Gordon, Milton M., *Assimilation in American Life. The Role of Race, Religion, and National Origins* (New York, 1966).
— "Assimilation in America: Theory and Reality." *Daedalus. Journal of the American Academy of Arts and Sciences* (Spring, 1961).

Gosnell, H.F., "Non-Naturalization: A Study in Political Assimilation," *The American Journal of Sociology* (May, 1928).

Grant, Madison, *The Conquest of a Continent* (New York, 1933)

Greene, Victor, "For God and Country: The Origins of Slavic Catholic Self – Conscience in America," *Church History*, Volume XXXV (December, 1966).

Handlin, Oscar, *America. A History* (New York, 1968).
— *Boston's Immigrants* (New York, 1969).
— *Race and Nationality in American Life* (Boston, 1957).
— *The American People in the Twenties Century* (Boston, 1963).

Hansen, Marcus Lee, *The Problem of the Third Generation Immigrant* (Rock Island, 1938).

Hartmann, Edward G., *The Movement to Americanize the Immigrant* (New York, 1948).

Hasselmo, Nils, "Den amerikanska svenskan: En översikt" (unpublished manuscript).
— "Language in Exile," *The Swedish Immigrant Community in Transition. Essays in Honor of Dr Conrad Bergendoff* (Rock Island, 1963).

— "The Swedish Language in Chisago County, Minnesota" (unpublished manuscript).
— "Language Displacement and Language Influence in Swedish America," *Swedish Pioneer Historical Quarterly* (April, 1963).

Haugen, Einar, *The Norwegian Language in America. A Study in Bilingual Behavior* (Philadelphia, 1953).

Hembygden. Historik av Chicagos svenska hembygdsföreningar. Century of Progress (Chicago, 1933).

Hemdahl, Reuel Gustav, "The Swedes in Illinois Politics." Ph.D. thesis (Northwestern University, Evanston, 1934).

Hicks, John, *Republican Ascendency, 1921–1933* (New York, 1963).

Higham, John, *Strangers in the Land. Patterns of American Nativism, 1860–1925* (New York, 1965).

Hilton, O.A., "The Minnesota Commission of Public Safety in World War I, 1917–1919" *(Bulletin of the Oklahoma Agricultural and Mechanical College,* Stillwater, May, 15, 1951).

Historical Review. District Lodge Illinois No 8, 1908–1943. Vasa Order of America (Chicago,1943).

Historik över distriktslogen Minnesota No 7, 1908–1935. Vasa Order of America (Minneapolis, 1935).

Hollingshead, August B., "Cultural Factors in the Selection of Marriage Mates," *American Sociological Review,* Volume 15 (1950).

Hoving, Johannes, *Den svenska kolonisationen i Amerika* (Stockholm, 1940).
— *Läsebok och uppslagsbok för Vasabarnen i Amerika* (Stockholm, 1935).

Hutchinson, Edward, *Immigrants and Their Children, 1850–1950* (New York, 1956).

Hägglund, S.G., "Svenskhetens bevarande i Amerika," *Augustana* (February 14, 1924).
— "Svenska språket vid synodalmötet i Minneapolis," *Augustana* (July 9, 1925).
— "The Swedish Demand," *Augustana Quarterly* (January, 1925).

Janson, Florence, *The Background of Swedish Immigration, 1840–1930* (Chicago, 1931).

Jenison, Marguerite E., *War Documents and Addresses* (Springfield, 1923).
— *The War-Time Organization of Illinois* (Springfield, 1923).

Johnson, P. Arthur, "National and International Relationships of the Augustana Synod," *After Seventy-Five Years, 1860–1935. A Jubilee Publication* (Rock Island, 1935).

Johnson, Emeroy, "The Duty of the Augustana Synod in Regard to the Swedish Language," *The Lutheran Companion* (February 9, 1924).
— *God Gave the Growth. The Story of the Lutheran Minnesota Conference, 1876–1958* (Minneapolis, 1958).

Johnson, E. Gustav, "Periodicals Published among the Mission Covenant People in America," *Covenant Memories, 1885–1935* (Chicago, 1935).

Johnson, Gustav E., "The Swedes of Chicago." Ph.D. thesis. Unpublished (University of Chicago, 1940).

Johnston, L.A., "Hvad Augustana-synoden i nationellt hänseende varit för Amerikas svenskar," *Prärieblomman* (1911).

Jones, Maldwyn, *American Immigration* (Chicago, 1960).

Jordan, Riverda Harding, *Nationality and School Progress. A Study in Americanization* (Ph.D. thesis, University of Minnesota, Bloomington, Illinois, 1921).

Jung, Norman O., "Chicago's Foreign Language Press in World War I." Unpublished dissertation (University of Chicago, 1959).

Kennedy, Ruby J.R., "Single or Triple Melting Pot? Intermarriage Trends in New Haven, 1870–1940," *The American Journal of Sociology,* Volume 49 (January, 1944).

Kilander, K.A., "Svenskhetens bevarande," *Augustana* (January 3, 1924).

Koblik, Steven, "Wartime Diplomacy and the Democratization of Sweden in September–October 1917," *The Journal of Modern History* (March, 1969).

von Koch, G.H., "Svenskarna i Förenta staterna," *Emigrationsutredningen.* Bilaga XX (Stockholm, 1911).

— *Emigranternas land. Studier i Amerikanskt samhällsliv* (Stockholm, 1910).

La Follette, Belle C., and La Follette, Fola, *Robert M. La Follette.* Vol. I–II (New York, 1953).

Lamm, Olof, "En skrivelse i nödhjälpsfrågan," *Nordstjernan* (November 12, 1931).

Larson, Edor, *History of Red River Valley Conference of the Augustana Lutheran Church* (Blair, Nebraska, 1953).

Lewis, Read, "Immigration Issues," *The Survey* (May 15, 1932).

Lindbergh, Charles Augustus, *Why Is Your Country of War and What Happens to You after the War Is over and Related Subjects* (1917).

Lindberg, John, *The Background of Swedish Emigration to the United States* (Minneapolis, 1930).

Lindblom, Ernst, *Stjärnbanerets land* (Stockholm, 1910).

Lincoln, Julius, "The Language Question," *The Augustana Synod. A Brief Review of Its History, 1860–1910* (Rock Island, 1910).

Linder, Oliver A., "Svenskhetens bevarande," *Svenska Amerikanaren* (November 25, 1926).
— "The Swedish-American Press," *The Swedish Element in America.* Volume II (Chicago, 1931).

Lindquist, Emory, *Smoky Valley People – A History of Lindsborg, Kansas* (Lindsborg, 1953).

Lindvall, C.A., "Vårt stora kulturarv," *Year-Book of the Swedish Historical Society of America* (1916/1917).
— "Har det svenska språket någon framtid i Amerika?" *Ungdomsvännen* (July, 1916).
— "Svenska språket i Amerika," *Year-Book of the Swedish Historical Society of America* (1915).

Ljungmark, Lars, *Den stora utvandringen* (Stockholm, 1965).

Lund, Emil, *Minnesota-konferensens av Augustana Synoden och dess församlingars historia* (Rock Island, 1923).
— "Huru skall svenskheten i Amerika på bästa sätt bevaras och förkovras." *Årsbok publ. av Samfundet St. Erik* (Stockholm, 1920).

Lund, Gene, "The Americanization of the Augustana Lutheran Church." Ph.D. thesis, unpublished (Princeton, 1954).

Lunden, Walter A., "Some Statistical Facts about the Augustana Synod," *The Lutheran Companion* (September 13, 1930).

Lundquist, Carl Hjalmar, *Är vårt land fullt neutralt? En svensk-amerikans åsikter ur freds-, humanitets- och neutralitetssynpunkter* (1916).

Lönnquist, C.A., "Vårt svensk-lutherska arv," *Korsbaneret* (1925).

Magnuson, P.M., *Our Civilization, Democracy and the War. A Study of the Political Sociology of the War* (St. Cloud, Minn., 1918).

Marcson, Simon, "A Theory of Intermarriage and Assimilation," *Social Forces*. Volume 29 (October, 1950).

Mattson, A.D., *Polity of the Augustana Lutheran Church* (Rock Island, 1952).

Mattson, Karl E., "The Theology of the Augustana Lutheran Church," *Centennial Essays. Augustana Lutheran Church, 1860–1960* (Rock Island, 1960).

McDonnel, Eleonor, "Shall We Close the Door," *Saturday Evening Post* (March 14, 1931).

Meixner, Esther, *The Teaching of the Scandinavian Languages and Literatures in the United States*. Dissertation (University of Pennsylvania, Philadelphia, 1941).

Meuser, Fred M., *The Formation of the American Lutheran Church* (Columbus, Ohio, 1958).

Miller, John P., *Vart togo de vägen?* (Chicago, 1945).

Mitchell, Broadus, *Depression Decade* (New York, 1947).

Mock, James and Larson, Cedric, *Words That Won the War. The Story of the Committee on Public Information, 1917–1919* (Princeton, 1939).

Morgan, Dwight, *The Foreign-Born in the United States* (New York, 1936).

Myers, William and Newton, Walter, *The Hoover Administration. A Document Narrative* (New York, 1936).

Nelson, Clifford and Fevold, Eugene L., *The Lutheran Church among Norwegian-Americans. A History of the Evangelical Lutheran Church* (Minneapolis, 1960).

Nelson, Helge, *The Swedes and the Swedish Settlements in North America* (Lund, 1943).
— *Nordamerika. Natur och kulturbygd* (Stockholm, 1935).

Nelson, Lowry, "Intermarriage among Nationality Groups in a Rural Area of Minnesota," *The American Journal of Sociology,* Volume 48 (March, 1943).

Norberg, P.G., "Svenskarnas Amerika och Amerikas svenskar," *Emigrationsutredningen.* Bilaga XX (Stockholm, 1911).

Norrlie, Olaf Morgan, *History of the Norwegian People in America* (Minneapolis, 1925).

Nothstein, I.O., "The Language Transition in the Augustana Synod," *The Augustana Quarterly* (July and October, 1945).

Nyholm, Paul C., *The Americanization of the Danish Lutheran Churches in America. A Study in Immigrant History* (Copenhagen, 1963).

Nylin, Henry, "History of Swedish Methodism in Chicago." Unpublished M.A. thesis (Northwestern University, Evanston, 1925).

Nystrom, Daniel, *A Ministry of Printing. A History of the Publication House of Augustana Lutheran Church* (Rock Island, 1962).

Nyvall, David, *Svenskhet i Amerika. Ett ord till mina landsmän om vad det vill säga att i sann mening vara en svensk i detta land* (1893).
— "Den svenska nationalkaraktären och dess amerikanisering," *Prärieblomman* (1903).
— "Svenskhetens bevarande," *Augustana* (December 22, 1921).

Oblom, Lorraine, "Determining Factors in the Growth of the Evangelical Mission Covenant Church of America." *The Covenant Quarterly.* Volume III (May, 1943).

O'Connor, Richard, *The German-Americans. An Informal History* (Boston, 1968).

Olander, C.M., "What Does the Present Situation Demand of Our Synod?" *The Augustana Quarterly* (January, 1930).

Olson, Adolf, *A Centenary History. As Related to the Baptist General Conference of America* (Chicago, 1952).

Olson, Ernst W., "A Word to Patriots in All Camps," *Ungdomsvännen* (August, 1917).
— *Augustana Book Concern. Fiftieth Anniversary, 1884–1934* (Rock Island, 1934).

Olsson, Karl, *By One Spirit* (Chicago, 1962).

Olson, Oscar N., *The Augustana Lutheran Church in America, 1860–1910. The Formative Period* (Davenport, Iowa, 1956).

Park, Robert, *The Immigrant Press and Its Control* (New York, 1922).

Pease, Theodore Calvin, *The Story of Illinois* (Chicago, 1965).

Person, Johan, *Svensk-amerikanska studier* (Rock Island, 1912).

Person, Peter, "A History of Higher Education among the Swedish Immigrants in America." Unpublished Ph.D. thesis (Harvard University, 1941).

Peterson, C.F., *Sverige i Amerika. Kulturhistoriska och Biografiska Teckningar* (Chicago, 1898).

Peterson, H.C., and Fite, Gilbert C., *Opponents of War, 1917–1918* (Madison, 1957).

Peterson, Mabel W., "The Story of the Reaction of the Evangelical Mission Covenant Church of America to Its Social Environment, 1910–1950." Unpublished M.A. thesis (Northwestern University, Evanston, 1955).

Pihlblad, Terence, "The Kansas Swedes," *The Southwestern Social Science Quarterly*. Volume XIII (1932).

Ranseen, M.C., "Augustana-synoden och the General Council," *Minnesskrift med anledning av Augustana-Synodens femtioåriga tillvaro, 1860–1910* (Rock Island, 1910).

Rom, Gudrun, "The United Charities of Chicago. Its History. 1857–1957." Manuscript (Chicago).

Rosenquist, Carl M., "Linguistic Changes in the Acculturation of the Swedes of Texas," *Sociology and Social Research* (January/February, 1932).

— "The Swedes of Texas." Unpublished Ph.D. thesis (University of Chicago, 1930).

Rydén, E.E., "What Has the Association of English Churches Accomplished?" *The Lutheran Companion* (October 15, 1927).

Schersten, Albert F., *The Relation of the Swedish-American Newspapers to the Assimilation of Swedish Immigrants* (Rock Island, 1935).

Schlesinger, Arthur, *Political and Social Growth of the American People, 1865–1940* (New York, 1947).

Schroeder, W.W., and Obenhaus, Victor, *Religion in American Culture* (New York, 1964).

Scott, Franklin, D., *Emigration and Immigration* (Washington D.C., 1963).
— "The Immigration Theme in the Framework of National Groups," *Immigration and American History*. Essays in Honor of Theodore C. Blegen, Minnesota University (Minneapolis, 1961).

Serenius, A., "Varför svenskan i Amerika," *Missionsförbundets Ungdomstidning* (May 21, 1912).

Simpson, Georg and Yinger, Milton, *Racial and Cultural Minorities. An Analysis of Prejudice and Discrimination* (New York, 1958).

Skarstedt, Ernst, *Svensk-amerikanska folket i helg och söcken* (Stockholm, 1917).
— *Våra pennfäktare* (San Fransciso, 1897).

Smith Carlson, William, *Americans in the Making. The Natural History of the Assimilation of Immigrants* (New York, 1939).

Stephenson, George, "The Attitude of Swedish Americans towards the World War," *Proceedings of Mississippi Valley Historical Association*. Volume X (1918/1919).
— *A History of American Immigration, 1820–1924* (Boston, 1926).
— *John Lind of Minnesota* (Minneapolis, 1935).
— *The Religious Aspects of Swedish Immigration. A Study of Immigrant Churches* (Minneapolis, 1932).
— "Rip van Winkle in Sweden," *Swedish Pioneer Historical Quarterly* (April, 1956).

Stomberg, Andrew, *Den svenska folkstammen i Amerika* (Stockholm, 1928).

Sundbeck, Carl, *Svensk-Amerikanerna. Deras materiella och andliga sträfvanden* (Stockholm, 1904).

Swanson, Charles, "Svensk-Amerikansk kultur," *Swedish-American Forum* (Dorchester, Mass., April, 1929).

Swanson, Roy, "Our Predecessors," *Swedish Pioneer Historical Quarterly* (July, 1950).

Söderström, Alfred, *Blixtar på tidningshorisonten, samlade och magasinerade* (Warroad, Minn., 1910).

Taft, Donald, *Problems Arising from Minorities. Our Racial and National Minorities Their History, Contributions and Present Problems* (New York, 1937).
— and Robbins, R., *International Migrations: The Immigrant in the Modern World* (New York, 1955).

Thörnberg, G.H., *Sverige i Amerika. Amerika i Sverige* (Stockholm, 1938).

Vasa Order of America. Historik, 1896–1946 (Worcester, 1946).

Vikingen. Golden Jubilee Number, 1890–1949 (Chicago, 1949).

Wahlgren, Erik, "Vårt svenska språk," *Svenska Kulturförbundets Minnesskrift* (1938).

Wahlström, M., "Svenska språkets framtid i Amerika," *Year-Book of the Swedish Historical Society of America* (1916–17).

Wallenius, C.G., and Olson E.D., *A Short Story of the Swedish Methodism in America* (Chicago, 1931).

Wallenius, C.G., "Svenska Kulturförbundet, 1924 till 1938," *Svenska Kulturförbundets Minnesskrift* (Chicago, 1938).

Vecoli, Rudolph, "Ethnicity: A Neglected Dimension of American History," *American Studies in Scandinavia* (Uppsala, Summer, 1970).

Wecter, Dixon, *The Age of the Depression, 1929–41* (New York, 1948).

Wessén, Theophilus, "Den svenska nationalkaraktären – en gåva till Amerikas folk," *Årsbok Publ. by St. Erik* (Stockholm, 1920).

White, C., *Administration of Public Welfare* (New York, 1940).
— *Research Memorandum on Social Aspects of Relief Policies in the Depression* (New York, 1937).

Whitney, Nathaniel, *The Sale of War Bonds in Iowa* (Iowa City, 1923).

Whittaker, Wayne, *The Rockford Story, 1852–1952* (Rockford, 1956).

Widén, Albin, *Vår sista folkvandring* (Falköping, 1962).

Wheeler, Wayne, "An Analysis of Social Change in a Swedish-Immigrant Community," (Doctoral dissertation, University of Missouri, 1959).

Witting, A.G., "Svenskheten och den äkta amerikanismen," *Meddelanden från Svenska Kulturförbundet i Amerika* (1932?).
— "En allmän svenskamerikansk samling," *Svenska Kulturförbundet i Amerika Minnesskrift* (Chicago, 1938).
— "Den rätta amerikanismen," *Svenska Kulturförbundet i Amerika Minnesskrift* (Chicago, 1938).

Wittke, Carl, *The German-Language Press in America* (Lexington, 1957).
— "Fissures in the Melting Pot," *The Immigration of Ideas. Studies in the North Atlantic Community.* Essays Presented to O. Fritiof Ander (Rock Island, 1968).
— "Immigration Policy Prior to World War I," *Immigration an American Dilemma. Problems in American Civilization* (Boston, 1953).
— *The Irish in America* (Baton Rouge, 1956).
— *We Who Built America. The Saga of the Immigrant* (Cleveland, 1964).

Woofter, T. J., *Races and Ethnic Groups in American Life* (New York, 1933).

Yinger, Milton, "Social Forces Involved in Group Identification or Withdrawal," *Daedalus. Journal of the American Academy of Arts and Sciences* (Spring, 1961).

Young, Donald, *Research Memorandum on Minority People in the Depression* (New York, 1937).

Youngert, S.G., "Augustana synoden och moderkyrkan i Sverige," *Minnesskrift med anledning av Augustana-Synodens femtioåriga tillvaro, 1860–1910* (Rock Island, 1910).

Zetterstrand, E.A., "Engelskans inflytande på det svenska språket i Amerika," *Ungdomsvännen* (June–August, 1904).

Zubrzycki, Jerzy, "The Rôle of the Foreign-Language Press in Migrant Integration," *Population Studies* (1958).

Åkerman, Sune, "Medborgarskapshandlingar som källa för anpassning i USA." Unpublished paper (Uppsala, 1970).

Öhman, S.G., *Augustana-Synodens självständighetsförklaring* (Worcester, 1918).
— "Vårt svenska arv," *Korsbaneret* (1924).

Name index

This biography includes only those Swedish Americans who were active in Swedish America during the period covered in this book and those contemporary individuals who had an articulated opinion about Swedish America. Mere references are not included.